SCIENCE AMONG THE OTTOMANS

SCIENCE AMONG THE OTTOMANS

The Cultural Creation and Exchange of Knowledge

MIRI SHEFER-MOSSENSOHN

UNIVERSITY OF TEXAS PRESS
Austin

First edition, 2015
First paperback edition, 2016

♾ The paper used in this book meets the minimum requirements of
ANSI/NISO Z39.48-1992 (R1997) (Permanence of Paper).

Library of Congress Cataloging-in-Publication Data
Shefer-Mossensohn, Miri, 1971– author.
Science among the Ottomans : the cultural creation and exchange
of knowledge / Miri Shefer-Mossensohn. — First edition.
pages cm
Includes bibliographical references and index.
ISBN 978-1-4773-0359-7 (cloth : alk. paper) —
ISBN 978-1-4773-0360-3 (library e-book) —
ISBN 978-1-4773-0361-0 (nonlibrary e-book)
1. Science—Turkey—History. 2. Technology—Turkey—History.
3. Science—Social aspects—Turkey—History. 4. Islam and science—
Turkey—History. 5. Science and state—Turkey—History.
6. Turkey—History—Ottoman Empire, 1288-1918. I. Title.
Q127.T9S54 2015
509.56′0903—dc23 2015010452

doi:10.7560/303597
ISBN 978-1-4773-1221-6 (paperback)

CONTENTS

PREFACE

This book unravels the story of Ottoman scientific endeavors. In 1877, the Ottoman Empire boasted the seventh-longest electric telegraph network in the world. As far as modern communication infrastructure, the Ottomans were among the most advanced nations at the time. Their progressive status is surprising, considering the common Western image of the Ottomans of the nineteenth and early twentieth centuries as backward and impoverished—a view that even many elite Ottomans shared. Yet the portrait uncovered by this volume is one of considerable curiosity and vibrant scientific and technological activity. Indeed, Ottoman society was among those cultures that successfully adopted new technologies and adapted them to their own needs. The Ottomans could also boast scientific independence, successfully producing their own technologies rather than relying on a foreign source for supplying a final product. Granted, the Ottomans could not claim any world-renowned invention or innovation; yet their many scientific and technological abilities sustained a six-hundred-year empire. Their successes (coupled with failures and misunderstandings) were humble, but their story is very human, reflecting universal experiences.

Communicating the full range of scientific and technological activities that occurred in the Ottoman Empire is a task for a competent team of specialized scholars, considering the spatial and temporal breath of Ottoman history. The outcome of their endeavors would be a multivolume work. Hence the scope of this study is limited to experiences with science and technology of Turkish- and Arabic-speaking Ottomans who produced, legitimized, consumed, and altered scientific and technological products. It weaves together teachers and students, patrons and men of science, the students of science and the users of science. The book highlights the numerous Ottomans who were engaged in science and technology as "doers" or "consumers," sometimes on a modest level, thus integrating laypeople as well. Intentionally, the book does not celebrate the outstanding geniuses and major discoveries, as by definition these were few and untypical of their times.

The book puts forward three main arguments. First, an "Ottoman science" did in fact exist, harboring unique features differentiating it from other scientific systems of the time. Planning and organization of the processes of scientific activity are embedded in cultural worldviews and prioritizations that are different in different places. This volume explains the various modes of operation, forms, and formats that made the science and technology conducted within the Ottoman realm indeed uniquely Ottoman.

The second main argument is that Ottoman society and culture were a fertile ground for diverse scientific activity. This contradicts common wisdom that still prevails in many academic and non-academic circles, namely, that after the medieval period's Muslim Golden Age, Muslims shut themselves off from other civilizations. This book on Ottoman science presents a different vista of scientific activity in a Muslim society from the fourteenth century through the beginning of the twentieth century. The assumption that the Ottomans were inherently opposed to inventions and innovations is challenged.

The third, more general argument is that Ottoman scientific activity suggests that excellence and innovation are not necessarily identical to invention as we understand it today, namely, cutting-edge creative breakthroughs. The term *generics*—that is, products that are comparable to patented brands in performance—is very useful here to conceptualize Ottoman preoccupation with science.

Like "my" Ottoman scientists, I too relied on the help and support of so many people. I am glad I am able to repay it by presenting them with this book and acknowledging their support here.

The project originated as a short textbook in Hebrew for a new Open University of Israel course on Ottoman history. I thank Professor Haggai Erlich and Dr. Tal Shuval, who invited me to write it. Drs. Yuval Ben-Bassat and Avi Rubin, who reviewed the textbook for the Open University, were encouraging and helpful.

While working on the textbook version I realized the acute need to write a monograph in English on this topic. For that reason I delved again into the sources. Along the way the manuscript went through a series of major transformations to supply colleagues and students with a book-length discussion of the processes that produced Ottoman science.

I owe a debt to my colleagues at the Department of Middle Eastern and African History at Tel Aviv University. Professor Uzi Rabi, the departmental chair during the period of writing the monograph, was a constant source of support, morally and materially. He also enabled me to offer seminars on science and technology in the Muslim world that were the beginning of the book. Professor Ehud R. Toledano, head of the Tel Aviv University Program in Ottoman and Turkish Studies, read a preliminary outline. I benefitted from his ideas. Dr. On Barak graciously shared with me his insights into science, technology, and modernization in the Middle East based on his own work on materials and temporality in colonial Egypt and coal in the Middle East; he also carefully read the whole manuscript.

With Dr. Keren Abbou-Hershkovitz, a friend and a colleague, I share an interest in Islamic science. I thank her for numerous discussions on numerous versions of this text. I enjoyed these talks and profited from them. With Dr. Rainer Brömer of İstanbul Üniversity's Tıp Fakültesi, whom I also think of as a friend, I shared many talks on Ottoman science and medicine around the globe: in Oxford, in Heidelberg, and in recent years in Istanbul, in- and outside the Ottoman archives. Dr. Sonja Brentjes of the Max Planck Institute for the History of Science, Berlin, is a very gracious colleague (in addition to being one of the more erudite and meticulous scholars I know). She answered several questions via e-mail and was willing to share her work by facilitating me with copies of publications I could not locate easily. During the conferences of "Translations, Translators, and Converts: Transmission of Knowledge in the Seventeenth Century Ottoman Lands" (Chicago, March 2013) and "Studies of Knowledge in Eurasia and Africa: Issues of Methodology and Future Perspectives" (Berlin, June–July 2014), I benefited from our talks on methodology and sources in history of Islamic science. Professors Tzvi Langermann (of Bar-Ilan University) and Robert Morrison (of Bowdoin College) listened to a description of the book on the shores of the Bosporus. I thank them for their interest and comments.

I would also like to express thanks to my students at TAU in the seminars "Science and Technology in the Muslim World." Together we tested ideas and evidence. Your questions triggered me further.

Along the way I benefitted from opportunities to present vignettes from this work in several conferences and workshops. In February 2008 I presented a paper at the European Social Science History Conference (ESSHC, Lisbon) on German-speaking health officials in the Ottoman Empire that became part of the my discussion on modernization and state involvement in scientific production. In May 2008 I participated in a panel on medical exchange in premodern Asia, from the Levant to Tibet, at the Annual Conference of Asian Studies in Israel (ASI, Jerusalem). In July 2008 I participated at the Three Societies Meeting dedicated to the theme of "Connecting Disciplines." It was a joint event of the History of Science Society, the British Society for the History of Science, and the Canadian Society for the History and Philosophy of Science. In both conferences I focused on what would become a major theme in this book: the flow of people, techniques, and knowledge East and West. This theme was also discussed in September 2011 in a Tel Aviv University Minerva Humanities Center conference organized by Professor Y. T. Langermann, who leads the working group on the migration of knowledge in the eastern Mediterranean during the late medieval and early modern periods. The most recent venue, in September 2012, was the fourth international conference of the Mediterranean World, "Domino Effects and Hybridization of the Mediterranean," held at 29 Mayıs Üniversitesi, Üskudar, Istanbul. In March 2013 I presented a paper on Ottoman translators within the framework of the University of Chicago symposium "Translation, Translators, and Converts: Transmission of Knowledge in the Seventeenth Century Ottoman Lands." A month later, in April 2013, I presented the sketches of what would become the first chapter on the categorization of knowledge in the framework of the research seminar of the Tel Aviv University Department of Arabic and Islamic Studies. In June 2014 I presented the main arguments of the book in the annual conference of the Middle East and Islamic Studies Association of Israel. I am grateful to the conveners and the participants for an engaging and fruitful dialogue.

Ms. Irena Fliter, Ms. Jennifer Poliakov, and Mr. Ido Ben-Ami, my research assistants and doctoral students, helped me in various ways in preparing this manuscript. Special warm thanks are due to Mr. Liran Yadgar, my previous research assistant, now completing his doctoral project at the University of Chicago. Liran was enthusiastic and helpful in assisting me to locate materials from abroad. I thank them for their dedication and willingness to devote time and energy on my behalf. Mrs. Hephzibah Levin, Shany Orian, and Judith Yacov took care of the linguistic/editorial aspect of the text. At the University of Texas Press I found experts who guided me through the editorial and production process. I thank Jim Burr and Alexis Mills wholeheartedly. I am indebted to Bill Nelson for producing the map.

I am happy to acknowledge the generous financial support from various institutions that allowed me to conduct my research and then write it up: the Israel Science Foundation (Grant #182/11); the Deutsch-Israelische

Stiftung für Wissenschaftlische Forschung und Entwicklung [GIF]—a GIF Young Scientist Grant (Grant #2172-1760.4/200); and the Department of Middle Eastern and African History.

Finally, I would like to mention my family. I especially think of my late father, Dr. Michael Shefer. He was able to see my first two books, and I am sure he would have been happy and proud to see a third. I dedicate this book to my younger daughter, Daphna. The first months after birth were not easy for her medically. Some of the insights brought here regarding the interface of knowledge, professional groups, and institutions were gathered as we spent much time with her in hospitals.

A NOTE ON TRANSLITERATION

The problem of transliteration in Ottoman studies is complicated because of the very broad geographical, cultural, and linguistic scope of the subject matter. Spreading over three continents for six hundred years, the Ottoman Empire was inhabited by members of many linguistic groups living alongside each other, including—in addition to speakers of Turkic dialects—users of Serbo-Croat, Berber, Hebrew, Arabic, Persian, Kurdish, and many more. Moreover, Ottoman society and culture enabled, indeed encouraged, routine crossing of language and cultural boundaries. The result was cultural mixtures and diversities. Such realties are hard to capture, and any single system of transliteration is found lacking either grammatically, phonetically, or aesthetically.

I chose a compromise that allowed me to achieve consistency as much as possible while emphasizing the theme of cultural diversity with regard to Ottoman scientific and technological realities of the early modern period and accurately reflecting the languages of the sources utilized here, which are mainly Ottoman Turkish and Arabic. In addition I tried to simplify forms as much as possible to make the text accessible to historians of science who are nonspecialists in Middle Eastern studies.

Throughout the book I make the case of the high level of Ottomanness of science in the Middle East of the Ottoman era, 1300–1922. With the Ottoman context in mind, I find it appropriate to write most terms and names of places and individuals in Ottoman Turkish forms. For the sake of simplicity, I rendered such terms and names in a modern Turkish form rather than following formal transliteration tables of Ottoman Turkish. In modern Turkish, *c* is pronounced as *j* in English, *ç* as *ch*, and ğ is unvocalized and lengthens the preceding vowel; ı (undotted i) sounds like *u* in the word *turn*; and ş is pronounced like *sh*.

At the same time, I give ample room to provincial-cultural variations, recognizing the Arab character of the Ottoman-Arab provinces. Therefore in cases where the context is Arabic-speaking, I have used Arabic forms. I also used Arabic forms in the context of the Islamic character of the region. Here the Arabic form expresses a universal component.

This dual system of transliterations allows me to make a distinction, for example, between *ülema*, scholars of religion in a Turkish-speaking site, and their colleagues in an Arabic environment, who are *ʿulamāʾ*. I write about *medrese*s and *vakıf*s, but discuss also endowments in Arabic-speaking environments and refer to them as *waqf*s. I refer to such Ottoman scholars as Ahmed bin Mustafa Taşköprüzade, who wrote much in Arabic but functioned in the context of sixteenth-century Ottoman bureaucracy. However, I also discuss Ottoman physicians such as Ṣāliḥ b. Naṣrallāh Ibn Sallūm, the seventeenth-century physician from Aleppo who rose to be the imperial head physician but still wrote only in Arabic.

SCIENCE AMONG THE OTTOMANS

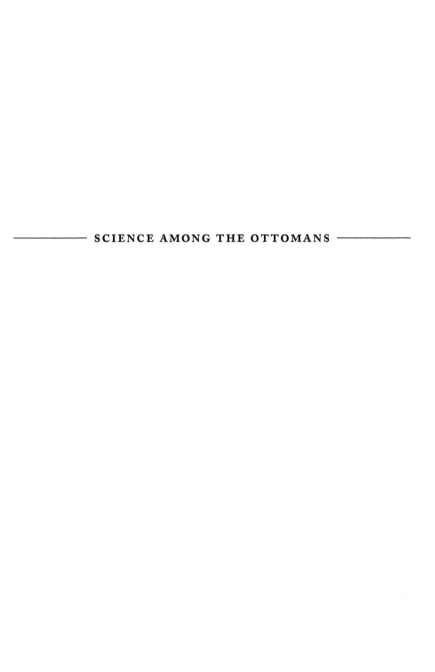

INTRODUCTION

What Is the History of Science?

The history of science has attracted lively scholarly discussion in the twenty-first century's opening decades, in part because the very identity of its subject matter has been opened to new interpretations. Karl Popper (1902–1994), one of the greatest historians and philosophers of science of the twentieth century, knew that the history of science was the history of impossible dreams, of obstinacy, and of error.[1] In other words, the history of science takes us back to past claims and beliefs, many of which we now know to be incorrect. Peter Dear, one of the leading historians of science of this generation, is less sure. He poses a provocative question: "What is the history of science history of?"[2] The modern definition of "science" is embedded in an ideology that it is something natural and hence universal. This definition assumes a very specific historical process that led to the correspondence of "science" and universalism. Our challenge is to abstain from this impediment. Hence the working definition for "history of science" involves an attempt to understand changes in the body of knowledge about the reality of our lives. It investigates the categories of thinking, proving, and experiencing that create, determine, develop, and change scientific knowledge. It is in an attempt to understand why people living in a specific era thought and acted in one way or another with regard to all matters concerning systemized knowledge.

THE HISTORY OF SCIENCE AND TECHNOLOGY

The historical analysis of scientific activity sprang from the self-perception of science as universal, aiming at the formulation of global generalizations. Those who share this view understand scientific work as an internal process tied solely by knowledge and science: ideas create new ideas, knowledge yields further knowledge. Historians of science, like scientists, regard the people who cultivate science and the institutions in which they work as external to knowledge, and thus they are not perceived as influencing the way in which science is practiced. "Pure" science is supposed to be uninfluenced by extraneous considerations, be they economic, social, or political. The world lies open before us for objective investigation, unfettered by outside influences.

This positivist outlook of both past scientists and historians of science was also accompanied by the perception that science develops in a single direction of advancement and progress. Scientific development was viewed as a positive procession, brought about by shining heroes and full of success stories. As long as internal processes were free of alien influences from external powers, there were positive accomplishments. A leading proponent of this approach was Karl Popper, who described knowledge and science as evolutionary. As he perceived it, knowledge is accumulated and progressive; we constantly move forward knowing more and understanding more.[3]

Nowadays, positivist conceptions of science and its narrative are considered naïve, maybe even dangerous. Historians of science fear that characterizing science as providing unconditional and mostly objective answers will sabotage the legitimacy of its products, which in most cases do not constitute a definitive answer or solution to a problem. Scrutiny may lead to contradictory observations, and different observers of established and fixed "facts" might suggest differing interpretations. The demand for "the truth" sets an unreasonable and unobtainable standard. Any scientific argument may be refuted on the pretext of being insufficiently scientific, less than wholly "true," or somehow connected to public policy that the critics find objectionable.[4]

The first significant change in this assessment should be ascribed to the work of Thomas Samuel Kuhn (1922–1996). In his book *The Structure of Scientific Revolutions*, Kuhn declared that in some instances, knowledge changes quickly, dramatically, powerfully, and profoundly. Hence, knowledge does not develop in a continuous linear progression, yet Kuhn still refers to "development" in which science upgrades, improves, and marches forward.[5]

Kuhn's contemporary Paul Feyerabend (1924–1994) had already asserted that knowledge is not accumulated and does not necessarily progress linearly. A student of Karl Popper, Feyerabend was also influenced by Kuhn, but he cautioned that "positive" knowledge or the desire to reach "the truth" may also create something monstrous. Indeed, the historical and moral discussion of Nazi sciences and the fruits of their research deal with a similar point: is knowledge acquired by monstrous means worthy of being channeled in positive directions, or, perhaps, is the very existence of such frightful research enough to negate its right to be applied, no matter how useful its applications may be?[6] In addition, Feyerabend indicates that scientists have no common tools or methods. His starting point was ethical: man's creativity must not be restricted. The result is that scientific work is not even and orderly; on the contrary, it involves a chaotic dimension. Understandably, Feyerabend described his perception of knowledge as "anarchistic."[7]

Kuhn, Feyerabend, and other philosophers and historians of science demonstrate the change in the field. In the past, historical and philosophical writing about science dealt with people and with knowledge, focusing on important people and their intellectual activity. Since the mid-twentieth century, however, the field has undergone extensive changes in the way scientific activity is perceived and, therefore, in the ways it should be studied. The kernel of the change involved awareness that theories may not last forever and the perception of science (and hence its study) as an interdisciplinary endeavor.

Science is tightly tied to philosophy, sociology, anthropology, cultural studies, psychology, economics, and other fields. Moreover, disparate spheres of knowledge are knit together in various deep and intrinsic manners. The ways in which knowledge is acquired in the various fields of science (physics, biology, chemistry, medicine, technology, and so forth) are similar to and influenced by one another. For this reason, it is impossible to learn the history of one field in a manner totally separated from the history of other fields of knowledge; the histories must be synthesized.[8]

Michel Foucault (1926–1984) is among the thinkers who best demonstrate the multidimensional nature of scientific research, although he did not deal with science per se. Foucault was a French philosopher who analyzed social institutions and the theory of systems of thought, but his work helps to understand scientific activity and the function of knowledge in general. He came under criticism for his overgeneralized historical analysis, but Foucault's central argument regarding power and knowledge formed a cornerstone in understanding how the ability to influence human behavior controls information and skills, and vice versa. Foucault was instrumental in understanding how institutions and bodies of knowledge such as medicine are used as a form of social control. Furthermore, he underlined how human discourse—the modalities and codes and signs embedded in conversation—shapes interaction; as a result, discourse is yet another tool to control communication, perception, and behavior.[9] Foucault's influence was substantial partly because of opportune timing. His criticism arrived during deep revision in historiography between the 1960s and 1980s. First arrived the "Linguistic Turn," a major development in Western philosophy that pointed out how language has the power to shape meaning: language is not transparent; rather, it is an agent in the comprehension and construction of reality. The "Cultural Turn" soon joined forces: this is a criticism from within the social sciences that shifted the emphasis toward meaning and away from realism.

The scientist's personal characteristics (personality structure and values) and scientific priorities (such as the standard work methods or questions considered urgent in his era), and likewise factors external to the scientist himself or the field (political, economic, and social circumstances), sow the seeds leading to the growth or rejection of an original idea that on (rare) occasions manages to transcend the hypothetical and provide a practical answer to a problem. In fact, theories are actually proven or refuted by these internal and external factors, and not on account of the success or failure of a laboratory experiment or the wording of a formula and an equation.[10]

With the growing perception of science as a complicated, integralistic, or holistic, process, the research about science becomes richer. Contemporary research outlines the circumstances that enable (or restrict) scientific activity and freedom of thought, including social connections, economic potential, religious concepts, cultural values, and political maneuvers. In other words, the history of science now deals with social networks, connections among ideas, institutions, and professional organizations. The current research ties the lone scientist into his social and professional environment, ideologies, and their influences on science. (Nationalism, for example, argues for involving science with questions of honor and national competitiveness rather than merely individual ambitions.) In addition, other aspects, such as power games, legitimacy, funding, knowledge, and applicability, have affected the history of science as well. Instances of double meanings and even scientific theoretical contradictions are all intermingled. This complex reality requires a completely different kind of investigation into scientific activity.

Recent research trends have given attention to marginal groups and previously marginalized sites of scientific activity—for example, the East. One example is the work of Kapil Raj, who demonstrated that modern science is not an exclusively European and Western creation. Raj clarified that a great part of "Western" knowledge between the seventeenth and nineteenth centuries was actually created far away from the European centers, in the New World or the colonies in Asia. In medicine, cartography, engineering, and other fields, the help of locals in sharing knowledge, skills, and tools enabled European university graduates to learn and improve their knowledge and then export it to Europe itself.[11]

Another example is a feminist reading of scientific research. In 1990 Dorothy E. Smith, a sociologist and feminist theoretician with interests also in education, claimed that women's experience of knowledge is radically different from the male hegemonic one.[12] Fifteen years later, in the introductory essay of a special *Signs* issue devoted to feminist approaches to social science methodologies, Sandra Harding and Kathryn Norberg called for transformation of the methodologies and epistemologies of scientific disciplines. Their concerns about conventional standards for "good research," and whether and how customary approaches to knowledge promote or obstruct the development of a more ethical research, are applicable to all fields of scientific works.[13]

The current discourse within the history of science and technology wishes to go further and integrates in a meaningful way the nonhuman factors in scientific process. David Bloor and the Strong Program, initiated in the 1970s in Edinburgh, regards the existence of a cooperatively functioning scientific community as an essential condition for scientific activity and argues against the philosophical view as a principle of scientific activity.[14]

The Bath School and Harry Collins are less historical and more social: Collins is a sociologist of knowledge in general, not specifically of science. He and his school focused on microsocial case studies of, for example, laboratories and experiments to show how scientists obey rules while performing experiments. In this way, norms, traditions, and patterns shape scientific activity.[15]

Bruno Latour, a French philosopher, anthropologist, and sociologist of science, contested both these British schools.[16] He was one of the developers of actor-network theory and maintains that scientific activity is the product of associations of people, ideas, and objects. In other words, the act of science includes semiotic as well as material and physical actors. The relationships between the elements are continuous and ever-changing.[17] His contribution is the insistence on the momentous role of nonhuman entities alongside human actors: only when they come together is there a scientific meaning. Protocols, machines, and materials are also crucial factors determining scientific outcomes.[18] Latour explained that physical entities are not radically different from a context made of colleagues, rulers, money, instruments, or body practices.[19]

In the Middle Eastern context, a posthumanistic influence (together with environmental postcolonialism) may be seen in Timothy Mitchell's analysis (influenced by Latour) of modernity, state formation, and economics and technology in twentieth-century Egypt. The opening essay of his *Rule of Experts* on Egyptian political and economic processes in the postcolonial phase of the twentieth century posits the question, "Can the mosquito speak?" He then examines how malaria and other nonhuman agents, which include artifacts as well as natural events, shaped forms and manifestations of power.[20]

Khaled Fahmy is another example of posthumanistic writing, here coming from a Foucauldian influence in the Middle Eastern context. Fahmy too is a historian of Egypt, albeit of an earlier period: his focus is nineteenth-century modernization and colonization. Fahmy traces political, legal, and social transformations in Egypt through the changes in the human body: physical, medical, aesthetical, and so on. He presents a revisionist narrative to the modernization, colonization, and cosmopolitanism of nineteenth-century Egypt by looking at the physical human body which moved, breathed, heard, and smelled—that is, the physical functions and senses that make up human activity and experience.[21]

A very recent example of posthumanistic writing is On Barak's monograph on transportation and communication in twentieth-century Egypt. Barak demonstrates how universal technologies (here: steamers, railways, telegraphs, tramways, and telephones) perform differently in various sociocultural contexts: in the West they were associated with standardization, promptness, and expediency, while in Egypt the very same technologies contributed to construction of a different sense of time.[22] His current research on the "coal-ization of the Middle East" situates the adoption of coal and the steam engine in a global context. It explores how the percolation of British coal into the Middle East simultaneously fueled the region's uneven modernization and, by offering new markets and coaling depots, enabled developments in steam navigation and politics in the colonies and metropolis alike, albeit along very different trajectories.[23]

My own position is meant to strike a balance between approaches that invest agency in nonhuman factors in scientific action and an anthropological influence that regards "culture" as a crucial category of analysis. Artifacts are not outside history; they are dependent on cultural context, and with it they change.[24]

Having started with "culture," I note how cultures laid the foundation for different and parallel trainings about knowledge and scientific endeavors, attached multiple goals to knowledge, and indeed accepted several modes of knowing that are the basis of how we assess evidence and reach conclusions. The exact varieties might differ from one culture to another, but the plural experiences of science and knowledge seem to be a recurring theme.[25]

THE HISTORY OF ISLAMIC SCIENCE AND TECHNOLOGY

Islamic science history has a long history of its own.[26] Comparing the historiography of Islamic science in western Asia to the historiography of Chinese science in eastern Asia is illuminating because of some basic similarities, at least during large parts of the twentieth century. The principles that governed these histories in the mid-twentieth century were text-based narratives of heroes, successes, and discoveries, of progress and the improvement of the quality of life. However, while the Islamic history of science is still a rather conservative field, whose discourse is shaped to large extent by these principles, the history of Chinese science is today at a very different place.

The study of science in Muslim societies did not have a central towering figure like Joseph Needham (1900–1995), the undisputed don of the history of Chinese science thanks to his series of monographs on Chinese science and culture.[27] The study of Islamic science, in contrast, was decentralized, characterized by a dialogue between several key scholars specializing in various bodies of knowledge in Muslim contexts.

Past and present scholars of Islamic science have also asked the question that Joseph Needham posed at the heart of his work: why did the West surpass the regions of Islam (or China) in science and technology despite the latter's much more promising historical start? They seem not to follow further the historiography of Chinese science and technology. Here Nathan Sivin introduced a new path of inquiry in his concentration on what happened within the Chinese scientific realm rather than on what was lacking. He further urged scholars to understand the different nature and meaning of "science" in the Chinese context.[28] His call for reflection was met, for example, by Benjamin A. Elman, who analyzed scientific contacts in the realms of astronomy, geography, mathematics, and medicine between Chinese literati under the Manchu dynasty and Jesuits and Protestants. His task, as he explained it, was to unify late Imperial China and early modern China, each of which was characterized by a distinct scientific impact, either Jesuit or Protestant. He titled his monograph *In Their Own Terms* to reflect his conclusion that despite the many borrowings, the Chinese produced their own science.[29]

Scholars of the Islamic world apparently did not engage with the post-Needham historiography and chose to focus on the "why not" question; they did so within the paradigm of decline. "Decline theory" centered on the theme of total Muslim weakness compared to that of the Christian West. According to this paradigm, after the Islamic golden age and the Abbasid dynasty in the Middle Ages, which were characterized by intellectual curiosity and innovative research, the desire for renewal was lost. Seclusion and introversion characterized all aspects of life and led to political decline, continuing through religion and economics and ending in culture and science. The decline did not stop except for a relatively short time during the so-called Ottoman golden age around the sixteenth century and during the rule of "Suleiman the Magnificent." (The title is, of course, connected to the way the period is perceived among the generations that followed.) According to this view, Western penetration into the Muslim world in the nineteenth century forced Muslims to shake themselves free from their apathy and join modernity. This notion asserts that without an external Western force, Muslim ignorance would have continued into the modern period.

A further claim in current scholarship on Islamic science, however, ties the European success to Islamic origins and maintains that the West's scientific breakthrough could not have happened without the decisive contribution of Muslim science. In this spirit, scholars study the Islamic sources of mathematics, astronomy, and European cosmology of the Renaissance period.[30] This claim is heard in both academic and public spheres, as in the popular 1001 Inventions exhibition, created by the British-based Foundation for Science, Technology and Civilisation (FSTC). It is evident that many both within and outside of academia think in terms of "breakthroughs," "enduring legacies," and "leaving a mark on the world."[31]

Like Needham, who discussed failures in the development of Chinese science toward modernization—and unlike Sivin—scholars of Islamic science focused on limitations in scientific achievements. They identified the roots of obstructions to scientific advances in different spheres of life. Some considered Islam to be a restraint that imprisoned science in mental chains from which it could not be liberated. Other scholars who shared the view of decline but did not necessarily tie it with religion per se pointed to external reasons that created a burden on Islamic science and technology, like the "infiltration" of "strangers" (meaning non-Arabs). In this context, scholars discussed the Turks' entrance into and domination of the Islamic world. Their starting point was the establishment of the institution of military slavery, the Mamluks, during the ninth century. The incursion of the Mongols in the mid-thirteenth century was described as the final blow, turning the Islamic world into a wasteland from which it was never able to recover.

The perception in such studies that non-Arabs contributed to the decline of science and technology in the Islamic world is connected to the scholars' academic specialization. They were Arabists in their training, orientalists in their outlook, and, sometimes, they were also armed with Arab-nationalist ideology.[32] As far as they were concerned, Islam and Islamic culture were, in essence, Arab. Interestingly, these Western academic scholars reflected the Islamic-Salafi stances of the figures they studied, like the Egyptian Muḥammad ʿAbduh (1849–1905) and other Muslim intellectuals and reformers, and blamed non-Arab figures for the relative inferiority of the Islamic world in the modern era: foreign intruders diminished the splendor of Muslim culture and adapted it to their inferior dimensions. These academics did not master Turkish and therefore were unable to read the relevant manuscripts in the Muslim-Turkic languages (like Ottoman and Chagatay). In their view, this obstacle was not a limitation. They did not value the scientific contribution of Muslim Turks and Persians from the start; thus, they did not expect to find significant new discoveries in the treatises they had written. In their opinion, the renunciation of such texts was insignificant.

The Encyclopedia of the History of Arabic Science, edited by Roshdi Rashed—one of the important scholars of Islamic-Arab mathematics—is one example of many of the trends described above. The encyclopedia is a comprehensive compendium containing no less than thirty essays by leading scholars. It is organized into three volumes: astronomy (theory and practice); mathematics and physics; and technology, alchemy, and life sciences. These general titles reflect the inclusion of essays on optics, music, botany, marine navigation, and more. The scope is truly impressive, and as a collection of essays, the encyclopedia serves as a good starting point for examining scientific activity in Arabic. The title is a clear declaration of the importance of scientific activity in Arabic in particular and of its contribution to global science in general. Even so, this collection, which was published in 1996 (although a large number of the essays had been written in the 1980s and were not updated), still almost completely ignores scientific essays in Persian, Turkish, and other Islamic languages.[33] Likewise, Rashed's current project, the "Scientia Graeco-Arabica," is a series of publications that includes the addition of key texts and intellectual biographies of role models in the transition of science and philosophy from ancient times to the *Arab* Islamic world (my emphasis), and thus traces the ongoing tradition from ancient to modern times, conducted apparently only in Arabic.

As this survey reveals, in most cases the scholarship of Islamic science gives the impression that terms like "beginnings," "progress," and "demise" dominated the historiography. The usual narrative was a linear history of either progress or decline. In recent years more and more scholars have called for a more critical examination of Islamic pursuit of science as both social and epistemological activity—a perspective that allows for multiple interpretations, approaches, and practices. In other words, the linear process is replaced by parallels and irregularities.[34]

THE HISTORY OF OTTOMAN SCIENCE AND TECHNOLOGY HISTORY

The survey of the historiography of Muslim science history explains why not too much has been done in the field of Ottoman science history.[35] The decline thesis inhibited Western historians from dealing with Ottoman science, and while many Turkish scholars were seriously involved with Ottoman science, they read and wrote only in Turkish. The unfortunate result was that they functioned in a closed discursive group: their scholarship was inaccessible to most Western scholars, and the Turkish scholars, on their part, almost never followed up on research in Western languages. Moreover, many Turkish scholars internalized the orientalist discourse and accepted the premise regarding Muslim decline and religion's responsibility for it. Such orientalist discourse found a place within nationalistic ideology, which openly advocated Turkish Western secular identity. Within this framework, Turkish academics related to the Ottoman past in science only from a very specific angle: the process of the Westernization of science or the infiltration of the West into the world of Islam via technology and science.

Adnan Adıvar's work on Ottoman science from the late 1930s and early 1940s, which is still considered a basic Turkish-language textbook in the field,[36] is a clear product of a national, Western, and secular political agenda. His monograph is aptly titled *Osmanlı Türklerinde İlim* (Science

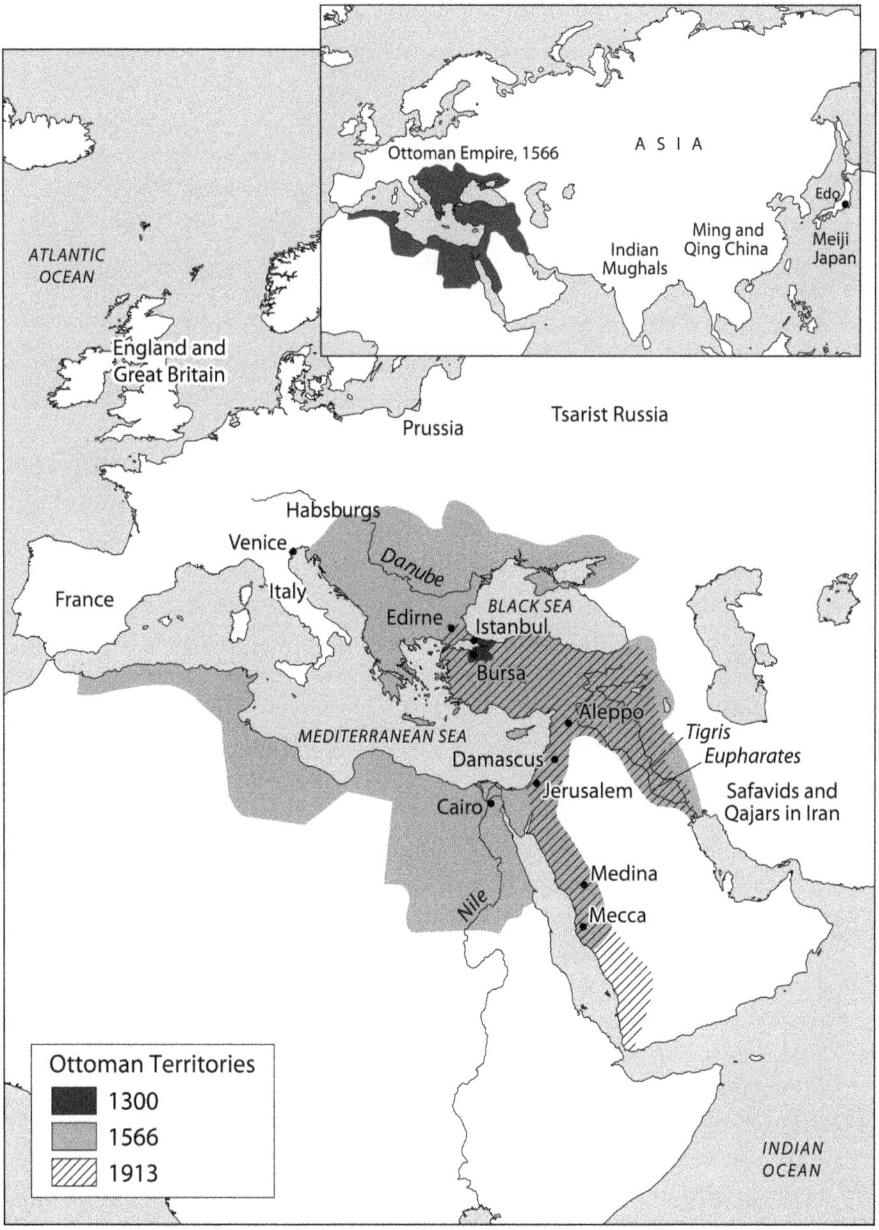

MAP I

The Ottomans and Their Worlds

among the Ottoman Turks). It has been printed in numerous editions since it first appeared in the early 1940s. Interestingly, the Turkish book is not the original work but a translation, with additions, from a shorter 1939 monograph that Adıvar wrote in French while exiled in Paris. The book embraces a variety of fields of knowledge and is arranged chronologically.

Adıvar proposed a clear criterion for assessing the quality of science: Ottoman science should be evaluated only according to the extent of its exposure to the West and the Ottoman willingness to adopt it, while popular science was classified as no more than a collection of superstitions. Adıvar's framework was widely accepted. Accordingly, two eras (and only two) were marked as worthy of study: the sixteenth century, considered the golden era, and the nineteenth century, during which accelerated modernization processes began.

Like many others of his generation and profession in the Middle East and worldwide, Adıvar was the product of a process that started during the nineteenth century: "science" as a global and universal endeavor had become equated with Western science, excluding both the Islamic East and Far East. The distinction (even antagonism) between "science"—that is, the higher order and systemization of truth—and "traditional knowledge," which was now reduced to "belief," did not appear before the nineteenth century.[37]

In covering success, or prosperity, or the growing dependence on the West, other writers have employed similar research methods: the discussion is text-based, focused on "famous" figures and their discoveries, and on scientific institutions or publication of key texts. The available Turkish scholarship includes studies of hospital architecture,[38] an illustrated surgical manual from the fifteenth century,[39] and the history of the reconstruction of the observatory in Istanbul. (This latter study is a rather rare exception of a Turkish academic publication in English for the benefit of the whole academic community.)[40]

A particularly prominent figure in our generation is Ekmeleddin İhsanoğlu. In the 1980s he established the History of Science Department at the University of Istanbul, and he was the founder of, life of, and spirit behind the Research Centre for Islamic History, Art and Culture (IRCICA) in Istanbul. Alongside his academic work, he has also been active since the 1980s in international Muslim organizations. Since 2005 he has served as general director of the Organization of the Islamic Conference (OIC), an organization of fifty-seven Muslim countries for economic, political, cultural, and religious cooperation. İhsanoğlu is mentioned here thanks to a long line of studies and bibliographies, most of which are not in Turkish, in order to appeal to their international target audience and thereby enhance the status of Ottoman and Muslim science's achievements.[41]

All of these works cumulatively have accrued vast knowledge, allowing the academic community to assess and analyze Ottoman scientific activity in political, social, cultural, and economic contexts. Recent questions touch upon science and state, science and society, science and international relations with Europe and Muslim countries in Asia, science and gender, and more. An encouraging sign is the long list of articles dealing with Ottoman science and technology included in *The Turks*. This encyclopedia of six thick volumes was published in Ankara in English in 2002 (obviously targeting an international audience). The encyclopedia lays out the history of Turks from the Asian plains of the Paleolithic era up to the collapse of the USSR and the founding of the Turkish Moslem republics in central Asia. Two of the six volumes are dedicated to Ottoman history. They contain a variety of articles written by Turkish and non-Turkish scholars about the relationships between Ottoman science and the world around the Mediterranean Basin, between the economic system and scientific activity, and between European travelers to the empire and local science. The encyclopedia also chronicles Ottoman attempts at aviation and constructing automatic motor vehicles, as well as other inventions.[42]

TOWARD A HISTORY OF OTTOMAN SCIENTIFIC EXPERIENCES

This book is about the social and cultural logistics that produced Ottoman science. Instead of focusing on "what"—that is, the finished product (unambiguously formulated, solid knowledge)—I focus on "how": the processes by which Ottomans were engaged with knowledge and the value invested in these procedures. There are many forms of knowledge and multiple ways of knowing. What was worth knowing for Ottomans in various times and places? How did Ottomans go about learning them? The book traces the different answers to these questions, the challenges to them, and the various sites of learning. The narrative here suggests that tracing the experiences Ottomans had with systemized knowledge serves as a guide to define what is behind the label "science" in the context of the early modern Middle East. It is thus a possible answer to Dear's challenge presented in the beginning of this introduction: "What is the history of science history of?"

I focus on producers and consumers of knowledge in elite circles but also outside of them. I approach this task by discussing the various types of Ottomans involved in scientific activity: Ottomans of different religious and ethnic affiliations; Ottomans living in diverse geopolitical locations, in the imperial center as well as in the provinces; and Ottomans from different social echelons. Additionally, I explore gender and discuss women as patrons of science and scientists, as well as female modes of learning. I also approach different experiences of knowledge: the theoretical sort that scholars or scientists gain through reading and writing, and the artisanal knowledge gained through practice and labor.

The structure of the book follows the various stages in the nonlinear processes that different Ottoman communities used to create and justify, transmit and transform, and use and manage knowledge for various purposes: concepts of knowledge, patterns of learning, transfer and transmission of knowledge, and state involvement in scientific and technological activities. Within each thematic chapter the narrative carefully notes changes along chronological lines. I also reflect on both subtle adjustments and moments of rupture in scientific experiences, along with continuation of such experiences through the Ottoman centuries.

The first chapter identifies the various sources of knowledge that nurtured the Ottomans over the years and the mechanisms of legitimation. It moves on to classify the bodies of knowledge following Ottoman epistemological criteria of theory and practice, religion and intellect, while also classifying the classifications and explaining their meaning. The chapter situates Ottoman scientific experiences at the center of a Eurasian scientific hub made up of the Islamic world, the Turkic-Mongol world, the Byzantine world, the Mediterranean world, and western Europe. My aim is to demonstrate that the Ottomans absorbed varied and multiple traditions from various geocultural sources.

The second and third chapters analyze the various people who were engaged in processes of creation of knowledge and then its dissemination: their social, geographical, religious, professional, and gender identities. Chapter 2 charts the institutions of learning, the pedagogy of teaching, and the professional groups involved in the various bodies of knowledge. Chapter 3 locates the intermediary agents who were the human carriers of knowledge across time and space, and explains how the processes of transference were implemented in the Ottoman context.

The fourth and final chapter connects scientific activity and the state by examining the personal contact of patronage and infrastructural projects, which were always controlled by the Ottoman state. The main issues in this chapter are power structures, the composite nature of formal and informal relationships, and modes of financing of Ottoman scientific experiences.

The discussion culminates in the conclusion with the question, "What was Ottoman science?" With the drive toward writing a global history of science gaining momentum, the book helps to note the distinct features of Ottoman scientific experience. The careers of two eminent Ottoman scholars serve as a platform to distill the patterns of scientific experience that were unique to the Ottoman scene, and at the same time called for contacts and connections with other Islamic and non-Islamic sciences. The binary categories from the school of "the west of the rest," in the form of "west" and "east" or "indigenous" and "global," are not helpful in explaining the Ottoman situation.

The following narrative relies on evidence found mainly in archival documents, scientific treatises, and various literary genres. This type of evidence is the product of states and elites wishing to perpetuate themselves. As such, the figures and their actions are not typical of common non-elite practices. In other words, the sources do not lend themselves easily to reconstructing Ottoman scientific experience from below, which is the aim of this book. Nonetheless, these sources reveal "the Ottoman mentality," to borrow Robert Dankoff's phrase from his lifelong study of Evliya Çelebi (ca. 1611–1682), the renowned Ottoman traveler of the seventeenth century.[43] "Ottoman mentality" is used here in the sense of the French term *mentalités*, which includes mindsets and social attitudes at the juncture of the individual and the collective.[44]

The sources expose prevalent patterns of conceptions and attitudes in Ottoman society, including the scientific and technological realms. Hence, although the heroes in the sources are usually unique individuals, they were in fact typical Ottomans of their day. They thus provide a view of the Ottoman mind from the inside.

Three intertwined themes run through the book, all connected with the Ottoman pursuit of science: movement and mobility of people, hybridization of identities, and crossing of boundaries.

People make knowledge moveable when they transmit, circulate, transfer, transform, ignore, forget, translate, erase, add, distort, and correct knowledge. Knowledge is ever-changing. It has to be "concerted" in order to be localized and thus succeeds in bridging the gaps of time, distance, and language.[45] This amazing phenomenon was created by two interrelated aspects of scientific activity: the cultivation of a variety of formats of intellectual exchange and the existence of numerous human agents of exchange. Knowledge was transmitted through translation, copying, circulation of texts, or even citations. Such practices provided a powerful site of contact and exchange and contributed to the shaping of a cosmopolitan sphere that was closely connected with the broader, universal Muslim community while rooted in local identities.[46]

Human agents through their very lives acted as a link between scientific networks, sometimes unintentionally. There were numerous causes, reasons, or circumstances that transformed various groups into de facto hybrids that were able to act as go-betweens and undermine the drive for purification of categories. Steven Epstein's *Purity Lost* shows how the islands of the late medieval eastern Mediterranean were sites of cultural exchange that framed self-identity in multicultural communities.[47] In addition to geographical pockets such as islands, linguistic skills, confessional or ethnic kinship, and unique political circumstances—all of which appeared in the Ottoman case—allowed and even called for mixed alliances.

Hybridization goes hand in hand with a related theme of crossing boundaries. Two opposite processes are discerned in the Ottoman scientific system: the erection of boundaries and categories, on the one hand, and the crossing of the very same boundaries, on the other. Several types of boundaries separated premodern scientific cultures and distinguished between disciplines and methods. At the same time, such borders were eradicated temporarily, made elastic, or at least modified to permit the acceptance of an alien type of scientific knowledge. The outcome was movement of people and their artifacts and thoughts across civilizations and countries. When movement was restricted (such trials were initiated on both sides of the border), these attempts proved futile in most cases. There was no real way to prevent leakage of knowledge from one side and its assimilation on the other side.

Cultural domains are not exclusive. Modern historiography ignored this fact for many years, but this is changing with a wave of scholars showing European contacts with the late medieval and early modern Muslim worlds. The themes vary: some relate to geography and worldviews;[48] others concern the cultural-mercantile contacts in the eastern Mediterranean,[49] the cultural configuration of the Renaissance,[50] or military technological rivalry.[51] But the leitmotif is the same: civilizations in Europe and Asia have crisscrossed each other in the eastern Mediterranean and central Asia for centuries. There was no iron curtain between East and West.

INTRODUCTION

ON INVENTIVENESS: AN OTTOMAN LESSON

A crucial argument that runs through this book is that scientific excellence and innovation are not necessarily identical with "invention" as we mean it today—that is, a cutting-edge, patent-like creative breakthrough. Modern society created, accordingly, the concept of "intellectual property" and the legal mechanisms to protect it. The Ottomans, however, relied on exogenous forces science-wise while being quite independent in production. The term *generics*—referring to products that are comparable to patented brands in performance—is very useful here to conceptualize Ottoman preoccupation with science (terms like *borrowing* or *imitation* are left aside as less helpful).

The Ottoman case brings the following lesson: innovation and creativity in science manifest themselves in many ways. This statement goes beyond discarding modern and Western dualistic reconstruction of innovation versus tradition as too simplistic and polarized. Even a call for a more nuanced look at Ottoman scientific experience is quite simplistic, as it ignores the powerful forces (whether social, financial, political, religious, etc.) that intentionally reconstruct this collision and nurture it. To make things even more complicated, the supposed collision between old and new is not new at all. Ottomans used it as well. Fifty years ago, Bernard Lewis discussed early modern Ottoman observers who used the antonyms "old" and "new" to criticize what they viewed as disappointing contemporary realities.[52]

It is common to start discussions regarding Islamic inventions, or lack thereof, by referring to the Muslim concept of *bidʿa* (innovation and, more precisely, a belief or an act that is unprecedented in the time of the Prophet Muḥammad). *Bidʿa* is the opposite of *sunna*, the lifestyle of Muḥammad, a model demanding emulation. A commonplace notion posits that the world of Islam is sealed to the West and purposely rejects any innovation or invention out of the desire to preserve text-based conservative tradition. In this spirit, a particular hadith is often quoted: "the most evil things are innovations; every innovation is an invention; every invention is a mistake; and all mistakes lead to Hell." This is a religious and theological statement, which was also practiced in daily life: conservative circles could use it as a pretext to reject coffee, printing, clocks, telephones, and female suffrage.

Such conservative rejection did not always succeed. In reality, the consensus in Muslim societies as to what constitutes a forbidden and dangerous innovation (*bidʿa sayyiʾa* or *bidʿa madhmūma*) and what is a desirable innovation that is worth adopting (*bidʿa ḥasana* or *bidʿa maḥmūda*) changed from time to time. Today's *bidʿa* have often turned into tomorrow's *sunna*.[53] Muslims throughout the centuries developed an extensive literature dealing with the different kinds of innovation—an attempt to distinguish between different types of innovation by means of complicated criteria. The aim was to enable a dynamic and flexible approach that could answer the changing needs of society.[54]

The Ottoman example laid out in the following pages demonstrates how a Muslim society actually coped with the question of innovation on the levels of both theoretical beliefs and practical daily life. The Ottoman attitude included aspects that we may categorize as acceptance and resistance simultaneously. Ogier Ghislain de Busbecq, the Hapsburg ambassador to the Ottoman court in the mid-sixteenth century, wrote that there was no other nation that displayed greater willingness to adopt practical inventions to fulfill its needs; at the same time, its citizens were filled with superstition, and it was impossible to persuade them to accept inventions that they considered to be compromising the principles of their faith or the authority of their religious leaders.[55]

Maybe de Busbecq's description should be taken more broadly to hint at a situation of "not only/but also," in contrast to the dichotomy of "either/or." Or maybe modern and Western dualistic categorization did not occupy the Ottomans too much (unless the discussion bore on theological issues). The *bidʿa* discourse is too narrow a prism to evaluate inventiveness in general, and the Ottoman case in particular. Industrious and imaginative minds and active production can manifest also in translations, adaptations, and improvements, and these are crucial as well to sustaining dynamism.

Methodologically, I draw on Keith Krause's model of scientific diffusion, but with a twist. Building on his research on Western military technology, Krause formulated the following process: innovations in science and technology and their diffusion are like waves; the wave starts in a period of rapid and intense changes. In the second stage, the innovations spread further to agents who adopt that knowledge and adapt it to their own requirements. The adapted knowledge is then passed on to third actors, who produce imitations with no claim to innovation or change. The final tier consists of the consumers of imported and finished products. Like waves, the exponentiation of knowledge starts with energy and fades toward the end, and like waves, the process is cyclical and happens again and again.[56]

Krause formulated this model to explain patterns in the transfer of knowledge, production, and commerce for military purposes. His model stresses that scientific activity and transfer of knowledge are complex processes that include different levels of action and creation. Krause's three-tier theory of military technology was criticized for sounding suspiciously like a substitute for "first" and "third" worlds.[57] I have no intention of re-invoking a simplistic hierarchy between supposedly homogeneous worlds. Instead I refer to Krause's model in order to highlight that any given society sustains different modes of engagement with scientific and technological activity; inventors and end users coexist. Indeed, very few Nobel laureates and outstanding, brilliant inventors exist. The end users, however, are countless and important partners to the circle of scientific activity. Krause's model helps us to evaluate Ottoman scientific activity as a whole and locate it along the scientific wave. The Ottomans did not invent many significant things. They did not revolutionize science and technology. They also did not stand out for making singular improvements to existing ideas and techniques. However, once they realized the efficiency and utility of a skill or the accuracy and veracity of an idea, they had the flexibility to assimilate those techniques and knowledge, and offer local production.

The ability to adopt and adapt science and technology was not even, however, in all fields of scientific activity or during all six hundred years of Ottoman existence. Ottoman self-sufficiency eroded during the nineteenth century. Ottomans moved consciously in some cases—for example, in their armaments policy—to importation of finished goods and reduced their attempts to domesticate technology. The reasons were apparently weak industrial and financial foundations in time of rapid change (rather than lack of expertise or materials), but either way it led to Ottoman vulnerability and eventually dependency.[58]

This book celebrates diligence, consistency, and independent thinking in small and large technologies. There is much more to science and technology than high-tech, and much to say in favor of popularization—perhaps even vulgarization—of avant-garde science and technology.

ONE

FRAMING "KNOWLEDGE" IN THE OTTOMAN EMPIRE

How did Ottomans view knowledge? What types of knowledge were they familiar with? What sources of knowledge did they consider legitimate? These questions invoke epistemological issues regarding the sources and types of human knowledge. The process of defining and organizing knowledge resulted in a hierarchy. It entailed inclusions and exclusions, acceptance and tensions. Certain bodies of knowledge were endorsed, while others were rejected or marginalized, and even for those bodies accepted there could be tensions and competition for recognition and status between people who were occupied with specific bodies of knowledge as theoretical constructs and their applications. In some cases, the categorization of what constitutes knowledge was not merely one of relative importance and utility but rather went deeper, to question to what extent, if at all, certain fields were worthy of being taught and included in the Ottoman intellectual environment. As that climate changed from time to time, Ottomans would always have to consider these questions.

A EURASIAN MATRIX: THE MULTIPLE CULTURAL SOURCES OF KNOWLEDGE IN THE OTTOMAN EMPIRE

The Ottomans interacted with numerous scientific traditions whose paths they crossed chronologically and spatially: those of the Islamic world, the Turkic-Mongol world, the Byzantine world, the Mediterranean world, and Western Europe. Previously, scholars tended to separate and segregate the Ottomans,[1] but this is not the case anymore. The Ottoman Empire is routinely connected either to Renaissance Europe or to the Far East, but in fact it was a situation of "not only/but also," in contrast to the dichotomy of "either/or." This singular situation positioned the Ottomans at the center of a very rich and complex matrix of diverse scientific worlds across Eurasia.

Every culture rests on the shoulders of the one that preceded it, and the Ottomans were no exception. But there was something unique to the Ottoman method: they were especially eclectic. The Ottomans engaged with multiple, varied traditions from different geocultural sources. The traditions varied not only in their sources, but also in their characters; some were written and others orally transmitted, some were erudite and others, folkloristic. Ottomans did not hide (or, perhaps, did not succeed in hiding) these layers. They mixed these traditions into a new creation, not necessarily always comfortably or devoid of tensions.

The Chinese zodiac and Persian and Mediterranean gardening are examples of an amalgamation and digestion of heritages resulting in unique Ottoman cultural and scientific traditions. Many Ottomans wrote on and practiced astrology and astronomy. To a large extent, they worked within the Islamic interpretation of astrology and astronomy as formulated by many generations of Muslim scholars and practitioners in the pre-Ottoman era. However, the Ottomans had a minor astrological tradition that linked to shamanistic cosmology from the plains of Asia.

Heads of animals were carved into the impressive entrance gate to the Seljukid school Gök Medrese in Sivas, which continued to be popularly used during the Ottoman era. The representation of animals is a dominant theme in Seljukid religious and "secular" architecture. Twentieth-century historians of art and architecture took great pains at identifying Seljukid figural images, explaining their origins, and deciphering their meanings. Now we know that there are several connotations to these stylized animals: astrological symbolism, indications of power, and references to cosmic mythologies. In many cases the Armenian and Georgian Anatolian influences are quite pronounced and visible.

However, in other buildings the carvings allude to a different set of concepts and meanings, and these are taken from central Asian shamanism. In the case of the Sivas *medrese* and mosques and mausolea from Kayseri and elsewhere across Seljukid Anatolia, the stone reliefs even echo fusion of Chinese astrology into the western Seljukid Islamic repertoire, as the carvings surprisingly resemble images of the animal cycle from the Chinese zodiac. There are also rare cases of dragons, some of which recall Chinese dragon representations from the Han period. Indeed, Chinese culture was part of the possible cultural and scientific basket in the original homeland of the Turkish tribes in the plains of central Asia who made their way eastward on the continent. Accordingly, evidence of the central Asian Chinese calendar system in the Islamic world appeared around 1000, at the time nomadic Turkish tribes from eastern and central Asia were moving into the Islamic world. During the period of the Mongol invasion (which started in Anatolia in 1240), artists, intellectuals, and bureaucrats had access again to Chinese culture. This phase might have stimulated existing ideas and concepts from earlier engagement with Chinese knowledge and models of the world. The artistic execution of the images on the Seljukid buildings, however, was taken from the repertoire of west Asia, the present seat of these Turkish Muslims.[2] Perhaps it is not accidental that the Sivas structure with a Seljukid interpretation of a Chinese zodiac symbol was named Gök Medrese, meaning "college of the sky."

The possibility of some symbiosis of Chinese science and Turkish-Islamic scientific horizons dates from a later period than the controversy regarding a famous prophetic saying (hadith) in which Muḥammad reportedly said, "Seek knowledge even in China." This hadith deserves an independent study as its history reveals the durability of ideas and preferences even while under attack for centuries by eminent critics. Just a cursory search in Islamic forums in the new media[3] or leafing through the formal publications of leading modern scholars[4] demonstrates that those who denounce the hadith (usually but not exclusively associated with Salafi cycles) find themselves referring to this hadith time and again. This dialectical mechanism spread and advanced the very idea the texts were trying to refute.

The debate surrounding the saying "Seek knowledge even in China" goes back to the eleventh and twelfth centuries, and to legal circles with a taste for adherence to the literal text. The controversy touches on two points. The first is whether the extreme measures of obtaining knowledge are desirable. The second point of criticism, and this is the one that interests us here, is whether the positioning of China as a symbol or a source of knowledge and truth should be accepted.[5]

Ibn al-Qaysarānī (d. 1113), a scholar of traditions and a Zahirite, was part of the "intense canonical process" of collecting prophetic traditions in general and compiling those of al-Bukhārī and Muslim in particular.[6] According to al-Qaysarānī, the hadith is rejected (*munkar*).[7] The Hanbalite scholar Abū al-Faraj Ibn al-Jawzī (d. 1201) from Baghdad followed a similar path. His *Kitāb al-Mawḍuʿāt* (Collection of fabricated traditions) includes a chapter (*kitāb*) devoted to knowledge which opens with the "Seek knowledge even in China" saying. Ibn al-Jawzī presented a few chains of transmission and then stated that this hadith was not authenticated.[8] The debate continued in later centuries and spread from Iraq to the Levant, and to other parts of the Middle East. Ibn Taymiyya (d. 1326), the forceful Mamluk Hanbalite scholar and theologian from Damascus and Cairo who sought the return to the scriptures, opined that these were not the Prophet's words.[9]

The participants in the debate were far from reaching a consensual approach. The Egyptian luminary Jalāl al-Dīn al-Ṣuyūṭī (d. 1505) stated his approval of this hadith while acknowledging the existence of a controversy. Al-Ṣuyūṭī's texts circulated widely in the Ottoman domains, and copies were found in the libraries and collections of the elite as well as in local mosques more accessible to a wider audience.[10] Al-Ṣuyūṭī was somewhat revered by his peers, who attributed to him a measure of sanctity.[11] He included the hadith in several treatises. In his *Al-La'ālī' al-Maṣnū'a fī al-Aḥādīth al-Mawḍū'a* (The artificial pearls of forged hadiths—an apt image for a text that discusses fabricated hadiths), al-Ṣuyūṭī returns to the objections toward this specific saying. He mentions sources and authors but summarizes the discussion by stating his own position, that for him this was a sound hadith.[12] As mentioned above, the protocols of refutation science—here with regard to the science of hadith—are instrumental in circulating the same knowledge. As Brinkley Messick observed in his seminal monograph *The Calligraphic State*, writing permits the preservation of memory and event. Ironically, by writing about what the author regards false, he also protects it from oblivion.[13]

The deliberations of Muslim scholars aside, the Seljuk *medrese* portal in Sivas and the continued use of the building under the Ottomans is one piece of evidence that China remained a possible source of knowledge for at least some Muslims as an abstract idea as well as a practical reality. This was part of a wider intellectual phenomenon, namely the late medieval and early modern western Islamic feeling of some affinity with Chinese worldviews. Persis Berlekamp has shown that magnificently by focusing on the illustrated wonders-of-creation manuscripts from the thirteenth to nineteenth centuries.[14]

The association of Ottomans with China never developed into a major scientific inspiration. Furthermore, it seems that there was no insertion of this source of knowledge into mainstream intellectual trends (not unlike the role assigned to the New World in the sixteenth-century Ottoman Empire).[15]

On the one hand there was persistent interest in China, as attested by several extant early modern Ottoman geographical and travelogue accounts devoted to this region. The texts reveal what the Ottomans knew about this periphery in terms of politics, society, culture, and the existence of Chinese Muslim communities. Ottomans were not indifferent observers, but able to interact with Chinese public spheres through the collective memory and knowledge of Ottoman travelers and merchants. Clearly, China was not a mere esoteric anecdote for the Ottoman elite.

On the other hand, the Ottomans' knowledge of China was framed by imperial self-perceptions. China was portrayed as a worthy model for a universal empire: it was prosperous due to its law-abiding society; it expanded territorially with just wars; and the diffusion of justice brought also even spread of wealth. The Ottomans' sensitivity to China was fluid as they reconfigured themselves as a universal power.[16]

Berlekamp's appraisal of the Tansūqnāma, the famous Ilkhanid illuminated manuscript of Chinese medicine in Persian (associated with Rashīd al-Dīn, the great Ilkhanid vizier and patron of arts and sciences), applies here to the Ottoman context as well. The evidence testifies not only to the breadth of the Ottoman encounter with Chinese science and culture during the premodern period but also to the limits of its depth.[17]

Garden culture provides another example of an amalgamation and digestion of heritages with the final outcome a unique Ottoman cultural and scientific tradition. Gardening is at the center of different domains of knowledge and practices: scientific discussion of agriculture and botany, material culture, social practices of leisure, means of making a living, and professionalism.

A developed and refined culture of gardens is a well-known characteristic of many Muslim societies. One interpretation of classic Arabic poetry claimed that, as a rule, Muslim Arabs were indifferent to nature,[18] though an abundance of other evidence from literature, theology, and mysticism, as well as archeological remains, indicates great awareness of nature (water, plants, animals, and topography). For Ottomans, gardens were thought to depict a love of nature, as well as to prove the existence of God and his involvement in the world he created. Nature was seen as God's gift to human beings. Gardens were also perceived as the place for man to exercise his desire to control nature and mold it beyond the limitations of climate and physical structure. In gardens, men can create a new world by themselves.[19] In addition to these particular reasons, based on local religious and cultural concepts that encourage gardening, there is a universal phenomenon of gardening as an aesthetic expression of and inclination toward beauty, and the wish to cultivate it.

Gardening is also a necessity, which led this body of knowledge to acquire a practical layer alongside the tradition of writing at a high level.

Muslim societies had a tradition since medieval times to write sophistically and theoretically about agriculture, botany, husbandry, and geography. The characteristics of the plants and animals were studied, their geographical origins were recorded, and their various uses as food, decoration, cosmetics, artifacts, and healing remedies were learned. These were also practical fields. Experimentation took place to create new species and study their characteristics. The knowledge gained satisfied the needs of agronomists, patrons, and merchants, and in turn also helped create further needs. We know of brisk trade (and strong competition) in special plants, new hybrids, exotic animals, and other natural commodities. Plants and animals fulfilled both functional and emotional needs: they helped to impress, to gratify their owners' collector's urge, to enrich their cuisine, and to satisfy intellectual curiosity.[20]

A bibliographical dictionary of the seventeenth century reveals that the Islamic tradition of learned writing about agriculture and gardening continued during the Ottoman era (although it was far from being a major field of interest). The identity of the lexicographer Katip Çelebi (1609–1657), an Ottoman official with a quest for learning, also attests to the contexts of bureaucracy and imperial policy. The study of nature, medicine, and botany "arose not from disembodied minds," as Harold J. Cook wrote with regard to the study of nature and medicine in the context of the Dutch naval commerce of the early modern period, "but from the passions and interests of mind and body united."[21] Cook wrote about traders of the Dutch golden age, but his argument could be extended to Ottoman bureaucrats who wanted to know and understand their world exactly because of their position as the machinery of an empire that made them acquainted with that world.

Katip Çelebi compiled a vast bibliographical encyclopedia of no less than 15,000 titles and 10,000 authors, information that was gathered over a period of twenty years.[22] He defines *ʿilm al-filāḥa* as a body of knowledge that deals with cultivating plants from germination to their full growth, and mentions four different essays on gardening written in Arabic and Ottoman Turkish in this period. He further notes that this knowledge is essential to humans. Man must improve the soil, irrigate it, protect it from rotting, and keep it warm when frost sets in. The effort required is great, and the dissimilarity from region to region is considerable, but the benefit in the form of grain and fruit is significant.[23]

Archival material and historical writings chronicle some of the very complicated and sophisticated irrigation practices that made it possible to convey water over dozens of kilometers and maximize the use of small amounts of water. Such techniques included dams, irrigation canals, aqueducts, wells, mechanical instruments, controlled flooding, and other systems. (Despite this knowledge, however, in enormous stretches of the empire, the yield of the land was not high.)[24]

Agriculture and general interest in plants also connected Ottoman interest in botany with medicine. As a rule, the Ottoman imperial gardens (unlike those in Europe) were not intended to enrich the cuisine of the owner or to provide medical assistance. The Ottoman hospital gardens were also not recorded as having a pharmacological purpose (in contrast to European hospital gardens and monastic gardens, which were at least to some extent medicinal). At the same time, we have a number of botanical essays from the Ottoman period that focus specifically on medicinal materials (*materia medica*). These Ottoman botanical works include descriptions of plants, ways of harvesting them, a discussion of their uses, and guidance on extracting their active ingredients.[25] The discussion did not concern only theoretical knowledge but rather dealt with commerce in the branch. Indeed, Mısır Çarşısı, the Egyptian market in Istanbul, offered both international imports and exports of botanical and mineral-based medicinal substances, including narcotic drugs.[26] Spices were sold then as they are to this day. The distinction between substances intended for cuisine and those for the pharmacy was occasionally equivocal.[27]

The plentitude of gardens of varying sorts and sizes throughout the Ottoman Empire is impressive. As might be expected, the most splendid of them were the imperial gardens, though many official and unofficial gardens were open to all. In fact, the most significant "green lungs" of the Ottoman city were often the cemeteries. Gardens also surrounded city hospitals and contributed to the healing process.[28]

Evliya Çelebi, the inexhaustible Ottoman traveler, enumerated the outstanding gardens and promenades throughout Istanbul. Evliya dedicated the opening volume of his ten-part treatise, describing his travels throughout the empire of his era, to Istanbul. In his view, green areas were fundamentally important spots to be noticed in the urban landscape, only slightly less important than the mosques and other public institutions he considered noteworthy. Hence, his writings deal extensively with gardens. Besides noting their locations, he also described their structure and explained that there were so many gardens that he could only mention the most important of them.[29]

Gardens in Istanbul were so tempting that at least one physician in the capital was noted to desert his patients in favor of relaxation in the many gardens along the Golden Horn Bay—the reason the imperial head physician (*hekimbaşı*) provided for the physician's dismissal. If indeed true, this episode tells us of the attraction of gardens; if it is merely slander, the context tells us that gardens could be used as a plausible and convincing argument to get rid of that physician.[30]

Indeed, not only in the capital but all over the empire, greenery and water were used to landscape urban space. Furthermore, the importance of gardens increased over the course of the eighteenth century, when a noticeable trend emerged to open private gardens for the benefit of the general public. This trend formed part of far-reaching process of change in the awareness of leisure time and the concept of private space.[31]

In green open spaces, people can relax physically and emotionally. Calmness, which is usually associated with the nonmaterial world, can be attained in these public spaces. Public gardens were serene, and the common behavior code was less strictly observed there in comparison to other public sites. Ottoman society emphasized public behavior characterized by self-discipline, simplicity (sometimes verging on the ascetic), religious conservatism, seriousness, and gravity. Although in society's higher echelons at least, hedonism was the accepted norm, Ottomans were always expected to carry themselves proudly and not lose control of their appetites for drink, food, or smoking. No thought of rebelliousness could materialize in public gardens, which people enjoyed under the watchful eyes of strangers. Here too, alongside release, the urban man's behavior was expected to be cultured and refined. Nevertheless, behavior was more relaxed. It was possible to rest, play, converse, and engage in love games.[32]

The relaxation and restfulness that characterized those enjoying the gardens in the Ottoman urban centers were perhaps connected to the informal structure and design of the gardens as open and asymmetric spaces. These gardens were different from the accepted Persian Muslim or Spanish Muslim gardens, which were influenced in turn by Persian motifs, based on the rigid form of *çahār-bāgh* (Persian, meaning "four gardens"): a clear and obligatory division of a garden into four quarters around a centrally located pool and fountain.

Generally, Persian motifs proliferated and were prominent in Ottoman architecture over a long period. Until the mid-sixteenth century, Ottoman art was founded on what Gülru Necipoğlu called "International Timurid Taste." She identified taste that was common to the dynasties that flourished following the Timurs in central Asia and were culturally influenced by Timurid aesthetics: the Ottomans, the Safavids in Persia, and the Mughals in India. Only in the mid-sixteenth century did the Ottomans form their own unique and independent artistic taste.[33] Nevertheless, over the course of the eighteenth century, there was a return to the Persian repertoire,[34] which of course had changed as well since the late medieval period.

Regarding gardens, however, the Ottoman style was different from the accepted norms in the Persian world. The Ottomans shared a common Persian tradition with the Iranian world; they shared the tradition of the ancient world, the Byzantine, and the Mediterranean, with the Italian renaissance. The Ottomans interpreted these shared traditions in a way that created gardens that were "Ottoman"—that is, gardens that were physical and social products of their culture.[35]

Such give-and-take between the Ottomans and other cultures demonstrates that the Ottomans were conscious of and interested in the different scientific worlds around them. A growing number of studies indicate an Ottoman sensitivity to cultures and geographies around them from the sixteenth century on. Since Cornell Fleischer,[36] scholars tie this phenomenon to a distinct Ottoman enterprise with a sense of imperial sovereignty, which included a universal claim.[37] It seems that scientific encounters and appropriation of various scientific heritages were part of the Ottomans' positioning as an empire, and how the dynasty envisioned its connection with the world.

THE OTTOMAN CONCEPT AND EPISTEMOLOGY OF KNOWLEDGE: THE TERM *ʿILM*

The term *ʿilm* was used by Ottomans to refer to knowledge (or wisdom) and science. It contains a rich world of meanings, ideas, and insights, and as such embodies the complexity of the concept of knowledge in Ottoman society. It has nothing to do with our own "science," but like "our" science, *ʿilm* was used by Ottomans to refer to intentional and systemized engagement with knowledge. Hence it is key in unfolding Ottoman conceptualizations and the boundaries and aims of their science.

The word *ʿilm* comes from Arabic. Franz Rosenthal (1914–2003) devoted his classic work on the concept of knowledge in the Arabic Muslim societies of the Middle Ages to its different layers, from the linguistic to the cultural. He distinguished between knowledge as an abstract term and as a tangible materialization. Rosenthal noted that the existence of a plural form of *ʿilm*, namely *ʿulūm*, semantically proves the perception that knowledge appears in different forms. He analyzed various types of knowledge—such as mystical revelation, philosophical thought, and education—as a guiding factor in social behavior (*adab*).[38] Rosenthal's work was continued by Dimitri Gutas (who was also appointed to Rosenthal's post at Yale University). Gutas illustrated to what extent the term is in fact equivocal: it has a wide range of different meanings and uses in the Arabic language during different periods and in various texts.[39]

The complexity of the concept of *ʿilm* during the Ottoman period is revealed, for example, in the *Thesaurus* of Franz de Mesgnien Meninski (1623–1698), a Hapsburg orientalist and a Polish diplomat.[40] He was born in the Lorraine region, received his education in Rome, and was later attached to the Polish ambassador's delegation to Istanbul, where he studied the Ottoman Turkish language. Meninski began serving as an interpreter for the Polish embassy in Istanbul and was finally even appointed ambassador. In recognition of his services, he was granted Polish citizenship, in honor of which he changed his name to Meninski, adding the Polish suffix *-ski*. Meninski returned to the Hapsburg Empire, to the court of the kaiser in Vienna, as the chief translator of Oriental languages and, after a few years, was also appointed as counselor to the kaiser. Besides his diplomatic work, he continued his work as a linguist. From 1680 to 1687, four volumes of his *Thesaurus linguarum orientalium* were published, complemented in 1687 by the *Onomasticon latino-turcico-arabico-persicum*. Together, these publications formed a huge lexicon in four languages: Latin explanations for Ottoman Turkish, Arabic, and Persian terms. Indeed, Meninski's dictionary reflects the Ottoman linguistic world of the upper classes in the seventeenth century.[41]

Meninski included various fields of knowledge under the term *ʿilm*. These definitions show his understanding of what knowledge is, and as is to be expected of an enlightened man in central Europe in the early modern period, his outlook and knowledge are founded on the classical definitions surviving from antiquity. Terms such as *art* and *profession* (which should be understood by their Latin meanings rather than their modern English ones) suggest the Greek perception that some knowledge is based in understanding and thought (*episteme*), whereas another kind is based in creativity, performance, and experience (*techne*).[42] These Greek concepts continued to influence understanding of knowledge in Europe well into the early modern period, Meninski's time. Even in the twentieth century, Michel Foucault and Martin Heidegger offered formative discussions regarding knowledge and ways of knowing and doing science based on reinterpretations of these classical terms.[43]

Meninski's concepts of *art* and *profession* were external to the Ottoman world, though the examples he brought in of Arabic, Farsi, and Ottoman Turkish synonyms for *ʿilm* in general and for *ʿilm* of specific kinds relate to the mental world of the Ottomans of his era. Meninski addressed knowledge of divinity, whose source is sometimes in prophecy (linking them with the terms *ʿilm-i ilāhī* and *ʿilm-i khodā*), alongside knowledge of arithmetic and poetry. He mentioned knowledge of Muslim theology (*ʿilm-i kelām*) alongside knowledge of magic (*ʿilm-i siḥr*). Thus, Meninski showed that the Ottomans linked knowledge of different kinds, from a range of sources and for a variety of purposes.[44]

What epistemological process qualified fields or notions as meeting the requirements of knowledge? In other words, how did the Ottomans know (or think or feel) that something known to them was indeed true? After all, we do not accept everything we read or hear as the truth; we receive each scrap of information at a different level of certainty according to its source and the manner in which it is transmitted. We now turn our attention to the variety of sources of legitimate knowledge in the Ottoman world.

Divine revelation (*waḥy*) posits Allah as the source of all human knowledge; Allah creates all knowledge and permits man to gain it. Moreover, the widespread perception was that the potential human capacity to comprehend and process information is restricted from the outset, so that even the things that God permits us to understand are, in fact, beyond our grasp, and we should not question what is beyond our comprehension.[45] The perception of Allah as all-knowing is expressed in the name al-ʿAlīm, one of "the beautiful names of Allah" (*al-asmāʾ al-ḥusnā*). This Qurʾanic term formed the developmental basis of the Muslim theological concept of the characteristics of Allah, including "the merciful," "the healer," and many more. These characteristics are defined with ninety-nine adjectives, some of them taken from the Qurʾan, and together the names include the various aspects of the divinity of Allah.[46]

The articulation of this perception was an answer to a different opinion that discussed God's will to control human creation and His limits. A central position within this latter perception was the Muʿtazila, a medieval theological school that influenced Islamic thinking for centuries. They upheld the doctrine of the created Qurʾan as they insisted on the eternal nature of God against a widely accepted claim that elevated the Qurʾan to a degree of un-createdness (similar to God) and its origin in a "heavenly tablet" (*al-lawḥ al-maḥfūẓ*). They also asserted the principle of the necessary justice of God: He wills and does only that which is good, and thus they limited the scope of God's actions. These debates were not fully resolved. While the Muʿtazila as a formal school disappeared, their ideas were perpetuated by other Islamic groups. During the twentieth century this movement was a center of rejuvenated intellectual debate in Egypt.[47]

Role models, some of which were attached to myths rather than concrete historical reality, were another legitimate source of knowledge. Ottoman society made mention of the names of its founding fathers in various spheres of knowledge. Beyond satisfying the curiosity of knowing who was the first physician, the first astronomer, or the first shoemaker, this was also a system that combined the body of knowledge and occupation with it in Muslim society through association with role models from the distant past. This legitimating process is not unlike the chain of narrators (*isnād*) that opens every hadith.

Logic and reason (*ʿaql*) provide additional important sources of knowledge, including in aspects of religion. Thus, for example, one of the sources of Muslim law involves drawing conclusions derived from the Qurʾan and from the hadith by way of analogy (*qiyās*). However, what can be learned from certain texts is limited, and this procedure ranks third in importance out of four. Moreover, certain theological perceptions can restrict the use of logic as a knowledge source.

Observations, experiments, and experiences (*tajārib*) are yet another source of knowledge, as they allow direct access to knowledge and its ratification. Elitists throughout Muslim history clearly voiced their disapproval of these more popular modes. They wanted to base knowledge only on the narrations of accepted and familiar role models. They thus distanced themselves from personal experience. Tension about the relative merit of sources of knowledge resulted also from the possible use of the senses as a foundation for knowledge. In fact, in order to use observation and experiment as a basis, the senses must be regarded as a reliable source. There should be no apprehension that senses may deceive us; rather, the narrators must be consensually regarded as actually transmitting a faithful and accurate message about the world. And indeed, some groups held that observation has no significance, as nature does not operate according to patterns that repeat themselves because the Creator is not limited by fixed patterns.

Finally, knowledge drawn from a **living tradition** or based on broad **popular consent** does not require the endorsement or justification of figures of authority but rather comes from below. The fact that something is accepted and familiar justifies its existence. Talismans, for example, and other magical acts were deemed "tried and tested" as confirmation of their potency and effectiveness.[48]

None of these sources of knowledge were exclusive. They overlapped and complemented one another in their dialogue, but rivalry and tension also existed between them. The plurality of ways to know things allowed creativity and more egalitarianism than the more formal and authoritative scholars would have liked.[49]

The career of Şerefeddin Sabuncuoğlu, a physician from Amasya in the fifteenth century, reveals the dynamics of combining sources of knowledge. Sabuncuoğlu titled his manual on drugs and their preparation *Mücerrebname* (The book of tried medications). This was the last of three medical treatises he composed. He explains, following common phrasing we see in many medical treatises, that he wrote the work in 1468 as an answer to a plea from colleagues that he put on paper his fourteen-year medical experiences in a hospital. The contents and structure of this short manual—with regard to types of drugs, their ingredients, and methods of preparation—repeat earlier Arab-Islamic examples of learned written pharmacopeia. At the same time he refers frequently to his techniques in preparing drugs and discusses efficacy based on experiments upon himself and animals.[50] The title and the numerous references to trials and observations attest to this as a source of pride for him.

Nevertheless, Sabuncuoğlu was of humble reputation and importance in his time. He had some contacts with Istanbul and the imperial court, or wished to establish such contacts. In his text he tells of a journey to Istanbul, and he dedicated an earlier treatise, devoted to surgery, to the reigning Sultan Mehmed II (reigned 1451–1481). His name and works were known to other Ottoman physicians of the period. Ibrahim bin Abdüllah, an early sixteenth-century Ottoman surgeon, mentioned Sabuncuoğlu in his own manual, *ʿAlaim-i Cerrahin* (The miracles of surgeons).[51] However, his career was in Amasya, not on an imperial scale. Only a few copies of Sabuncuoğlu's works exist. His profile is one of a common Muslim physician in Ottoman Anatolia of the fifteenth century. And among such practitioners it was quite common to insert conclusions drawn from personal trials and observations into learned treatises that tapped into sources of theoretical knowledge.

The combination and integration of sources of knowledge was possible among professional scholars (here we saw such an example in the works of one Ottoman physician), as well as among educated Ottomans. Evliya Çelebi, a gentleman and traveler, described the physicians' guild in Istanbul in a way that shows how different sources were intertwined.

Evliya described in detail an impressive parade of the guilds in the Istanbul city center in the mid-seventeenth century. He stated that all of

Istanbul's guilds of the period participated, and divided them into fifty-seven groups and a total of no fewer than 1,001 professional associations (a poetic expression of the fact that the number of guilds was immense rather than a number that should be taken literally). The parade was intended to display the successes of the various guilds and obtain recognition of their professional level and organization from both the public and the government. Indeed, Ottoman authorities wanted to oversee commercial life and artisanship in the city by inspecting the guilds' activities. It is no coincidence that the Sultan Murad IV (reigned 1623–1640) personally supervised the colorful parade. Thus, a public event of popular entertainment was cloaked in political significance, like other mass celebrations in the capital. Evliya documented the parade—its participants and the processional order—addressing the relative importance of the professions, the fields of specialization in each profession, the tools that characterized each, and other issues. He also noted the name of the founding father of each profession in which such existed role was known.

In the paragraph devoted to the physicians' guild, Evliya mentioned that medicine was an ancient profession, whose patron in earlier periods was Lokman.[52] Evliya did not have to explain who Lokman was, as he was an extremely well-known folk hero for his readers, famous for his intelligence, wise leadership, and longevity.

In other sources we find the description of a figure legendary in the pre-Islamic peninsula. In Sura 31 of the Qur'an, which bears his name, Luqmān (the Arabic version of the Turkish Lokman) is described as someone who holds a natural monotheistic faith in times and a place of paganism; he is an ideal father who both reprimands and advises his son. According to the Qur'an, Luqmān's wisdom was given by God, and following the Qur'anic example, Muslim tradition has attributed many proverbs and idioms to him. In many ways, then, Luqmān became the Arabic-Muslim equivalent of Aesop. Indeed, in Persian literature, Luqmān is described as being the ideal ascetic.[53]

The Turks were also familiar with the character of Luqmān. In addition to his recognized functions in Arabic and Persian literature, Luqmān appears in Turkish folklore as an Arab physician (*hekim*, the Turkish version of the Arabic word *ḥakīm*), and in this role he appeared in Evliya's account. One of the tales about him, still circulating in modern Turkey, associates Lokman with supernatural healing.

The story tells of Mehmed the Mad, the spoiled child of an Egyptian king, who pretends to be the great physician Lokman from Arabia in order to heal the wife and daughter of the king, and the wife of the Grand

Vizier, of the affliction of snakes. First, he causes them to grow horns and later treats them, before returning to his own country to resume his throne for a prosperous reign.[54] In another popular story, Lokman is referred to as a great physician, and the only one who can prescribe remedies for the ill-fated Latif-Shah, a ruler of Iran, who was separated from his wife and children for sixteen years and later reunited with them.[55]

Evliya's survey of the sources of medical knowledge and the manner in which this knowledge is transmitted combines divine revelation, oral folklore, wisdom, and exceptional individual capabilities in the field of medicine. Combined, they create legitimacy for medicine as a realm of knowledge and as a profession. All these spheres—the philosophical, cultural, and social—determined the boundaries of knowledge in Ottoman society. Indeed, these boundaries involve a powerful notion of what is right and wrong with knowledge, but should be understood as quite elastic rather than defined in a clear and unequivocal manner.

CLASSIFICATION OF KNOWLEDGE IN MUSLIM SOCIETIES

The notion that knowledge can come from different sources, can be of different types, and can serve various goals—as well as the reality that, indeed, a variety of bodies of knowledge existed alongside each other—led from the ninth and tenth centuries onward to the classification of knowledge (*marātib al-ʿulūm*). Thus, another scientific sub-sphere was born: the discussion of the organization of knowledge and its various disciplines. The discussion was held on both theoretical and bibliographical levels, explaining methodologies and division of subject matters, as well as listing what had been written in a specific field.[56]

Ottomans continued to prepare such lists, which reveal Ottoman intellectual cultures—the dialogues with different traditions and shifts through time. In the year AH 909 (1502–1503) the royal librarian in Topkapı, the imperial palace, compiled a catalogue in Arabic of the holdings of the palace library for Sultan Bayezid II (reigned 1481–1512; the manuscript is now in the Oriental Collection of the Library of the Hungarian Academy of Sciences).[57] The list is very enlightening. The text is written in Arabic, as was customary in the Arab-Islamic genre of bibliographical lists. The arrangements of disciplines likewise seems to follow previous lists. The 7,200 titles mentioned, however, suggest a wide, maybe Islamic universal alignment of the Ottoman Empire: the texts are written in Arabic but also in Persian, Ottoman Turkish, and Chagatay Turkish. This reveals that the early sixteenth-century Ottoman cultural canon was still very much within the Persianate-Timurid world, even before the Ottoman conquest of the Arab Middle East and the intellectual shift it brought.

This is the viewpoint from the royal palace. Looking to wider circles of readers among state officials, seventeenth-century Katip Çelebi's bibliography *Kashf al-Ẓunūn ʿan Asāmī al-Kutūb wal-Funūn* (The revelation of thoughts: Names of the books and the sciences) is an appropriate source. An extremely high number of copies were prepared throughout the empire, and it was known in Europe since the late seventeenth century (although Guy Burak suggested recently that the text's usage and influence may have been humbler than currently assumed).[58]

Katip Çelebi provided quotes from earlier bibliographical sources, which he was careful to acknowledge and which attest to his intellectual and literary lineage continuing from previous periods. One of his sources was Ahmed bin Mustafa Taşköprüzade (1495–1561), a prominent and prolific Ottoman writer.[59] Taşköprüzade's treatises are among the most important sources pertaining to the first three hundred years of the empire's history. Of particular significance is *Miftāḥ al-Saʿāda wa-Miṣbāḥ al-Siyāda fī Mawḍūʿāt al-ʿUlūm* (The key to happiness and the light to mastery of subjects of knowledge), which Katip Çelebi emulated and often quoted. He drew critical information from Taşköprüzade's *Miftāḥ al-Saʿāda*, and more importantly, Katip Çelebi followed Taşköprüzade's assessments of the significance of a specific body of knowledge.[60]

In the *Kashf*, Katip Çelebi organizes the branches of knowledge alphabetically. Such an organization facilitates easy referencing and dictionary-like usage, but it does not tell the user the relations between the different branches of knowledge, as does Taşköprüzade's *Miftāḥ al-Saʿāda*. In a separate treatise Katip Çelebi sketched succinctly the divisions of knowledge relevant to the man of culture and how they relate to one another. In *jāmiʿ al-mutūn min jall al-funūn* (the comprehensive list of texts on the exalted sciences) Katip Çelebi refers to "the tree of sciences" (*shajarat al-ʿulūm*). He used the metaphor of a tree and visually drew branches to supply a bird's-eye view of all knowledge.[61] Here he followed Taşköprüzade's perspective of knowledge (who in turn recapitulated previous conceptualizations of knowledge), sometimes verbatim, including the tree metaphor. Taşköprüzade presented his taxonomy of human knowledge in words, rather than in drawing, using terms like *boughs*, *branches*, *sprays*, and *cluster of grapes* to explain the categorization of knowledge, its sources, and subjects.

In language, too, Katip Çelebi followed the steps of his predecessors:

his dictionary is written in Arabic, and most of the treatises mentioned were, indeed, written in Arabic. Alongside the continuation of the Arab-Islamic tradition we can assess also an adaptation to unique Ottoman features. One of the shifts was linguistic: more than a few books listed by the compiler were written in Persian and Ottoman Turkish. Furthermore, the bodies of knowledge discussed in the dictionary are arranged in Ottoman alphabetical order rather than Arabic, although the language of the text is Arabic: the three letters that end the dictionary are *waw-ha-ya*, instead of *ha-waw-ya*, the familiar order of Arabic dictionaries. This is just scraping the surface of the Ottoman intellectual mind-set, as this and other Ottoman bibliographies are only beginning to be closely investigated.

Identification of different fields of knowledge and their classification creates a hierarchy. Muslim writers sought to classify knowledge by field and status according to its perceived importance and value.[62] Alongside classification, attempts focusing on the theoretical status of bodies of knowledge, social distinctions and status evaluations of the various knowledge realms developed as well. These distinct intellectual, moral, and social appraisals were interwoven.

Biographical lexicons—documenting the education of their heroes and their activity as students, teachers, and treatise writers—clearly demonstrate that some spheres of knowledge were much more popular than others. Religious sciences, for instance (namely those directly connected to the religion of Islam, such as Qurʾan, hadith, law and jurisprudence, and theology, as well as auxiliary fields [e.g., Arabic language]), were studied by more people who may have studied other fields of knowledge, too. "Religious sciences" were catalogued as such, for they were understood as deriving from divine revelation and being pursued for the sake of understanding divine revelation. Following the same categorization, those fields that were not religious were classified as "rational fields," since their source is not God but, rather, humankind's ability to perceive the world from varying points of view.

The internal stratification was based on a number of criteria beyond mere classification according to the field of knowledge: some scientific activities were more highly valued than other activities in the same sphere of knowledge. The measure of importance attributed, for example, to writing an essay relied not only on the broad sphere of knowledge to which the essay belonged but on the readers to whom the essay was directed: an essay addressed to an educated and selected public was more highly valued than an essay intended to satisfy the needs of a wider audience of laypersons.[63]

Scholars long viewed the nonreligious sciences as marginal to Islamic thought. This status was supposedly portrayed in the biographical dictionaries from the Middle Ages and later periods and reinforced by other sources, such as bibliographical literature, leading scholars of Islamic science to claim that the Muslim intellectual climate from the Middle Ages onward was so intolerant of non-Muslim knowledge as to almost negate it. According to this thesis, clear separation existed between religious sciences and the remaining scientific spheres. According to historians of science, enlightenment, and education in the Islamic world, rational scientists' measure of cultural respectability and even the extent of their religious orthodoxy were questioned.

A key figure in this discourse was George Makdisi.[64] His claims were rejected long ago, but when raised in the 1980s, they significantly influenced many researchers. For instance, Abdul Hamid Ibrahim Sabra claimed that the Greek sciences actually became acclimatized in Muslim society, yet they were treated with a measure of distance.[65] Historians sharing this line of thought assumed that the rational spheres were identified with *ʿulūm al-awāʾil*, meaning "the sciences of the firsts": in this context, the Greeks. The term thus referred to the sciences that came from the Greeks, which Muslims adopted in the Middle Ages and translated into Arabic directly from Greek or, more usually, via Aramaic. Many a modern scholar has imagined connections between the non-Muslim source of certain sciences and their secondary importance. Moreover, scholars who supported this thesis explained that in the intellectual climate that (supposedly) based itself exclusively on divine revelation, the distance between marginalizing the importance of a specific body of knowledge and doubting its legitimacy is rather short.

AMALGAMATION OF BODIES OF KNOWLEDGE IN MUSLIM SOCIETIES

Simultaneously with the establishment of borders and boundaries separating spheres of knowledge, the sciences became interconnected because many people studied several fields of knowledge, including a combination of religious and rational sciences. Certain fields of knowledge combined and supported one another, while others merely existed in parallel. This phenomenon has been customary among Muslims since pre-Ottoman times, and we know of many polymaths.

The biographical dictionaries compiled by Muslim scholars in the late Middle Ages and early modern era reveal a consistent presence of rational sciences in the education of scholars, even if not with the majority of them or as a central topic. Some *ʿulamāʾ* studied astronomy and astrology (in the premodern era, astrology was considered a science like any other). Others studied arithmetic and algebra. After all, arithmetic and algebra are the basis of *ʿilm al-farāʾiḍ*, literally "knowledge of portions," which refers to the Islamic law of inheritance, dealing to a large extent with the calculation of the fixed shares of all heirs to an estate according to religious law. This accounting work was complicated and sometimes necessitated several divisions and redivisions, and was considered a sub-branch of the sciences of numbers.[66]

Recent years also yielded new insights on the ways in which the content of both religious and scientific discourses shaped mutual interactions during the late medieval and early modern periods,[67] although our current understanding with regard to the Ottoman case is far more limited.

We do know, however, that collections of Ottoman libraries point to the integration of different fields of knowledge on the library shelves. Even medium-sized Ottoman libraries with limited collections displayed a mixture of hadith and Qurʾan interpretation, Arabic philology, philosophy, history, medicine, mysticism, literature, and poetry. Collections also included treatises in several Muslim languages. In libraries in the Balkans, for example, we find good representation not only of Arabic and Ottoman Turkish, which might be expected, but also of Farsi.[68]

The Egyptian Aḥmad al-Damanhūrī (d. 1778) provided an extraordinary example of the enormous variety (at least in the contemporary opinion) of spheres of learning that existed. His academic curricula and mores reflect al-Azhar of the eighteenth century.[69] Al-Damanhūrī was proficient in four schools of law, and his biographer went on to say that his expertise in each of them surpassed that of those who specialized in only one of them (as was the common practice); he also occupied himself with alchemy, philosophy, and medicine. Al-Damanhūrī wrote essays in all these spheres of knowledge, including interpretation of the Qurʾan as well as an essay on logic, and all this while still serving as a Shaykh al-Azhar—Egypt's senior scholar (and a very busy one at that). Two important Muslim scholars of his time considered him truly eminent in his vast knowledge and a multidimensional scholar. One was his student ʿAbd al-Raḥmān al-Jabartī, an exceptional scholar in his own right (more on him in the conclusion).[70] The second was Muḥammad Khalīl al-Murādī (d. 1791), who composed a biographical dictionary (and was himself a scholar of Muslim law in Damascus who combined knowledge of religious law and Sufi mystic knowledge).[71]

Al-Damanhūrī was a typical scholar of his time in his diversified scholarly interests, balancing practical science with religious scholarship. It seems, however, that his contemporaries were impressed by the number of spheres he combined and with the extent of his command of all of them, not by his integration of spheres of knowledge that were seemingly (perhaps wrongly in modern opinion) very remote from one another. Furthermore, he came from humble origins as an orphan from rural lower Egypt who did not enjoy the background of an illustrious family. Al-Damanhūrī's background makes his success even more extraordinary, and this tells us about social and political patterns of career paths, and the bond between vast scholarly expertise and upward mobility.[72]

The popularity and importance attributed to bodies of knowledge changed from time to time. Similarly, the degrees of popularity of the combinations were neither fixed nor inflexible. We learn this, for example, from the fact that during different periods, the character of the person described in the sources as the ideal physician (*al-ṭabīb al-kāmil*) was depicted differently. The Arabic sources in the Middle Ages present the physician-philosopher as the ideal combination. They used the Greek model of ancient times to create a contemporary model and quoted Galen (Aelius Galenus), the Greek physician and philosopher who lived in the second century. Galen influenced medicine in the Middle East and Europe for hundreds of years beyond his lifetime with his articulate presentation of the synthesis of various medical theories that were based on the theory of temperaments and humors and the need for physical and mental equilibrium. Among his many influential treatises is a short essay promoting a training program that Galen initiated to be executed in the future, for "the best physician, who is also a philosopher." Arab Muslims were familiar with the essay's Arabic translation, and even if they did not read it directly, the ideal that it suggested (like Galen's entire body of work, which was translated into Arabic) became a widespread criterion for evaluating the qualities of a "true" physician in Muslim society in the Middle Ages.

At times, the discussion regarding the perfect physician was more theoretical than practical. In practice, often the "physician" was the person his (or her) patients regarded as such and were willing to pay a fee to, rather than the person who had indeed completed the curriculum of the required classical medical texts per se. Nevertheless, the issue of who is a physician-philosopher was tremendously significant in establishing status and reputation in society. The authors of the biographical dictionaries justified their choice of whom to immortalize in their lexicons by drawing a flattering comparison with a physician-philosopher, for example, a man with the status of Ibn Sīnā (Avicenna). An unflattering comparison, on the other hand, enabled physicians to accuse one another of being charlatans. Lawrence I. Conrad and later on Peter Pormann showed how a personal disagreement between Muslim physicians in the medieval period, a theoretical medical argument, or professional struggle could lead to denunciating rivals and competitors as frauds, even when the adversaries were skilled professionals.[73]

Whereas sources from the Middle Ages portray the physician-philosopher as an ideal, later, beginning with the Mamluks and during the Ottoman era, the sources seemed to promote a different ideal. The Ottoman biographical lexicons from the sixteenth through the eighteenth centuries (the medical system changed in the nineteenth century with the introduction of European medicine, and, accordingly, so did the method of evaluating a physician; hence this period is excluded here) refer to the physician-jurist rather than the physician-philosopher as a perfect example of medical practice. The early modern lexicons document many physicians who also studied *fiqh* (Muslim divine law), while *fiqh* scholars also studied medicine.[74] During the Ottoman era, we no longer find lexicons dedicated to physicians (while at least three are familiar to us from the Middle Ages: the lexicons of Ibn Juljul of tenth-century Andalusia; the Egyptian-born al-Qifṭī, who worked in al-Shām between the twelfth and thirteenth centuries; and the Syrian Ibn Abī Uṣyabiʿa of the thirteenth century). In the Ottoman period, however, physicians were included in lexicons dedicated to *ülema* and Sufi *şeyhs*; such was the editorial choice of the authors of the biographical dictionaries.

The life story of Ibn Shamāqa (the appellation of Muḥammad bin Muḥammad bin Aḥmad [d. 1610]), from the city of Homs in Syria, is a representative example of an Ottoman combination of law and medicine. Ibn Shamāqa was a *mujāwir* (literally "a neighbor"), meaning someone who lives in the vicinity of a sacred place.[75] Ibn Shamāqa chose to live in Mecca (in his case, for ten years) out of devoutness and a desire to live close to the holy Muslim sites. He finally returned to Syria and studied chemistry and medicine in Damascus, but then continued on to Egypt to study grammar and Muslim law. Ibn Shamāqa attached himself to the senior *ülema* in Istanbul. It was these connections, perhaps, that assisted him in initially being granted administrative positions in the *medrese*s: he was appointed as a *mütevelli*, the trustee of an endowed institution. Ultimately, he also received teaching posts in these *medrese*s.[76]

The shift from physician-philosopher to physician-jurist did not dispense with the ideal image of the perfect physician taken from antiquity. As in the medieval period, biographies (*tarājim*) of Ottoman physicians in the early modern period continued praising physicians for being the "Galen (or Hippocrates) of his period." Two seventeenth-century chief physicians (*raʾīs al-aṭibbāʾ*) in Damascus were heralded with such a description. One was Muḥammad Ibn al-Ghazāl (d. 1626). He was born in Homs, studied in Tripoli, and then reached Damascus, where he ascended to the position of head physician.[77] The second was Yūsuf, who was originally from Tripoli but moved to Damascus and became head physician there until his death in September 1693.[78] However, the physician biographies of the period had shifted aims; they were now focused on praising the medical professionalism of their subject, and did not necessarily see him as the hero of the biography or as a certified philosopher.

The biographical lexicons of legal and medical scholars do not inform us of their subjects' actual career track. Some were theologians who added medicine to their broad knowledge; others were physicians who wished to expand their knowledge in the spheres of religion; and there were probably also those who became better informed in both these fields out of curiosity and interest, while making their living from a completely different source. Ismāʿīl bin ʿAbd al-Ḥaqq of Syria (d. 1592/1593) combined these traits. He studied Qurʾan with the senior teachers of his generation in Syria while learning medicine from his grandfather, among others. He served as a Shāfiʿī judge at the local courthouse,[79] and from there he was promoted to the position of chief physician.[80] Medicine was considered to be an appropriate body of knowledge for a respectable, educated man of religion, and, surprisingly, many physicians considered jurisprudence—of all the religious sciences—to be a field worthy of specialization.

Medicine itself was a field consisting of several medical theories and practices that existed alongside one another and that were mutually influential. Medical practitioners had to choose one of the bodies of knowledge covered by the overall term *medicine* or combine them with one another. Modern researchers have tended to categorize three separate systems that together formed the medical system in premodern Muslim society: the Muslim version of the Greek medicine of humors; folk medicine handed down from generation to generation, based on experience with herbs; and the Muslim prophetic medicine, which was similar in content to the Greek-Muslim medicine of humors but depended for legitimacy on the sayings of the Prophet Muḥammad (hence the name "prophetic medicine": in Arabic, *al-ṭibb al-nabawī*, and in Ottoman Turkish, *tibb-ül-nebevi*).[81]

Some theologians integrated religion and religious law into prophetic medicine. An outstanding example of this is Jalāl al-Dīn al-Suyūṭī, the renowned Egyptian-Mamluk theologian. Al-Suyūṭī wrote prolifically and is known for his works in the fields of religious law and Qur'an interpretation, among others. But he also wrote about *al-manhaj al-sawī wal-manhal al-rawī fī al-ṭibb al-nabawī* (the proper road and the thirst-quenching spring of prophetic medicine), which achieved popularity in the Middle East and was also acquired by Ottoman sultans for their libraries.[82] Apparently, the integration of prophetic medicine with bodies of knowledge whose business is faith and religious practice was natural to theologians. Indeed, the numerous theologians who engaged with the medicine of humors reveal that this combination was apparently not only possible but also quite normative.

The drive toward interaction of different bodies of knowledge went deep. In addition to the amalgamation of sciences side by side, the integration could mix methods and knowledge. If early Muslim legal scholars kept their distance from philosophy, early Ottoman legal scholars (1300–1600) understood theoretical Islamic jurisprudence as based on Greco-Islamic philosophy in general and Aristotelean logic in particular. They tried to prove Aristotle's theory of sciences applicable to Islamic law. They presented their area of interest as based on premises, the validity and certainty of which could be collaborated externally. Even the very concept and standard of what knowledge and science were could merge Islamic and Greek attitudes.[83]

TENSIONS DUE TO FUSION OF BODIES OF KNOWLEDGE: THE DISPUTE REGARDING THE STATUS OF PRE-ISLAMIC SCIENCES

The integration between the various spheres of knowledge should not mislead us: the dispute regarding the status of pre-Islamic sciences, which was significant and long-standing, began at an early stage (apparently already in the ninth century). Some of the prominent figures rejected a deep integration of Greek thought and Islamic religious thinking. Philosophy and astronomy, in particular, drew special attention over the years in the controversy as to whether the bodies of knowledge in question were worthy and necessary, or perhaps were actually misleading spheres of knowledge that caused moral damage. The controversy around these fields demonstrates the wide spectrum of attitudes toward the various bodies of knowledge. Moreover, these attitudes also changed from time to time, according to the specific intellectual climate in each society.

Philosophy: Criticism and Guarded Acceptance

Philosophy—a sphere of knowledge that deals with existence and reality, as well as the capacity to understand and discuss them—came to the Muslim world from Greece. There were those in orthodox Sunni circles who were somewhat critical and perhaps even apprehensive about this body of knowledge. Sunni Muslims warned of the slippery slope of asking questions they thought would cause weaker believers to deny the existence of God. Abū Ḥāmid Muḥammad ibn Muḥammad al-Ghazzālī (1058–1111) provided one example of such criticism by reacting negatively to Gnostic and other trends that doubted the act of divine creation, the physical existence of the world to come, and special divine knowledge. At the same time, in his criticism he allowed for "harmless" philosophy. He referred to that which recognized the existence of divine revelation, one which stays as a power in the world even after creation. This sort of philosophy found a place in the mainstream Sunni world and not just in occults and subversive movements.

In his spiritual autobiography *al-Munqidh min al-Ḍalāl* (The deliverance from error) (an intellectual analysis of his spiritual growth, as termed by W. M. Watt),[84] al-Ghazzālī questioned blind religious conformism while advocating closeness to God and purity of heart. He clearly rejected philosophy. He noted divisions among philosophers—materialists, naturalists, and theists—but observed that all of them deserved the stigma of unbelief and godlessness. He did conclude, however, that the philosophical sciences (like mathematics, logic, and physics) had nothing to do with religion by means of negation or affirmation of belief. In his opinion, it was metaphysics that harbored the greatest evil: he claimed metaphysicists were deceitful and overestimated their cleverness with no humility regarding human ability to discern right and truth from wrong and error.[85]

Nevertheless, in his refutation of philosophy and philosophers, al-Ghazzālī also made them better known in the Islamic world. Michael E. Marmura, who translated and edited al-Ghazzālī's treatise on *Tahāfut al-Falāsifa* (The incoherence of the philosophers), noted this paradox. Al-Ghazzālī highlighted the conflict between philosophy and more traditional Islamic beliefs; however, in order to refute Muslim philosophers, he had to explain them. In fact, he explained them so clearly that he rendered abstract and difficult ideas accessible to laypersons. After him,

Muslim theologians found it necessary to discuss philosophical theories, and Islamic theology (*kalām*) became more and more involved with philosophy.[86] Thus, from al-Ghazzālī onward, philosophy continued to exist in the Muslim realm, even if relatively marginally.[87]

Hence, a complicated reality combining acceptance and apprehension of philosophy existed during the Ottoman era. In conjunction, it seems that at the time, philosophy or subfields in philosophy moved toward the heart of intellectual life by comparison with previous periods. On the one hand, concern was still apparent, even if relatively concealed, that philosophical investigation might lead to a crisis of faith. The biographical lexicons document cases of religious conversions (albeit only a few) that resulted from delving deeply into philosophy. Certainly, the biographical lexicons immortalize exemplary role models from the perspective of the Muslim community, which produced and used these lexicons. Thus, the religious conversions discussed are always conversions to Islam (after all, anyone perceived of as denying the faith practiced by the community would not be recorded in this kind of lexicon). Nevertheless, these cases of conversion to Islam prove that it occurred to the Ottomans that philosophy is certainly likely (in the case of conversion to Islam) or may (in the case of leaving Islam) encourage a man to question his faith to the point of abandoning it.

The biography of Ishak el-Rumi, a physician from Anatolia who lived in the sixteenth century, reflects this. "El-Rumi" indicates his Greek Orthodox Christian origin. As part of his medical education he also studied philosophy and logic, which led to his conversion to Islam. He abandoned medicine and specialized in theology and Islamic-Hanafi law. The story of the recognition of the superiority of Islam over other religions (in al-Rumi's case through studying philosophy) is the reason that this unknown physician is mentioned in two important biographical dictionaries: one written in the empire's center in the mid-sixteenth century and the other in Syria in the mid-seventeenth century.[88]

And, indeed, we know from various sources that philosophers and logicians, some of them high-ranking scholars in their time, were active in the Ottoman Empire. One example is the inclusion of the body of knowledge known as philosophy (*ʿilm al-falsafiyāt*) in the seventeenth-century bibliographical lexicon *Kashf al-Ẓunūn*. The entry devoted to philosophy is not too long by comparison to the other fields: (only) two pages in the first Ottoman printing in Istanbul in AH 1310 (1892–1893) are devoted to philosophy, but it is longer than the space dedicated to other fields, like agriculture (discussed above). The compiler of the bibliography delineated the fields that constitute philosophy, distinguishing between four principal types: mathematics (*riyāḍiyya*), logic (*manṭaqiyya*), physics (*ṭabīʿiyya*), and metaphysics (*ilāhiyya*). Katip Çelebi also named the subfields that constitute each field; for example, geometry, arithmetic, and music were branches of mathematics, while political philosophy was part of metaphysics. He noted twenty-three essays dealing with the different fields of philosophy, all written in the twelfth to fifteenth centuries. Hence, most of the essays are pre-Ottoman, and only one is clearly attributable to Anatolia: the author bears the moniker "El-Akshahrī," meaning that he came from Akşehir in central Anatolia, then a village or small town renowned in popular culture as the home of the satirical figure Nasreddin Hoca/Juḥā.[89]

Certain fields of philosophy actually developed during the Ottoman era, especially the field of logic, as shown convincingly by Khaled El-Rouayheb.[90] The number of essays steadily grew from the fifteenth and sixteenth centuries into the seventeenth and eighteenth centuries. The titles of the essays describe works of interpretation, summaries and synopses of existing treatises, though the genre does not have to be misleading. "Summary," "synopsis," and "interpretation" perhaps hint at restoration of existing knowledge and acceptance of traditions. However, the contents of the essays from the Ottoman era demonstrate innovative thinking and criticism of earlier philosophers, and are not at all characterized by lack of progress.

In *Relational Syllogisms and the History of Arabic Logic, 900–1900*, Al-Rouayheb showed how Ottoman logicians in the seventeenth and eighteenth centuries communicated between themselves in lively discourses without worrying too much about hostile views to logic, although these certainly existed. Hüseyin Khalkhali (d. 1604), Mehmed Emin Şirvani (d. 1627), Musa Pehlevani (d. 1720), Mehmed Tavuskari (flourished around 1748), Ismail Gelenbevi (d. 1791), Hocazade Abdallah Kilisi (d. 1886), and other mainstream scholars assessed, discussed, refuted, and developed logic. Their summaries and abbreviations were part of an intellectual-scientific tradition. They intended to study and explain this tradition, and while doing so tradition lent itself to animated and innovative discussions. Practices of citing, quoting, and copying also provided a powerful site of scientific engagement.[91]

In the realm of logic, this kind of scientific activity led to the Ottoman abandonment of classic Aristotelian concepts. The Ottoman logicians understood that the Aristotelian tools were inhibiting them, while they wanted to develop more complex syllogisms. For example, they dealt with deductions founded on underlying suppositions that are unrelated to one another—arguments with which Aristotelian logic could not cope. In the nineteenth century, the number of Ottoman treatises on logic was especially large, judging from the great number of them that have persisted to this day. While some of these treatises are not of a particularly high quality, others are quite excellent. Whatever the quality, these works testify to the Ottoman interest in logic and the development of the field toward growing sophistication and independent thought.

Astronomy, Astrology, and Their Sites in- and outside the Sultan's Court

The sciences of astronomy and astrology included various fields of interest that are not consistent with the fields in their modern sense: popular astronomy, stemming in part from pre-Muslim Arabs in the pre-Islamic period and focusing on stars; religious cosmologies inspired by the Qur'an and the hadith; Greek astrology; philosophical literature that dealt with the essence of the world; applied astronomy that used mathematical tools to solve problems involving the position of the stars, determining the time for religious ceremonies; and theoretical astronomy, which dealt with cosmography on the basis of mathematical models, devoid of connection to philosophical questions.

After the eleventh century, the distance between the fields of astronomy (*ʿilm al-hayʾa*) and astrology (*ʿilm al-nujūm*) began widening. In Katip Çelebi's seventeenth-century bibliography they appear as two separate bodies of related knowledge. Astronomy was described as an attempt to understand all the bodies that constitute the universe, astrology as understanding the influence of heavenly conditions on the physical reality of the human world and the attempt to foretell future positive and negative events by observing heavenly configurations.[92]

The multiplicity of intellectual concerns and artisanal skills under the headings "astronomy" and "astrology" shows that, according to the Muslim perception, the study of the skies was not limited only to the heavens but rather embraced the entire universe and the way in which the heavens conducted a dialogue with the subheavenly world below them. Islamic astronomy aimed at bringing higher precision to knowledge drawn from earlier traditions. This obligation led to significant development of the instruments required for observation and calculation, and for arranging the observation posts and recording the results. This process eventually led to the establishment of large-scale observatories.

The actual reasons for interest in astronomy/astrology were varied. Clearly, there was interest in knowledge for knowledge's sake, but there were also reasons connected to the specific content of astronomy and the uses made of it. Astronomy was a means to glorify the divine creation by scientifically understanding the sophisticated way in which the universe functions. Astronomers and astrologers provided useful services to the Muslim community: they fixed the religious time of prayers and holidays, prepared calendars and maps, calculated the precise direction of prayer to Mecca, and cast maritime navigational instruments and astrological forecasts. All these services made astronomy and astrology important and brought those involved in it prestige and a livelihood.[93]

During the Mamluk period, many treatises were written in all branches of astronomy (although only a few astrological treatises from this era exist). The institution of *muwaqqit* (timekeeper) was also inaugurated in this period. Now there was a well-organized group of professionals who fixed the religious time in sophistication and precision. They were employed at different mosques and schools, and thus came under the protective wing of religious patrons and the *waqf* (endowment/trust) institutions. It started in the second half of thirteenth-century Cairo and from there spread elsewhere in the Mamluk sultanate. Later on, the institution expanded into the Ottoman Empire and continued there until the nineteenth century. Those appointed as *muwaqqit* were honorably supported and held the post in comfort, so they did not necessarily have to make a living from other branches of their craft.[94]

Astronomy and astrology were certainly popular among Ottoman Muslims, as proven by the large number of texts and instruments for observation and calculation that have survived to our time. Indeed, the bibliographical dictionary of Katip Çelebi contains several entries that focus on subfields of astronomy/astrology. These included, for example, the science of using the astrolabe and the science of observing the heavenly bodies by means of instruments, among other practices.[95]

As astronomy and astrology were widespread, they were also much debated among scholars and bureaucrats. Popular as they were, from the palaces of the elites to the neighborhood mosques and bazaars, the tension surrounding these topics and the professionals who engaged with them, including the efforts to suppress them, is apparent from the medieval period and continued all the more forcefully during the Ottoman period. There existed no authoritative texts on astronomy and astrology, and explicit references could not have existed in the scriptures, traditions, or formative legal discussions. The pro-astronomy/astrology faction exploited this fact to its advantage: if no prohibiting tradition on the matter existed, then people were permitted it. Formal permission was one thing; social acceptance and consensual legal approval were another. The lack of a clear statement against astronomy and/or astrology could not preclude distrust from other, just as powerful factions.

This is a different situation from what Daniel Stolz has noted regarding later Ottoman Egypt, where he notes the existence of three distinct cultures of astronomy: the Islamic astronomy of *ʿulamāʾ*, the state astronomy of viceregal servants, and astronomy in the newly established Arab press. The reality for actual people—in their education, careers, and ways of understanding astronomy—was that these cultures frequently blended. Yet these astronomical cultures emerged in particular sites and traditions.[96] In the early modern Ottoman world, even in the same intellectual and social milieu and space, there were opposing sentiments regarding stargazing.

Once again, a mid-seventeenth-century example emerges from the biographical dictionary of Katip Çelebi, who summarizes the claims of opponents to astrology. He quotes Taşköprüzade, who referred to fourteenth-century Ibn Qayyim al-Jawziyya and others who opposed astrology; immediately afterward, though, he gives details of the astrological essays with which he is familiar.[97] Interestingly, he provides astronomy much less space than he gives to astrology,[98] less, even, than the space given to the entry about knowledge of talismans (*ʿilm al-ṭilasmāt*), which Katip Çelebi defines as knowledge of the means to combine earthly and celestial/heavenly powers.[99] However, astronomy seems to have been regarded as a "proper" field, perhaps the more respectable sphere of knowledge from a religious standpoint.

The foundation of an imperial observatory in Istanbul in the sixteenth century and its closing and destruction two years later is another scene where we observe the separation and integration of astrology and astronomy, the simultaneous acceptance and disapproval, and how the two factions of pro-astronomy/astrology and anti-astronomy played out their rivalry. The fate of the observatory illustrates this labyrinth of attitudes and interests.

The observatory was opened in 1577 on the crest of Galata Hill, on the way to the Tophane neighborhood in Istanbul, and operated under the aegis of Sultan Murad III (reigned 1574–1595), the Grand Vizier Sokollu Mehmed Paşa, and the sultan's former teacher, Saʿdüddin Hoca.[100] The observatory came to be identified not with these noted patrons but rather with the scholar who ran the institution, Takiyüddîn (1521/1525–1585). The observatory was well equipped and employed some townspeople in various professional capacities. The splendid observatory was immortalized in *Şāhīnşāhnāme* (The book of the king of kings), whose author has not been identified clearly. The essay in rhyming Persian prose commemorates Murad III's successes on and off the battlefield. Illustrations added to the manuscript emphasized specific topics in the written material and enhanced the manuscript's material value. The illustrated and written description of the observatory provides additional evidence of interest in the institution, its fame, and its connection to elite patronage.[101]

Takiyüddîn's observatory was not a mere caprice of the sultan and other members of the court but part of a widespread phenomenon in Istanbul and well beyond its confines. Significant astronomical activity also existed in towns like Bursa, the first capital of the Ottoman Empire, and Kütahya, a provincial town in west Anatolia where astronomy was taught, studied, and written about, and an observatory also operated.[102] In the Greek-speaking regions, educated people, some of whom were clerics, wrote many essays dealing with astrology/astronomy in an attempt to foretell and explain natural disasters that periodically wreaked havoc on the region.[103]

The geographical and religious dispersal of astronomy/astrology informs us of the measure of activity in the field and the extent of its integration into the Ottoman intellectual climate in the early modern era. Nevertheless, the practitioners of astronomy and astrology needed also to defend themselves quite constantly, which explains the short lifespan of some of these projects.

The observatory in Istanbul was active for only a short time, and the beginning of its end is symbolically connected to a significant event that was of both astronomic and astrologic importance: the appearance of a comet in the skies over Istanbul in 1577. The commentaries on its appearance and a series of events linked to the phenomenon reveal the tensions surrounding astronomy and astrology during the Ottoman era and, incidentally, also demonstrate the involvement of the two fields with one another, despite repeated attempts at separation and professionalization.

With the appearance of the comet, Takîyüddîn prepared an optimistic forecast for the sultan. He not only was an astronomer and the administrator of the imperial observatory but also served as the *müneccim-başı* (the imperial astrologer)—a post at the sultan's court—a fact that points to the Ottomans' support of astrology and those who dealt with it. The context of astrological prognostication was still important for astronomy. It was a normal aspect of practice and thinking in the Islamic world and Europe.

Takîyüddîn interpreted the appearance of the comet as signifying a period of successes, including victories on the battlefield against the Safavids in Iran. From the Ottoman perspective, however, reality was not that rosy. The Ottoman army did indeed defeat the Safavids. Furthermore, the war, fought from 1578 to 1590, ended with a number of significant achievements: the Ottomans annexed Azerbaijan, established a fleet on the banks of the Caspian Sea, and formed a direct and contiguous connection with the Uzbeks (a Turkic-Sunni state in central Asia in the region of present-day Uzbekistan, which was also the enemy of the Persian Shiite Safavids). However, a year after the comet appeared, there was a serious outbreak of plague in Istanbul that took many lives, including members of the imperial family: Mihrümah Sultan, the daughter of Sultan Süleyman and the aunt of Murad III, was among the fatalities.

Such misfortunes for the empire were fertile ground for nurturing general opposition to Takîyüddîn, the stargazer and astrologist. Şeyhülislam Şemsüddin Efendi, the imperial chief *müfti*, who had opposed the observatory from the outset, made the connection between the institution, the horoscope prediction, and the outbreak of the plague. It would be a mistake to see his opposition as being solely on religious grounds. He questioned the relevance of astronomy and astrology as a kind of Islamic knowledge, and claimed that this activity was always an expression of evil for those who preoccupy themselves with it—and that the life of anyone who initiates the construction of an observatory will come to an unnatural end. He claimed that astrology and astronomy are an attempt to investigate divine miracles, and God finds ways of expressing his dissatisfaction with whoever dares to reveal the secrets of the universe and attempt to divert the fate that God has determined. For this reason, Şeyhülislam warned that the disasters would not cease as long as the astronomical activity continued; he also prophesized that an earthquake would befall the empire (indeed, the center of the empire was and still is a high-earthquake-risk zone). However, he also had a political agenda: he was the political rival of Sokollu Mehmed Paşa and Saʿdüddin Hoca, among the patrons of Takîyüddîn and the observatory. Ultimately, he convinced the sultan, who sent Kılıç Ali Paşa, admiral of the Ottoman navy, to close the observatory.[104]

Although the observatory itself was demolished, the activity of astronomers and astrologers in Istanbul and elsewhere in the empire did not stop. Hundreds of essays were written on both topics.[105] In the first half of the nineteenth century an astronomer/astrologer from Ankara, Müderriszâde Saʿdüllah el-Ankaravî, used his scientific expertise to position himself within Ottoman political culture. He was well connected with the social elite, and was both a scholar and an Ottoman official in Ankara and its environs. As an astronomer/astrologer who was also a bureaucrat, he discussed the utility of horoscopes of prominent people in the context of the Tanzimat provincial administration to make sure the nominees were suitable to a new and reformed system.[106]

Well after Takîyüddîn, *müneccim-başı*s continued serving at the sultan's court. A total of thirty-seven people occupied this position following the institution's establishment during the sultanate of Bayezid II (reigned 1481–1512) and before it was ultimately abolished (only in 1924) with the end of the Ottoman Caliphate. They continued to face criticism each time their horoscopes failed to materialize. Thus, Mehmed Çelebi, the empire's chief astrologer in the seventeenth century (d. 1631), was asked why he had not predicted the death of Sultan Ahmed I (reigned 1603–1617). He rejected the claims and referred his rivals to a manuscript that had been placed in the Topkapı palace treasury for safekeeping. The essay was examined, and it became clear that he had indeed explicitly addressed the sultan's death. (Some of his manuscripts have survived to this day.) Nevertheless, his eminence and reputation for being trustworthy and knowledgeable did not save Mehmed from having to defend himself. His career preceding his appointment to the palace as *muvakkit* at the Şehzade Mosque in Istanbul (The Prince's Mosque that Süleyman I built in 1543 in memory of his beloved son, who died at the age of twenty-two, apparently from the plague) reflects that the integration between the crafts of astronomy and astrology had not disappeared.[107]

The roles of the *müneccim-başı*s involved a mixture of the study of theoretical astronomy with determining prayer times, the fast of Ramadan and festivals, and the preparation of horoscopes. As the one to fix the empire's religious schedule, the *müneccim-başı* was responsible for all the *muvakkit-hane* institutions, situated close to the principal mosques. Even after mechanical clocks were introduced in the Ottoman Empire and became commonplace in the nineteenth century, religious time was still fixed by traditional astronomers under the supervision of the *müneccim-başı*.[108] As chief astrologer, the *müneccim-başı* and his staff primarily served the sultan, but they prepared horoscopes for all the members of the imperial family and other key figures in the empire. (Some of the noted astronomers in Europe, like Johannes Kepler [1571–1630], earned their living not from "scientific" work but rather from the horoscopes they wrote, as Kepler did for the Hapsburg kaisers.)[109] Moreover, they prepared horoscopes for the empire itself: they determined fortuitous times for holding significant events like ceremonies of ascendance to the sultanate, festivals to mark births and weddings, and the departures of ships on voyages. The staff also recorded extraordinary astronomical occurrences—including solar and lunar eclipses, and the appearance of comets and unidentified objects in the skies—as well as earthquakes and fires. Beyond just presenting information on these events, the *müneccim-başı* was in charge of interpreting their significance. In this capacity, he and his staff were responsible not only for fixing the time but also for evaluating the quality of time, and whether it bode good or bad luck.[110]

MEDIATING MECHANISMS OF RECEPTION

The desire and ability to absorb ideas and skills into the Ottoman scientific system were controlled by various mechanisms that influenced the speed, volume, and mode of reception. Parallel operation of different levels of acceptance and rejection occurred. The slow entrance of European mechanical clocks into the Ottoman Empire demonstrates this realm. Ottomans were already familiar with mechanical clocks from the end of the fifteenth century, principally as an Italian product, but their widespread use did not begin at the time. Even during the eighteenth century, wall clocks (grandfather clocks) or hanging clocks were not necessarily accepted items among the Ottomans. Clocks, for example, were included in the imperial parades in which the sultan's wealth and status were demonstrated by parading the valuable gifts he received from foreign rulers.[111] Indeed, only in the nineteenth century did Ottomans successfully assimilate clocks as a product of European technology; they then became part of conceptual changes with regard to time and space.[112]

Another mechanism of control was integration. As Maurice Cerasi notes with regard to Ottoman architecture and use of space, the Ottomans adopted French Rococo and Italian Baroque, but did not surrender to these styles; instead, they used them for their own architectural and functional needs, and suited them to the Ottoman taste, thereby creating a style authentically Ottoman but distinct from that of the classic period.[113] They demonstrated willingness and the ability to assimilate new ideas and techniques as long as these were contained within the Ottoman intellectual world. Hence, what we see in this regard is not a break with the past but continuity. In this period, the early modern era, the new knowledge—or knowledge that could be understood as being new—was not seen as a challenge to basic concepts. In fact, it was perceived as complementing or combining with the Ottoman worldview. Or perhaps an understanding existed (even if subconsciously) that certain ideas might threaten the world order, and so certain innovations were repressed (for example, the first appearance of printed matter, discussed in Chapter 3).

A third mechanism filtered scientific exchange through the prism of closeness and resemblance between Ottoman and other systems of science and technology. This framework enabled significant dialogues with other distinctive systems while viewing them as internal discourses within the same worldviews.

Evliya Çelebi, the indefatigable Ottoman traveler of the mid-seventeenth century, tells a story about brain surgery in Vienna that demonstrates this complexity. According to Evliya, he visited Vienna in 1665 as a member of a delegation to the Hapsburg kaiser Leopold I (1640–1705) on behalf of Mehmed IV (reigned 1648–1687). During his stay in Vienna, he visited the hospital near the St. Stephen Cathedral on the banks of the Danube. The hospital was especially renowned at that time and, among others, treated patients from the imperial family. Evliya was impressed by the hospital's surgeons as a particularly clever and skilled team: in his view, they were comparable to Pythagoras and Ibn Sīnā. He described a brain surgery in detail. The forehead was cut across, from ear to ear, and he was amazed at the clean incision: not one drop of blood flowed. The top of the skull was removed with forceps, and Evliya was invited to look inside. He saw the brain, blood, and a lot of fluid as well as the bullet stuck in the brain tissue. The Viennese surgeon carefully extracted the bullet with forceps. A sponge soaked in wine was used to clean the internal wound, the top of the skull was replaced, and the head was bandaged with strips of leather. Ants were laid on the incision to suture and heal the wound, and all the incisions and holes in the head were covered with a thick paste. The smell of incense and drops of wine near the nostrils and body massage with clay for an hour aroused the patient from a deep sleep. His first meal was chicken soup and wine. Fifteen days after surgery, the patient was released from hospital and presented to the emperor.[114]

Of interest in understanding the Ottoman state of mind regarding European science is Evliya's attitude toward the surgery. He was amazed at the physicians' skill and astounded by the daring surgery and penetration into the human body; however, he certainly thought that the procedure was possible in "his" medicine as well. In Evliya's view, the surgery in Vienna was an impressive peak of achievement in medical ability, but not beyond Ottoman knowledge and capability.

At the time, Ottoman medicine was still based on the Galenic concept of humoral balance in its translation to Muslim-Arabic and subsequent

Ottoman adaptation. The Ottomans built on the surgical practices of al-Zahrāwī, an eleventh-century Andalusian,[115] improving his techniques and equipment. Two Ottoman adaptations of al-Zahrāwī were carried out in Anatolia during the fifteenth century, a rather early phase in writing in Ottoman Turkish: the more famous one was that of Şerefeddin Sabuncuoğlu in the mid-fifteenth century;[116] the other was an anonymous manuscript from the last quarter of the fifteenth century.[117] Europe, however, began to move on, even if its separation from Galen and his concept of humoral equilibrium was far from a total break. The surgery Evliya witnessed occurred a hundred years after the anatomical revolution of Andreas Vesalius and Renaissance artists like Leonardo da Vinci (1452–1519) and many others. In Evliya's era, the Englishman William Harvey (d. 1657) discovered the human blood circulatory system. This period saw many discoveries and medical procedures being carried out for the first time.

Evliya was unaware of this still subtle current and did not see the widening discrepancy that was growing between the two health systems. As far as he was concerned, Ottoman medicine was sophisticated and of high quality, like the system he had observed in Vienna. In this spirit, Evliya related with what esteem his medical knowledge had been received in Vienna: when he was invited to look at the opened head of the patient, Evliya immediately complied, though he covered his mouth and nose with a handkerchief. The local surgeon was surprised, and Evliya explained that he did not want to sneeze or cough so close to the open wound. The Viennese surgeon was impressed and cheered, "Bravo!" Certainly, Evliya did not avoid taking pride in his actions throughout the text, but even this exaggeration is evidence of the mood of the writer and his time. Evliya examined Viennese medicine and was impressed by it, maintaining his opinion that his own Ottoman system not only was of the same quality, but shared a professional language with the European one.[118]

During the nineteenth century, the mechanism of mediating reception by way of a discourse of closeness was no longer relevant. Now Ottomans thought about the two scientific systems—namely, the Ottoman and western European—as separate and different. At the end of the Ottoman period, Ottoman philosophers suggested another means to reconcile new sources of knowledge by thinking of technology as value-free. Ultimately, in practice, it proved impossible to separate Western technology, for instance, and Western perspectives with regard to the social order and political organization, even though they believed that such separation was possible. Regardless of whether this intellectual solution proved satisfactory or not, it reveals that the discussion regarding the multiple nature of *ʿilm* never ended, with each generation reinterpreting it.

Ziya Gökalp (1876–1924), for example, one of the important philosophers of the end of the Ottoman era, also sought to integrate Western and Turkish culture. Gökalp, who was active in the Young Turks as well as the Unity and Progress Committee, was Pan-Turkish and one of the fathers of Turkish nationalism. He perceived of the Turks as an integrating link between the East and West, and considered it possible to assume this role without losing Turkish cultural characteristics in which he took great pride. Gökalp was part of a discourse prevailing among Ottoman literati in the second half of the nineteenth century that focused on change, transformation, and adaptation. For them it was perfectly sensible to take knowledge and techniques that had originated in the West and implant them into the Ottoman context by its Ottomanization. Hence Gökalp dealt exclusively with *how* to achieve this goal; he had no doubt regarding its feasibility.[119]

The debate in which Gökalp participated—without addressing the issue of whether his position was logical or naïve—suggests that Ottoman society's struggle toward the end of the nineteenth century and early twentieth century was with a process that included cultural and social changes as much as technical and scientific ones. Gökalp and others wanted to control the process: they wanted to be able to adopt Western technology on one hand, yet prevent the Ottoman-Turkish-Muslim identity from being erased on the other. At least certain segments in Ottoman society exhibited real enthusiasm for the West, termed *gharbzadegi* ("Western sickness" or "Westoxication," to use an Iranian term from the 1960s, which relates critically to the adoption of Western social and economic patterns). Certain Ottoman groups also internalized the orientalist dialogue about the world of Islam in general and about the Ottoman Empire in particular: they accepted the dichotomy between East and West, including the subjective evaluation of the inferior status of the East as compared to the progressive, modern, and cultured West.[120] At the end of the nineteenth century and the beginning of the twentieth, the Ottoman press exhibited satirical ridicule toward the extremists in both camps: those who almost unquestioningly adopted Western fashion without a sense of proportion and those who rejected anything European just by mere virtue of its being European.[121]

The Westernization process was more complicated than just accepting it without bounds and without question. The treatise on European astronomy by nineteenth-century Abdüllah el-Shukri ibn Seyyid Abdülkarim el-Konavi in the early modern era demonstrates this. He aimed his *Tanqīḥ al-ahshkāk ʿan tawḍīḥ al-idrāk* (The correction of doubts about the clarification of perception) to the teachers at the Ottoman *medrese*s and presented them with the new cosmology (*hayʾa jadīda*): the Copernican heliocentric model, placing the sun at the center of the solar system. The verbal explanation was accompanied by a drawing of the planets circling the sun. El-Konavi also addressed the newer discoveries from the end of the eighteenth century and the beginning of the nineteenth century: the existence of a belt of asteroids between Jupiter and Mars and the planets Uranus and Neptune. In contrast, he ignored the works of Galileo, Kepler, and Newton. Principally, although other Ottoman authors did support the Copernican system, el-Konavi rejected heliocentric analysis in favor of supporting the traditional geocentric model, with Earth in the center. El-Konavi thought that astronomy should be part of traditional general education and included in this the knowledge taken from Europe—but only partially.[122]

Scholarship dealing with intellectual life in this period points out that assimilation of certain Western values took place—for many Ottomans, out of choice and under their own control. But this process also took a heavy toll. It left a reality that connected technology, science, and a Western worldview with traditional priorities and local identity, inflaming inner tensions that were rather complicated: criticism, embarrassment, and confusion; curiosity and restraint; jealousy, contempt, and a sense of superiority; and shame and a sense of inferiority.[123]

It is appropriate to end this discussion of the Ottomans' nineteenth-century debates by pointing out that it was a particular intellectual phenomenon rooted in specific circumstances, and at the same time it also represented continuity of Islamic discourse of *ʿilm* among traditionally educated Muslim scholars. I invoke here Foucauldian terms to conclude this chapter by saying that mechanisms of reception, conceptualizations of knowledge, and categorization of sources during the nineteenth century were different and a break from previous epistemological discourses; however, the very same nineteenth-century discourse also belonged to the Ottoman epistemological notion of *ʿilm*. What *ʿilm* meant was subject to historical change, but its configuration in a way that allowed the historical action of knowledge(s) proved a consistent pattern.

TWO

WHERE AND HOW DOES LEARNING TAKE PLACE?

In the absence of quantifiable data about learning among the Ottomans, we must turn to the impressions and estimations of both Ottomans and Europeans. For the sixteenth and seventeenth centuries, sources regarding the Turkish-speaking areas mention that at least a quarter of the urban population could read and write in Turkish and knew, at worst, those Arabic chapters of the Qur'an pertaining to prayer.[1] Nelly Hanna describes the existence of a vibrant and educated urban middle class in Arabic-speaking Cairo of the early modern period. She notices a spread of written colloquial language and suggests it was a dominant factor in the spread of literacy. In fact, around 1600 there was a definitive and significant rise in the spread of texts on the whole, with a proliferation of texts on different subjects written in colloquial Arabic. This linguistic choice was made even by educated authors with a mastery of Arabic. Hanna also points to the growth of trade as contributing to the spread of literacy.

The spread of literacy was spatially uneven. In some urban centers—for instance, Jerusalem (a place of pilgrimage and religious importance but not a site of major trade or industry)—members of the Muslim community were illiterate more often than not.[2] The rural population, which constituted the majority in Ottoman society, is sadly usually outside the scope of the sources.

This reality of literacy in varying degrees, spatially and temporally, invites us to reflect on the contents of education of various social groups (and not just among the elite) and the means to acquire it. How did they learn? Where did they learn? This chapter traces the patterns of teaching and learning in the main centers of the Ottoman Empire, in both the Turkish- and Arabic-speaking domains.

PEDAGOGY

The Ottoman discourse on education continued a tradition dating back to the Arabic Middle Ages. Discussions on the subject took place in various genres: medical treatises on pediatrics, essays on education and pedagogy, legal discussions on the status of the child in the community and in the family, and letters of condolence to bereaved parents.[3]

A glimpse at the Ottoman discourse on pedagogy is possible through Ottoman hagiography—descriptions of the lives of saints. Using legends, the *menaqibname* literature (literally, "the book of virtues") documents the qualities of saints and heroes as lessons and examples worth following. The *sira* literature—that is, the biography of the Prophet—is the most outstanding example of this kind of literature. Although religious in its aims and contents (the text deals with beliefs and rituals, orthodoxy and heterodoxy), the *menaqibname* literature also discloses social and political values, including ideas about childhood. The childhoods of the saints, as represented in stories, form the background for their special role in society. Like any other aspect recalled about a saintly hero, his childhood is seen as a model to emulate with regard to the treatment of children. The idyllic description of the Prophet Muḥammad's childhood, including his schooling years, informs us, for example, that the relationship between teacher and pupil was shaped in an extremely hierarchical manner. In the hagiographic Ottoman version of the Prophet's biography, the teacher is described as an authoritative, coercive, and commanding character. Children were taught in a rigid framework of obligations. A substantial portion of the teaching was based on memorizing material and reciting it countless times (and not necessarily on the basis of a deep understanding of what was learned). Teacher-pupil relations revolved around the pupils' fear of punishment, including physical retribution.

The hagiographical literature characterizes the teacher-pupil relationship in the classroom by rigidity. Hence children's games were described as valuable. For example, experience in a children's space—playing in the street without the presence of parents or another adult authority—was considered important to the child's development. Boys were encouraged to be mischievous and playful and to compete in various sports, such as wrestling (popular in Ottoman society). Ottoman writers described children's games as reflecting adult behavior (competitiveness, a struggle for social status and prestige) and not mere play, devoid of "serious" goals. However, these ideas are perhaps linked to the identity of storybook heroes: after all, it was unlikely that saints, especially Muḥammad, would have a "regular" childhood. For this reason, his hagiography does not relate to childhood as a different or separate period. Ideas about being patient with children, nurturing the emotional connection between children and parents, and appreciating children as innocent and natural (and sometimes irresponsible) are expressed in *menaqibname* literature. In Ottoman society, play was not only considered normal but also inherently valued: through play, children were thought to put their abilities to the test and learn their limits from the process.[4]

Instruction: How?

Multiple methods existed for acquiring knowledge and education in Ottoman society: autodidactic, formal schooling, home learning with a private tutor, and apprenticing to an artisan. Many Ottomans were taught by a private tutor during childhood and individually or in groups as adolescents. The reality of instruction was complex. Many individuals learned in a variety of ways in accordance with their economic capacity, the accessibility of training, and their way of life or personal leanings—all of which obviously change through time.

No single mode of acquiring knowledge or learning a specific profession enjoyed a monopoly. This reality resulted in competition between the different paths and, in fact, between the people who followed different educational methods, regarding who possessed "real" knowledge. For example, as noted in Chapter 1, Ottoman doctors hurled the epithet "charlatan" at each other in order to label a rival unworthy because of inferior training (at least in their eyes), among other accusations.[5]

When evaluating a professional's worth, Ottomans did not necessarily view previous training as a crucial criterion. They cared only about a professional's abilities at that time, not his or her previous studies. This tendency is apparent, for example, in legal suits against physicians for what we today call "medical malpractice." Disappointed patients sued, complaining that their physicians had not complied with the contract between them: the accused physicians had received payment for full recovery but had not delivered the goods. Court deliberations in such malpractice cases were predictable: the *kadi* clarified the details of the contract between the patient and the physician regarding the diagnosis, what was promised, and the agreed fee; he reviewed the treatment actually given and its results and, where necessary, consulted an expert witness regarding the extent to which the treatment given was customary in cases like the one being deliberated. In this procedure, while the status of the defendant physician in the local professional community was examined, according to the Muslim court records (*sijill*, in Arabic), no examination was conducted of the physician's precise training in the past, at least openly.

Women also studied, and at every stage of life, as girls, adolescents, and adults. Amongst the elite, girls would study with a private tutor at home, as did boys. Among the lower classes, education was acquired at a communal institution adjacent to the mosque or church, or at home in learning circles for women throughout the neighborhood. Both men and women arranged and taught at these learning circles. Even the Orthodox writers, who were the most stringent regarding appropriate moral behavior, allowed women to leave their homes for reasons of education, and certainly when the intention was religious education.[6]

Instruction: Where?

Alongside multiple pedagogical methods of learning, Ottomans also used multiple sites of learning. Some of them were intended to be used primarily as sites of learning, but mosques and libraries were also used. Before the reforms of the nineteenth century, the accepted practice in Ottoman society was to send children to school around the age of seven to acquire the basic education of a Muslim believer. Known variably as *kuttāb* and *maktab* in Arabic and *mekteb* in Ottoman Turkish, such schools were the Muslim equivalent of the Jewish cheder (or heder). Indeed, among Ottomans, circumcision and entering school were two seminal events or rites of passage in the transfer from infancy to childhood.[7]

Elementary education principally involved religious training aimed at instilling the knowledge and the skills required to observe the religion of Islam as a ritual- and faith-based system. Hence, the goal of instruction was mainly technical. Therefore, the major part of the teaching in the *kuttāb* was devoted to memorizing passages from the Qur'an. Reading and writing skills were taught in the local language. Arabic, the language of Islam, was studied only where it was the prominent local language, so children elsewhere memorized the religious texts in Arabic without necessarily any real understanding. They also studied a little arithmetic, history, and geography. In practice, great variance existed between the content and the level of study in the different *kuttāb*s. No system of coordination or unification was implemented to determine content and enforce its application. Rather, each school centered on the character and authority of a senior teacher. The level and teaching content of each parochial school were determined exclusively on the basis of the abilities of each school's specific teachers.

The Ottoman *medrese* (the Turkish version of the Arabic term *madrasa*) was the institution responsible first and foremost for acquiring deeper knowledge in the field of religion. However, at least to some extent, it offered a broad education as well. For those who desired a wider understanding, some *medrese*s could also provide the comprehensive knowledge required by polymaths. This was the impression of one eighteenth-century observer, G. B. Toderini, a learned Jesuit who lived in Istanbul from October 1781 to May 1786. He described the grandness of Ottoman *medrese*s (he referred to them as "accademia"), noting generally how magnificent *medrese* buildings were and how impressive the professors were. He then elaborated on some of the more famous and centrally located *medrese*s in Istanbul at that time, organized according to the chronology of their establishment, from the schools of Mehmed II to those of Abdülhamid I (reigned 1774–1789). More importantly, Toderini described Ottoman *medrese*s as institutions devoted to all the sciences, where religious studies such as *tafsir* and hadith were taught alongside astronomy and geometry.[8]

Indeed, solid evidence exists that astronomy and mathematics were sometimes taught in some Ottoman *medrese*s, and even in Sufi lodges of *tekke*s and *zaviye*s. Geometry and astronomy were mentioned as separate courses in the curriculum; algebra was usually part of arithmetic rather than an independent field of study.[9]

Perhaps Ottomans included the sciences in *medrese* studies in continuation of the Timurid model from Samarqand, the most important Muslim cultural center in the fourteenth and fifteenth centuries under the Chingissid-Mongolian dynasty.[10] However, Nebi Efendizade, an eighteenth-century Ottoman *müderris* (a teacher in a *medrese*) from Uşak in western Anatolia, offers evidence to the contrary in his recording of standard curricula. The list of topics included Arabic morphology, grammar, and syntax; logic and rhetoric; jurisprudence; theology; and hadith and Qur'anic exegesis. Interestingly, exact and rational sciences did not appear in any of these lists.[11]

At present we are unable to estimate the extent and significance of the Ottoman phenomenon of combining the religious with the rational. Some historians, mainly Turkish ones, suggest that nonreligious studies (including arithmetic, geometry, astronomy, music, chemistry, medicine, agriculture, and geography) were almost (but not quite) as important as religious studies at the *medrese*.[12] However, the extent to which nonreligious subjects were routinely taught in the *medrese*s and their relative importance in the curriculum can still be questioned. To put it differently: although many *ülema* did indeed combine religious learning with natural sciences, the exact sciences, or other spheres of knowledge, we do not know how their own diverse knowledge was related to their *medrese* education and teaching. Ultimately, even if a given teacher taught a religious *ʿilm* in the *medrese* and, from his biography, we know that he was an expert in other fields as well and even that he also taught these other subjects, given our current state of knowledge it would be a mistake to assume that he necessarily taught those nonreligious subjects at the *medrese* specifically. As in the pre-Ottoman periods, teaching and learning took place at a variety of locations.[13] Therefore, well-founded evidence would be required to establish any trend of concentrating the teaching and learning of a broad variety of subjects, especially in the *medrese*s of all places.

Many Ottomanists studied at the *medrese* to broaden their knowledge and education. They were literate and educated, but not professionals. Just as many students, if not more, viewed the *medrese* as a vocational school. Training at the *medrese* was an essential stage in two principal career tracks. One was the religious professions. The most prominent of these positions in the Ottoman Empire were teaching and judging, but also included delivering legal opinions (*iftāʾ*) and preaching in mosques (*waʿẓ*), among other options. The second career track was clerical work in the Ottoman administration. Both tracks relied on a common combination of fields of knowledge at the *medrese*s: religious subjects, such as Qurʾan interpretation, law, and theology, and auxiliary fields, such as Arabic language, including grammar, syntax, and more.

Indeed, training at the *medrese* was an essential stage in the career of a professional man of religion. At the beginning of the empire, in the fourteenth century, no tradition of religious instruction had yet emerged in Anatolia. Thus, the first *ülema* in the empire had to travel to the traditional learning centers throughout the Middle East in Syria and Egypt. (An analysis of these journeys to acquire knowledge will follow.) Over the course of the fourteenth century, the first Ottoman *medrese*s were established, and it became possible to obtain Islamic knowledge locally. By the time of Mehmed II, the conqueror of Constantinople, a local tradition of religious studies had already begun to develop. To this, Mehmed II added a hierarchy of the various teaching institutions throughout the Ottoman state. This development continued vigorously, and by time of Süleyman's reign in the mid-sixteenth century, clear career paths were expressed in the level of teachers' salaries and students' stipends. The more esteemed an institution was, the higher the sums that were paid there. As expected, the *medreses* in the capital were held in higher regard than those in the provinces. Among the three capitals (Bursa, Edirne, and Istanbul), Istanbul was the most highly regarded, and in Istanbul, the highest rank was the sultanic imperial *medreses*. The first of these were the eight *medreses* of Mehmed II (known thereafter as *sahn-ı seman* or *semaniye*; that is, "the eights"). Later on, the *medreses* that Süleyman included in his complex outranked Mehmed's as the most prestigious.[14]

The inclusion of the *medreses* in the hierarchical system coincided with attempts to coordinate the contents of teaching and define obligatory standards. As in the past, the instruction centered on texts selected by the teachers; consequently, great discrepancies could develop between educational institutions and even within an institution based on the tendencies of the teachers. This chaotic nature was characteristic of the medieval *medreses*, and the Ottoman state sought to regulate them.

Regulations concerning the Ottoman *medreses* were passed in several phases, or maybe they had to be ratified several times when previous regulations were not strictly followed. In the sixteenth century, a collection of regulations (*kanun-name*) was prepared for the *ülema* and their students. In this period we see a drive for systemized restructuring and development of an imperial hierarchy throughout the Ottoman ruling institutions, including the religious establishment, the *ilmiyye*. During the reign of Süleyman, career paths and hierarchies became clearer than they had been before. Within this context, it became relevant for the *kanun-name* to define ranks, standards, and fixed curricula for every level, from the lowest entrance position upward. This compilation contains lists of basic texts that the students had to read. They were prohibited from proceeding to the following stage until they were tested on required texts and received a confirmation from the teacher (*icazet*); the teacher of the following stage was also supposed to check that the new student did, indeed, have certification of having completed the earlier stage, and if not, he could not allow him to attend classes. Moreover, the regulations declared that the *medreses* were to be inspected, and teachers not abiding by the regulations would be dismissed. A 1598 sultanic decree (*nişan*) from Murad III ratified these regulations.[15]

Nebi Efendizade, the name by which Ali bin Abdüllah el-Uşşak (d. 1785/1786) was known, was an Ottoman *medrese* teacher (and as such, an official in an Ottoman bureaucratic institution) who recorded a curriculum that was accepted in his period. His writings attest that the hierarchy and more or less uniform curricula envisioned in previous Ottoman centuries had become a norm. His *Kaside fi-l-kütüb el-meşhure fi el-ulum* (Qasida on famous book of knowledge) introduces a form of rhymed lyric poetry with an elaborate meter, as well as listing textbooks and authors studied in Ottoman *medreses*. He recorded a three-level hierarchy: beginners started by reading summaries (*ikhtiṣār*); intermediate students read midlevel texts (*iqtiṣād*); and advanced students were required to read detailed, in-depth treatises (*istiqṣāʾ*). In turn, each stage was divided into three substages.[16]

It appears that in the early modern period there was a drive toward regulating teaching methodology and constructing graduated and structured progress. The regulations were implemented in the *medreses* throughout the empire (not only at its center). Yet, at the same time, a certain fluidity was the norm and allowed for differences in educational content stemming from a variety of reasons. One such reason could be a school's inclination toward mystical Islam (or lack thereof).

Erzurumlu İbrahim Hakkı (d. 1780) produced different ideal curricula from Nebi Efendizade. He too was a teacher in an Ottoman *medrese*. He came from Erzurum in eastern Anatolia (hence his name), but he also visited Istanbul, where he received an audience with Sultan Abdülhamid I. In addition to being a religious scholar, İbrahim Hakkı was a Sufi leader, a *şeyh*, teaching a mystical theory and practice. Indeed, his list of curricula combined religious and legal subjects with Sufi texts. In his vision, the *medrese* and the *tekke* had much in common. His distinction between the two institutions of learning—one for Orthodox Islamic learning and the other for Sufi Islamic learning—is blurred.[17]

The *medrese*'s institutional regulation during its Ottoman phase (the implementation of a hierarchy, a drive toward consensual curricula, and the transformation of *medrese* education into a requisite component in the careers of *ülema*) differentiated Ottoman *medreses* from medieval ones. The disparity has to do with the exact role assigned to this institution. Before the Ottomans, during the Ayyubid and Mamluk periods, the *medrese*'s social importance stemmed mainly from its responsibility for creating and preserving status; most of the teaching and learning was carried out elsewhere.[18] In the Ottoman period as well, belonging to *medreses* in general and to the prestigious ones among them in particular bore social significance; yet the Ottoman *medrese* was an educationally active institution, and religious education was obtained there first of all.

Medreses were also an important part of the training of some Ottoman administrators, as demonstrated by the biography of Mustafa bin Abdüllah

(1609–1657). He is almost unknown by this name, but the names and titles for which he became famous indicate his diverse career and education: we refer to Haji Khalifa, who was none other than the celebrated Katip Çelebi. He was given the title "Haji" as a show of respect for one who has observed the obligation of pilgrimage to Mecca, the hajj; "Khalifa" (or "Kalfa") is the title of honor granted to a clerk in the Ottoman administration. Katip Çelebi was a historian, geographer, and bibliographer who served as an Ottoman official in the army finance division. In this position, he accompanied the army on its travels in Anatolia, the Caucasus, and the Middle East, including Murad IV's campaign to reconquer Baghdad.

During his lifetime Katip Çelebi fused the education of the *mekteb* and *medrese* and the Ottoman administration. He began his studies at the age of five or six, and by the time he was fourteen, he had become an apprentice in one of the offices of the Ottoman financial bureaucracy. There he learned bookkeeping and the *siyakat* (the secret code used by financial clerks to codify sensitive financial information to hide it from unauthorized eyes). All through his administrative career with the army, Katip Çelebi continued to pursue his religious studies. Most of his studying took place in the capital, though he knew how to take advantage of the stops the army made on its campaigns, which allowed him to study with other prominent *ülema*. In the city of Aleppo, for example, he studied while on journeys to Iraq. Twice while he was in Istanbul, he also took time off from his bureaucratic work and devoted himself fully to attending the lectures of the *ülema* in the capital city. He used the inheritance left by his father—a soldier in the Ottoman army—to take leave from his regular work for the benefit of his studies. A few years later, after being bypassed for a promotion he expected, Katip Çelebi had an altercation with his superior and resigned. Again he returned to study at the *medrese*, and only after some time did he seek a new position as an administrator. Katip Çelebi interested himself not only in the sphere of religion. His unquenchable curiosity included an interest in the history, geography, and cartography of Europe and the New World. He read the works of his period through translations from Latin. He was a prolific writer in Arabic and Ottoman Turkish in his fields of interest, which also included contemporary issues of his day.[19]

Two particular examples illustrate the nature of Katip Çelebi's twenty-two works.[20] The first, *Tuhfet ül-kibar fi esfar el-bihar* (The gift of the great and noble on naval campaigns), dealt with war at sea. He wrote the treatise in 1656 after the Ottoman navy was defeated by the Venetians.[21] His last treatise, *Mizan al-haqq fi ikhtiyar al-ahaqq* (The balance of truth), charts in twenty-one chapters the principal theological and moral issues dividing Ottoman society at the time—for example, music, smoking, dancing, and more. He attempted to present a balanced, tolerant perspective. His starting point was that beliefs and customs that have already become rooted in society cannot be uprooted, and there is no reason to cause difficulty to the community and put the public to tests it cannot withstand.[22]

Clearly, Katip Çelebi was an intellectual, even a philosopher in the opinion of his peers, who also addressed practical matters that interested the state and society. He is an extraordinary example because of the scope of his knowledge and the variety of spheres in which he was involved. From this standpoint, his education was not representative of the standard Ottoman education of the early modern era. Yet he provides an interesting example of how the fields of interest and the skills of an Ottoman official were combined with the outcomes of *medrese* education; in this, Katip Çelebi was a product of his time.

Indeed, *medrese*s were flourishing, spreading throughout the Ottoman Empire. One incentive to found more schools was to offer more study slots to the numerous students who kept knocking on *medrese* doors. But establishing more schools only postponed the problem: along the way, the number of trained students outnumbered the number of available jobs. The *medrese*s were able to accept many more students than the Ottoman work establishment could offer employment, whether as professional *ülema* or as clerks. This bottleneck caused great bitterness, not only because of graduates' unemployment through no fault of their own, but also because the Ottoman state was ultimately forced to provide for them for long periods, which caused social tensions.

From the sixteenth century onward, the *softa* (*medrese* students) are mentioned in Ottoman sources as a rabble, sometimes uncontrolled, which participated in or even initiated uprisings in the capital city. They took part in the July 1703 uprising directed against Şeyhülislam Feyzüllah Efendi and his patron, Sultan Mustafa II (reigned 1695–1703). Known as the Edirne event, the rebellion led to the sultan's removal from power. Feyzüllah Efendi's fate was worse: after being tortured in prison for two months, he was decapitated in front of the mob in one of the city squares of Edirne. The *softa* also participated in the spring 1909 uprising against the Young Turks and their political organization, the Committee for Unity and Progress. The protests aimed, among other things, to renew the power of Sultan Abdülhamid II (reigned 1876–1909), which had diminished with the renewal of the parliament in 1908. The rebellion was suppressed at a cost of dozens of fatalities in the capital and brought about the total removal of Abdülhamid from power. He was replaced by Sultan Mehmed V Reşad (reigned 1909–1918). One reason for the active rebelliousness, to the point of violence, was the students' concern for their social and economic future as they saw opportunities for advancement diminishing.[23]

Schools were an especially important institution for learning but not the only one available for Ottomans who wished to learn. Mosques and libraries also functioned under certain circumstances as possible schools. The personnel in these establishments acquired further duties over time, one of which could be teaching. In the eighteenth century it became increasingly common for some libraries to expect the librarian—initially the keeper and conserver of books, with a grasp of bibliography—to also be a qualified teacher. To the requirements of good skills in writing, decorating, cleaning and mending books, and loaning and recalling books, scholarship was now added.[24]

Apprenticeship

Mekteb and *medrese* institutions offered principally religious knowledge and reading and writing skills, thereby training the next generation of Ottoman religious and administrative officers. Where could Ottomans get training in a different profession? There were no vocational schools.

The activity of the medical school and hospital in the Süleymaniye complex in Istanbul was extraordinary rather than the rule. There may have been a few other medical schools; for example, the *medrese* at the Edirne complex of Bayezid II (reigned 1481–1512) may have actually been a medical school. Evliya visited the institution in the mid-seventeenth century and clearly regarded it as a medical school (*medrese-i etıbbâsı*). He even highly praised the level of the teaching, as well as the students and the extent of their dedication to healing people.[25]

Circumstantial evidence for the fact that some *medreses* might have offered medical training may also be found in their proximity (or occasionally even attachment) to hospital buildings. Moreover, ornaments at the school connected to the Istanbul hospital named after Hürrem Sultan—the preferred concubine and later the wife of Süleyman I—raise the question of the school's potential history as a medical training establishment: the walls of the school were decorated with what seems to be a medical theme. Perhaps the snakes on the exterior walls of the Hürrem *medrese* are a veiled reference to Asclepius, the Greek god of healing and medicine; if so, might this be evidence of the medical role of the *medrese*?[26]

Even if we accept the inconclusive evidence that a few *medreses* were acting as medical schools, only a handful of *medrese*s in the Ottoman Empire specialized in medicine or taught medicine in addition to bodies of religious knowledge. The picture is clear: there were hardly any professional medical schools, just as there were no vocational schools for many other professions, prior to the educational reforms of the nineteenth century.

If this was the case, where could a person train as a physician? Or as a carpenter? For fields that were perceived to be crafts (*ṣināʿa* in Arabic; *sinaet* in Ottoman Turkish), the answer was an apprenticeship. Physicians struggled constantly to be recognized as professionals rather than craftsmen—not always with success—and the apprenticeship model applied to them as well. Work as an apprentice made vocational schooling unnecessary, not only because the apprenticeship institution already existed, but also from a conceptual point of view: clearly, the way to study fields that were perceived as crafts (and not as founded on a theoretical body of knowledge) was to learn by experience, not from studying books and theories. (Anyway, books and theories did not always exist regarding such professions.)

Young people commenced their apprenticeships during their teens. This was also considered an important stage in the life of a young Ottoman: the start of organized, fixed employment was perceived as the end of childhood and the beginning of adulthood.[27] Apprentices (*şakirdan*) were found in a wide range of workplaces: stores, workshops, hospitals, and studios in which various artifacts and art objects were manufactured. Apprentices worked and studied within a professional guild or with a relative. Many instances have been documented in which dynasties of specialists were created in specific professions, which were handed down from father to son or from mother to daughter (or more rarely, across genders). In such cases, there was an overlap between guild connection and family ties.[28]

The Palace and Harem as Institutions of Learning

The imperial palaces served as training institutions for their many servants, who were in fact the cadre for the future military-administrative elite. The palace institution's role was to prepare a new generation of officers and administrators by means of a preliminary selection of excellent candidates. Careful selection processes, whereby only the most talented were chosen throughout the tutelage process, ensured that only those who excelled would reach the upper echelons and serve the dynasty in various capacities. The most renowned school operated in the Enderun, the inner service in the third and most private court at Topkapı, the imperial palace in Istanbul. Other schools existed at the various palaces in Istanbul and Edirne. The school at Topkapı was unique: under the supervision of the white eunuchs who ran the palace, the youths received tutelage by personally serving the sultan himself. They lived under an especially strict, military-like regimen. It was forbidden to speak in a loud voice in the sultan's presence, and the trainees had to communicate between themselves in a special sign language.[29]

The palace school trained officers and governors, as well as excellent craftsmen. One graduate of the imperial school was Mimar Sinan (1490–1588), who was perhaps the greatest Ottoman architect. As a youth of Christian-Greek origin, he was recruited in the *devşirme* (the enlistment of Christian youths into the Janissaries unit), converted to Islam, and circumcised. He trained at the palace as both a soldier and an architect. He excelled on a succession of campaigns, participating, for example, in the journey to Rhodes, Belgrade, Hungary, and Baghdad. He built a series of facilities for the army's use: bridges, fortifications, aqueducts, and more. His accomplishments brought him to the attention of Sultan Süleyman, who ultimately appointed him to the post of chief imperial architect (*mimar-başı* [master builder]). He occupied the post for decades, during which he designed hundreds of buildings throughout the empire (more on him and his buildings as state infrastructure in Chapter 4).[30]

Parallel to the palace school, a similar institute was run in the harem, which trained young women to serve as suitable companions to the sultan and his mother (*valide-i sultan*), as well as senior women in the harem. They could also leave the harem to become wives to future elite males at the palace, in the Ottoman administration and army. The harem school followed the design of the male model. Europeans compared the lifestyle in the palace and harem schools to a monastic regimen: in both, strict discipline was implemented, and the solemn atmosphere demanded, among other things, complete silence. The harem school, like the palace school, was a very detailed, hierarchical system with similar ranks and advancement tracks. In both schools, the students and staff had the status of slaves (female concubines and male slaves). Thus both schools enlisted people from outside the Turkish-Muslim population. White concubines came from the Balkans, eastern Europe, and the Caucasus, and black concubines were brought from Africa. This network paralleled that of the male slaves of the sultan's *devşirme*.

Female concubines learned various crafts like sewing, embroidery, dancing, and music, including singing and playing instruments. They also received guidance in the religious principles of Islam. This ambitious educational system left the concubines with no free time, since in addition to their studies they worked in the service of the other women: cleaning, cooking, entertaining, and doing maintenance work around the harem. The harem lifestyle stressed the importance of perseverance and diligence. Only the most senior women were granted a life of greater ease, and only a few were able to rise above the status of indentured workers. But even when they reached that stage in their lives, they were supposed to continue occupying themselves with needlework, embroidery, and music, which were considered noble and delicate occupations.[31]

Ṭalab al-ʿIlm

The search for knowledge (*ṭalab al-ʿilm*) was understood to be the religious obligation of every Muslim and incorporated the physical aspect of travel with an initiated search for teachers, texts, and knowledge (*al-riḥla fī ṭalab al-ʿilm*). Many hadiths praised the search for knowledge, hailing it as "walking in God's path" (*fī sabīl allāh*), and encouraged Muslims to explore to the ends of the universe. China is mentioned in this context as an example of how far it is appropriate or even recommendable for a Muslim to go for the sake of knowledge (an example that was rejected in some corners, and still is debated in modern times).

The hadith was popular and proved durable, at least as a literal trope, alongside another corpus of sayings discouraging travel in pursuit of knowledge for the wrong reasons. The eleventh-century al-Khaṭīb al-Baghdādī—a religious scholar (especially of hadiths), historian, and biographer—devoted a treatise to the phenomenon of travel as a pattern of transfer of knowledge. He disapproved what he regarded as the degeneration of the practice as it involved greed, and travel for knowledge blended with trade and commerce.[32]

In reality many Muslims from the eighth or ninth centuries onward did not live the spirit of the saying and accumulated knowledge locally.[33] Ignaz Goldziher, in his classic *Muhammedanische Studien*, pointed out that the value of travel eroded through the centuries, and during the eleventh century, the *ijāza* (a license to transmit) replaced the *ṭalab* practice as the major system of disseminating knowledge and texts.[34]

Nevertheless, traveling was a major social enterprise in the premodern Islamic world. Networks of travel and trade have often been viewed as central to understanding interactions among Muslims, the Ottoman world included. In her book *Travel and Artisans in the Ottoman Empire: Employment and Mobility in the Early Modern Era*, Suraiya Faroqhi showed that many Ottoman subjects were mobile, although the established wisdom claims most Ottomans stayed put. Even before the nineteenth century, when migrations and deportations were common, Ottomans moved a lot and in various contexts. Some moved on their own accord, and some were moved at the sultan's command: rural dwellers abandoned their farmland and went to the cities because of climatic changes; peasants left to join the sultans' armies as mercenaries; nomads and seminomads migrated nonstop as part of their lifestyle; merchants traveled within the empire, and long-distance trade also took them outside it; pilgrimage to holy sites was common among Muslims, Jews, and Christians; forced recruitment (like *devşirme*) and resettlement (*sürgün*) were common policies; high-ranking officials were sent routinely to new offices within the empire or outside it as diplomats; artisans traveled for work; slaves were moved as items of property.[35]

Here we are concerned with travels in search of knowledge as a socially and culturally significant phenomenon for individuals and for the community. It was a tool to create a social hierarchy for those who were interested in building themselves as sources of authority and legitimacy. Within local communities, travels in search of knowledge encouraged local identity and pride. For the Muslim *umma*, travels were a means of transmitting and transferring ideas and topics to communities in order to unite all the Muslim nations. Indeed, journeys with the principal goal of seeking knowledge were a prominent characteristic of daily life in medieval Muslim society.[36]

Ideas that expressed appreciation for the search for knowledge appeared in Ottoman society from its early days. Prior to the development of the local Ottoman tradition of religious studies and the establishment of an institution (the *medrese*) that made local religious study possible, Anatolian *ülema* were forced to travel to the world's traditional Islamic centers. This was an essential stage in the dissemination of Muslim religious knowledge in Anatolia. The biographies of early Ottoman religious officials testify to this pattern of acquiring knowledge and building a reputation. A representative example is the life story of Molla Şemsüddin el-Fenari (1350–1431), one of the outstanding religious figures in the time of Bayezid I (reigned 1389–1402). His biography is included in the Ottoman "Who's Who" *Al-Shaqā'iq al-Nuʿmāniyya fī ʿUlamā' al-Dawla al-ʿUthmāniyya* (The windflowers of the Ottoman Empire scholars). This encyclopedia was collected in the sixteenth century by Ahmed Ibn Taşköprüzade, a religious scholar and Ottoman official in the period of Süleyman "the Law Giver." Ibn Taşköprüzade mentions that Molla el-Fenari initially studied in Anatolia, but only after studying for some time in Egypt and returning to Anatolia did he reach prominence as a most senior religious official.[37]

The pattern of seeking knowledge changed in the centuries that followed the early Ottoman period. From the sixteenth century on, the paths of training and the establishment of the status and authority of the religious and administrative Ottoman elite reveal local patterns of study and careers rather than long journeys for extended periods of time. These journeys posed real difficulty for many reasons, hence the inability of many to carry out such an ideal. One hurdle was the financial cost of the journey itself and the loss of time away from work. Another hurdle was the need to overcome topographical obstacles, climatic constraints that limited travel to certain seasons of the year, a scarcity of means of transport, bad roads, and other challenges.[38]

In addition to financial and physical hardships, potential cultural obstacles to travel should be noted. One such hurdle is the language barrier. Although all Muslim scholars had to know Arabic in order to access the religious text, conducting a conversation in the language is a totally different skill. Many had to acquire another language, in some cases because in their official duties they had to engage in direct contact with people who spoke other languages. This was especially true for Arabic-speaking communities who needed Turkish in order to communicate with the ruling establishment. However, even if certain segments in society were indeed bilingual, most Ottomans were not.[39]

The language barrier hints at a deeper hurdle in the way of cross-cultural journeys and intellectual exchanges: namely, local pride, which may have inhibited some from valuing knowledge originating in a different place. The Egyptian *ʿulamāʾ* held the level of religiousness and the quality of scholarship in other Islamic areas in disdain. Their contempt for the Ottomans is evident in the attitude of Ibn Iyās (ca. 1448–1524), an Egyptian chronicler from Cairo from the end of the Mamluk period and the early Ottoman years. On many occasions Ibn Iyās described Ottoman men of religion as contemptible people known to commit vile injustices. He applied to them such phrases as "having but little knowledge" (*qalīl al-rashmāl min al-ʿilm*) and being "more stupid than donkeys" (*ajhal min al-ḥimār*).[40] This sense of superiority was by no means a new phenomenon. In pre-Ottoman Egypt, it was quite common to refer to local institutions as the hub of Islamic knowledge, perhaps (as Sam Gellens suggests) as continuity to a Pharaonic perception of Egypt as the center of the universe.[41] If that was a common opinion, one can understand why

Egyptian scholars abstained from studying at the Anatolian *medrese*s or even in the closer (and older, Islam-wise) al-Shām. Nevertheless, in the opposite direction—traveling to study in Cairo, one of the ancient centers of the world of Islam—was a familiar route to the *ülema* of Anatolia and Syria. Yet in the sixteenth century Anatolia became an important site of religious learning. From then on there was no need to travel; it was now a matter of choice.

Despite all these difficulties, travels continued. Many individuals left no trace of their forays, but there are the outcomes of scientific exchange to attest that individuals did travel, and their ideas traveled with them. One such outcome is the Mings' attempt to procure Ottoman rifles. In the late sixteenth century, Japan invaded Korea, and China's ruling Ming dynasty (1368–1644) found itself in an inferior position due to the superiority of Japanese weaponry. In a sixteenth-century Chinese treatise discussing the means to gain the upper hand, the author compares minutely, in both words and diagrams, three types of rifles: European, Japanese, and Ottoman. He refers to the length, weight, power, and methods of holding, aiming, and maneuvering of each, concluding that Ottoman firearms were of better quality.[42] The war in Korea ended in a peace treaty, and there was neither time nor reason for the Mings to equip their army with new Ottoman rifles. However, the intimate technological knowledge revealed by a bureaucrat in the Ming administration indicates that examples of Ottoman rifles and/or detailed descriptions of them had made their way from western to eastern Asia by means we cannot reconstruct.

If people are known to have traversed long distances, but many are anonymous to us, can we at least say something about the contexts of their travels? Many combined a pilgrimage, which demanded a break from the routine of daily life, with the opportunity to attend lectures at the various *medrese*s en route to the hajj. This combination allowed non-elite craftsmen and students who set out to Mecca to experience studies with new teachers. Sufi networks played an especially crucial role in facilitating transimperial travel and the concomitant social and political connections associated with the pilgrimage. Sufi lodges supplied the physical structures and buildings—the actual sites of interactions. Sufi masters and disciples were the human conduits and mediators that forged the social contacts. In the early modern period, the Naqshbandiyya was a major Sufi agent of transmission of sacred knowledge and social organization from central Asia west to the Ottoman world.[43] At the turn of the twentieth century, *naqshbandi* lodges in Istanbul were a primary locus of Ottoman interactions with central Asians and a major hub of their diasporic networks.

The Russian expansion and the new transportation technologies brought broader segments of central Asian society into sustained contact with the Ottoman world. The Sufi *tekke*s where they lodged linked these travelers to one another, to places in the Ottoman world, and to the Ottoman state.[44]

There were other life circumstances that brought about opportunities to travel and study. We recall the biography of Katip Çelebi. An Ottoman bureaucrat, he accompanied the army on several campaigns in the Middle East in the mid-seventeenth century and took advantage of the opportunity to study at the *medrese*s in the main cities of Syria.

There were also those who set out in search of new ways to make a living. One such person was a sixteenth-century architect by the name of Mimar Yusuf. He served Akbar (reigned 1556–1605), the third Mughal ruler, and claimed to have had a hand in Akbar's building projects in Agra and Delhi. Mimar Yusuf was educated in Istanbul by no less than Mimar Sinan, the most famous Ottoman architect (discussed in the following chapter).[45]

Shaykh ibn ʿAbdallāh (d. 1631/1632), a physician from the Hejaz, is another example of a traveler. He studied medicine and other spheres of knowledge in Arabia but did not remain there. At the beginning of the seventeenth century, he traveled to India, where he found his way into the Mughal court as a physician.[46] Shaykh ibn ʿAbdallāh was important enough for contemporaries to include him in *Taʾrīkh Khulasat al-Athr fī Aʿyān al-Qarn al-Ḥādī ʿAshar*, a biographical dictionary of the great people of the eleventh *hijri* century (the end of the sixteenth century and most of the seventeenth century) in Syria. Yet his short biography includes few details and arouses considerable curiosity: Why did he set out on a journey? What, in particular, drew him to Mughal India? Perhaps the Mughal pilgrims, who went on the hajj each year, fired his imagination or exposed him to new possibilities connected to his profession? And how did the dictionary's compiler, the Damascene Muḥammad al-Muḥibbī, find out about him? Did Shaykh ibn ʿAbdallāh ever return? Did he keep in touch with his family? Was he, perhaps, recorded in the dictionary just because he was unique and his life story was unusual?

Dozens of Persianate *ülema*, artists, and artisans traveled into the Ottoman Empire and were co-opted into Ottoman society. Among them were scholars in Qurʾanic exegesis, hadith, and *fiqh*, as well as physicians, historians, musicians, philosophers, mathematicians, astronomers, painters, calligraphers, and members of countless other professions. Some of them came originally from Anatolia and the Levant to study in Timurid Iran, Khorasan, or central Asia. Some returned after a period, while others stayed for good. They moved in different contexts, either individually or with groups en masse. Some ran away from Iran because of political or other factions; others traveled voluntarily; many others were deported. Following the old and common tradition of seizing the cultural assets of a conquered regime to display total and glorious victory, the Ottomans practiced *sürgün*—the state-organized transfer of groups. As they did after the conquest of Mamluk Cairo in 1517,[47] the Ottoman armies took with them many administrators, scholars, artists, and artisans on their return from campaigns in western Iran in the environs of Tabriz. (A similar fate was experienced by scholars in the eastern domains of the Safavids, in Herat, which came under Üzbek invasions.) In the sixteenth century, due to the eminence of the personalities involved and their considerable number, they enriched Ottoman culture, but perhaps left a void in Safavid intellectual life.[48]

For obvious reasons, the best-documented actors and mediators were those who traveled under diplomatic or royal patronage. Indeed, there were two persistent legacies of travel. One was of elite travels and cross-cultural contacts. A second legacy involved journeys of countless individuals lacking pomp. Most of them are unknown to us today because they were not considered important. When the empire became an important center of knowledge, Istanbul was a magnet for intellectuals from all over the Muslim world who wished to enjoy the imperial city and, perhaps, hoped to win the sultan's favor. A prominent example is Alaüddin Ali bin Mehmed Kuşçu, a brilliant mathematician and astronomer born in Transoxania in the fifteenth century. He served several rulers in central Asia and the Caucasus before emigrating to Istanbul.

Ali Kuşçu studied in Samarkand at the observatory of the Timurid governor, Ulugh Beg (1394–1449), who like all princes in the Timurid house was well educated. His court revived Turkic literature, patronized art and architecture, and was intellectually interested in religion, and he was personally a gifted practitioner of mathematics and astronomy. Ulugh Beg assembled dozens of scholars to discuss mathematics and astronomy, solve theoretical planetary problems, and devise instruments.[49] His fame as an astronomer resulted in a European myth based on an early modern misunderstanding rather than a historical truth—namely, that Ulugh Beg laid a sundial in the church of Ayasofya in 1437 using the height of the domed space.[50]

As a young person, Ali Kuşçu was one of Ulugh Beg's students, although for a period he had to study elsewhere, in the Kirman (in south-central Iran). Departure on a journey that involved teaching and studying was sometimes instigated more by political intrigues than by the need to seek new teachers. Ali Kuşçu returned and ultimately became the observatory's administrator. He continued his patron's *zīj* tables and interpreted them: these astronomical tables detailed astronomical observations and calculations that served as practical guides to understanding the positions and arrangements of the heavenly bodies. When Ulugh Beg was assassinated by his sons, Ali Kuşçu sought out new patrons, moving west to the Caucasian region, western Persia, and eastern Anatolia. There he enjoyed the favors of Uzun Hasan (Uzun the Tall), ruler of the Ak Koyunlu dynasty (a confederation of Turcoman tribes in the Diyarbakir region called "the White Sheep" throughout the fourteenth and fifteenth centuries). His new patron appointed him as a diplomatic representative to Mehmed II, the Ottoman conqueror of Constantinople, who tried to enlist him to his own service. Ali Kuşçu first fulfilled his assignments on behalf of Uzan Hasan and then immigrated to Istanbul with his family, funded by the Ottomans.

Ali Kuşçu served as an escort and companion to the Ottoman sultan, who took an interest in the sciences. The sultan granted him a teaching post at the *medrese* at the Ayasofya, the Byzantine church that became the imperial mosque in Istanbul. He earned a very high salary: a daily stipend of 200 *akçe* (Ottoman coins made of silver). At the *medrese* and the court, Ali Kuşçu continued his work in mathematics and astronomy. As was accepted in the premodern era, he combined these fields with astrology and wrote several treatises that Ottomans were still reading in the sixteenth and seventeenth centuries. The manuscripts of some of them are to be found, to this day, in the library at the Ayasofya, where he taught.

Ali Kuşçu died in 1474 in Istanbul. He was honored by being interred in the capital's Eyüp quarter, not far from the tomb of Abū Ayūb al-Anṣārī, a friend of the Prophet Muḥammed (*ṣaḥāba*). He was killed in the attack on the walls of the Byzantine city at the end of the seventh century and was regarded as the patron of the city of Istanbul.[51] The journey that started in Samarkand ended here, by Istanbul's old walls.

A similar pattern of educated Muslims belonging to various elite circles going on journeys and connecting with another Muslim society manifested also with regard to Ottoman contacts with the Indian subcontinent. Ottoman contacts with Muslim rulers in India date to the late fifteenth century, when the Ottomans exchanged gifts and letters with the Bahmanid kings. During the sixteenth century, especially after the establishment of Ottoman rule in Egypt and the Arab peninsula in 1517, contacts with Muslims in India and points east intensified. Giancarlo Casale termed this period the "Ottoman Age of Exploration." The Ottomans had maritime technology, a political ideology, and intense intellectual interest in the outside world.[52] They were familiar with the local Indian Muslim rulers who had sought refuge in Istanbul from the invasions of both the Portuguese and the Chagatai armies from central Asia, who would later become the Mughal dynasty. Even later, the Ottomans established direct relations with the Mughals themselves, although neither party was terribly interested in the other: the Ottomans were more concerned with their immediate neighbors, and the Mughals were preoccupied with Indian affairs. The somewhat limited formal and informal contacts between the Ottomans and Muslims in India were not mutually exclusive: espionage, diplomatic embassies in the capitals, and Mughal hajj contingents were linked, in many cases, by the same people and events.[53]

One Ottoman bureaucrat threatened to immigrate to India unless he was promoted. Mustafa Ali (d. 1600), who was also a historian, did not receive the advancement he deemed himself worthy of, while others (less qualified, in his view) were preferred. This was one reason for his distaste of what he perceived to be the immoral realities of his days. Ali complained to the sultan and hinted that he would relocate to India, where men of learning such as himself were highly regarded. Ali never carried through with this threat, which perhaps was an empty one from the beginning since he was an Ottoman gentleman through and through. He had always taken pride in his identity and worked hard to improve Ottoman morality and the Ottoman state; would someone like this be able to leave his milieu? Regardless, the option of leaving the Ottoman world for India was a real possibility for the Ottoman elite.[54]

Another Ottoman historian and bureaucrat, Mustafa Naima (1655–1716),[55] mentions the individuals who fulfilled the task of envoys in the Mughal-Ottoman exchanges of embassies and gifts. All those selected for this task were members of the Ottoman elite. Not all of them were successful, naturally, especially when the Ottomans deviated from their ancient custom of sending a knowledgeable, eloquent, and witty person from the *ülema* or bureaucracy (or so was Naima's bitter assessment). In some cases, Naima explains, a person was nominated simply for having the right connections, not necessarily the right skills.[56] Apparently, the diplomatic mission to India was a coveted position that people pulled strings in order to secure.

NEW EDUCATIONAL INSTITUTIONS AND A NEW TYPE OF EDUCATION IN THE LONG NINETEENTH CENTURY

Numerous formats for teaching and learning existed in the Ottoman Empire prior to the nineteenth century. They coexisted and created a plurality that allowed individuals to carve out their own paths based on social, cultural, and financial abilities. This educational diversity changed over the course of the nineteenth century. In this period, education played a significant role in the reforms of the sultans and the viziers that led toward a centralized and modern Ottoman state. The goals were to bring about uniformity, unity, efficiency, and discipline. Hence, a new system of education was devised to train the young generation in accordance with the state's new needs in regard to knowledge and life skills, as Istanbul defined those requirements.

Ottoman educational policies of the nineteenth century were founded on the various beginnings that occurred throughout the eighteenth century. These ripened into a comprehensive, intensive, and complex process in the nineteenth and early twentieth centuries—a fluid transition rather than a rupture. In daily life, the differences between "new" and "old" institutions, between "religious" and "secular" institutions, and even between "military" and "civilian" institutions, were more blurred than not.[57] For many contemporary Ottomans, such distinctions were probably quite meaningless, and these terms were not used to describe the system's characteristics. This does not diminish the fact that a long process led to a very different type of education in the Ottoman Empire, as we shall see shortly.

The lengthy evolution of the new education system required great patience before its results could be noticed, let alone enjoyed, in the form of a new generation of Ottoman youths with the desired education and skills: the state had to open new institutions, decide on content and methods and implement them, train the required teaching staff, and then wait a few years for the first cycle of students to complete their studies. In light of this situation, the Ottoman state took two other steps in the meantime. Initially, European experts were invited to train Ottoman army units in European warfare skills. The intention was to have the experts train the army in a particular and defined skill, after which they would go back home. The second method was to send Ottomans to learn the required subjects in the capitals of Europe at state expense. After completing their studies, these students would take up positions in the Ottoman administration and army. In both cases—missions of foreign experts to the empire or missions of Ottoman students to Europe—the aim was to resolve the shortage of skilled manpower quickly and to be aided by the trainees as agents in the process of reform.

The arrival of European delegations of experts in the nineteenth century was the Ottoman state's first step in the process of adopting Western methods. The use of Europeans as suppliers of professional services was actually not a new phenomenon but the continuation of a long tradition documented in the early Ottoman centuries as well. Individual mercenaries and random prisoners of war were co-opted into the administrative system as the Ottoman state went through a process of bureaucratization in the course of the fifteenth and sixteenth centuries. Ottoman sources record the *taifa-yı efrenciyan*—literally, the group of Europeans—who served the empire on a regular basis, openly and officially, for long periods. These were professionals in varied fields, from physicians and craftsmen (watchmakers, for example) to mercenaries for the army.[58]

In the period of Selim III (reigned 1789–1807), authorities recognized the need to refresh and renew the army, and so they invited delegations of European experts to improve the armed forces. Already in the 1780s, naval technology experts had been invited to the empire. The navy had been identified as one of the weakest links in the Ottoman military and was therefore one of the first targeted for adoption of Western know-how and technology. The delegations from France, Sweden, and Great Britain were especially prominent; however, there were also Hapsburg subjects and French and Venetian citizens who taught the Ottomans new shipbuilding techniques, methods of training the crews, use of artillery, and other techniques.[59] As in the past, the Ottoman state was skilled at identifying specific problems, like weakness in the army, and foreign missions were perceived to be a quick practical solution. The innovation in the eighteenth century was the intensity with which the Ottomans came to rely on European abilities and their recognition of European superiority over local know-how. Only over the course of the nineteenth century did the Ottoman state progress to more comprehensive and deeper social assessments.

As noted above, the second step in the rapid short-term training of the military and administrative elite involved student missions to Europe. During the period of the Sultan Mahmud II (reigned 1808–1839), carefully chosen Ottoman students were sent to study selected professions like engineering and medicine in the European capitals. The first four students were sent to Paris in 1827. Mehmet Ali Paşa, the Ottoman governor of Egypt, had sent a large delegation to Paris a year earlier after having sent a few individual students even before; apparently, this served as an incentive for the sultan in Istanbul.[60]

As previously discussed, given the problems identified with the army, military educational reforms were the first priority, and cadet officers were the first to be sent to the various European capitals. Moreover, the new schools that were opened in the center of the empire were patently for military purposes.

The first military schools had already been established during the eighteenth century. The educational program in these newly opened schools openly instilled knowledge and methods taken from Europe and not local Ottoman knowledge. An engineering school was established in Üsküdar on the Asian side of Istanbul, and the site also included a military training base. The school was part of a broader development designed to reestablish the Ottoman artillery corps (*humbaracıyan*).

The project of introducing major changes in the Ottoman artillery was entrusted to Comte Claude Alexandre de Bonneval (1675–1747), a French nobleman distantly related to the Bourbons. He had excelled in the French army but, after a political and financial conflict, turned to serve other European rulers. After a further dispute at the Hapsburg court, de Bonneval began serving the Ottoman Empire during the reign of Ahmed III (reigned 1703–1730). He converted to Islam, apparently to avoid extradition to Vienna, and adopted the Muslim-Turkish name "Ahmed." He rose to prominence under Mahmud I (reigned 1730–54) and served the Ottoman court in military affairs against the Hapsburgs, the Hungarians, and the Poles while also conducting diplomatic contacts with the Swedes. Among other roles, de Bonneval was appointed commander of the artillery corps (*humbaracıbaşı* [master gunner]). He acquired the rank of *paşa* (with two horse tails), which established him at the level of provincial governors (*beğlerbeği*). With the political changes in the Ottoman court, however, he lost this position. De Bonneval died in Istanbul as he waited for permission from the French king to return to France. His adopted son, Süleyman Ağa, also a Frenchman who converted to Islam, succeeded in securing the post his father previously held as commander of the artillery corps. Süleyman Ağa then created a new unit, "the corps of mathematicians," which matched the new requirements of the army.[61]

The three institutions—the engineering school, the bombardiers, and the mathematicians—did not last for long, but they began a tradition that was adopted by the reforming sultans and viziers of following generations. This was, in fact, a multilayered tradition: new institutions, new contents, and European tutorship. Later in the eighteenth century, in 1773, the school of mathematics was reopened for the navy. It served a model for similar engineering schools for the army in 1793, medical academies in 1827,[62] music schools in 1831, war sciences studies in 1834, and other fields. Mainly, the military schools gave the impetus for a new, broad education system.

The nineteenth-century system was indeed "new." It was a program that presented a new way of thinking of the nature of education. The education reforms created a learning environment that was new in its contents, its sociocultural atmosphere, and its physicality. The system evolved over a few decades during the Tanzimat of the nineteenth century, but during the Hamidian and the Young Turks periods, we can trace the extent to which it formed part of an ambitious agenda of social engineering to reintegrate alienated segments and peripheral regions into the empire under a centralized administration. Through the education system, the Ottoman elite sought to create "Ottoman citizens": new political individuals in the Ottoman scene. Then the state aimed to mobilize them for modernization as the elite perceived it, including changes and variations in these concepts along the way. At the same time, the education system offered a means to assert authority and maintain stability.[63]

Socially, the new institutions were aimed at many social sectors to whom traditional educational institutions had not been accessible in the past. One example would be the introduction of simpler Ottoman Turkish instead of the complex Arabicized and Persianate Ottoman of previous centuries (more on the language issue in the next chapter). Another example is the intentional spread of the new education system in the provinces, especially the non-Muslim and non-Turkish ones. For example, Abdülhamid II opened special schools for the sons of leading tribal notables, both Arabs and Kurds.[64] In the Balkans, Ottoman officials advised the opening of hundreds of schools of all levels, including teaching-training schools to make the system viable in terms of staff.[65]

During the last decades of the Ottoman Empire, the expansion of education included female students as well. Ziya Gökalp, the ideologist of the reforms of the late Ottoman period and the early republic, explains the context. Gökalp was pan-Turkist or a Turk nationalist rather than Ottomanist per se, but his state of mind was typical in elite circles at the time. Gökalp targeted young women as having a crucial role to play in the progress of society, culture, and civilization.

Gökalp's comprehension of "progress" stemmed not from looking outside to a European or Western modernity but from an inward-looking investigation of Turkish-ness. He wished to unravel the pristine Turkish past, and here is where women were so important: they were the repository of the Turkish essence. Women, he concluded, must be emancipated and educated to allow them to carry out this decisive task.[66]

New schools were built throughout the empire. They were no longer necessarily located adjacent to mosques, and their physical organization was different from the traditional setting of the *mekteb*. Classes were smaller and organized according to age groups instead of being held in large spaces that hosted multiple ages. The arrangement of study time was likewise distinctive from previous methods. The physical and temporal setting was a requisite to an efficient pedagogical process promoting the new contents: a set of virtues, such as regularity, punctuality, and efficiency. These were deemed the tools required to promote modernization.[67]

For the first time in the Ottoman Empire, the education system was indeed a binding "system." Schools were structured according to the hierarchical model of the West. Elementary or primary education (*ibtidai*) had to be completed in order to transfer to a secondary school (*rüşdiye*) and finally high school (*idadi* and *sultani*). The new educational model was a state-governed system: educational and pedagogical techniques were decided upon at the center and implemented through the provinces (although discrepancies occurred between territories).

Alongside all these features, the very new system had numerous connections and meaningful convergence with the older institutions. For instance, the new school included traditional Ottoman teaching staff and learning formats alongside new techniques and concepts. Ideally, an Ottoman citizen was supposed to be able to find an education of any inclination within the state system. The new Ottoman state education never succeeded in canceling the traditional system or making it disappear altogether; in fact, the state never wished to hide, evade, or close the older system (there was no ideology of secularization). Traditional schools, the *mekteb*s and *medrese*s, continued to exist side by side with the new system, and continued to attract many in Ottoman society. Informal patterns of education likewise continued. Palace and harem education continued as well during the last decades of the empire. Memoirs of elite Ottoman women attest to its continuity, with changes due to the spirit of the new times. For example, the harem of Mehmed IV Reşad (reigned 1909–1918) employed a professional female teacher, Safiye Ünüvar, for the education of the princes and princesses.[68]

The conflict was not between "old" and "new" but between the Ottoman system(s) and the private educational institutions external to the state system. In the second half of the nineteenth century, non-Muslim educational institutions became a significant alternative for educating young Ottomans in many regions, including the Balkans and Arabic provinces. Some institutions served the main minority groups: Greeks, Armenians, and Jews. Some minority schools, like some of those that served the Greek-Orthodox communities, were hundreds of years old. These institutions predated the educational reforms of the nineteenth century. Other schools for minority groups were established by foreign institutions. The Alliance Israélite Universelle, a Paris-based organization founded in the 1860s, is an example. Alliance promoted Jewish self-defense and self-sufficiency through education and professional development. By the beginning of the twentieth century, the organization opened around a hundred schools in the Ottoman Empire and North Africa.[69]

Foreign educational institutions were also established by Christian missionaries of European and American origins, both Catholic and Protestant. In particular, these missionaries focused their efforts in the Arab districts. Other schools were established throughout Anatolia and the Balkans, and, by the First World War, also in the capital city, Istanbul. Many thousands of institutions were established at all levels, from elementary school to college. Their influence in increasing the number of students was considerable.[70]

A large number of missionary institutions made it their goal to educate girls and young women. In 1835, the first permanent Protestant-American school for girls opened in Beirut and served as a model. In many cases, these institutions preceded the local Ottoman ones intended for female students; they probably also provided an impetus for local authorities to offer Ottoman institutions for this group so as not to "lose" the opportunity to mold the mothers of the future. Not unlike Ziya Gökalp, the missionaries regarded women as the ones who would shape the moral, spiritual, and intellectual atmosphere in the home and society. Hence, their education was regarded as even more important than that of boys. And, indeed, many of the women students were trained as teachers in order to be instrumental in bringing about social change. These schools taught in the local language and provided the most basic education in reading, writing, arithmetic, and the "feminine" professions, such as singing, sewing, and drawing (not unlike the imperial harem school of centuries before). Upon acquiring mandatory skills, girls could go on to higher-level classes in algebra, geography, science, and foreign languages.[71]

Even as the educational map within the Ottoman domains changed drastically, students were still sent to European capitals. In the first part of the nineteenth century, such missions were seen as ad hoc, temporary solutions until the local education system could offer the education needed by a new Ottoman generation. However, throughout the nineteenth century, Ottomans continued to pursue higher studies abroad. They resided in all the main intellectual centers of Europe, participating in literary circles and then returning home with new modes of thinking. Intellectuals and journalists in exile have been considered intermediaries between the intellectuals and literati of Europe and the Ottoman Empire. Yet students also took part in this exchange. In the classrooms as part of their official studies, or during their intellectual, literary, or political activities, they were exposed to social and political thought in contemporary Europe: ideologies such as nationalism and liberalism; political frameworks such as democracy; emerging scientific disciplines such as social sciences. (The latter proved crucial in the intellectual trajectories of numerous Ottomans.) Some of the Ottoman students in Europe from the 1870s onward became leading reformers and modernizers, adapting intellectual categories developed in the social and psychological sciences to their own Ottoman ends.[72] Studying in European capitals became a modern *ṭalab al-ʿilm*.

The parallel functioning of several types of schools and the educational paths both locally and abroad were not without tensions. Such coexistence involved competitiveness with regard to prestige, the implementation of educational worldview, influence over the society of the future, and the earning of a living. There was a battle for education and for the direction that society should take.[73]

The biography of Mustafa Kemal Atatürk, the founder of the Turkish Republic in the twentieth century, reveals the reality of various educational possibilities after the changes and reforms of the nineteenth century. Atatürk himself would describe his education in retrospect as the outcome of a dichotomy between tradition and modernity, but by then he was already committed to his modernizing agenda. However, his studies led him as a child and then teenager from one type of school to another, which, despite differences in curricula, shared subjects and teaching staff; one could thus maneuver between the various schools.

Mustafa was born around 1881 in Salonica to a lower-middle-class family in the Muslim Turkish quarter. Although his military and political career is documented in detail, a considerable lack of clarity exists regarding his parents and his early years, during which, of course, the man he would become was still unknown. Ottoman Salonica was at that time a prosperous cosmopolitan city with religious, ethnic, and linguistically varied communities, composed of Jews (about half of the city's population), Muslims (the second largest community), and Christians of various kinds—from Greece, Armenia, and the various Balkan communities. Despite the cosmopolitan atmosphere, each community conducted itself autonomously and developed its own institutions, including its educational institutions.

When the time came for the young Mustafa to go to school, his parents were divided over which institution he should attend. Theirs was a dispute about the kind of education the child should receive: should Mustafa study at the neighborhood religious school, where he would acquire a principally religious education, or at the modern elementary school that had recently opened in Salonica? The respective schools each involved a different education track, with separate curricula and teaching staff.

Mustafa's mother, Zübeyda, was a devout Muslim who wanted to enroll her son in a traditional school. Indeed, most of the children in the city still attended this type of school or institution. In contrast, Mustafa's father, Ali Riza, supported the new education system. He had formerly been employed as an Ottoman customs officer and had served in the army for a short period. These experiences were the product of his identification with the Ottoman state and in turn encouraged this identification. One way or another, Ali Riza wanted to give his son the kind of modern Western education that was considered important to the future of the Ottoman elite and to give the young child the tools to socialize with this elite. The argument ended with a creative solution, according to Mustafa's own memory, years later: the child was welcomed into the traditional school with all the children of the neighborhood in a very impressive ceremony, to the satisfaction of his mother; a few days later, he left the *mekteb* in favor of the Şemsi Efendi School, the elementary school his father preferred.

The family problem was solved, but the tension did not stop. The new Şemsi Efendi School aroused great criticism in Salonica. The school was explicit about giving students a Western education with Western tools. The school environment was characterized by rigid discipline. Staff and students observed military etiquette, including saluting one another. Traditionalists in the Muslim community objected to the school and the values it symbolized. Incidentally, the school belonged to the Dönme, the Muslim-Sabbatean community that led the educational revolution in Salonica (more about this community as a transfer agent of knowledge in the next chapter). The school's sectarian affiliation might have played a role in the opposition against it, which was considerable. In the school's first years, (occasionally violent) gatherings and demonstrations took place, causing the school to close for periods of time. Nevertheless, in spite of the difficulties brought to bear and the early years marked by skepticism and suspicion, the school survived and functioned for many years. It even became a model emulated by other schools, in the Dönme community and outside it, and won imperial medals from the sultans.

After graduating from the Şemsi Efendi School, Mustafa wanted to continue his studies at the military academy. His mother (his father had since died) actually enrolled him in a civilian high school that prepared its students for a career as officers in the Ottoman administration. At this point she had become accustomed to Western education for her son and did not try to return him to the religious track. However, without her knowledge, Mustafa took the entrance exams at the military academy in Salonica and presented her with a fait accompli. This was Mustafa's first step on the road that, in time, turned him into an Ottoman officer.[74]

As in the previous centuries, education was a significant factor in Ottoman society. As before, it was a means of individual mobility. In the empire's last decades, the new education system turned into a major agent of change for larger groups.

THREE

THE TRANSFER OF KNOWLEDGE TO, FROM, AND WITHIN THE OTTOMAN EMPIRE

An instance of knowledge that originated in one culture appearing in another culture is evidence of a transfer or transmission of knowledge between those two cultures. Appearance alone, however, is not enough evidence to prove that a meaningful transfer of knowledge has taken place. Transfer of knowledge may result in barren transmission inasmuch as knowledge can migrate but not be picked up by anyone.[1] A successful integration of knowledge requires one of two approaches: either transforming knowledge of a foreign culture into something different, or transforming the foreign culture into something similar. Journeys of knowledge are more than the movement of people, ideas, and instruments. Successful flows of knowledge are the outcome of motion and content, which includes adaptability and change in people, ideas, and instruments.[2]

So it was in the specific case of movement of knowledge within the Ottoman Empire among Ottomans and between Ottomans and others, and the first chapter discussed multiple others that Ottomans engaged with: it was a multifaceted intellectual, social, and physical process. The previous chapter discussed patterns of learning available in the Ottoman Empire, including physical travels. Here we explore the cross-cultural fluidity of knowledge through sifting and selection, translation, citations, copying, and circulation of people, ideas, and instruments.

There is never-ending movement of knowledge via circulation and transition between multiple sites. Each site appropriates from others, and while doing so also produces new knowledge. Although there are obvious asymmetries between sites and agents and transition, they were all actors engaged in circulation of knowledge. The model envisioned here is of a bidirectional exchange rather than one of a hegemonic center giving birth to "original science" that peripheries simply copied and reproduced.[3]

OTTOMAN LITERACY

The principal way to assimilate knowledge and then transfer it is through literacy, that is, the ability to read and write. Many—but not all—cultures considered the ability to read and, often, to write as a primary requisite for learning and education. However, in this narrow meaning, the definition of literacy is lacking. For what does "knowing how to read and write" mean?

Among the pre-Islamic Arabian tribes, for instance, oral transmission, memorization, and the spoken word were highly appreciated. With the advent of Islam, literacy acquired significance—especially with regard to the scriptures, but also more generally.[4] Also, in other medieval monotheistic cultures, the literal landscape was complex and crowded. Literacy fulfilled different needs in different communities, even in the same broad culture. Literacy was sometimes tied to knowledge of a specific language (Arabic, Hebrew, or Latin), which may have been different from the vernacular spoken language, but it could also be a skill, like scribbling one's name; it was related to religion and religious education but not restricted to it.[5] In our contemporary modern society literacy demands a high level of reading and writing skills. We are expected to create and understand innuendos in the text and connect them to prior knowledge we have on the subject under discussion. In other words, beyond understanding the text, we are expected to be able to consider and evaluate the material.

Beyond the varying definitions of "knowing reading and writing," the term *literacy* itself is now understood differently. In its broad significance, literacy is the ability to carry on effective communication with people in order to perform properly in society and culture. To do that, we have to develop skills in various ways of communicating: written, visual, and verbal. Different channels coexist, and oral channels, for instance, certainly exist also in societies with writing, although they function differently than in societies where oral tradition has to bear the full burden of cultural transmission. There is interface between the registers, between individuals who perform differently in various modes, and between societies that emphasize different characters of communication.[6] For this reason, the term *integrative literacy* has become common in recent years, meaning the efficient use of a number of channels of communication simultaneously. We add technology to this basket, which of course changes from era to era. In the contemporary world, the computer is the cornerstone of literacy. The computer and other new electronic devices are not only channels of communication but also agents of change in language. The new technologies stress short and immediate communication (e.g., text messaging), thus encouraging expression in brief, uncomplicated units.

In Ottoman society, literacy was expressed in three main forms: reading and writing; memorizing, speaking, and listening; and by visual means. In each of these ways, people could read individually or in groups, in the private or public domain, in silence or aloud (group reading and vocal performance were quite important). In many instances, the means of literacy were combined. For example, the visual appearance of a written text was highly significant and influenced how it was absorbed. Images enriched and empowered the text, and sometimes were independent of it.

Reading and Writing in the Ottoman Lands

Ottomans, especially the elites, consumed books. In *Picturing History at the Ottoman Court*, Emine Fetvacı established the existence of a broad group of people in and around the court who acquired and read books. In addition to the imperial family, administrators, imperial household servants, and male and female trainees formed the audience for books. This community bought books, borrowed books from libraries, and circulated books. However, books were rendered most valuable by their use as objects with social functions. Illustrated manuscripts, in particular, were a status symbol.[7]

Early modern sources depict the Ottoman elite as bibliophiles with varied interests. But how many Ottomans could actually read such books, let alone write them? We have no quantitative information. The varying estimates of European travelers consolidate around an approximation that a quarter of the empire's urban population was literate. But what was the extent of their literacy? According to Patrick Russell (1726–1805)—a Scottish physician, Arabist, and natural scientist who lived in Aleppo for a decade—many among the elite in Aleppo did not read and write fluently. Their reading skills were limited, and they had difficulty writing. Russell's disapproval can be read between the lines, but he found encouragement in the young generation, which had been more thoroughly prepared to read and manage their own correspondence in professional and private matters. Nevertheless, he added, the better-educated young generation also preferred the assistance of professional secretaries for more skillful writing.[8]

Reading and writing among women was even more limited. Women did study, but by comparison with males of a similar class, fewer women were educated. Even a woman who was fortunate enough to study typically learned less in terms of the content and extent of her studies. The women of the Ottoman harem, for example, could read and write. The harem also operated a school, and the senior women were taught to read and write Ottoman Turkish. Yet even the imperial women did not have a full command of the skills—or so is the impression from personal correspondence between family members preserved in the Topkapı Palace archive. Large numbers of letters written to the sultans—who were their husbands, sons, brothers, and fathers—accumulated in the palace archive. Some of the letters were so polished in style and handwriting that one suspects that the writing itself was not performed by the women; could it be that the letters were dictated to skilled scribes? In many other instances, the text of the letters includes errors in grammar and syntax. Moreover, the handwriting is not necessarily flowing and meticulous in regard to the size of the letters and the spacing between words. As for the language used, it is not always idiomatically correct, nor does it uniformly demonstrate a command of expressions, sayings, phrases, and idioms. Such mistakes are characteristic of people writing in a language that is not their mother tongue. (Indeed, except for princesses born in the harem, most of the women were not Turkish or Muslim by birth: they were daughters of foreign dynasties or concubines from the Balkans, eastern Europe, and the Caucasus.) Apparently the women themselves wrote these letters.[9] Even if the women of the palace, at least the higher echelons among them, knew how to read and write at a reasonable level, they were a representative example of neither the majority of women nor the majority of Ottoman men.

Russell offers three explanations for limited Ottoman literacy. One suggestion involves the norms of writing official letters. The rules of writing were complicated and required a precision of style that was difficult for anyone who was not a professional in the field—including those who were well educated. Russell's second explanation was that the existence of a large professional bureaucracy actually hindered the spread of skilled writing. Elite people could turn the task over to seasoned clerks instead of writing themselves, saving them time and energy. In the long run, this practice brought about the identification of writing with clerks and reduced its status to menial work, hence too inferior for an aristocratic man of honor. The third reason was the complexity of written language. The written cultural language was significantly different from and much more complex than the language in daily use. Literary language was difficult to master to the degree befitting the author's status.

The Ottoman Empire was the home of numerous vernacular languages. In this polyethnic empire, polyglottism was the norm among subjects and members of the elite alike.[10] The number of languages within the Ottoman lands was overwhelming. In the beginning of the twentieth century, after the empire lost most of its European territories, the list of only the most significant languages included Turkish, Arabic, Armenian, Bulgarian, Greek, Ladino, Serbian, Syriac, Albanian, Kurdish, Rumanian, and Caucasian languages. To these local languages, French should be added as well, at least in the later Ottoman period.[11] For the previous centuries, the list should also include the Balkan languages, like Serbo-Croatian, as well as North African tongues. Because the state never sought to impose Ottoman Turkish on its subjects, the conquered peoples did not forsake their traditional languages, and the list of languages spoken in the Ottoman world was indeed staggering.

The imperial language, Ottoman Turkish, was used by the bureaucracy, and anyone who wanted to approach the imperial organs had to avail himself of it. Ottoman Turkish also became an important literary and scientific venue for the imperial elite, and in order to court elite patronage, it was wise (although not mandatory) to use it. But mastering the language was a very difficult task.

Ottoman Turkish was the amalgamation of three philologically very different languages: Turkish, Arabic, and Persian. It drew vocabulary in addition to syntactical and grammatical structures from all three. The contact between these languages continued a trend that had begun in the time of the Seljuk Turks. Their migration from the plains of Asia to the Middle East around the year 1000 included Islamization, which brought along with it a permanent impact of Arabic. Geographically, they passed through Iran, where they learned political administration. The Seljuks continued to employ Persian administrative officers after gaining control of the Islamic Middle East (from the Arabs). The Seljuks of Rum, the Seljuk sultanate in Anatolia, followed this cultural trend, and the Ottomans in turn continued Persianization at full force. In addition to drawing on languages used by Muslims, Ottoman Turkish incorporated vocabulary from European languages, mainly Italian (in the realms of insurance and navigation, since the fourteenth century) and French (since the late eighteenth century, in the realms of politics and administration).

Unique linguistic mixing created Ottoman Turkish. Such hybridity resulted in a very rich language, which also yielded two major disadvantages. One of them was the complexity involved in standardizing style and written modes. It was not uncommon to find several spellings of the same word. Considering that Ottoman Turkish is written in the Arabic alphabet, which is suitable for a Semitic language but does not answer the needs of the Turkish language with its different system of consonants and syllables, inconsistency of spelling is to be expected. Another problem was the ever-growing gap between Ottoman Turkish and its basic components, namely Arabic, Turkish, and Persian. As Ottoman Turkish increasingly became the language of the imperial officialdom and a realm of literary activity, it acquired growing artistic flare. Ottoman Turkish became elaborated and complex rather than pragmatic, simple, and functional.[12]

Ottoman Turkish was not the only language to develop several registers. Arabic, the major Middle Eastern language, is known to transform into almost completely distinct spheres: spoken language is diversified by many dialects, whereas the written language attempts to be uniform and to observe traditional rules of grammar and syntax. The case of Latin in medieval Europe was quite similar. A not particularly well-educated person from a rural or even an urban area would not be able to converse in Latin with the elite. However, the reality of Ottoman Turkish was more problematic than that. The peculiarities of the formal Ottoman language made it inaccessible to all but the most educated. Complicated grammatical forms and vast vocabulary required years of formal education to master, making it too cumbersome for utilitarian daily use. Consequently, Ottoman Turkish was not widely spoken and was mainly used in writing.

The complexity of Ottoman Turkish as an obstacle to a broad education was discussed among the Ottomans. In the fifteenth and sixteenth centuries, a literary movement demanded a turn to plain Turkish (*Türki-i basit*). This demand was voiced in reaction to another school that advocated the use of literary Ottoman language, characterized by its incorporation of Arabic and Persian vocabulary and grammar, which were not in everyday usage. Poets and authors intentionally used rare words from the dictionary, including those originating in Persian and Arabic, to embellish their work and impress readers with their vast knowledge. There were always authors who used simple language, taking the spoken language as their basis; however, more and more authors produced works of prose and poetry that contained Arabic and Persian grammar and vocabulary, sometimes to an excessive degree. Indeed, every Persian and Arabic word could potentially become an Ottoman word; no restriction existed. Thus, literary production displayed ornamental and artistic talents, distancing itself from simple structures. Ultimately, the early modern *Türki-i basit* movement did not succeed.[13]

Meaningful attempts to simplify the language had to wait until the nineteenth century as part of the reorganizational reforms. One of the goals of the Tanzimat was to create a simple and efficient language for the government's administrative requirements and the population's everyday needs. In 1839, Mahmud II delivered a speech in the opening ceremony of the imperial medical school in which he claimed that it was no longer necessary to use French as the language of instruction. His aim was to quickly create the possibility of a full education, including science, in simple Turkish.[14]

The Young Ottoman intellectuals and bureaucrats of the second half of the nineteenth century continued to pursue the project of systemization and simplification of Turkish. İbrahim Şinasi (1826–1871) and Namık Kemal (1840–1888), as well as other prolific authors and journalists, wrote articles in which they were not shy about publicizing their ideas. Furthermore, the language they used to publish their ideas was supposed to serve as a model for the type of simple Ottoman Turkish they were aiming at. They targeted the language and its orthography as realms particularly in need of reform. The Young Ottomans noted the insufficiency of the Ottoman alphabet and suggested the adoption of the Latin alphabet as more appropriate for the Turkish language.[15]

Efforts toward simplification of the written language continued all the more vigorously during the period of the Young Turks and under the Committee for Unity and Progress. Now there were more voices in favor of Turkification of Ottoman Turkish than for its simplification. These two distinct processes had a lot in common in the practical sphere, but the ideologies that motivated them were different. Simplification of Ottoman Turkish was still well within the Ottoman state of mind: it wished to preserve the language, but in a more accessible format to reach mass readers. In fact, some of the leading figures in the Young Ottoman era included Arabic and Persian vocabulary in their simpler Ottoman Turkish. Turkification, however, is a different story: it stemmed from nationalistic ideology and aspired to openly express Turkish culture in a language accessible to all and a substitute for Ottoman elitism.[16]

For most of recorded time, the ability to read (and write) has been limited to a small elite who control access to their knowledge, their texts, and their shared language of references and symbols—an observation Benjamin Fortna used to begin his book *Learning to Read in the Late Ottoman Empire and the Early Turkish Republic*.[17] He reminds readers that the lion's share of reading was linked to perpetuation of statecraft. The educational reforms of the nineteenth century were aimed at widespread reading when literacy became synonymous with modern society, bringing about economic advancement and cohesion. (In the transition from the late Ottoman Empire to the early Republic, cohesion was identified with nationalism.) Indeed, the Ottoman educational system introduced, at least to an extent, a simple new language (*yeni lisan*). The choice to base it on the vernacular of Istanbul suggests that the elitist feelings of decision makers in Istanbul had changed not in substance but only in format.

The steps taken over several decades to simplify Ottoman Turkish did not result in a "pure" language. The influence of Arabic and Persian was still quite substantial. Furthermore, during the nineteenth century the reception of European vocabulary was accelerated; these foreign terms were either translated into Ottoman Turkish or transliterated. However, these steps did bring about an unprecedented degree of literacy in Ottoman lands. New commercial and career opportunities were perhaps the most readily observed of the changes that literacy induced; the more subtle ones were challenges to established social, political, cultural, and economic authority.[18]

The Craft of Writing

A standard of professional writing in Arabic—including everything connected to size, shape, and proportion—has been in existence since around the year 1000. Instructional books for Middle Eastern Muslim clerks in the Middle Ages mention the names of six principal scripts, *al-Aqlām al-Sitta* (literally, "six pens"), from which additional variants developed. Because of the importance of the Arabic language for religious and other reasons, it was the first to undergo the process of professionalization described here, but calligraphers also developed fonts for Persian and, afterward, for Ottoman Turkish. The fonts were designated for specific languages and were adapted to the various materials to be printed on (paper, cloth, leather, pottery, metal, or stone) and to the various purposes of writing they were dedicated to, whether religious, literary, clerical, or artistic. Some scripts stressed the joining of letters in cursive writing, while others favored letters that were squared, angled, and separate from one another. Even if the apparent purpose of writing was utilitarian, and not to decorate and embellish, all writing had an element of design. The criteria for judging the quality of the font included a combination of elegance and beauty on the one hand, and simplicity, uniformity, delicacy, speed of writing, and legibility on the other. These are issues of both technique and aesthetics. The outward appearance was considered an inseparable component of the text, creating dialogue between the reader and the text.[19]

As in many other cases of nuanced dialogue with past traditions and parallel cultures, the Ottomans continued the Arabic and Persian traditions in the art and craft of writing. They adapted the Six Pens, the six principal scripts, to their needs and taste. They also sharpened the precision and mathematical dimensions of the letters, creating unique styles. A key figure in this process was Şeyh Hamdüllah (1436–1520). He was a renowned calligrapher in the court of Mehmet II and especially in the court of Bayezid II, whom he had attended since Bayezid was a prince in Amasya. Şeyh Hamdüllah's school trained important calligraphers for the Ottoman court, and among his students were members of his own family. They were still serving the Ottoman bureaucracy at the beginning of the seventeenth century.[20]

The evolution in Ottoman calligraphy occurred in conjunction with the construction of a bureaucracy in the Ottoman state throughout the fourteenth and fifteenth centuries. Complex relationships evolved between calligraphy and bureaucracy. Calligraphy had to develop to include methods and shapes that facilitated the work of the clerks; throughout the history of the empire, some calligraphers were absorbed into the bureaucratic and religious establishment, so they were well experienced in the practical aspects of writing. The religious administration and the administrative establishment "raised" professionals who were interested in writing, refining their skills and adapting them to their own requirements.[21]

Eventually the two spheres of creators of books and patron-bureaucrats who enjoyed books merged. The careers of Kalender Paşa (d. 1616) and Nakkaş Hasan Paşa (d. 1623) combined excellence in calligraphy with success as administrators and officers. They were not the first to combine such career paths, but do illustrate that combining the art of writing with high-ranking office became popular and accepted. Both men served in the imperial treasury, foundry, and palace, and still were involved as artists or supervisors for a large number of illustrated books. They were responsible for developing a new visual style for the Ottoman court and attained their posts due, at least in part, to their artistic or cultural accomplishments.[22]

The process witnessed here is one of canonization of literary arts. The sifting, refining, and elaborating of existing styles brought about a stylistic evolution of Ottoman calligraphy. A widespread saying in the Muslim world testifies that Ottoman calligraphy was regarded as attaining the highest level of its art: "The Qur'an was revealed in the Hijaz; it was best recited in Egypt and best written in Istanbul."[23]

The process of canonization in calligraphy included a "division of labor" between the different types of scripts and writing designated for each of them. *Nash* (literally, "copying") was the clearly preferred writing style for essays. *Sulus*, which specialized in larger fonts, was handwriting that stood out and suited display; other handwriting styles (not necessarily belonging to the Six Pens group) served the Ottoman scribes, the *katiban.*

The Divani script was used for writing decisions of the Imperial Council, the *divan-ı Hümayun.* Divani satisfied the internal needs of the clerks and was used, for instance, for the *mühimme defterleri* (literally, "registers of important affairs"). In these notebooks, abstracts of decisions deliberated in the Imperial Council were recorded. These included copies of orders issued to Ottoman officers throughout the provinces.

Outgoing official Divan documents used Celi Divani. This stylistic evolvement was used for the sultan's decrees (*fermans*), appointments, instructions, and diplomatic correspondence. In this style, the letters are intertwined with a slight upward slope. At the end of the line, on the left side, the text is drawn in a clearer, rounded upward sweep, reminiscent of the bow of a ship; hence the style is known as "boat."

For financial matters the Ottoman clerks used a secret script known only to those in the relevant departments of the imperial administration. This script, the *siyakat*, was inherited from the Anatolian Seljuqs. The Ottomans refined and adapted it for managing the entire empire's accounts. The object was to keep sensitive financial matters in the hands of treasury clerks who could be trusted to keep secrets and thus protect the empire's interests. Treasury officials were cognizant of the fact that the use of a secret script strengthened their status because critical financial information was not accessible without their cooperation.[24]

In addition to using distinct scripts, official Ottoman documents were differentiated by their dimensions and colorfulness. Regular documents, account books, copies, and internal correspondence were written in black or red ink; original documents addressed to people outside the administration were colored, and besides black and red a document might be written in blue, green, and gold. The internal documents were executed by scribes who were not commemorated: various people wrote in a uniform script and did not add their signature. The more splendid documents were created by a team of calligraphers: experts at writing, technical drawing, and illustration who worked together in a calligrapher-illustrator *nakkaşan* group. The senior members were renowned artists, but they did not sign their work either; unlike the lower clerks, however, they developed unique styles that were documented by their peers, which allows us at least to identify their schools.

Cooperation between calligraphers was required for complicated documents that contained different styles of writing and painting. Decrees from the sultan were composed of three parts. On the uppermost part of each document, including the *ferman*s, the Arabic word *huwwa* (He) appeared in small letters: an abbreviated call to Allah. Below, but still in the upper portion of the *ferman*, a more prominent section appeared: the *tuğra*, meaning the sultan's seal. The seal was composed of four parts: the designed letters of the text, the lines elongated upward, loops on the left side, and prominent lines on the right side. In especially elegant signatures, the text was written in colors, and the spaces between the letters and shapes were decorated with flowers and colorful arabesque. The text included the name of the reigning sultan, his father's name, and the ruling titles: Mongolian "Khan"; "Shah," taken from the Persian political world; and "the eternal winner" (*al-muẓaffar dā'imān*). The document text itself was written below the seal. The choice of colors (whether nonblack colors would be used and, if so, which colors and what portion of the text would be written in each color) changed from document to document, according to the letter's importance and, perhaps, the personal decision of the calligrapher as to which would create the most favorable impression. The document text itself would be written before the *tuğra* was prepared. The *tuğra* was turned over to the illustrating staff, who specialized in this work. All the aspects of form shared a common goal: to communicate with the reading and viewing public and create an additional aura of importance and authority with regard to everything connected to the document's content and the status of those mentioned in it—first and foremost the sultan, whose word was communicated in the document.[25]

Each Ottoman script required suitable writing implements: pens or brushes with different heads that were rounded, straight-cut, or pointed, depending on the desired result. Raw materials for writing had to be prepared. Inks were valuable, especially the colored ones. Gold, blue, and green, which were especially expensive, were stored in the Imperial Treasury and supplied directly to the illustrators and calligraphers, and were kept separate from more mundane materials such as paper, pens, and black and red ink.[26] All of these tools imposed a heavy financial toll, in addition to the difficulties of writing and reading. While in Europe the invention of the printing press had enabled cheap, fast mass copying of texts, in the Ottoman Empire the complex system of scribes and manuscript preparation continued to operate.

Printing

Handwriting presented an additional difficulty for reading and writing in the Ottoman Empire. Historians of Europe agree that the printing revolution was an essential factor in making European society literate. Printing contributed to the success of the Reformation, the scientific revolution, and consolidation of the national languages and cultures in all the countries of central and western Europe. Printing was one of the significant factors that enabled Europe to leap forward to its hegemonic status in the world.[27]

The technique of printing entered the Ottoman Empire in a gradual and intricate way. The empire's first printing house was established in 1493, about half a century after the first Bible was printed by Johannes Gutenberg in Mainz, Germany. It was built by the brothers Samuel and David ben Nahmias for the Jewish community in Istanbul. Other printing houses were then established in all the central Ottoman cities. Founded by non-Muslims, they printed books for the various Jewish and Christian communities (the Greeks and Armenians, in particular) in their respective languages. While the sultans permitted other printing activity by non-Muslims for their communities, those same sultans—for example, Bayezid II in 1485 and Selim I in 1515—expressly forbade Muslims to print books in Arabic letters. The community of the Muslim majority continued using manuscripts. Only in 1729 was the first Muslim printing house opened. What made it a "Muslim" printing house? The fact that it received the approval of the Muslim ruler, in this case Ahmet III (reigned 1703–1730), to print books written by Muslims, for Muslims, in Ottoman Turkish written in Arabic letters.[28]

The initiator and promoter behind the first Muslim printing house was İbrahim Müteferrika (ca. 1674–1745), an Ottoman diplomat of Transylvanian origin.[29] He converted to Islam as a youth and served the Ottomans in a variety of roles. Among his numerous jobs, he served as an intermediary and contact person with the Hapsburgs due to his familiarity with the relevant languages. He imported six printing presses from Europe to his home in the Fatih neighborhood of Istanbul and began experimenting with printing the Arabic alphabet even before receiving official permission to do so. In 1726 he submitted a memorandum to the grand vizier, Damad İbrahim Paşa, in which he exhibited his technological capability and discussed the many benefits of printing books in Ottoman Turkish.

İbrahim Müteferrika was not the first Muslim Ottoman to suggest printing to the court. In the middle of the seventeenth century, İbrahim Peçevi (1574 to ca. 1649–1650), a historian and Ottoman administrative officer and a member of a family that served the Ottoman military for generations, claimed that printing would benefit Ottoman society. Peçevi emphasized the speed with which it would be possible to produce books after the exhausting work of setting the presses was completed. He was informed enough to quote the names of Gutenberg and his city, Mainz, when discussing the innovation of printing, and to state the date of 1440 according to the Christian era. Peçevi stressed that the printing press was an invention (*ijad*), and one made by heretics (*küffar*). Nevertheless, he said, it was a good thing (*uz*).[30]

It was only a hundred years after Peçevi that Müteferrika's memorandum regarding the benefits of printing received any attention. The memo raised eleven points, including the following benefits of the printing press: the growth of knowledge and its dissemination among an increasing number of Ottomans; the ability to restore knowledge easily (a manuscript can be destroyed in wartime, as the Mongolian conquest of the Islamic world and the Reconquista in Spain clearly demonstrated, but a lost printed book is easy to renew and reprint); the reasonable costs of printing compared to those of preparing a manuscript; the lifespan of a printed book compared to that of a manuscript (handwriting ink faded, unlike print); and the return of the book industry to Muslim hands after Christians had controlled it. Müteferrika persuaded the grand vizier and the sultan, and he received approval to establish a printing house in 1727.

Between 1729 (the year in which the first book was published) and 1742, when Müteferrika's printing house was abandoned, it printed seventeen titles, producing at least five hundred copies of each. Certain titles were printed in a thousand or more copies. Müteferrika published only dictionaries and books on history and geography; the license he received clearly stated that he was not to print Muslim religious texts. The printed material included prose alongside illustrations and maps. Two of the six presses in the printing house were designated for the latter kind of work.

İbrahim Müteferrika was not the only one printing in Ottoman Turkish. Ahmet III's *ferman*, which permitted the operation of a printing house, was intended not only for Müteferrika. Another beneficiary was Said Effendi, the son of an Ottoman diplomat, Yirmisekiz Mehmed Çelebi Efendi (d. 1732), the famous ambassador to France. Said Efendi—himself a future ambassador to Sweden and France, and future grand vizier—accompanied his father on his missions to Paris and returned in October 1721, apparently bringing a printing press back with him. Even later in the eighteenth century, after the initial operation of the printing house had ended and, also, after the death of Müteferrika himself, others continued to work in his printing house. Even in the second half of the eighteenth century, the printing house published some titles, although reduced in number. Some of these were republications, and work progressed slowly between long intervals.

The beginning of activity in the printing house was the product of a very specific cultural atmosphere: the climate of "the Tulip era" at the beginning of the eighteenth century. This period was characterized, at least in the imperial capital, by a culture of leisure and more obvious consumerism, cosmopolitanism, religious tolerance, and valorization of philosophy. This is the period Harun Küçük termed "early enlightenment in Istanbul."[31]

As the century progressed, Ottoman society faced economic difficulties at home and military problems along its borders, though attempts at reform were made to improve the situation. Societal mood changed, heating the public debate pertaining to printing. The outcome was a narrowing of the space allotted to printing activity until the final closing down of the institution.

The erratic start of printing in the Ottoman Empire had multiple causes. For example, there were significant technical difficulties related to Arabic (as well as Persian and Ottoman Turkish) calligraphy. Arabic, Persian, and Ottoman orthography posed real challenges for typesetters because of the rounded and connected letters. The letters also change shape depending on their location in the word (beginning, middle, or end), the preceding letter, and whether they are joined or not. This requires the addition of vowel and punctuation marks. The system of punctuation marks required for Arabic printing may add up to several hundred individual signs, which would require additional aides to position the fonts correctly for them to be joined together. Indeed, the Arabic printing press that was prepared for Napoleon around 1800 included more than 700 signs.

The technological and cultural transformations that delayed an Ottoman printing culture should not be taken to mean that printing in Muslim languages was unfamiliar to the Islamic world. Printing was even used as an efficient and inexpensive way to prepare talismans or to decorate cotton cloth. In fact, Muslims were acquainted with printing in general and printing Muslim languages in particular from the tenth or eleventh century. Chinese technology–based printing appeared as a passing episode in Ilkhanate Persia at the end of the thirteenth century in an attempt to introduce printed banknotes that were familiar in China. Later, in the fifteenth century, bookbinding techniques that resembled printing were used in Persia and Egypt for inexpensive leather bindings.

In Europe a solution was found for the technical difficulty in printing Arabic letters that would suit the printing technique of Gutenberg. With the encouragement of Pope Gregory XIII (held office 1572–1585), the printing house of Medici specialized in foreign languages, including Arabic. Medici books included translations of the Bible and New Testament, Ibn Sīnā's *Canon of Medicine*, and the geography book of Muḥammad al-Idrisī from Norman Sicily. Books were also exported to the Ottoman Empire, and the Ottomans made use of them.[32]

Technical difficulty, as great as it may be, can be overcome in most cases if the atmosphere is ripe for the appearance of a solution. That solution may already exist but face implementation difficulties for cultural and social reasons. In fact, the obstacle to the speedy acceptance in the Muslim Middle East of the printing press was a combination of several interconnected cultural and social factors. Let's look at these points in detail.

Because the craft of writing was held in such high esteem as a cultural creation, an aversion existed to printing. Ottomans had maintained a connection between writing and authority and legitimacy, especially concerning religious texts. Each printing of Arabic letters raised this legitimacy problem from the outset. Moreover, a professional group of clerks (scribes and copiers) depended on writing for their livelihood.

The preparation of manuscripts was considered desirable in several ways. Fine manuscripts for elite consumption enjoyed high cultural standing. Accordingly, copiers of fine manuscripts were classed, according to one (self-serving) tradition, with those whose place in heaven is assured. Printed books, on the other hand, were believed to be the work of Satan, and, in general, print was considered to resemble the poisonous oleander bush.[33] The French orientalist Antoine Galland (1646–1715) said he came across printed books in the markets. One could purchase Ibn Sīnā's *Canon*, but no one wanted it, and like other printed books, it gathered dust on store shelves. Manuscript copies of the same works were easily and quickly sold, though for a higher price than that of the printed versions.[34] The activity of İbrahim Müteferrika did not alter this attitude.

Parallel to the incentive to continue producing fine handwritten manuscripts, another process arose during the seventeenth and eighteenth centuries regarding the production of lower-quality manuscripts, which Nelly Hanna identified as "vulgarization" in manuscript copying. The market opened up to manuscripts prepared intentionally using a lower quality of calligraphy and lower-quality paper in order to price them competitively in comparison with the new, cheap printed books. These manuscripts were also produced with newer and speedier techniques to likewise offer an attractive product commercially, but at the expense of aesthetic quality.

As the volume of manuscripts increased, many people became involved in writing, copying, and buying them.[35] The appearance of print in Europe translated in the early modern Ottoman context to a reduction in the costs of handwritten manuscripts, not to the appearance of books.

Printing presented a new way of creating and organizing texts on paper. A straight-ruled text is dramatically different from the common physical structure of many types of Arabic and Ottoman Turkish written documents—the visual image that Messick called "spiral." In this type of handwriting, the text is indented toward the center of a page; if the bottom is reached before the writing finished, the writing continues in the wide margins, including rotations of the page. This organization of space was more than a matter of design: it was the sign of authority. Typed texts offer a different relation between form and content, with straight lines and ruled margins predetermining the way content is put on paper. It forces uniformity, with no individual mark that goes back to the contents of the document and its author and his/her knowledge, professionalism, and authority.[36]

The possible printing of the Qurʾan made that an especially more pointed question. The Qurʾan was handed down by word of mouth to Muḥammad, and even after he put it in writing and the binding canonic text was created, it was still handed down verbally from generation to generation. Reciting the Qurʾan from memory—in fact, singing the Qurʾan—is an important component in the religious education of a Muslim to this day. Indeed, as discussed in the previous chapter, verbally conveying the Qurʾan and reciting it from memory were the principal pedagogic method of the *mekteb*s and *medrese*s.

Narrating from memory created close personal relations between teacher and student. Printed books created an alternative to this intimate conveyance of knowledge, raising questions regarding the authority and legitimacy of knowledge. Fear arose that an unintentional error in a holy text could mislead the unlearned. Handwriting can always be corrected or a single manuscript destroyed; however, printed text, which by its very nature is issued in large numbers of copies, posed the danger of an irrevocably unfixable error. Thus, printing was delayed, initially, out of what Muslims believed was the necessity to protect the faith. For the same reason, and stemming from the desire to revive the faith and the community, Muslims finally did decide to adopt printing. It was precisely this increasingly vital and imperative need of the Muslim community to preserve its faith that İbrahim Peçevi and İbrahim Müteferrika spoke of. While in their time the need was not perceived to be sufficiently urgent in many communities, by the nineteenth century, a consensus did develop around the necessity to reform and thus preserve their faith. The Qur'an had already been printed around 1537/1538, albeit a Venetian edition for missionaries. A Qur'an printed by Muslims for Muslims did not appear until 1787, in St. Petersburg.[37]

The attitude to printing was also a professional issue because it endangered the livelihood and identity of a socioprofessional group of considerable power. The Ottoman Empire was run by bureaucrats: an "army" of officials. It was a state of craftsmen and merchants that was run on documented bookkeeping. It was a society that consumed books, with many people making their living from the crafts of book publishing: manufacturing paper and ink, preparing writing implements, creating the writing itself, drawing illustrations, and bookbinding. According to the estimation of Luigi Marsigli, an educated man from seventeenth-century Bologna who was held as a prisoner of war in a paşa's home until his liberation in 1682, there were 80,000 manuscript copiers in Istanbul.[38] The numbers recalled by Evliya Çelebi, the seventeenth-century Ottoman traveler, are more modest. However, Evliya also described the organization into guilds of all the professions dealing with book crafts and discussed how stores were distributed throughout the city.[39] This, then, refers to a significantly powerful pressure group.

Fuller acceptance of printing only occurred during the nineteenth century, by the end of which at least seventy-seven printing houses were operating in Ottoman Turkish in Istanbul.[40]

Reading and Writing in Illustrations

Reading takes various forms with multiple types of "text." Comprehending one type may require several corollary literacies. Reading a written text demands certitude in linguistic matters (such as grammar and syntax), in culture (to decipher symbols and relate to ideas), and in visual signs (to be able to interpret images diverging from orthography of letters). Visual literacy in the premodern era refers mainly to body language, maps, and drawn pictures. Later literary forms and technologies introduced cartoons, photographs, movies, videos, and other visual forms.[41]

Miniatures in manuscripts provide one example of Ottoman conceptual visual representations, and they point to the copresence of visual and linguistic models of literacies. Relationships between image and text were varied, depending on the specific genre of the text and its changing artistic, political, cultural, and social functions in the Ottoman context. In manuscripts of illustrated history, for example, images were closely related to the verbal accounts. They were especially popular in the second half of the sixteenth century, but less so in later periods, when albums seemed to have replaced them as the main artistic-cultural product. This preference occurred in tandem with a new Ottoman understanding of books, illustrations, and word–image relationships. In albums the paintings took center stage: they had more narrative power and were independent of the text.[42]

In pharmacological treatises (and in other scientific works as well), the connection between the written word and the illustration was intricate, and the precise role of the illustration is not always clear to modern readers. Sometimes it appears to be a didactic tool intended to visually describe the raw materials (*materia medica*) to the reader and facilitate identifying them in nature. The visual tool enriches the description with details for which the text has no room or which it is unable to convey in words; such details may be conveyed easily in images. Yet there are cases where the illustration does not resemble the original in nature and, in fact, is more misleading than helpful for purposes of identification. One possibility was that the goal was actually to artistically embellish the text with no scientific pretension for a new interpretation, or a pedagogical presumption to offer an auxiliary tool. In some cases, the illustrations may have slowly changed in each copy, even when a didactic intention existed. Alterations may have occurred when the illustrator did not pay attention to small details, was not aware of their importance, was unfamiliar with the original living plant, or operated according to aesthetic standards and was not, in fact, faithful to the original. Katib Çelebi, also a cartographer among his numerous skills and fields of interest, complained about the very poor quality among Istanbul copiers. Given their lack of experience or understanding, he had to explain to them the importance of keeping the drawings in the same shape and place as in the original; apparently, they had made major repeated errors.[43]

Map charting is another example of Ottoman conceptual representation and requires visual certitude. As Karen Pinto has put the matter, "Mapmakers are writers too. Instead of words they use lines and keys and toponyms and symbolic codes."[44] The Ottomans made several different types of charts. Practical nautical charts and portolans (navigational maps based on compass directions and estimated distances) were used by sea captains.[45]

Ottoman cartographers called upon a host of sources in terms of cultural origins and types: Arabic-Islamic cartography was their main source, but also European mapmaking traditions (mainly Italian, but also Spanish), in addition to products of material culture in general. These traditions merged somewhat along the way. From the second half of the sixteenth century the Islamic maps gradually assumed a European outlook, with changes in the accompanying text following later. Ottomans also tried their hands at copying European maps. They likewise acquired European globes. Abū Bakr al-Dimashqī (d. 1691), for example, infused a substantial amount of geographical and cartographical knowledge of Islamic elite culture into material appropriated from the translation of the Dutch father and son Willem and Johan Blaeu's *Atlas Minor*, published in Amsterdam in the middle of the seventeenth century. However, the borrowing from and engagement with Islamic and Ottoman traditions was the more influential process.[46]

Ottoman maps were quite easily bought, produced by a local guild of cartographers, the *esnaf-ı haritacıyan*. Evliya Çelebi referred in his detailed mid-seventeenth-century description of Istanbul to fifteen mapmakers in eight shops. Evliya remarked that they were fluent in several languages, including Latin (he mentioned this language explicitly), and knew astronomy and geography. Evliya described the maps they sold sailors and emphasized the significant details included in the maps and their variety. The maps depicted celestial bodies; the ports, islands, and coasts of the Mediterranean and Black Sea; major lakes and rivers; and other inland topographical information, such as mountain ranges.[47]

Piri Reis (d. 1554) is the most famous representative of Ottoman cartography (based on his number of Google hits, one scholar recently half-jokingly said Piri Reis is now more popular than the famous sultan he served, Süleyman I). Piri Reis launched his career as a mariner-corsair, then served as an Ottoman captain, eventually rising to excel in the more theoretical side of his professions: cartography and writing on navigation. He combined his vast experience with Italian and Catalan sources, including a map made by Columbus, to map the shores, including a series of Mediterranean city views. His world map reveals that in addition to the tradition of the Mediterranean portolan chart, he was anchored in the tradition of the world map of the age of great discoveries. Yet his knowledge of traditional Islamic mapping was equal to his familiarity with European maps. All of his maps were presented in a lavish, colorful manner, including legends, intended to impress a potential elite recipient rather than serve as a useful tool for a common sailor. Indeed, he wrote his major book, *Kitab-i Bahriyye* (Book on seafaring; a first version completed in 1521 and a second in 1526), when he realized that all of the relevant information he wished to include could not actually be drawn on a map. He then produced a volume of texts and charts, detailed descriptions of the entire Mediterranean, and an introduction discussing navigation, oceanic geography, and ongoing voyages.[48]

Matrakçi Nasuh (d. ca. 1564) was another Ottoman who drew sixteenth-century Ottoman town views, but from a very different angle than Piri Reis. Nasuh was a mathematician, historian, and calligrapher/painter who emerged from the palace school—not an autodidact corsair climbing up slowly, like Piri Reis. Nasuh accompanied the army during the Süleymanic campaigns and created documentary paintings of the townscapes and countryside through which the campaign progressed. We have only the illustrations themselves to draw from in seeking to understand his perspective. The talents for observation and recording that Nasuh displayed as a miniaturist were, unhappily, not reinforced by his efforts as an author. His books involve no collaboration or interesting interplay between the written page and its visual support. The miniatures are preoccupied with subject matter more ritualistic and ceremonial in tone than informative. This is not to say that his maps are not realistic, but at the same time they carry a fantastical aura.[49]

Visual certitude evolved to acquire understanding in new formats of images and idealized visions. New technologies and mass media promoted new visual objects to be learned. Advertisements and satirical cartoons in the late Ottoman press demonstrate the wish of authors to develop communication via images, interlaced with the need of the readers to push further their ability to make sense of images.[50]

TRANSLATIONS AND TRANSLATORS AMONG THE OTTOMAN ELITE

The phenomenon of translating into Turkish is documented from the thirteenth century, and the most ancient manuscripts that have survived to this day are dated to the fourteenth century. Except for the Qur'an, no known testimony exists of translation into Turkish in earlier periods. The administration of the Seljuq states, including the Seljuq sultanate of Rum in Anatolia, was conducted in Arabic and, mainly, in Persian. It was only during the thirteenth century that Turkish patrons began to show interest in Turkish translations. The translated books covered an impressive variety of fields: medicine, geography, history, *edeb*, mystical Islam, zoology, astronomy, dream interpretation, and, of course, the religious sciences, such as the law, Qur'an exegesis, and others.[51]

With the rise of the Ottoman state, translation gained momentum: more Turkish patrons appeared, and they were interested in reading in their own language. A burgeoning enterprise grew up around the translation of scientific texts into Ottoman Turkish for an elite audience. Pre-Ottoman Turkish had traditionally been used in the Muslim world as the language of the bureaucracy since the entry of Turkish clans as rulers of the Muslim world from around the year 1000. Under the Ottoman Empire, however, Ottoman Turkish (which is different from Anatolian Turkish) added a cultural scientific role to the layer of administrative usage. Ottoman Turkish was the language of the elite; anyone who sought their recognition and patronage had to display his work in their language. Morphological, phonetic, and lexical analysis reveals the transition from old Anatolian Turkish into Ottoman Turkish. Translations, alongside the writing of original treatises directly in Turkish, for the first time created a significant body of knowledge in the Turkish language. This process started during the fourteenth century, with the inception of the Ottoman state, but gained momentum from the fifteenth century onward as the state rose to become an empire. It is not a coincidence, for instance, that during the second half of the fifteenth century two surgical manuals were written in Ottoman Turkish for the first time.[52]

Works of various languages were translated into Ottoman Turkish in accordance with the multicultural world within which the Ottomans lived. Treatises were translated from Greek, Latin, Arabic, and Persian, among many other source languages. The translation process, at times, weaved several languages together, merged sources of knowledge, and synthesized cultural worlds. Translation is not a "thing" but a process requiring people to make a certain piece of knowledge accessible and relevant in a different language. Hence, "translation" in the Ottoman context was more than "word for word" mediation of the text. Ottomans practiced diverse strategies of translation, some of which involved intervention in the text.[53] As translation studies with an eye on "the cultural turn" have shown, translations were strongly influenced by the needs of the recipient culture. Hence, translation into Ottoman Turkish could mean several different things. It indicated a wish to communicate within and across languages. It was also a marker of a form of spoliation, cultural dependence, and independence at the same time.[54]

The process by which two Ottoman medical treatises in the seventeenth century came into being demonstrates this complexity. Şemsüddin Itaki was born in the 1570s in Şirvan, a border area between the Ottoman Empire and the Safavid state. The wars of the 1620s forced him to leave his dwelling, and ultimately he immigrated to Istanbul. His introduction to the elite patronage was *Teşrih-i ebdan ve terjuman kibale-yi al-falasufan* (The anatomy of body parts and an explanation of the philosophers). The essay attracted the interest of the vizier Topal Recep Paşa, who as an expression of his patronage bestowed upon Itaki the prestigious title of Guardian of the Sacred Mosque in Mecca. The little we know about him derives mainly from autobiographical notes he inserted in his medical treatise.[55]

Itaki's essay on anatomy followed the familiar traditions of Ottoman Galenic-Muslim medicine. It was based on the work of eleventh-century Ibn Sīnā and thirteenth-century Ibn al-Nafīs (a legal scholar and physician). The structure of the treatise abides by the accepted norms: it opens with a presentation of Galenic humoral theory in its Muslim Arabic adaptation, and goes on to describe the parts of the body in order. The body parts were sorted into two groups, according to Ibn Sīnā's classification: simple organs (meaning of similar structure, like blood, bones, and muscles) and more complicated organs (like the digestive and respiratory systems).[56]

At the same time, Itaki presented information regarding certain organs and perceptions concerning the human body as a whole that deviated from customary knowledge at that time. This was evident in the anatomical drawings that accompany the essay. As in other medical-anatomical treatises, we find the skeleton, nerves, arteries, and veins, and the development of the fetus. But Itaki displays these features in a way that combined two different traditions. It was clear that he copied drawings that had first appeared in *Teşrih-i mansuri*, an anatomical treatise in Persian by the Timurid Ibn Ilyas of the fourteenth century. To this he added drawings and knowledge he acquired from a completely different source: anatomical treatises from Renaissance Europe.

While the connection between Itaki's work and an earlier Persian source seems reasonable and likely, it is less clear to us how treatises from Italy and Spain reached him. Did he read them in the original? We have no evidence that he knew European languages. Perhaps someone translated them for him? We have no idea who the translator might have been. Did he read the original or, perhaps, only see the illustrations? These questions remain unanswered.

Even if we cannot re-create the connection between Itaki and European anatomy, *Teşrih-i ebdan* clearly proves that the author saw the European treatises: Itaki copied from *De humani corporis fabrica* (The structure of the human body) by Vesalius from 1543, as well as from the 1556 *Histo-*

ria de la composición del cuerpo humano (A description of the composition of the human body) by the Spanish anatomist Juan de Valverde.[57]

The anatomical drawings from the Renaissance are the product of an art form that is completely different from that of Muslims. The Muslim illustrators worked in two dimensions in an attempt to convey the idea and avoided attempting to achieve realism; in Europe, on the other hand, from the time of Leonardo da Vinci, anatomical drawings attempted to express precise physical reality in three dimensions. However, the more essential difference was the rift that began to develop between European and Ottoman medical outlooks. Though not yet marked, the gap did already exist. The two medical systems had once both followed the Galenic medical tradition from antiquity, but now they were growing apart. In the Renaissance period, Europe had confronted the Galenic tradition, argued with it, and criticized it; in Ottoman medicine, this tradition was still a crucial foundation.

In Ottoman Turkish, Itaki brought together knowledge and perceptions that had originated in the Persian- and Arabic-speaking Muslim world and in Latin writings from Europe. His terminology within the Ottoman Turkish text was mostly, like his sources, in Arabic, though from time to time he added translation to Ottoman Turkish and occasionally included Persian terms. From this point of view, Itaki is an important link in the creation of Ottoman Turkish medical-scientific terminology.

Another treatise that took a winding road was that of Ṣāliḥ bin Naṣrallāh Ibn Sallūm (d. 1670), a native of Aleppo who became the companion of Mehmet IV (reigned 1648–1687) and chief physician of the empire (*hekimbaşı*). Ibn Sallūm prepared a long essay on therapy and hygiene entitled *Ghāyat al-itqān fī tadbīr badan al-insān* (The greatest thoroughness in treatment of the human body).[58] The original tract was written in Arabic, Ibn Sallūm's mother tongue, but it was soon translated into Ottoman Turkish for the benefit of the Istanbul elite, hence the existence of an Ottoman Turkish version (which was apparently widely copied and circulated, to judge from the numerous surviving manuscripts).[59] Ibn Sallūm's work was later translated into Persian.[60]

The treatise of Ibn Sallūm is written in the tradition of Islamic medical treatises, but as in the case of Itaki, he was clearly influenced by European sources as well. In Ibn Sallūm's case, this was chemical medicine, associated with Paracelsus, a physician and chemist from Basel (d. 1541). Ibn Sallūm acknowledged his indebtedness to Paracelsus and aptly titled the fourth and last part of his book *al-Ṭibb al-jadīd al-kimyawī aladhī ikhtaraʿahu barkākīlsūs* (The new chemical medicine which Paracelsus invented).

Paracelsus introduced a new and subversive approach in European medicine in the sixteenth century. (By the end of the seventeenth century, when it entered the Ottoman Empire, the sting of chemical medicine had dulled a little and was no longer avant-garde.) He suggested a method of treatment based on chemical materials (poisonous drugs) and not on botany, which had been accepted since ancient times. It was part of the deep revision he sought to introduce to the understanding of the human body and was very critical of Galen's theories.

Ibn Sallūm was quite familiar with treatises of the disciples of Paracelsus from the late sixteenth and early seventeenth centuries: Oswald Croll (1563–1609) and Daniel Sennert (1572–1637). A comparison between their treatises and Ibn Sallūm's prescriptions for diseases of the cataract and trachoma are evidence of the direct and unequivocal connection. Ibn Sallūm's style is a translation (usually abbreviated) of the early treatises. The prescriptions include materials whose source was the New World (America) and thus foreign to Middle Eastern Muslim medicine. Ibn Sallūm also placed more emphasis on the chemical means of preparing medications (distillation, for example) compared to the literature accepted at the time.[61] However, Ibn Sallūm's engagement with these texts was highly surgical. Although he regarded Paracelsus's recipes as effective, he more or less left Paracelsian philosophy out.[62] In the words of Harun Küçük, while "data" traveled well, medical theories did not.[63] Ibn Sallūm's treatise was copied many times in its Arabic and Ottoman Turkish versions under the patronage of the Ottoman elites.[64] Although it did not inspire a major change in clinical realities during Ibn Sallūm's time, later on, during the eighteenth century, chemical medicine became a possible alternative to humoral medicine, at least in Istanbul.[65]

Along the lines of continuity in Ottoman interest in European medicine and ability to subsume it, at least up to a point, it is possible to discern two directions of change throughout the centuries. First, an interest in foreign languages, or at least the recognition of the need to be fluent in them, increased among Muslims. Second, the status of western European languages (French, for example) as a translation source rose with time. Polyglottism always characterized the early modern Ottoman Empire. Travelers remarked on the "cacophony" of languages in the imperial Ottoman centers, likening the situation to the Tower of Babel, and commented that conversation over dinner in elite circles could move between as many as thirteen different languages.[66] Even though it was more likely for non-Muslim Ottomans to become polyglots, and there were many translators acting as intermediaries, it should not obscure the polyglot character of the Ottoman world—a norm that many viewed favorably, including Muslims.[67]

Mahmud II's speech at the festive opening ceremony of the Imperial School of Medicine in Istanbul in 1827 addressed the fact that the school's teaching language would be French. In his speech, the sultan claimed that the students' acquisition of a foreign language had not been a goal in itself. His intention was that they should acquire proficiency in reading French only in order to understand the textbooks, because there were no books in "our language." The principal, Dr. Karl Ambrose Bernard, an Austrian, also spoke a foreign language. Polyglotism was an ad hoc, temporary necessity. According to Mahmud II's vision, the first students would ultimately translate the textbooks into Turkish: that would be their mission in addition to serving the empire as physicians. The speech was published in the imperial official newspaper, which frames contents as the state's ideology. To complete the picture of this occasion, the ceremony took place on March 14, 1827, designated in republican times by the medical community as Medicine Day to celebrate the introduction of Western medicine into Turkey.[68]

Muslim Ottomans indeed took up the gauntlet. Şanizade Mehmed Atallah Efendi (d. 1826) was just one of the people who rose to this challenge. Şanizade had many interests and skills: he was a scholar of religion, a physician, and a historian; he wrote poetry and was a watchmaker; and he was fluent in Arabic, Persian, French, and apparently Italian and Latin. After experimenting with a smallpox vaccination on cows and finding it safe and efficient, he recommended that the sultan start a general inoculation campaign in Istanbul. His book *Mirat-ül-ebdan fi teşrih aza-ül-insan* (The beautiful appearance of the organs in the anatomy of man's body parts) is the first printed medical treatise in Ottoman Turkish and contains the first precise anatomical diagrams in this language. In his book *Tarih* (History) he covered the years 1808 (the rise to power of Mahmud II) through 1820–1821. Şanizade's *Tarih* reveals a certain leaning toward Western knowledge. Some of the subjects it covers include parliament as a political method, isolation and quarantine as a medical health precaution, and insurance as an aspect of economics and commerce. In order to write about these new subjects in Ottoman Turkish, Şanizade had to create new terminology, especially in the fields of medical science.[69]

Şanizade was a member of a growing group of Muslim intelligentsia who considered knowledge of foreign languages (principally European) important in order to learn directly, without intermediaries, about the world that surrounded the Ottomans. Some of them were the product of the Bab-ı Ali Tercüme Odası (the Translation Office of the Sublime Porte). This governmental bureau, founded in 1821, was one of the first new ministries established by Mahmud II as part of the reorganization of the imperial central administration and the transition from an institute of scribes and secretaries (*kalemiye*) to one of professional civilian administration (*mülkiye*). The imperial translation office replaced the old method of translators and, in time, was used as the foundation of the modern Ottoman foreign office. Talented young men were enlisted by the organization, which functioned as a kind of school for diplomacy and foreign languages. For the first time, these positions were filled by Muslims and not, as in the past, by non-Muslim Ottoman subjects.[70]

One commonality among all these different translators is that they were *elite* Ottomans. (Not to mention the commissionaires involved; the next chapter will address the crucial role of patronage in scientific activity.) They were Muslims who served the Ottoman Empire in various capacities, as *ülema* and/or as bureaucrats. They were like the Ottoman bureaucrats who coveted positions as emissaries to Mughal India, discussed in the previous chapter. Many (although not all) were born in the Ottoman Empire; those who immigrated were incorporated into the Ottoman elite social institutions. Translations were carried out by the imperial head physicians and chief imperial astronomers, historians, and geographers, as well as by official court interpreters.[71]

Translation and translators, however, like foreign travel (discussed in Chapter 2), affirm the picture of intellectual and physical contacts between Ottomans and their Muslim Asian and European neighbors as an ongoing phenomenon encompassing many people in many different circumstances: Spanish Jews, Greeks educated in Italy, converts to Islam, but also *ülema*. Some were "star" scholars, but they were the minority. Consider the case of Itaki (discussed above), whose journey was shorter than Ali Kuşçu's: he traveled "only" from the Caucasus to Istanbul. The context of the respective journeys could not have been more different: Kuşçu was an esteemed, invited guest whom the sultan very much wanted to recruit; Itaki was a refugee from the wars between the Ottomans and the Safavids, although he too rose in the ranks of the religious institution and succeeded in attracting patronage.

MARGINAL GROUPS AS AGENTS OF KNOWLEDGE

Conduits of translation were diversified. In her work on the dissemination of European knowledge and technology in eighteenth-century Istanbul, sociologist Fatma Müge Göçek pointed to the decisive role played by three specific social groups.[72] Interestingly, these groups were marginal segments of Ottoman society—nationally, ethnically, and religiously.

The first social group she identified was the foreign nationals (some of whom lived for long periods in the Ottoman Empire). This group was far from cohesive since people came to the empire under very different circumstances: as diplomats, traders, adventurers, scientists, and prisoners. Their presence became increasingly prominent over the passing centuries and lent the Ottoman capital a cosmopolitan atmosphere. The foreigners did not keep to themselves, and local communities developed personal and professional ties with them, despite limitations of language and other constraints imposed by the authorities.

The second group to serve as agents disseminating Western science and technology within the empire was one that acted as the necessary intermediaries when the authorities imposed difficulties in direct contact with Europeans. The intermediary role was filled by minority groups, mostly Jews, Armenians, Greeks, and Christian Arabs. The relative importance of these intermediary groups and the specific role they played varied from time to time. Jews, for example, were important in trade, medicine, and diplomacy in the sixteenth and seventeenth centuries, while in the eighteenth century their power diminished. Another group's influence became more prominent in intermediary roles in the eighteenth century: that of the Phanariote Greeks from the Fener quarter of Istanbul. Traditionally, they served as interpreters at the sultan's palace, but in the eighteenth century, members of this group were also appointed as governors in the Danube region. Their status and roles afforded them special freedom of movement among foreign nationals, non-Muslim Ottoman nationals, and the Ottoman elite.

The third group that Göçek refers to consisted of eminent Ottomans who connected the other intermediaries to the imperial power seat. Their roles as officials and senior bureaucrats, diplomats and courtiers, naval and military commanders placed them at the cutting edge of relations with Europe and Europeans. For instance, they staffed the ad hoc embassies to Mughal India or the Hapsburg. For other Ottomans, they provided an example to emulate; the elite's adoption of foreign ideas and techniques was one of the pipelines that connected the European world to a wider population in the empire.

Göçek's analysis was mainly a social explanation of the ways in which interactions between the Ottoman Empire and Europe unfolded in one special locality, namely Istanbul. She showed how various groups in the capital mediated between the empire and Europe. Institutions and groups aside, it was *people* who actually made these contacts possible by mediating between languages and cultures. People transferred ideas, texts, and equipment. Furthermore, such fruitful contacts occurred throughout the Ottoman urban sphere, not in Istanbul alone. In fact, as we shall see below, contacts of significant volume and intensity were taking place in the provinces. Also, as demonstrated above, Ottomans were in scientific dialogue with Muslim societies as well, including Iran under both the Safavids (sixteenth and seventeenth centuries) and the Qajars (nineteenth and twentieth centuries).

The dragomans, Ottoman interpreters, came into being as a result of contacts between the Ottoman world and Europe, defying categories and boundaries of religion, language, ethnicity, and "nationality." These were either non-Muslim native Ottomans (mainly Greeks, Slavs, Armenians, and Sephardic Jews, but also Roman Catholics, whose importance rose during the second half of the eighteenth century) or naturalized Europeans (Venetians are a prime example). Only the French and the Hapsburgs regularly employed a sizeable number of their own nationals, trained in schools in Paris and Vienna to be professional orientalists, but they too had to depend on the service of local and localized dragomans.

Dragomans had both language abilities and social and professional contacts. (They usually came from well-to-do families in their communities.) More importantly, they were motivated to put these skills and contacts to social, commercial, legal, and diplomatic use. They were able to weave a strong network of patronage and commerce serving the Ottoman state, the foreign consulates, and themselves.[73]

The power of the dragomans lay in their networking and the importance of their services. The basic service they offered was translation, hence the Arabic/Ottoman title *tercümen* (translator), later corrupted in European languages into *dragoman*. They translated both correspondence and oral exchanges. Later on, however, they became negotiators and interpreters of cultures, advising foreigners on manners and propriety.

The dragomans' unique ability to act as go-betweens rested with their hybrid character: they were alien but loyal and entrusted with sophisticated and confidential assignments. In order to sustain such a precarious position, they had to be very cautious in their personal conduct. Several Ragusan dragomans were fired for their violent nature and what their employers regarded as a debauched lifestyle (drinking, playing cards, falling into debts, fornicating, and the like).[74]

More crucial than a dignified and controlled demeanor, however, was the talent and power to foster multiple identities. Once the dragomans lost their cosmopolitan or transnational identities, they lost their positions as intermediaries. Many Levantine Catholics opted to become naturalized Europeans during the nineteenth century, sometimes even being incorporated into the European nobility. Such a resocialization process turned them into foreigners, and as a result they lost the confidence of Ottoman authorities.[75]

The dragoman phenomenon was found in all of the empire's major urban centers. In fact, during the eighteenth century, their presence in the provinces grew in both absolute numbers and a widening scope of activities. In Aleppo in the 1790s, approximately 1,500 people claimed to be dragomans or their servants/assistants. In Salonica in the same decade, 72 people were officially registered as dragomans or their servants, but the actual number was higher.[76]

In addition to its spatial dissemination, the dragoman phenomenon endured until the late Ottoman Empire. Well into the nineteenth century, foreign embassies relied on the services of local dragomans to interpret and conduct exchanges with the Ottoman court. Dragomans carried out official and unofficial duties that required the ability to negotiate complex and diverse cultural affiliations. As in previous centuries, they were more than translators: they were intermediaries and negotiators for both the embassies and the Ottomans. In such a unique position, and in order to maintain it, their identities were particularly eclectic, even intersecting.[77]

Dragomans were not found only in diplomatic and commercial spheres. Another kind of dragoman was present at the Muslim courts. They served as intermediaries between the qadi and non-Turkish speakers who, depending on the exact geographical location, could be non-Muslims in regions under Ottoman rule, or Muslims who did not share the language of the Ottoman elite (as in the Arab provinces, where an Arabic Turkish interpreter would have been needed).[78]

The city of Salonica illustrates the dynamic that enabled acculturation and cross-convergence between East and West, between Ottomans and Europeans, between the center of the empire and other centers, and between Christianity, Islam, and Judaism, as well as the cross-fertilization of ideas, texts, and instruments. Moreover, Salonica demonstrated a process in which minority groups in particular (as opposed to the majority Muslim group), in a provincial town far away from the imperial center of Istanbul, were able to be especially productive and effective agents of knowledge exchange. Through this process, activities of marginal groups in the provinces were able to influence the whole empire. The background of such an intrinsic process was Salonica's ever-changing ethnic composition and cultural life.

Salonica was the main port city in the Ottoman Balkan from the time of its conquest, in 1430, until the First Balkan War, in 1912. With a protected bay, overland transportation routes connecting it to the Balkan centers (and, in time, also to the imperial Ottoman centers), and a fertile rural region rich in quarries, Salonica retained its prestigious status from ancient times and up to the modern era. During the Ottoman period, it was a bustling city of handcrafts and trade, with local handcrafts flourishing alongside international imports and exports via the Mediterranean Sea. Salonica was prominent in textile manufacture: coats for the janissaries and large towels for the hammams (baths) were manufactured there. Quarries in the immediate environs of Salonica made the manufacture of jewelry and production of silver utensils possible, as well as the production of gunpowder. Wheat, tobacco, wool, cotton, and wood were sent to Istanbul, Egypt, the Mediterranean islands, and the ports of Europe. Goods transported overland included coffee and rice, which came from Egypt; soap, flax, and citrus fruit, which came from the Aegean Islands; slaves and hides from North Africa; and tailored textile products from Europe.[79]

From a religious, ethnic, linguistic, and socioeconomic standpoint, Salonica was a heterogeneous city. This description applies to almost every other Ottoman urban center, but it seems that Salonica was characterized by being especially vibrant and colorful. In Salonica, the three Abrahamic faiths converged. Salonica was an important Muslim city. The qadi of Salonica was one of the nine senior qadis in the Ottoman Empire; only those of Istanbul, Mecca and Medina, Bursa, Edirne, Damascus, and Cairo preceded him in importance. Yet despite the city's clear Muslim identity, Jews composed the largest ethnic group from the beginning of the sixteenth century and formed the majority of the population, according to census counts.[80] The local rabbis were famous throughout the Balkans, to the extent that Salonica was called "Jerusalem of the Balkans." The city had also been a Christian metropolis since the fourth century and was subordinate to the Greek Patriarch, initially in Constantinople and later in Istanbul. Alongside the Orthodox Christians, who were affiliated with the eastern church, Salonica had a large presence of Catholic traders who came from western Europe.

In Salonica, religious and ethnic boundaries were often blurred. The local Gypsies exemplify this situation. Both Christian and Muslim Gypsies resided in the city, and despite the religious divide between the two groups, their similar lifestyles led others to consider them one community (both socially marginalized and highly stigmatized). The Gypsies are an especially clear example of blurred religious-ethnic boundaries, but not the only one. The Albanian community was also heterogeneous, composed of Muslims and Christians. Yet like the Gypsies, the various Albanians were regarded as a single ethnic group, perhaps because of what appeared to be a common lifestyle of banditry.[81]

As Mark Mazower's book *Salonica, City of Ghosts* has shown, Ottoman Salonica never existed "for" any one particular group; instead, the various parts of the city coexisted in continuous tension—but also in continuous synergy.[82] (Victoria Hislop has offered a literary approach to the multicultural city's terminal moments in the twentieth century in her novel *The Thread*.)[83] Against this colorful background, given the coexistence and somewhat blurred boundaries of various groups, Salonica was an especially fertile location for the transfer of knowledge and technology. Its geographical location and sociocultural characteristics provided a climate that encouraged such contacts. Moreover, as a port city, Salonica experienced constant movement of people bearing books, manuscripts, instruments, and ideas.

The biography of Shlomo ben Ya'akov Almoli reflects the spirit of the era and the place, and testifies how one group of intermediaries, the Jews of Salonica, were well rooted in various cultural worlds. Almoli, who earned his living as a physician, was born before 1485, apparently in Spain or, perhaps, already in Ottoman Salonica, where he published his popular treatise on the interpretation of dreams. The treatise was copied by hand many times and also printed in many editions up through the twentieth century; it was even translated into Yiddish, Persian-Hebrew, and English. From 1516, Almoli lived in Istanbul, where he was a member of one of the rabbinical courts. He died sometime after 1542.

Orphaned at a young age and unable to afford a private teacher, not even for Talmud (a point he complained about quite often in his essays), Almoli was self-educated. He also protested that books were expensive, were repetitious, and did not offer new knowledge or refreshing insights.

Unable to attract students and make a living as a teacher, Almoli labored on an ambitious project that never materialized in full: an encyclopedia of all the knowledge that an educated Jew should possess. Although he failed to complete this project, we have access to an abstract he prepared. This essay and his book on the interpretation of dreams present the profile of a polymath: breadth of knowledge; an understanding of learning as a broad, comprehensive process; and interests in different areas of Jewish knowledge as well as general humanist fields. Almoli incorporated numerous sources, including the Bible, the Bavli Talmud, Sephardic interpretations of the Talmud, Kabbalah, Jewish philosophy, Muslim philosophers (such as eleventh-century Ibn Sīnā and twelfth-century Al-Ghazzālī), in addition to Socrates, Plato, and Aristotle.

This broad approach to knowledge—combining various fields and different cultural worlds (Spain and the Ottoman Empire), the use of classical sources, and the rejection of magic and wizardry—justifies viewing Almoli as a Jewish polymath during the heart of the Ottoman Empire.[84] Such a broad intellectual profile perhaps appears unrealistic to modern readers, yet instances like these did occur. Almoli's biography is a fairly typical intellectual profile of an early modern Ottoman Jew, a hybrid of various worlds.

Numerous other polymaths like Almoli existed in the Ottoman sphere. Some were formally within Ottoman domains, as was Ilyās ibn Ibrāhīm al-Yahūdī al-Ishbānī (the Arabic appellation of Eliyahu ben Avraham), another Spanish-Ottoman Jewish physician. He wrote a treatise on the bubonic plague in Arabic and dedicated it to Selim I (reigned 1512–1520). The contents present knowledge and methods prevalent in both the Christian and Muslim cultures. Ilyās/Eliyahu studied medicine with his Jewish family in Iberia, practiced side by side with Spanish Christian colleagues, worked as a doctor in Naples after his expulsion from Iberia in 1492, and then settled in the Ottoman Empire, where he presented himself to the Ottoman Turkish elite by way of a scientific treatise in Arabic. In his treatise, Eliyahu ben Avraham quotes openly from authorities of different cultures, intentionally presents different or even contradictory positions regarding the bubonic plague, and relates himself to various medical trends and practices, showing no favoritism for any particular school of thought.[85]

Almoli resembles Eliyahu ben Avraham in his engagements with different cultural and scientific sources. However, his social standing is of interest. Unlike other elite figures, Almoli was not necessarily a well-known figure in his time, demonstrating that engagement in such heterogeneous scientific sources, and transfer of ideas from different cultural worlds, occurred widely, and not just among the most privileged elite.

This spread of hybridization within Salonica's Jewish community made these Jews agents of transmission and integration of knowledge in the Ottoman Empire. In sixteenth-century cosmopolitan Salonica, refugees expelled from Spain and Portugal met up with the local community. They were joined by Jews from Italy, some of whom were originally from Iberia; physicians and philosophers among this latter group read Latin. The Jews of Salonica mediated between the different cultural worlds like a link connecting two distinct intellectual and social networks, Ottoman and European. Jews were both a source of friction between the cultures and religions and a mediating factor forming a bridge between them. As part of both the Ottoman and the European network, they earned the trust of both. Contact and the dissemination of ideas were made possible on the basis of this trust. In Salonica, they translated European treatises of interest to astronomers from Latin to Hebrew. They took these treatises with them to Istanbul when they went there to trade or to carry out their activities in the Jewish community and on its behalf.[86]

Of course, Salonica was not the only place such an Ottoman-Jewish enterprise could happen—either in the Ottoman Empire or outside it. Jewish actors in scientific exchanges across the Mediterranean were not necessarily formal Ottoman subjects but were nevertheless important members of Ottoman social and cultural networks. Take Moses Galeano of Crete, which at his time (late fifteenth and early sixteenth centuries) was under Venetian rule. (Only in 1699 did the Ottomans conquer this Mediterranean island.) He was a physician and a scholar of astronomy who wrote in Hebrew and Arabic. Galeano's writings reveal his familiarity with medieval Islamic astronomers, such as the fourteenth-century Damascene Ibn al-Shāṭir, whose theories strongly resemble portions of Copernicus's work. Galeano also knew Latin. He spent time in the Veneto, Italy, around 1500, and was in direct contact with Christian intellectuals. Copernicus was in Padua at that time, and although it is impossible to prove they were in direct contact, Galeano was in contact with other European astronomers. He also spent considerable time in Istanbul and had ties with the court of the Ottoman sultan Bayezit II. He was part of a network of Jewish scholars who were conduits in selling and transferring texts between Crete, Istanbul, and Italy. Altogether, circumstantial evidence suggests he was an intermediary link between medieval Arabic and early modern Ottoman Islamic astronomy and Renaissance Europe.[87]

Salonica, while not the only place such things could happen, was nonetheless an enduring one. Even in the Hamidian period (marked by Sultan Abdülhamid II's reign), toward the end of the nineteenth century, Salonica was still a meeting place of ideas and people. Again, the Jewish community played an important role. Of particular note in this context was the community of Jewish origin, the Dönme, which was born from a critical event in Jewish history: the movement of Shabbatai Tzvi in the seventeenth century and the phenomenon of converted Jews thereafter. The Dönme community developed a unique identity and religion that were neither exactly Jewish nor quite Muslim. Different social systems—including intracommunal marriage and independent institutions, such as mosques and cemeteries—isolated the community from both the Muslim majority and the Jewish minority. One especially important institution in forming the group's identity was the Dönme's communal education system.

During the Hamidian period, the Dönme established new schools that emphasized progressive values, enlightenment, and excellence. The dress code combined items of apparel from Europe (trousers, neckties, jackets) with the fez hat that Mahmud II had introduced to replace the traditional head covering, the turban. The students—male and female—studied foreign languages (French and German), sciences, and accounting. The pedagogic methods were innovative for that period in the Ottoman Empire: students sat on chairs at a table rather than on the floor, as was customary in traditional schools, and the Ottoman language was studied with the help of punctuation and vowelization marks to facilitate reading. In addition to classroom study, students participated in physical education and sports. The schools were a reflection of the international business community, which sought to train members of the next generation to become, in body and soul, what they perceived to be modern business people: educated, independent, and aware of their self-worth.

The community's schools were intended mainly to serve the community, but their worldview was the complete opposite of isolationism: the goal was meaningful integration in the Ottoman realm. Graduates were assimilated into the imperial systems of commerce and administration, and helped create a required cadre of Ottoman nationals of a new type. Other schools in Salonica and throughout the empire regarded the Dönme schools as a model for emulation, and three different sultans (Murad V, Abdülhamid II, and Mehmed V Reşad) awarded medals of excellence to the Dönme in recognition of their contribution.

The Dönme schools accepted outside students, allowing their impact to reach well beyond the immediate community. One such pupil was Mustafa Kemal—in time, Atatürk. The previous chapter discussed his Salonica education to highlight the parallel existence of different kinds of educational institutions in the latter days of the Ottoman period. Here we refer to another aspect of Mustafa Kemal's basic education: his preparatory school was Şemsi Efendi, the first modern school of the Dönme community.

This first school was named after its founder, "the Enlightener," which later acquired symbolic significance. At the beginning of the republic, Şemsi Efendi was described (by Atatürk as well) as one of the positive forces working to liberate society from the constraints of religion and move it along the path of secularity.

The basis for this modernity, enlightenment, and progress was Islam as a belief and a legal system. The curriculum at Şemsi Efendi, as in other Dönme institutions that followed it, emphasized Islamic faith and morals as a foundation for the identity and success of its students in a modern, technological, and competitive Ottoman world. Islam was perceived as the foundation for a strong work ethic, accuracy, reliability, loyalty, and commitment to family, community, and society—all essential qualities (in the Dönme worldview) of a productive, progressive life.[88] In this way, the community that had turned its back on Judaism integrated a modern, Western, and cosmopolitan identity with Islam and became a model to emulate for the majority Muslim community.

THE PASSAGE OF TRAVELERS AND KNOWLEDGE TO AND FROM THE EMPIRE

The physical and practical aspects of journeys (as opposed to the symbolic ones) formed the basis of travel of knowledge. Travelers journeyed from place to place, carrying with them texts, techniques, instruments, and ideas. They made the acquaintance of locals, befriended them, taught them, and learned from them. The process was both conscious and unconscious.

In terms of numbers, Europeans were the largest group of travelers to the Ottoman Empire. Some continued on to the Far East, while others returned to Europe. From the sixteenth century on, travel for the purpose of learning was especially noticeable. Travel was a scientific project that was meticulously prepared in advance. Its goals included meteorological and astronomical observation, precise recording of dimensions and weights, archeological and architectural surveying, gathering of manuscripts, and learning of languages. In their travels and correspondence regarding their travels, European scientists formed the "Republic of Letters": a social-intellectual network of educated Europeans who met in person or on paper. This scientific-social activity began in the capitals of Europe but spread to the Mediterranean and also included the Ottoman Middle East.[89]

The journeys of education and the meetings they made possible with locals and other intellectuals created a liminal zone, an intercultural space where cooperation existed among people who in their usual life circumstances would not have mixed. In this special situation, they met and became acquainted by virtue of their human commonality. Knowledge in all its forms was an expensive and valued commodity to the extent that it provided the local "vendors" in the Middle East, including the non-Christians among them, an entrée into the prestigious realms of the European-Christian social network.[90]

Aleppo of the eighteenth century, which provided an example of Ottoman literacy at the beginning of this chapter, is also a case in point showing how the Republic of Letters existed in the Levant and enabled broad and comprehensive intercultural migration. At that time a series of visitors from various European nations made their way to Aleppo, among them English, Scottish, Dutch, French, and Germans. They met among themselves and with the city's Ottoman elite (including prominent religious figures, the governor, and so on). They discussed their fields of interest, gathered information, collected manuscripts, and learned about the city's history and natural resources. An example of their work is *The Natural History of Aleppo*, written by Alexander Russell (1715–ca. 1768) and edited in a second edition with an addendum by his young half-brother, Patrick. The book goes into great detail describing the city and its surroundings, flora, fauna, mineral deposits, climate, and natural phenomena, such as earthquakes and epidemics, as well as the city's Ottoman-Syrian institutions and lifestyles. Those who left Aleppo and returned to Europe, or continued on their journeys throughout the empire and Asia as far as India, maintained close contact with friends and colleagues by means of extensive correspondence.[91]

Like Muslim travelers in the framework of *ṭalab al-ʿIlm*, the phenomenon of European travelers in the empire included people of varied social backgrounds traveling for a variety of purposes—sometimes for various purposes at once (either integrated with each other or in conflict), and even for changing purposes over the course of the journey. The search of knowledge was only one of several objectives. The travel of pilgrims or missionaries was completely different from travel for the purpose of learning. Others engaged in pleasure or business trips. Among the travelers were diplomats, adventurers, pilgrims, missionaries, traders, mercenaries, felons, naturalists, hostages, and slaves. Some of them swung through the empire quickly, but others remained for long periods and integrated into local life.[92]

İbrahim Müteferrika exemplifies integration into the Ottoman system: a Transylvanian convert to Islam who adopted a Turkish identity, he became an important Ottoman official. Mentioned earlier for his printing press, his biography matters here because others like him arrived in the Ottoman Empire or were brought in by force (as slaves or prisoners) and became an inseparable part of Ottoman society, even of its elite.

Women were a special kind of traveler.[93] Women who traveled shared some similarities with male travelers, but they were also vastly different—for example, in their sources of information: women were able to mix with local women and exchanged completely different information, based on other sources, than that exchanged by men.

Lady Mary Wortley Montagu (1689–1762), wife of the English ambassador to the court of Ahmet III, was one of many female agents of the transfer of knowledge between the Ottoman Empire and Europe. Wortley Montagu was known for her literary activities in England as well as for the campaign she led in the popular press, among the members of the Royal College of Physicians, and at the royal court in favor of widespread inoculation against smallpox—a most dangerous and contagious disease. Her brother had died of it in childhood, and she too contracted it. Despite her recovery, her face was disfigured, and her unsightliness (in her eyes, at least) led her to seek a cure.

On her travels, Wortley Montagu established contacts with local women, residents of the harem elite as well as the popular healers. In Edirne, she met "old ladies" who specialized in a unique procedure that impressed her very much. As part of the coming-of-age ceremony for local Muslim youths, these women inoculated them against smallpox. (Montagu's account aside, no direct evidence exists of these young men being inoculated.) She describes witnessing variolation: taking material from the blister of a sick person and purposely inoculating a healthy individual. She described how popular healers nicked four or five capillaries on a youth's arms, chests, and foreheads and infected the scratches with pus taken from the smallpox sores of patients. The boys did, indeed, get ill after the treatment and suffered from high temperatures for a few days, but they recovered and never again contracted smallpox. The treatment was especially popular in the fall months, when it was festively celebrated. Wortley Montagu was so impressed that she had her own son inoculated before she began her publicized campaign to introduce inoculation into England.[94]

The inoculations that Wortley Montagu witnessed in Edirne (which was also performed in other areas around the Ottoman world)[95] were performed by infecting people with the disease itself, which was efficient but very dangerous. Many complications were possible and could even lead to death. With such a contagious disease, every inoculation poses a risk to the community. The method finally adopted worldwide was, indeed, different, resulting from the work of Englishman Edward Jenner (1749–1823) and based on cowpox, not smallpox. After carrying out observations at English farms, Jenner, who was a country doctor, concluded that people who were infected with cowpox were less seriously ill than those who contracted smallpox—and also developed immunity to the more serious disease. Of course, Wortley Montagu did not yet know of Jenner's work, but her campaign to introduce mass immunization against the illness apparently aided Jenner's later acceptance in England. The story of smallpox inoculations illustrates the movement of knowledge across space but also across social circles: a popular custom in the Ottoman Empire was discussed in "high-level" learned scientific circles;[96] in the Ottoman Empire it was a practice among women, and the agent of knowledge who had promoted the migration of this specific knowledge was a woman, whereas in England it was mainly men who discussed it.

European travelers were agents who entered the empire. Ottoman travelers were agents who left the empire and, like their European peers, took an interest in foreign worlds and documented their curiosity, their difference and foreignness, and their imagination. Their numbers were small compared to the European travelers, but they still were part of a phenomenon that was more common than supposed. Like their European counterparts, the Ottoman travelers came from socially diverse backgrounds. They belonged to different religious communities, and were motivated by different reasons and circumstances to leave the Muslim empire. From their essays, it is possible to learn of their broad knowledge of Europe, their deep understanding of European societies and cultures, and their ability and willingness to conduct a dialogue with Europe while being cognizant of both their similarities and differences.[97]

The tireless seventeenth-century Ottoman traveler Evliya Çelebi is an obvious example. He joined the entourage of Ottoman governors, serving as their escort on missions throughout the empire and beyond, reaching as far as Vienna. He is an especially well-known example, among other reasons, thanks to his long and detailed travelogue, the *Seyahatname* (Book of travel). He stood out for his breadth of knowledge, interest in new places and people, and thirst for travel. In many respects, he was quite unusual.

His account, however, describes prevailing conceptions and attitudes in Ottoman society, what Robert Dankoff terms "Ottoman mentality."[98]

There were, however, other sorts of Ottoman travelers who formed the Ottoman mentality in a different way. Among these were the early modern Cairene "middle class" that Nelly Hanna resurrected from oblivion (we were not aware they consumed so many written manuscripts and documents, and produced so much, until her research); the eighteenth-century networks, especially widespread, of Armenian merchants who connected the capitals of Europe, Istanbul, Anatolia, the Caucasus, and Iran;[99] and the cosmopolitan networks of Dönme merchants around the turn of the twentieth century.[100]

Yet another context of travel and movement of ideas was diplomacy, and here too intellectual activity probably had not been the main motivation. Professional, career diplomats, ad hoc ambassadors, translators, and unofficial people who were sent on diplomatic missions negotiated the different cultural worlds they traveled. This varied group of people was interested in Europe and kept records, transmitting knowledge to the empire and translating it into concepts of the Ottoman world.[101]

The Ottoman mentality was the product of numerous individuals, even if the extent of their travels was modest, their intellectual horizons not that broad, or their standing below that of the imperial Ottoman elite. They may not have been intellectuals in the sense of being professional scholars oriented toward learning. Their worldview could have been pragmatic and practical rather than idealistic or theoretical. But the juxtaposition of all this human energy created conduits for movement of knowledge to, from, and within the Ottoman Empire.

FOUR

STATE IN SCIENCE

On Empire, Power, Infrastructures, and Finance

The previous chapters depicted the world of curious Ottoman scholars—their families, communities, and social institutions—and how these affected the contents and directions of Ottoman scientific activity. Now we add an additional protagonist to the equation: the state and its distinct approach to planning and administration, science and technology included. This brings to mind Michel Foucault's term *governmentality* in the context of the rise of the idea of the modern state which governs at every level, not just the administrative or political. The techniques of control that are part of the art of government expand, and include, for Foucault, also organizing knowledge, science, and technology.[1] While it is helpful to think of techniques and procedures that were designed to govern the conduct of individuals and groups in science, the term is also problematic in the Ottoman context. Foucault identified a process in only one direction—namely, state apparatus coercing from above—whereas the Ottoman scientific experience should be understood as interaction between multiple actors around state apparatus.

This chapter demonstrates that the involvement of the Ottoman authorities (in both their private and official capacities) was extensive and significant. In discussing the state in science, I am referring to sultans, viziers, *paşa*s, eunuchs, other court officials, and powerful women at the court. These people formed the ruling institutions of the Ottoman Empire and ran the machinery of the state. My concern is not so much the intellectual atmosphere, but bringing to the forefront dynamics of power relations and patterns of funding for scientific activities.

State involvement is best revealed in the patronage system linking scholars with members of the elite. This system institutionalized preference for specific scholars and certain fields of activity. Via patronage, members of the elite could bring their influence, sometimes indirectly, to bear on scientific and technological ventures, and the direction of their development.

Another aspect of state involvement in Ottoman scientific experience is transportation and communication infrastructures. Such large projects were always executed under the wings of the Ottoman state.

THE PATRON AND THE SCHOLAR: *INTISAP* AND *WAQF/VAKIF*

Sonja Brentjes has shown that Islamic courtly patronage for the ancient sciences (her focus was mainly mathematics and medicine) continued in the Arab and Persianate postclassical worlds.[2] Building on that, I add here the Ottoman case, which Brentjes did not explore in depth.

The Ottoman elite patronized science as a body of knowledge and those who engaged with science as a social practice, establishing endowments on their behalf, organizing and financing scientific activity, and offering the physical sites for scientific activity—including palaces, *medrese*s, or the scholars' private homes.

Patron-protégé relationships (*intisap*) were characterized by dependence and loyalty, and revolved around benefit, gratitude, and obligation.[3] These were personal relationships, often close, even intimate, with inherently unequal power and status among the partners. The patron was committed to helping his protégé and promoting his interests through support of the latter's work and livelihood, and the protégé, on his part, compensated the patron with his services and helped in promoting the patron's interests. Protégés were trustworthy and loyal providers of services to their patrons. Patrons supported their protégés financially and politically, while the latter in turn helped their patrons advance their own political and financial status; and indeed, as patrons' power grew, so did their capacity to promote their protégés and offer them economic and physical security. This social arrangement featured a constant exchange of goods and services. Patrons and protégés related to one another in a tangled network of lateral relations combined with hierarchy and power.

Muslim households could also be quite varied. They could (or could not) rely on familial ties. The social group could (or could not) also be a residential unit. Many of those involved were men, but women participated in such relationships as well. Active and influential female patrons supported both male and female protégés; female protégés acted under both male and female patronage. Ambitious rulers and governors, senior administrative officials, and women from the elite all functioned as patrons. Patronage could be taken up by individuals, families, royal courts, or institutions.

These multibranched relationships formed the basic social and political units that composed premodern Muslim societies. This political and economic pattern was particularly widespread in the Ottoman Empire, where belonging to these networks was a significant component of individual identity in the organizational patterns of social activity and the political power structure.[4] The connection between protégé and patron was not legally contractual but was binding. Both parties could negotiate their standing. It was even possible to dissolve the connection and move on to a different one, or even to maintain several complementary relationships. However, the fundamental need to participate in such a relationship for motives of social profit, funding, and cultural immersion always existed.[5]

Patronage was expressed in various forms: stipends as a kind of salary to enable scientists and artists to set aside time for their activities; ceremonial awards of symbolic items; collections of artifacts or existing learned treatises; orders to produce specified new artifacts; and allocation of space for scholars and craftsmen to work in and produce within the palace, court, or an endowed institution. Patrons were able to direct and influence scientific activity in these ways.

Patronage in art, architecture, and the sciences had been very common in Muslim societies since the beginning of the early Middle Ages. An elaborate terminology evolved in Arabic to denote the different types of ties, benefits, and services that formed the different layers of patronage. The social practice of patronage became more elaborate over time, with a growing variety of patrons and protégés. From the late medieval period—that is, the Ayyubids and since—this included scholars, among several groups of civilians, in contrast to the earlier period, which was characterized by a more military type of patronage.[6]

In the Islamic world, as elsewhere, patronage was always a significant force in the development of science and art. With regard to the Ottoman world, we currently know more about the artists and artisans who were attached to well-known patrons than about the scholars who were pursuing science. However, the evidence allows us to assume that the modus operandi was similar.

Patronage of art and science was based on respect for the skills and knowledge of the artisans and scholars, and for the products of their labors. Behind the great moments in art and science we can find many instances of incentives offered by prominent patrons who demanded excellence. This demand and the need to always stand out from the rest encouraged competition and, at times, even bitter rivalry.[7]

This brutal competition for recognition and livelihood meant that scholars and artists had to excel in their vocation to reap the fruits of acceptance for themselves and their profession. Competition and jealousy between artists in the imperial court—including suspicion of each other's innovations, ultimately escalating to murder—formed the basis for the plot of Orhan Pamuk's *Benim Adım Kırmızı* (My name is Red).[8] The elite sponsors, on their part, enjoyed the prestige they acquired from patronizing the arts and sciences: it was important for building their status and power. They had much to gain from being associated with great scientific work. The more renowned a court became for its wealth, power, and refinement, the more artists and scientists it attracted, including those of the highest caliber.[9]

The rulers were the most influential patrons, and their tastes were a model for emulation that filtered down and penetrated society throughout the country. Gülru Necipoğlu showed how Ottoman identity changed during the period of Süleyman I and became more introverted; the change was demonstrated in art and architecture and the artifacts produced by the imperial workshops of the capital, the agents for transmitting the new fashion to the broader Ottoman elite and the provinces.[10]

Rulers, however, were far from being the only patrons of scientific work. As Emine Fetvacı has shown with relation to history writing and book making,[11] the bureaucratic class was also active and effective in expanding its patronage to scholars. In the Ottoman case, it seems, an especially wider array of individuals were able to insert themselves into the social practice of patronage, and in a very visible way.

The patronage system was one of the key factors in setting standards for excellence in the context of scientific work; this perception shaped the expectations of patronage in return. Excellence in the Ottoman scientific context combined conscious alignment with existing traditions and aspirations of renewal. This is what Marshall Hodgson termed "conservative florescence." In the early modern Islamic world, old traditions were fused and recast. There were major modifications, but usually within established lines.[12]

Indeed, totally new channels of creative activity had lower chances of securing the social recognition and financial backing of a patron. Patrons looked for the legitimacy acquired from an association with accepted heritage. Consequently, many scholars adapted themselves, maybe even unconsciously, to such expectations.

As in our modern world, economic policies of research have direct impact on the quantity and quality of results. Patronage is the premodern version of modern governmental funding of research, and according to supporters of the free market, it is not necessarily a wise policy, for either science or the economy. Terence Kealey, a British biochemist, is one of the clearer (and more provocative) voices on this issue. In his book *The Economic Laws of Scientific Research* (1996), he challenged the Baconian model of scientific and technological advance. It was Francis Bacon (d. 1626) who first proposed the "linear" model of technological advance, according to which governments fund academic research, which yields pure science, which underpins applied science or technology—all of which contribute to economic growth. In his alternative model, inspired by Adam Smith (d. 1790), Kealey suggests governments should allow laissez-faire mechanisms to drive results further. He claims that private funding of research within universities and the development of de facto universities (R&D departments) within industry breed positive competition that fosters science and technology, and increases countries' rates of economic growth.[13]

In 2008, Kealey returned to his thesis that entrepreneurs create a better research environment, but this time from a Darwinian perspective. In *Sex, Science and Profits* he emphasizes mistakes, good and bad luck, demands and necessities—rather than comfortably planned experiments—as the important engines of scientific and technological advances. As in Charles Darwin's theory of evolution, so in science and technology: the inventions, institutions, and products that best function in their environment will outcompete the others. If natural selection is not allowed to take place in science and technology, redundant, biased, and even false knowledge and skills will survive and reproduce. In other words, external factors such as governmental funding actually obstruct scientific progress.[14]

This is not the place to discuss the questionable moral dimensions of Kealey's model.[15] However, it is appropriate to consider his observation regarding the consequences of the dependence of academic science. Kealey argues that governmental hold of universities results in tyranny, curtailing researchers' freedom. Kealey refers to political pressures, but mostly he discusses how governments guide academic science and technology in specific directions, preventing evolution and development in others (which may be more relevant to the private sector and economic growth). Furthermore, in the current academic-economic system, scientists tend to work for recognition rather than the advancement of science.

In Kealey's analysis there are clues to understanding the characteristics of scientific output within the Ottoman patronage system, which compensated scholars who excelled in what Marshall Hodgson refers to as the "culmination," "delicacy," "complexity," and "subtlety" of the preexisting culture.[16] My own understanding of the process gives more value to experiments with new ideas, techniques, and social structures of scientific experience. Patrons changed; new patrons entered the system; new abilities and machines were acquired; and all that shifted the Ottoman scientific experience in ways that were not necessarily aligned with what had gone before. Social recognition and funding were also available to those who challenged accepted knowledge. Yet social patronage as the basic structure of scientific experience directed such activities to venues of continuation of the past that did not totally break with it.

The patron-protégé relationship not only was a financing factor and a means of social organization but also provided a physical location for activity. One important site was the *medrese*s, and in this context we must address the *waqf/vakıf* institution as a system that funded and managed schools. Amy Singer's studies reveal a great deal of Ottoman society's charitable work, including the expansion of its formal activity through endowed institutions.[17] The belief that allocation of one's property for public benefit is a religious act of charity that brings man closer to his god developed in the early Muslim centuries. By the Ottoman era, *waqf*s/*vakıf*s were common and took care of a wide range of communal services. In fact, the endowment became the principal tool of social charity. At the same time, these endowments honored the names and memory of generous donors and strengthened mutual commitment between the elite and the common ranks. One of the appropriate goals of the *waqf*s/*vakıf*s was occupation with knowledge and the people who involved themselves with knowledge.

According to Avner Ben-Zaken,[18] the *waqf/vakıf* system explains how science flourished in the early centuries of the Ottoman Empire and how its importance dwindled in the empire's latter centuries. Ben-Zaken suggests examining scientific activity in the Ottoman Empire as socioeconomic activity and not specifically as a cultural or intellectual product. He points to political, social, and economic structures that enable (or prevent) private and institutional scientific investigation in Muslim society. According to his thesis, the centralist structure of the Ottoman Empire enabled reinforcement of its control, and thus the empire could accumulate vast economic surpluses. These extra funds could be directed to support a wide range of significant intellectual activities.

This ability of centralized government and economic surpluses to finance the *waqfs*/*vakıfs* in general and the *medreses* in particular changed around the year 1700. During the seventeenth and eighteenth centuries, the empire suffered economic crises, and the political structure began a process of decentralization. Ben-Zaken notes two processes that negatively influenced scientific activity. The first was that local rulers became stronger as the empire's central authority weakened. For the first time, local rulers enjoyed the right to tax villagers in their provinces in return for an advance payment of a fixed land tax to Istanbul (the *iltizam* system). However, they were allowed to tax only a defined region, which was small compared to the entire empire, and their power to enforce the taxes was relatively limited. For both these reasons, they did not have significant surpluses that might have been directed to scientific activity. The second process was the rise of an agriculture-dependent market. The budget of the *waqfs*/*vakıfs* came largely from agriculture, but they could no longer cope with competitive forces in the market and their financial strength weakened. *Waqf*/*vakıf* administrators took steps to manage their finances more circumspectly in order to survive, and this necessarily reduced the *medreses*' activity.

Medicine under Patronage

Medicine was one of the fields in which the choices of the elite highly influenced scholarly activity. The Ottomans inherited from previous Muslim periods an Arab-Muslim medical tradition that viewed Galen's humoral medicine as the most learned and scientific of the time. The other medical theories and practices that existed in the Ottoman world (folk medicine and religious medicine) were just as popular among the elite as they were in other social segments. However, only physicians writing and treating within the Galenic framework as interpreted by generations of Muslims were supported by patrons. Indeed, the only medical institutions supported by the elite were hospitals that implemented Ottoman humoralism. Within this medical theory, the elite patronized new treatises, innovative ideas, and novel technologies.

One example of the influence of the patronage-protégé dynamic in the changing directions of science is the relationship between Sultan Mehmet IV and his personal physician and friend, Ibn Sallūm. The latter is renowned for authoring a medical encyclopedia by the name *Ghāyat al-itqān fī tadbīr badan al-insān*. The previous chapter discussed this treatise as an example of the tortuous translation and cultural assimilation route from Latin to Arabic and Ottoman Turkish and then to Persian. Here we emphasize the patronage of the sultan as an important factor in the acceptance and circulation of this treatise.

Ibn Sallūm was born in Aleppo in Syria, where he studied medicine and rose to become the local head physician. Later he emigrated to the capital, Istanbul, where he also attained fame due to his professional medical skills and social graces: the sources describe him as a pleasant-tempered man, an interesting conversationalist, an engaging storyteller with a fine singing voice. All these qualities brought him to the attention of the ruler, who assigned him to his court. Ibn Sallūm excelled at the sultan's court as well, again because of his combination of professional and social skills. His reward was appointment as the imperial chief physician. In this protective environment, he wrote a treatise that combined traditional structure and medical knowledge common in learned Ottoman medicine with new knowledge about chemical medicine from sixteenth- and early seventeenth-century Europe. Ibn Sallūm used chemical methods to prepare medications; moreover, in his prescriptions, he included medicinal materials from America.

Ibn Sallūm's innovation is limited. Some of the prescriptions were copied from treatises written in central Europe. He prided himself on including new medical knowledge, but in fact his medical outlook remained Gallenic-Ottoman. Ibn Sallūm adopted a few techniques from chemical medicine but rejected that paradigm's more fundamental principles, including its perceptions of the human body and how it functions. Yet innovation (even if it was combined with a familiar medical tradition) was exactly what brought Ibn Sallūm prestige and fame. The sultan, to whom Ibn Sallūm dedicated his treatise, was impressed. Mehmet IV rewarded the physician with a ceremonial robe to express his satisfaction, esteem, and benevolence.[19] Such an award of a splendid item of clothing at an official ceremony before an audience was a common practice in premodern Muslim society (as in other parts of the world). It was a means of showing preference for a noted personality and showering him with gifts and acclaim.[20]

Ottoman medical theory did not experience a turning point in the seventeenth century, but the clinical reality began to change during the eighteenth century, and a major theoretical shift occurred in the nineteenth century as the Ottomans moved from Ottoman humoral medicine to European medicine. The change was brought about under the aegis of the Ottoman imperial court and elite. Hospitals erected in the mid-nineteenth century in Istanbul demonstrated the decision of the Ottoman elite to promote medicine of a new kind. In 1845, Valide Sultan Bezmiâlem (d. 1853), the mother of Abdülmecid I (reigned 1839–1856), constructed a hospital and mosque in the capital's center.

Bezmiâlem's enterprise was firmly anchored in the Ottoman patronage tradition. Several outstanding women in the imperial family preceded her in building hospitals as charitable institutions and located them in the most important city centers of the empire, like the capital in Istanbul or Mecca, Islam's holy city. The structure and administration of the hospital also resembled Ottoman hospital tradition. The endowment deed specified that the hospital would offer free medical services for foreigners and the poor among the city' s Muslim community.

Under the traditional cloak, however, the content of Bezmiâlem's institution was new. It implemented European medicine of the nineteenth century and not the Greek humoral medicine in its Ottoman form, as was practiced in all previous Ottoman hospitals. More so than in the past, the hospital was subject to the continuous supervision of the central bureaucracy, in accordance with the Tanzimat spirit that sought to enforce centralized organization on state institutions. Moreover, the professional team at the hospital consisted of graduates of European institutions or new local institutions run in the European spirit.

Bezmiâlem's hospital was established after several decades during which the Ottoman elite openly introduced Western medicine into the empire. At the turn of the nineteenth century, a new medical system was inaugurated for the military with the help of European experts. Such was the naval hospital built by Selim III with the help of the Italians. The military medical school built by Mahmud II adopted French as a teaching language and was administered by a Viennese physician. Bezmiâlem's hospital was an important step toward disseminating European medicine among the broad civilian population and not only within narrow military circles—all this under the patronage of the sultan's mother, as part of the authorities' intentional policy.[21]

The Zeynep Kamil Hospital, founded in 1876 on the Asian banks of the Bosporus, continued the trend begun at the Bezmiâlem hospital. The 1876 hospital, like Bezmiâlem's hospital from 1845, was founded as an endowed institution for the city's Muslim community. The framework was traditional Muslim Ottoman charity, but the content was European medicine. In both hospitals some of the personnel had received training in

Europe or in new Ottoman medical schools. The Zeynep Kamil Hospital, however, went further. In an innovative spirit, the 1876 hospital was arranged structurally according to the pavilion system of European hospitals of that period. Such spatial organization enabled relatively easy expansion, as opposed to building a large central structure in which all the activities would be located. From then on, new Ottoman hospitals were formed according to the pavilion system.

The Zeynep Kamil Hospital also continued the tradition of Ottoman elite patronizing learned medicine, which during the nineteenth century translated into European medicine. In both cases, the initiative for the hospitals came from the elite. The Zeynep Kamil Hospital was constructed by a husband and wife. He was the former Grand Vizier, Yusuf Kamil Paşa; she was Zeynep Hanım (Lady Zeynep), the younger daughter of Mehmed Ali Paşa, the Ottoman governor of Egypt in the first half of the nineteenth century. As in Ottoman benevolence tradition, a private initiative mixed with public policy. This endeavor introduced a significant development: patronage of hospitals with a European flavor was now in the hands of the broader Ottoman elite, and not just those of the well-defined imperial family.[22]

Military Technology under Elite Patronage

Ottoman military technology, too, was developed within patronage that influenced the venues in which this technology was thought of, executed, and written on in the Ottoman Empire. As in medicine, the sultan's patronage carried special importance in developing such technologies; however, it was not only the sultans but also other key figures in the Ottoman military and administrative elite who changed the face of Ottoman warfare in their time. Together they demonstrate the close connection between military technology and elite patronage.

Sultan Mehmed II was described by his modern biographer, Franz Babinger, as one who focused most of his attention throughout his thirty-year reign on warfare. Art, architecture, literature, and science were fields of secondary importance for him and the elite surrounding him. This is the image procured from a comparison between Mehmed II, his father Murad II (reigned twice, in nonconsecutive years: 1421–1444 and 1446–1451), and his son, Bayezid II (reigned 1481–1512). Mehmed II wrote poetry: he left a *divan*, a collection of poems (eighty in number). Mehmed II was even unique in that his poetry was written in Ottoman Turkish and not Persian, as was accepted at that time. He enjoyed spending time in the company of poets, scholars, and *ülema*, whom he encouraged to converse and argue in their fields of expertise. We discussed above how Mehmed II invited mathematicians and astronomers from central Asia to his court. But these fields of arts and sciences were important only between wars and when the sultan was older, and fatigue and illness obliged him to take a break from warring.[23]

Indeed, Mehmed II is associated with various innovations connected to military technology in the broadest sense. He was keenly interested in European literature about military matters—an interest so well known in Europe that authors of treatises on these subjects dedicated them to the Ottoman sultan and sent him copies of their works directly. European rulers also sent the sultan copies of treatises on military topics to win his favor and please him. However, attempts to prevent the flow of contemporary updated military knowledge from Europe to the Ottoman Empire also took place, led by the Pope and the Italian states, which were in direct conflict with the Ottomans. Ultimately, however, these attempts were in vain.[24]

Mehmed II was especially interested in maps. Karen Pinto suggests the sultan had been a visually oriented person since childhood, in addition to being passionate about art and war in general.[25] He used the maps for practical, ideological, and aesthetic purposes. Contemporaries suggest maps gave visual rendering to Mehmed's present and future world dominion.[26] Meanwhile, he was the first important ruler-conqueror in history to make practical use of maps for military strategy. Since Mehmed II, cartography developed into a tradition within the Ottoman military. The needed intelligence on enemy environment was derived from reconnaissance and local informants. The extant maps demonstrate that detailed, militarily relevant information was depicted on maps and plans for operations like invasions and sieges.[27]

Mehmed started another tradition that lived on in the Ottoman central bureaucracy. Starting with him, Istanbul consulted European cartography to gain firsthand information about Ottoman European territories and frontiers. The Ottomans were surprisingly up-to-date. In 1573, during the reign of Selim II, one of the Porte's interpreters ordered from Vienna two copies of an atlas (containing uniform maps and supporting text) that had been published merely three years before.[28]

Mehmed II and his court were familiar with several geographical and cartographic traditions, including contemporary European mapmaking, mainly Italian, while also being interested in Ptolemaic texts (named for the second-century scholar Claudius Ptolemy). The court commissioned the project of translating several Greek cartographic treatises and maps into Arabic. Translations from Greek to Arabic and individual Greek manuscripts survived at the Topkapı Palace library. They were an intentional collection of science and philosophy that combined down-to-earth military involvements with Renaissance intellectual tastes.[29]

Mehmed was also the patron of Muslim cartographers (and following him, generations of Ottomans patronized Muslim geographers and cartographers). He sponsored the copying of a series of medieval Arabic geographical treatises containing stylized, decorative maps. Under the sultan's aegis, a selection of Arabic essays from the Middle Ages on geographical topics—essays that included elegant and ornamented maps—were copied and re-edited. Some of these manuscripts were deposited in the imperial palace libraries, while others were made available to the public through libraries in the new mosques in Istanbul. One assessment posits that the Timurid scholar Ali Kuşçu was most likely was the person who encouraged Mehmed II to take an interest in maps founded on Muslim geographical knowledge. Through his connections with Islamic centers of learning outside the Ottoman state, the sultan could have acquired maps and geographical texts in Arabic, or Ali Kuşçu may have brought them with him on his escape from central Asia. Some of the new Ottoman-Islamic maps from this period were found in the Ayasofya collection, where Ali Kuşçu resided and taught.[30]

Another military technology that interested Mehmed II was artillery. There is no precise information regarding the introduction of firearms into the Ottoman Empire, although it is clear that they entered through the Balkans and the Italian city-states during the fourteenth century.[31] The important issue is not their first appearance in the Ottoman scene but rather the point at which this technology was first used significantly, in a sufficiently great quantity and with enough efficiency so as to influence the outcome of battles.[32]

Before proceeding with the varied and intricate interactions between state patrons of firearms and technicians and soldiers, it should be stressed that even though the manufacturing of firearms was a state monopoly, the number of artisans manufacturing firearms privately multiplied rapidly toward the end of the sixteenth century. Villagers increasingly used firearms despite strict orders forbidding their use by the *reaya*, the non-elite segment of the Ottoman Empire. There were also periodic raids to enforce this rule by confiscating all firearms, but the orders and raids could not bring the arming of the population to a halt; with the constant and even growing demand for firearms, there was an increase in production, and vice versa.[33] In other words, the audience and market for the technological know-how discussed here with regard to Ottoman firearms were much wider than the Ottoman elite and those directly affected by it.

In many cases, sources attribute the integration of firearms in the Ottoman army to Mehmed II, which might tell us more of his image than of historical realities. Mehmed II was the first sultan to erect a state foundry for casting cannons (Tophane-i Amire) in Istanbul. The Ottoman plant was based, apparently, on a Genoese factory located on the slopes of Galata, which was the seat of the Genoese merchants from the pre-Ottoman era.[34] Mehmed II was also assisted by a number of European cannon specialists whom he employed at his court. A familiar example is Urban, the Hungarian cannon expert (according to different sources, he originated from Germany or Romania). Urban's cannons (especially the gigantic ones) played a decisive role in the conquest of Constantinople in 1453. Urban had defected from the Byzantine army when he did not receive the appreciation he expected, and Mehmed II welcomed him with open arms. Mehmed heaped a multitude of gifts on him and promised him an especially high salary; in exchange, Urban promised to cast cannons that no wall, including the fortifications of Byzantine Constantinople, could withstand. Within three months, near Rümeli Hisar—the citadel on the European side of the Bosporus—Urban did, indeed, cast a canon of vast dimensions that helped enforce the siege of Constantinople in preparation for its conquest. Thereafter, he cast the greatest cannon of all, which did indeed break down the walls of Constantinople.[35]

Urban was not the only military expert Mehmed II employed. Another renowned European at his court was Jörg of Nuremberg, a gunner who was taken prisoner by the Ottomans in Bosnia and served them for twenty years, until he escaped to Venice and, finally, to the court of the Pope in Rome.[36] At the same time, Mehmed II also made intelligent use of local craftsmen, who worked independently and separately from the foreign experts.[37]

Foreign advisors were an inseparable part of the Ottoman military and navy since the time of Mehmed II. They worked for the Ottomans through a complex network of patronage: some were associated with the sultan, but many formed part of lower-rank Ottoman groups, like viziers, *paşa*s, admirals, and so on. Foreign experts in the Ottoman military were a very heterogeneous group. They came from many European countries and very different circumstances: some were prisoners of war who were forced into the Ottoman Empire; others were deserters, mercenaries, converts, or adventurers who approached the Ottomans on their own initiative.[38]

Foreign advisors were the principal agents in adopting European military know-how, doctrine, and technology.

If in the early centuries the Ottomans relied on coincidental assortments of advisors, toward the end of the eighteenth century they began to organize and coordinate the activities of foreign experts. At this point the personal patronage between an Ottoman elite member and his foreign protégé added another layer, one of a more bureaucratic, impersonal relationship between the state machinery and a group of experts. Along with military preferences and considerations of individuals who were at the helm of the Ottoman state, there was now a process of creating an organizational memory that influenced decisions regarding the military's needs and priorities.

The Ottomans initiated a series of delegations that systematically transferred knowledge and skills in the areas they believed their own knowledge to be deficient.[39] Delegations from various countries were invited to help the Ottomans carry out reforms in various military concerns. The goal was to enrich the Ottomans with the most up-to-date military expertise. Numerous delegations were invited so as to avoid dependence on a single source of guidance. European countries, on their part, wished to establish a foothold in the empire and wanted to increase their influence on its decision-making centers by means of these delegations. In such a context, the German-speaking French, English, Italians, and Swedes were prepared to send delegations of professionals to the empire.[40]

The contribution made by European experts was sometimes quite limited: there were language and, principally, cultural barriers on both sides, which made interaction difficult. Some of the experts served as double agents: they served the Ottomans, but then reported on them to their dispatchers in Europe, so the Ottomans could not always place their full trust in them. Ultimately, the reforms initiated by the Ottomans themselves were more significant. At any rate, the presence of military delegations became familiar in Istanbul and in the empire's other political-military centers. The delegations themselves changed, but their presence was firmly fixed. Some of the professionals who manned the various delegations stayed for many years, learned Turkish and Turkish culture, and formed enduring relationships with Ottoman officers.

France offered long-term technical military assistance, which materialized through the continuous coming and going of numerous officers and technicians. (This phenomenon was discussed above in the context of changing educational options in the Ottoman Empire.) One of the people most identified with French investment in Ottoman science and technology (at least amongst Europeans) was Baron François de Tott (1733–1793), a French artillery officer of Hungarian origin. De Tott first arrived in the empire to serve as secretary to the French diplomatic delegation, and he learned Turkish in Istanbul. Years later he was sent to the Crimean Peninsula as the French consul and ultimately served as a military advisor to Mustafa III (reigned 1757–1774) and briefly also to Abdülhamid I (reigned 1774–1789). A bitter defeat of the Ottoman navy at the hands of the Russians in 1770 at Çeşme, near Izmir on the banks of the Aegean Sea, led the Ottomans to seek his assistance in reforming their army. Indeed, he arranged a series of reforms: improving the fortifications along the Straits of the Dardanelles as a defense against further invasion by the Russian navy; building new military schools; and forming a new artillery battalion that would specialize in rapid fire and easy mobility. De Tott published memoirs of his lengthy service to the empire, and his essays became a formative source that shaped the French perspective of a weak and passive Middle East all through the nineteenth century.

In the Ottoman Empire, in contrast, de Tott left a lesser impression. Ottoman sources depict him as a minor contributor to military reforms, and perhaps that is a more realistic description of his career in the Ottoman Empire. Indeed, there were numerous French experts who, just like de Tott, played an important part (even if not the principal role) in reforming the Ottoman army. De Tott was just one among several Frenchmen with similar career paths employed by the Ottoman state. This more reserved judgment of de Tott may have resulted also from tensions between political factions of the Ottoman elite. De Tott was involved in Ottoman politics, and rivals could have portrayed him negatively in contemporary sources. Moreover, his image was shaped by the debate over whether it was at all appropriate for the Ottoman state to obtain the assistance of foreign advisors and, if so, from which nations it was considered advisable to seek such assistance.[41]

The military contacts with German-speaking Europe were no less long, deep, and complex, starting with the Ottoman-Hapsburg military rivalry in the early modern period. The confrontations-cum-negotiations took place at several sites. One of them was Istanbul, where members of the court and the bureaucratic (diplomatic) and military elite met with Hapsburg representatives. Another site of Ottoman-Hapsburg engagement was along the 1,000-kilometer border through what is now Croatia and Hungary. The Ottomans who were exposed to the contacts there included those sent from the imperial center, local Ottomans (Hungarians, Transylvanians, etc.), Hapsburg exiles in the Ottoman domains, and soldiers in numerous fortresses. Since the beginning of the sixteenth century Ottomans were aware of changes in the Hapsburg weapons and ammunition, and organization and training of the military, and had infused these into their own system, but not necessarily as effectively.[42]

With the formation of Prussia and later Germany in the nineteenth century, the Ottoman engagement with German-speaking military systems intensified, diversified, and accompanied the Ottoman army through the long nineteenth century until the First World War. A series of delegations and, among them, dozens of Prussian and Bavarian officers were invited to the empire for the benefit of the navy and ground forces. They were generously financed by the empire. Among the first was Helmuth von Moltke (1800–1891). His involvement in the reforms of the nineteenth century was broad, spilling over from strictly military topics. Von Moltke mapped several regions in the Ottoman Empire and published his geographical and cartographical studies in both Europe and the empire. His charts of Istanbul, specifically, formed an essential step toward reconstructing the capital city.[43]

Among the Prussians who arrived toward the end of the Ottoman era were Wilhelm Leopold Colmar Freiherr von der Goltz (1843–1916),[44] Friedrich Freiherr Kress von Kressenstein (1870–1948),[45] and Otto Liman von Sanders, (1855–1929).[46] The three officers reached the empire before the First World War and became so influential that during the war they commanded Ottoman units on the eastern front. Von der Goltz was called out of retirement and received command of the front in Iraq, where he died of typhus in Kūt al-ʿAmāra a short time before the Ottomans defeated the British in 1916; Kress von Kressenstein served in Palestine, in the Suez Canal; and von Sanders was in command at Gallipoli before he, too, reached Syria-Palestine.

SCIENCE AND TECHNOLOGY AND THE OTTOMAN STATE INFRASTRUCTURE

Changes in Ottoman medicine and military technology demonstrate the ways in which patronage of the elite in general and of the sultan in particular engineered processes connected with science and technology. However, machines and techniques had their own agency, shaping in turn the Ottoman state organs.

The firearms industry—discussed above in the context of an elite patron who pushed for integration of new military technology—is a classic example of the reciprocal relationship between the state and technology. The introduction of firearms into Europe played a decisive role in the transformation process in the early modern era involving formation of states out of the weak medieval political entities. Some scholars view the entrance of firearms as the "military revolution," whereby relationships changed between state and society, and between cultures.

This process occurred in both Europe and the Islamic world. Marshall Hodgson claimed in his classic *The Venture of Islam* that it was no coincidence that circa 1500 there emerged three Islamic empires of unprecedented magnitude: the Mughals in India, the Safavids in Iran, and the Ottoman Turks. In all three, gunpowder played decisive roles (albeit not exclusively) in the formation of effective centralized systems.[47] Only the rulers of large, centralized states could afford the technology of firearms and the new means of protection it necessitated.

The thesis regarding the relationship between firearms and states was moderated over time. The common perception today holds that a process of change (rather than a dramatic event) alters the structure of a state, a society, and an economy. Nevertheless, it is still agreed that relationships between state and military technology were (and are) of great significance to both the state and technological innovation.[48]

The example of firearms is only one of many. Projects in transportation and communications from different periods of the Ottoman Empire show that the state was always involved in initiating and executing large-scale infrastructure projects that both served and challenged the centralized state.

Public Buildings, Roads, and Bridges: The Example of Sinan

Sinan (born around 1490) served as *mimar-başı*, the official court architect, for no less than fifty years, from 1537/1538 to his death in 1588.[49] A long life and the opportunity to work during one of the Ottoman Empire's cultural and economic zeniths enabled him to erect hundreds of buildings of various kinds.

Sinan was born into a Turkish-speaking Christian family from Anatolia and was enlisted by the *devşirme* during the reign of Selim I in the early sixteenth century to serve in the Janissaries. His name is apparently an abbreviation of the nickname Sinanüddin (meaning "the steel spearhead of faith"), which was quite common among the Janissaries, all of whom were new converts to Islam. Sinan was trained as a carpenter and participated in military campaigns under Süleyman I in Belgrade, Vienna, Mohács, Baghdad, and Corfu. He thus gained experience in building and maintaining military structures until his appointment to the post of imperial court architect.

Sinan built mosques, *medreses* and *mektebs*, mausoleums, *imarets* (soup kitchens), hospitals, palaces, bathhouses, bridges, and roads. He built impressive individual and complex structures. Sinan was responsible for not only the architecture of the structure but also the interior design. His two largest projects were the Süleymaniye in Istanbul and the Selimiye in Edirne. The Süleymaniye, a complex of fourteen buildings around a majestic mosque on a steep hill in Istanbul, was built for Süleyman I between 1550 and 1557. The Selimiye was built for Süleyman's son, Selim II, between 1564 and 1575. In the newer mosque, Sinan attempted (unsuccessfully) to surpass the central dome of the Ayasofya in height and diameter.

As an architect, Sinan also built and maintained aqueducts, dams, and reservoirs. Part of his responsibility was to ensure a consistent supply of water to his buildings. Only after his time were the responsibilities of the architect separated from those of the commissioner of the waterworks, who was subordinated to the office of the chief architect.

Beyond the quantity and variety of his works, Sinan was an architect of the highest level in planning, execution, and aesthetics. He knew how to address Ottoman tradition. He was practical in repeating works, while at the same time he revealed creativity and suggested innovative elements in design and engineering solutions. All these created a new peak in Muslim architecture. He became so renowned that many buildings were actually attributed to him in retrospect, though it is doubtful that they were the fruit of his own planning and execution. In some cases, apparently, Sinan only provided the sketches of a general idea, and the execution was in the hands of a lower architect in the field. In other cases, the connection to Sinan was, possibly, imagined in an attempt to benefit from his reputation without any real historical basis.

Sinan is not, perhaps, a representative example of the careers of most Ottoman architects: he is a well-known figure who overshadows those who preceded and succeeded him. The anonymity of other architects is evident, for example, in the large number of buildings whose architects are unknown, and we cannot necessarily establish who built one particular building or another. This is where the difference between Sinan and his contemporaries is evident. In Sinan's case, later generations know with greater certainty how to attribute specific buildings to him, or else do so out of wishful thinking. However, despite Sinan's extraordinary status, his career is composed of patterns that repeat themselves in other life stories as well, namely:

- Architects operated within the framework of an office subordinate to the sultan's court. This was the institution that headed building projects, with individual architects acting on its behalf rather than as independent artisans.
- Architects were trained in palace schools and then acquired their skills in the various branches of the administration and army.
- Architects belonged to the administrative-military elite, the Askeri group.
- Architects were organized into a hierarchical group, as expressed in their titles and salaries.
- Court architects throughout the empire received instructions and orders from the central authorities in Istanbul.
- Court architects were contractors who realized the ideas of their patrons. They did not initiate buildings and had to execute their patrons' wishes regarding the identity of the structure, its location, and its style. Even the most senior among them had only limited artistic license.

Together, these points emphasize the extent to which the activity of building strategic infrastructure, both military and civilian—like water conduits, transportation, and public buildings—and thereafter the ongoing maintenance were executed by the Ottoman state even in its premodern phase. During this period, as Sinan exemplifies and as seen with the elite patronage of scholars, the involvement of the authorities was not institutional but rather personal: members of the elite, motivated by social obligation and what they understood was expected of them, took it upon themselves to initiate such activity.

The Architects of the Long Nineteenth Century: Different but Similar

A jump ahead in time to the nineteenth century reveals both the lines of continuity and the lines of difference. Evidence exists of the continuing personal involvement of the sultans and other senior members of the Ottoman elite in public works construction, but the organization of the involvement and its justification were different. In previous centuries, state representatives administered state infrastructure as a personal charity that also carried political significance. In the nineteenth century, such construction was considered a public-political act, performed by official bodies as part of broad state policy, but an act that also involved the significance of personal charity.

The agenda of the nineteenth century aimed at rebuilding an empire and fostering modernity. The restructuring of the state apparatus regulated and set a standard across institutions, including building construction. The various court and elite building projects for both official and private purposes transformed physical sites, social action, and the iconography of the Ottoman Empire.

A further change with regard to architecture involved a change in stylistic characteristics, partly in response to cultural encounters with Europe. Already during the eighteenth century, the Ottoman elite had appropriated Baroque forms. Istanbul's Nuruosmaniye Mosque by the Covered Bazaar marks this change. In the nineteenth century, notes Zeynep Çelik, France and the Ottoman Empire were connected in a shared world of imperial ideology, technology, and strategy.[50] Such a cultural dialogue and experiments led the Ottomans to introduce a neo-Classical style during the nineteenth century. The architectural pluralism was evident on various levels, from visual setting, to decorations, to form and usage of space. These were new interpretations of traditional elements.[51]

The Ottoman Armenian Balyan family of architects was instrumental in executing many such new-styled projects. During most of the nineteenth century, members of the family built hundreds of buildings for the Ottomans: palaces, mosques, pavilions, and other lesser royal buildings, as well as public buildings.[52] The religious projects were especially noteworthy, for they were designed by architects from a non-Muslim minority. Until that point, court architects had been either Muslim-born or converts, like Sinan. Now—during the long nineteenth century—the Ottomans employed non-Muslim Ottomans and also non-Ottoman architects for their royal projects. The Balyans did not start this trend but symptomize the change and gave further impetus to a major professional shift in architecture that started in the late eighteenth century.

The Balyans' stylistic taste was flamboyant and highly eclectic yet original, while interpreting and synthesizing historical forms of Ottoman architecture.[53] The family was rooted in both the Ottoman and French worlds. Some of them became architects within the traditional Ottoman system. Other members were sent to France to study in Paris and then returned to Istanbul and were recruited into the palace's architecture corps.

The fame of the Balyans, our knowledge of different family members, and the ability to associate particular sites with specific members (rather than with the family as a whole) are both a symptom and an agent of the change in the perception of architecture as an art form and not just a practical and functional craft. The anonymity of a bureaucratic institution, as was the case with the earlier court architects' corps, was replaced with appreciation of the merits and singular contribution of architects-cum-artists.

Their individual input notwithstanding, the Balyans and other architects of the period were still commissioned by the state and executed projects initiated by the imperial elite. Sutlan Abdülaziz (reigned 1861–1876), for example, was said to have personally approved the plans for his new palace, the Beylerbeyi on the Asian shore, which the Balyans built for him in the 1860s. Ottoman art historian Filiz Yenişehirlioğlu describes the outcome as an imaginative ensemble that fused Islamic ideology, Ottoman culture, Western political concepts, and a European way of life.[54] The new projects were managed in the public sphere in order to direct public action. Since the eighteenth century, the rise of a middle class and the march toward modernity led Ottoman society to look for new foci of urban life. Patterns of intimate domestic interaction were replaced by more public ones, occurring in coffeehouses, taverns, gardens, and squares. The state led the process of a growing public domain: the reincarnation of old imperial gardens as public parks became routine; coffeehouses were commonplace in new endowments. The state and elite transformed the use of private and state land to offer new communal focal points in the urban fabric to contain public activity, control public behavior, and maintain order.[55] All these projects reflected a different Ottoman state and society and the new tastes and artistic preferences of the elite; the architects of the new age contributed their input, but still basically executed commissioned projects.

Telegraphs, Clocks, and Trains: The Story of the Nineteenth Century

In the sixteenth and seventeenth centuries, the Ottoman state was already taking care of the empire's main roadways within the cities and between them. Central roads (certainly in the large cities) were cleared and often paved, as well as inspected by various bodies to ensure that they were traversable. The state also organized navigation on the large rivers (i.e., the Danube, Nile, Tigris, and Euphrates) and along the Bosporus. In Istanbul, sailing was a readily available means of urban transportation. The state also cared for the principal interurban roads to ensure trade and the movement of couriers and the army. Inns for refreshment and changing horses were erected at central points on the roads for use by official state couriers, merchants, and travelers. Interurban transport was carried out by beasts of burden, principally camels but also horses and donkeys or wagons pulled by horses or oxen. In many cases, parallel use was made of the various means of transportation, so it appears that most roads were well maintained, enabling the passage of wagons.[56] Nevertheless, communities were still isolated, and movement between them was rather limited. Difficulties of climate and topography, the condition of the roads, dangers in the form of bandits, and also the financial cost of transportation severely limited the movements of people and knowledge from place to place. The result was a preference for the local: local products, traditions, festivals, and so on.[57]

Over the course of the nineteenth century, a new reality developed thanks to a network of railways and telegraph lines that were laid throughout the empire. As opposed to Europe, but similar to China and Japan, these were separate systems in the Ottoman Empire. In many instances, the telegraph was able to reach locations where the railway was still unfamiliar and vice versa.[58]

Developers of communication and transportation projects in the nineteenth century had to cope with two interrelated obstacles: the cost of the projects and the financial risk involved in them. In order to execute projects like these, capital had to be raised from the public, and the state had to provide guarantees. The state was prepared to commit to a large project if it suited its national interests, and the authorities had to interpret whether the interests justified such large-scale investment. In fact, in many instances, such projects were not only national, but international, and hence required complicated cooperation. The projects succeeded (or failed) thanks to businesspeople who knew how to make the connection between advanced technologies and political requirements, and could interpret the changing international map and present stable business plans. If they were hasty and hoped for quick profits, the plan usually collapsed.[59]

The telegraph system was introduced to the Ottoman Empire in 1839, when the technology was only in its infancy. An agent of Samuel Morse (1791–1872, known for having contributed to the invention of the telegraph and the code named for him) visited the sultan's court in Istanbul, but the equipment did not function well and left a negative impression. A further, much more successful attempt to introduce the telegraph took place in 1847. This time the demonstration impressed Sultan Abdülmecid, and the telegraph came into use during the 1850s.[60]

The Crimean War (1853–1856) provided leverage for advancing the technology. The war made essential speedy communication between the allies (against Russia) and between the forces and their military commanders in the Crimean Peninsula. These circumstances brought about the establishment of the Ottoman telegraphic network, which connected the main centers of the empire—Crimea and the Balkans among them—and connected the empire with the European system, which also included the submarine cable to the Black Sea.[61]

The next large telegraph project was the transcontinental network to Iraq. The project's local goal was partly directed by the persistent Ottoman policy to enforce centralized rule on a province that was difficult to manage, for example, because of its autonomy-seeking tribes. The international goal was to connect Europe to India. The project was the subject of dispute among the European countries and among various factions in the empire. Factions disagreed, for example, as to whether the route should run through the Tigris Valley or that of the Euphrates. Moreover, laying the cable required fixing clear and binding boundaries in Iraq for the first time in history to determine where the cable ceased to be Ottoman and became Qajari-Persian; traditionally territorial boundaries had never been clearly defined or applied. Another issue was which country would hold the concession. Both Britain and France coveted it and promoted their interests at the highest level. Britain even began laying a submarine cable that would circumvent Iraq, out of concern that its French rival would take control of the intercontinental cable. The Ottomans, for their part, were prepared to consider a new submarine cable that would circumvent Iraq, but stipulated as a condition that it would also connect Alexandria to Istanbul. The connection of these two cities was a most urgent task for the empire because it would also ensure that the new cable to India would go through (and not circumvent) Istanbul. Ultimately, the project failed for technical reasons; shortly after it commenced, the cable broke and could not be salvaged. This led to reconsideration of the proposed intercontinental cable through the Tigris Valley.[62]

Finally, in 1877, the empire operated the seventh-longest telegraph cable network in the world. The telegraph system brought about a communications revolution throughout the empire, created new employment for operational and maintenance personnel, and changed the face of Ottoman diplomacy.[63] The system radically transformed the nature of communication between Ottoman subjects and the imperial center. Telegraph was used to besiege the center with petitions from the provinces, as the new medium brought about expectations of efficiency and expediency.[64]

The period of Abdülhamid II was a further step in the link between state patronage and the spread of new means of communication. The underground projects in Istanbul (the Tünel), the Hejaz railway between Damascus and Medina, and the Baghdad railway, which was supposed to be the foundation for the ambitious Berlin-Basra line, are the largest and best-known examples, though many smaller local projects were also realized.[65] The reason for this patronage was the sultan's policy of enforcing an Ottoman Sunni-Muslim identity throughout the empire to unite and centralize the Ottoman Empire as a means of repulsing external Western pressures; to strengthen the sultan's personal status at home; and finally, to establish the image of the sultan as Caliph with all the religious and political significance of being the ruler of all Muslims, all over the world, even beyond the political boundaries of the Ottoman Empire.[66]

The clock towers are one of the technological projects most identified with Abdülhamid. These had been introduced into the empire in the sixteenth century, but during the Hamidian period they fulfilled many more significant and sometimes contradictory roles. The project began as a one-time event, a festive way of celebrating the Silver Jubilee of the sultan's reign. Within a few years, however, dozens of towers embellished the public areas of Anatolia and the Arab Middle East.[67]

The Hamidian clock towers were both functional and ideological. The clocks were double-faced: they marked Western time (*alafranga*), which was characterized by dividing the day into a fixed length (of twenty-four hours, each lasting sixty minutes), but also traditional Muslim time (*alaturca*). The combination allowed the Hamidian state, as Avner Wishnitzer showed,[68] to enforce uniformity, obedience, and regularity, which were so important to the drive for centralization; to express Islamic identity publicly through the towers; to advertise an attempt to calibrate interaction with the outer world while holding on to indigenous traditions; and to continue notions of sultanic rule as clock towers visually showed the sultan's benevolence to his subjects. The towers were dedicated to the community, as were mosques or any other charitable institutions. (Elite philanthropy persisted as a religious-cultural ideal, a social practice, and the physical concrete reality of sites.)[69]

In fact, clock towers embodied gift exchange, a very powerful political and cultural tool in Ottoman society since its inception. Some towers were donated by the sultan, while many others were products of local initiative. Towers were built to attract the sultan's attention, to be in his good graces, and to promote local interests. They were so successful exactly because they served both imperial and local interests: those of the central bureaucracy, the palace, the provincial administration, and local communities. Thus, on the ground, from the point of view of the local urban communities who constructed these clocks, the focus was on civic and urban identity and pride.

The Hejaz Railway project also demonstrates the complex activity of the sultan and the systems of the state, sometimes in combination and sometimes as separate entities. Abdülhamid II was personally involved in the Hejaz Railway project. This was common knowledge, and contemporaries referred to the project as the Hamidian Railway (a wordplay in Arabic: *al-sikka al-Ḥamīdiyya* also means "the praiseworthy railway").[70] Besides being the moving spirit behind the project, the sultan also invested his private fortune in it by, for example, purchasing tracts of land for the railway line in the Jordan Valley on its route southward from Syria to the Arabian Peninsula. Indeed, the precise route of the railway branches becomes understandable when the identity of the owner of the tracts of land in certain regions (the sultan himself) is taken into account. The route of the branch on the western side of Jordan River crossed the Yarmouk River and turned in the direction of Samakh (today Israeli Tzemakh) at the southern end of Lake Tiberias, and then southward to Bīsān (Beit She'an) at the junction of the Jordan and Jezreel Valleys. The topography on both sides of the Jordan River is flatland, so the final selection was apparently connected to the will of the sultan to ensure that the railway would cross his lands. In this way the sultan could closely supervise the project's execution and after its completion also enjoy the fruits of the new transportation by developing agriculture on his lands.[71]

Abdülhamid's policy of purchasing land for himself as a private individual led to his becoming the owner of the largest landholdings in the empire. Indeed, he fastidiously improved his property. Abdülhamid's motivation was two-pronged: he was, of course, interested in the financial profits, but he also exploited his land to realize political policies intended to strengthen the empire's sovereignty. The lands were carefully selected according to their strategic locations. It was then possible to use the sultan's private lands to build new cities, to settle nomads in permanent settlements and bring their clans under a certain measure of supervision, to settle Muslim refugees from the Balkans and Caucasus, and to defend sensitive border regions by preventing others from seizing control of them.[72]

The projects that the Ottoman State promoted from the nineteenth century onward in the fields of transport and communications became international endeavors in several different aspects. The technological complexity and high financial costs were beyond the reach of the Ottomans. The empire was obliged to several projects simultaneously and, of course, had to deal with the ongoing financing of its institutions. All this took place under a growing cloud of difficulties, the result of the absence of balanced budgeting throughout most of the nineteenth century. In order to obtain funding, the state turned to its inhabitants, requesting and sometimes demanding that they donate monies. Elites were expected to imitate the sultan and contribute large sums of money. Lower-rank state employees, civil and military personnel, were requested to donate a portion of their salary to the Hejaz Railway.[73]

Effective propaganda aimed at the empire's Muslim population succeeded in soliciting donations from civilians. An excellent example of this propaganda's success is a 1900 book in Arabic by Muḥammad ʿĀrif ibn al-Sayyid al-Munīr al-Ḥusayn al-Dimashqī, a scion of a well-to-do family in Damascus. The author refers to the Hejaz Railway as "increasing and eternal happiness" (*al-saʿāda al-nāmiya al-abadiyya*) and discusses the multifold advantages for Muslims. The book reflects intense identification with the Ottoman Empire in general and the project in particular, probably the product of a previous successful campaign among the Ottoman Arabs; it became a means of attracting further support.[74]

At the same time, the Ottoman state needed external financial backing and tapped into two different reservoirs. On one hand, toward the end of the nineteenth century and the beginning of the twentieth, the Ottoman state nurtured pan-Islamic sentiments in accordance with Abdülhamid's posing as the Caliph. The Hejaz Railway was presented as a pan-Islamic campaign, and Muslims outside the Ottoman borders were urged to contribute. The project did, indeed, fascinate broad audiences and gain wide Muslim attention. The shah of Iran contributed a large sum, and many Muslims from as far away as India and Burma in the east and Morocco in the west added their humble funds.[75]

While tapping into Muslim support, the empire also took advantage of various European countries for many infrastructure projects, borrowing money and enlisting technical help in the form of professional personnel and machinery. Even the Hejaz Railway, heralded as a Muslim project, involved European expertise and banking. The Ottoman state found several willing allies in Europe. In addition to France, Germany, Italy, and Belgium, the lesser colonial forces were present as well in the manpower.[76]

The German engineer Heinrich August Meissner (1862–1940) oversaw the construction with an iron fist. He worked for several years in the Ottoman Balkans and Anatolia in construction of railways, rose to senior executive posts, and eventually was appointed chief engineer to the Hejaz

Railway, the largest Ottoman technical project. His linguistic abilities (he knew Turkish well), his sense of tact and diplomacy with his Ottoman superiors, and his managerial skills made him indispensable. Yet European technological expertise in this project went deeper than Meissner's work at the top: his task force included both Ottomans and Europeans. In fact, for long periods, only half of the workers were Ottomans. However, as the project progressed south, reaching the proximity of Mecca and Medina, where no non-Muslim can enter, Muslims were preferred over foreigners. By that time there were qualified Ottoman engineers whom Meissner was able to employ.[77]

European countries were interested in increasing their involvement in the Middle East and expressed willingness to invest in the technological infrastructure in order to strengthen their authority in the region. Such civilian projects complemented the military ones, whose history goes back to the eighteenth century. Daniel R. Headrick, already in the early 1980s, claimed that science and technology have always been significant tools of an empire. Both were marshaled to assert authority—through their marriage to appropriate motives.[78] Recently, Martha Hanson has shown how medical maps of China were manifestations of imperialist powers whose function was to distill knowledge and legitimate colonial control.[79] Nineteenth-century Ottoman infrastructure is a case in point for both the Ottomans and the European powers.

SCIENCE, STATE, AND THE STATE ABOVE IT: THE (SEMI)COLONIAL CONNECTION

The involvement of foreign powers in transport and communication projects toward the end of the Ottoman Empire was different in character, aims, and intensity compared to earlier periods. The difference was the result of the new colonial context that had been introduced into European Middle East policy during the nineteenth century. Under the colonial umbrella, science and technology, toward the end of the empire, were sometimes implemented in different countries simultaneously. Now, more than ever, cooperation and the flow of Eastern and Western knowledge resulted from the states' interests and not only from personal contacts and human curiosity. The colonial mantle created a new kind of relationship between scientific activity and the state.

The complicated relationship between science and technology and the state(s) explains various projects: why they were executed, how they were carried out, and when they were realized. For example, the introduction of modern roads in Alexandria at the turn of the twentieth century—including the choice of specific materials and technology regarding asphalt pavements, drainage, and illumination—is fundamentally tied to the social and political processes that linked Egypt, the regional Ottoman reality, and the British colonial presence.[80]

The case of Istanbul, a city not under direct colonial influence, was similar, although the scale obviously was much greater as Istanbul was the capital of an empire. Zeynep Çelik regarded the nineteenth-century plans to regenerate Istanbul as "grand schemes"—a witty expression to simultaneously refer to the deviation from the ordinary Ottoman use of urban space (the huge magnitude [maybe megalomania] of some of the plans) and convey the aura of intrigue and contrivance. The plans to transform Istanbul, the Ottoman capital, into a Western-style capital were specific and included spatial rearrangement, visual realignment, and new infrastructure. The plans that remained on paper and the projects that were realized were the outcome of a subtle and delicate dialogue between impositions and internal forces and heritage. Hence, some of the architects invited to offer new urban forms and outlooks never actually visited Istanbul. Maybe it was a condescending European attitude that led them to consider it unnecessary to study the actual site and its topography and current reality before imposing their vision from above. It seems, however, that the Ottomans who commissioned such plans did not intend necessarily to follow through with them; they were aware these plans did not really correspond with the actual needs and abilities of Istanbul. However, the Ottoman elite wanted to situate their capital with the rest of great European capitals, like Paris and Rome, which were rejuvenated during the second half of the nineteenth century. The elite were interested in concrete and practical measures to administer and regulate the capital better in terms of communication and transportation. At the same time, the Ottomans considered themselves part of the European discourse on modern image and design.[81]

Along with construction of transportation and communication infrastructure, the establishment of quarantines and isolation camps in the Middle East as a defense against epidemics also formed part of the complex (semi)colonial fabric. In the nineteenth century, several outbreaks of new and especially virulent worldwide epidemics occurred, including typhoid and cholera, both severe digestive tract illnesses with high contagion and mortality rates. Cholera progresses quickly, and an infected victim can dehydrate and die within hours due to uncontrollable severe vomiting and diarrhea. During the nineteenth century the mortality rates were about 40–60 percent. Typhoid, by comparison, was a lighter malady: mortality rates were "only" 5 percent among children, but rose to 25 percent among teenagers and adults, and climbed to 50 percent among the elderly.[82]

The intensity of these outbreaks and the means to limit, control, and contain them were brought about by advancements in technology and scientific knowledge. In the realm of transportation, new inland and naval routes were opened. The opening of the Suez Canal in 1869, accompanied by a rousing fanfare, was a significant step in the Middle East. With the development of transcontinental and maritime transport, the nineteenth-century world became "smaller" than ever. Travel became speedy, available, efficient, and cheap in comparison to the past.

The period witnessed an unprecedented intensification in the movement of people, commodities, and ideas across the globe. Among the unwanted travelers were illness and epidemics, which also acquired greater mobility along the immigration and trade roads, the routes of pilgrimage, and tracks of military advance. The uncontrolled movement of illness was not a new phenomenon, of course, but the new means of transportation created a new reality of a world without borders, according to the perception of people of the nineteenth century. It was a question of volume and velocity: with the steamboats, more people traveled so much quicker that disease carriers were able to infect people in faraway places, whereas before they often fell victim to disease before reaching their destination. This was the first wave of modern globalization.[83]

In the realm of scientific medicine, during the second half of the nineteenth century the transmissibility of disease transformed from a hypothesis into a certainty. In order to cope with the globalization brought on by transportation and diseases, several international conferences were called toward the middle of the nineteenth century to deal with matters of health and sanitation. In practice, these were European conferences whose main interests were European. Their goal was to promote international cooperation to protect Europe from the spread of diseases that were likely to reach Europe from outside its borders. The means were familiarly colonial: borders were charted between Europe (and the West) and the rest of the world, and methods of quarantine and isolation were decided on for "the other" in the East, who—they believed—was the source of new diseases.

The region believed to be especially threatening to Europe's health was the "gateway to the East": the area we refer to today as the Middle East connected Europe to India, the subcontinent, which was the source of cholera. Disease reached Europe through Russia as well, but the pilgrimages to Mecca and Medina were perceived as being especially dangerous. In such mass events, conditions were unsanitary, providing a fertile ground for the outbreak of epidemics. Moreover, the hajj season brought together pilgrims from the Indian subcontinent, generally accepted as the source of cholera even before the scientific discoveries, with pilgrims from all over the Muslim world. In such mass events clothes and bodily fluids were likely to transmit the disease, usually without any awareness.

The outbreak of cholera among Muslim pilgrims in Mecca in 1865, which culminated in epidemics across Europe and North America that struck millions of victims, brought about a shift in international opinion to favor the restriction of importation.[84] To prevent the spread of other epidemics from Mecca and Medina, European countries forced the Ottoman Empire to set up transfer terminals in its territory, for example on the coast of Sinai. At these stations, pilgrims returning from Mecca were isolated under difficult conditions for several weeks in order to allow time for symptoms of illness to appear, if indeed they had been infected.[85]

While formally agreeing, European powers in fact showed a double standard, and cooperation in implementing actual anti-epidemic steps was sometimes ambivalent. The British colonial rule in India, for instance, banned Indian Muslim pilgrims from making the pilgrimage to the hajj in Mecca in times of cholera outbreak.[86] Yet the British also understood the political risk of agitating their Muslim Indian subjects by restricting access to the hajj, a fundamental Islamic practice. They also thought about their worldwide mercantile projects, were afraid to upset their Muslim populations, and were apprehensive about the possibility that international mechanisms might diminish their sovereignty in India.[87] Britain and the other European powers also engaged in rival attempts to establish influence in the region of the Ottoman Empire.[88]

In Ottoman Palestine, as in other Ottoman provinces, the local administrative bodies (*majlis al-idāra* in Arabic; *meclis-i idare* in Turkish) were responsible for taking active measures against public health hazards and agricultural diseases. The cases of Haifa and Jerusalem demonstrate how local agencies were hard-pressed to deal with disease. The authorities could make use of several European hospitals that had been established in the province since 1839, with the beginning of the Tanzimat reforms. Some of these hospitals were identified with specific countries (British, German, French, American, Prussian, Russian, Habsburg, and Italian) or with religious communities (Jewish, Catholic, Anglican, and

Protestant). But the local municipality was responsible for dealing with the extensive responsibilities regarding health and sanitation. In fact, of all its responsibilities, the municipality was most concerned with health. Indeed, public cleanliness was imperative for maintaining public health and preventing the spread of disease. The local administrative bodies had to achieve the goal of clean streets with limited authority and restricted funds, while coping with frequent interventions from local European consuls who expressed concern over the well-being of their citizens in the Ottoman province.[89]

The provincial *majlis*es corresponded intensively with the imperial center regarding health measures in general and communicable disease in particular. Such matters were not just a local concern, but rather became imperial worries due to their international consequences. Hence, the central government involved itself in the precautions required for preventing the spread of epidemics in Ottoman Palestine and monitoring the general health situation in the region. As the Ottoman bureaucracy evolved and became more professionalized throughout the nineteenth century, health-related edicts came from several specialized ministries: not only the Ministry of Interior (Dahiliye Nezaret), but also the Ministry of Military Schools (Mekatib-i Askeriyye), which included a medical school.[90]

Ottoman Palestine was perhaps a more sensitive case, but more or less the same events occurred in other Ottoman provinces, as the example of Beirut illustrates. This province was created as late as 1888, and both the imperial center and the local urban literate elite fused content and form to this administrative-political unit. Health measures were of special importance in creating municipal governance. Quarantines in particular were highly contested and had to be enforced with military force on many occasions. Yet the authorities insisted. In addition to specific sites used as quarantines, usually closer to the port, they even introduced on a basis of need a *cordon sanitaire*, a sanitary line around the border of the municipality of Beirut. The city was under (almost) constant siege.

Beirut, a busy Levantine port city, was prone to epidemics due to the growing numbers of travelers, pilgrims, and merchants visiting its shores. Practical and functional aspects aside, the imperial center wished to establish a firm Ottoman hold in the Arab provinces, present Beirut as an ideal urban microcosm and an exemplar of order for the international audience, and establish a dominant mercantile and tourist spot in the eastern Mediterranean (an aim shared by the local elite as well). For these purposes, extensive and frequent correspondence was maintained between the local authorities and Istanbul. Under the fear of an upcoming epidemic, the exchange also carried a sense of urgency. On top of it, French and British experts were called upon not just to advise in times of crisis, but also to participate on a routine basis in the work of health inspection and health boards. Some of these foreign doctors were local residents, teachers in the Christian colleges and/or practitioners in the missionary medical institutions; other experts came directly from the European mainland.[91]

At this stage, the Ottoman Empire was politically, economically, and militarily weakened. Previous scholarship has explained that the enormous human and financial efforts invested were aimed at presenting a modern and scientific Ottoman face, and therefore the empire cooperated with these international health initiatives. However, a large percentage of the Ottoman elite bureaucracy, certainly those involved directly with the reforms, believed wholeheartedly in the idea of a family of nations based on unity and equality of culture. For them, science and technology were of paramount importance, as in the late nineteenth century they were crucial criteria in gaining membership into the club of progressive nations. This was an abstract concept that was not necessarily anchored in specific, realistic political and economic realities.

Science and technology in the late Ottoman Empire were embedded in the specific realities of the state apparatus in the late nineteenth and early twentieth centuries: its political and financial abilities, its infrastructure, and its priorities. At the same time, these features also exhibit continuity of notions about legitimacy and perhaps also the necessity of involving state bureaucracy in how science was done.

The involvement of nonscholars in science is not unique to the Ottomans; however, the organized manner in which nonscholars were actively involved in shaping science and technology due to their formal positions and rank in the bureaucracy, which this chapter has shown, was uncommon prior to the modern state. Today we have governmental bodies such as ministries of science and technology. This is a formal and practical application of the concept that the human assets of the state should and must be channeled to contribute to its quality of life, social and economic resilience, and personal and national security. These state institutions involve people who may (or may not) have a formal background in science, and who may (or may not) have practiced science and technology professionally. Not their scientific credentials, which may not exist, but rather their bureaucratic function is what gave them authority to define, categorize, evaluate, and fund science. They thus played a pivotal role in systemizing and organizing what and how things are done in science. In the

Muslim world prior to the Ottoman case, as well as in other premodern states, personal and patrimonial patronage of scholars and science was a major form of action in the scientific scene. The Ottoman case, however, is one of the first cases where we can trace formal, impersonal bureaucratic formats as an important feature of scientific experience as early as the early modern period.

CONCLUSION

Ottoman Science

The journey in this book has moved back and forth between broad universal perspectives and the specific Ottoman outlook, and between the different worlds that nourished the Ottomans. The object of this concluding section is to emphasize the unique Ottoman characteristics: the traits that turned a system of knowledge and practices—enriched by Muslim, Arab, Anatolian, Turkish, Persian, Asian, Byzantine, Mediterranean, and European traditions—into something unique to the Ottoman mind.

A TEACHER AND A STUDENT: MURTAḌĀ AL-ZABĪDĪ AND ʿABD AL-RAḤMĀN AL-JABARTĪ AS OTTOMAN SCIENTISTS

Murtaḍā al-Zabīdī, whose contemporaries in the Arab Middle East regarded him as a monumental figure, was born in India in 1732, immigrated to Yemen in the middle of the century, and then moved to Cairo, where he died in the plague of 1791. He was the most successful eighteenth-century scholar-migrant from the Indian Ocean: some of his teachers preceded him, but al-Zabīdī's achievements surpassed theirs. Given his extraordinary erudition, he occupied a unique place among the *ʿulamāʾ* of his generation. His authority rests with two major literary projects, which are also the largest of their kind. His *Tāj al-ʿArūs min Jawāhir al-Qāmūs* (The bridal crown of the pearls of the dictionary) was the most comprehensive Arabic lexicon in the classical tradition of Arab-Muslim philology and lexigraphy. Al-Zabīdī followed the important medieval dictionaries, like Ibn al-Manẓūr's *Lisān al-ʿArab*. His other major accomplishment was *Itḥāf al-Sāda al-Muttaqin* (Gift of the god-fearing Sayyids), a distinctive commentary on al-Ghazzālī's *Iḥyā' ʿUlūm al-Dīn* (The revival of religious sciences), an eleventh-century manual for Muslims covering topics from routine daily life to matters of belief, ritual, piety, and purity of heart.

Equally important was the magnitude of his networks. Al-Zabīdī was at the center of an especially intricate and widespread social and professional web. He truly enjoyed meeting people, who flocked to his house in Cairo, especially during the pilgrimage season. Unlike other Cairene scholars, he mastered several languages and hence had the skills to allow such direct contacts: in addition to Arabic, he knew Ottoman Turkish, Persian, and some Georgian. He interacted with different social and professional groups, and his contacts included courts and ruling houses (including the Ottoman sultan Abdülhamid I), provincial and rural notables, military officers and civilian bureaucrats, and middle-class (and lower-standing) people. His geographical interests encompassed all the major Ottoman centers but stretched impressively outside the Ottoman domains, from western Africa to North Africa and the Balkans, the Black Sea, the Caucasus, central Asia, India, the Hejaz, and the Sudan.

Al-Zabīdī was a loyal Ottoman with many contacts among the Ottoman elite. He also identified with the state and integrated culturally and socially. Textual evidence in his Arabic works confirms that he had an Ottoman Turkish readership beyond that of Arabic speakers. He mentioned senior Ottoman *ülema* from previous centuries who would have been familiar to Ottoman Turkish speakers rather than Arabic readers in Egypt. He also referred to events in Ottoman history, such as the conquest of Constantinople and Crete, which more significantly impacted the core area of the Ottoman Empire from the Balkans to central Anatolia than they did Egypt. At the same time, al-Zabīdī cultivated a pan-Islamic identity. His works express a sense of unity that transcended contemporary political borders. Rarely did he mention contact with a non-Muslim, and he had minimal exposure to Europe and Europeans.

A noted feature of his intellectual and religious interests was al-Zabīdī's close contacts with Sufi *tarīqas* (brotherhoods). He nurtured and valued his relationship with the orthodox establishment while associating and fully identifying with the Sufi milieu. He was active in several *tarīqa*s but did not belong exclusively to any of them (let alone found a new branch). Al-Zabīdī merged different prevalent epistemologies in the Muslim world—theology, prophetic tradition, and mysticism—and he wished to fuse disciplines and harmonize legal and religious studies with the natural sciences. He not only wrote but also conducted his life this way. His contemporaries could consume through him different types of knowledge and tap into different sources of Muslim legitimacy.[1]

One of al-Zabīdī's numerous students was very impressive himself: ʿAbd al-Raḥmān al-Jabartī (1753–1822), an Egyptian polymath who also wrote the biography of his teacher and mentor. Both student and teacher shared interesting similarities in their perception of knowledge and its diverse manifestations. Their careers, as a social process, unfolded in similar fashion.

Al-Jabartī was a member of a well-known Egyptian *ʿulamāʾ* family that originated from the Horn of Africa in the region currently known as Djibouti and immigrated to Egypt at the beginning of the sixteenth century. Al-Jabartī's father was a wealthy Ottoman official and a scholar. He was very well connected in Egypt, as well as in other Ottoman provinces and imperial capital, Istanbul. ʿAbd al-Raḥmān was the only son, out of many children, who survived childhood illnesses and reached maturity. Therefore, he inherited all of his father's wealth, did not have to earn a living, and was able to devote his time to studying and writing. He held no official position, but ʿAbd al-Raḥmān created a name for himself as a leading scholar, maintained that reputation, and cultivated connections with religious figures of diverse schools. He associated with both Al-Azhar followers, attracted to their orthodoxy, and numerous Sufi *tarīqa*s, identifying with their mystical outlook.

Al-Jabartī wrote three treatises dealing with Egyptian history that express different attitudes toward the French conquest. In the first essay, *Taʾrīkh Muddat al-Faransīs bi-Miṣr* (The history of the French in Egypt), from 1799, al-Jabartī appeared impressed by the advanced French technology. His positive impression cooled over the years. In *Maẓhar al-Taqdīs bi-Zawāl Dawlat al-Faransīs* (The appearance of sanctity: The end of French rule) (1801), al-Jabartī was already writing under the influence of the French defeat at the hands of the Ottomans and the British. In the third and last chronicle, *ʿAjāʾib al-Āthār fī al-Tarājim wa-al-Akhbār* (The wondrous works of biographies and chronicles), he sounds rather reserved, even ironic or cynical.[2]

Al-Jabartī addressed science and technology in all three essays. He provided an especially detailed description in his chronicle *ʿAjāʾib al-Āthār*, which is broad and comprehensive and covers 133 years of Egyptian history, from the end of the seventeenth century to the French conquest. In the text, al-Jabartī combined dozens of references to the local *ʿulamāʾ* who excelled in a various fields of knowledge. Such integration, even fusion, between religious and rational fields, discussed in Chapter 1 with reference to biographies of Anatolian and Syrian *ʿulamāʾ* from the sixteenth to the eighteenth centuries, was relevant to the Egyptians during the long eighteenth century as well.

Al-Jabartī referred in detail to French science and technology. Unlike his teacher, he was in direct contact with Europeans and was interested in observing them. His writings portray Egypt as a site for the practice of the sciences in the late eighteenth century. He had an avid interest in mathematics, astronomy, astrology, medicine, and divination techniques, usually grouped in contemporary Arabic sources under the heading "uncommon sciences" (*al-ʿulūm al-gharība*). He wished to explore the natural and supernatural worlds, and utilize this knowledge in matters of governance and legitimacy in Egypt.[3]

Al-Jabartī's numerous references to French science and technology include, for example, comments on French medical administration—what we would have termed "public health." Al-Jabartī mentions the custom of not burying the deceased close to residential areas and discusses how the French impose quarantines in outbreaks of plague. They stipulated against funerals in times of pestilence, ordered the burning of clothes worn by deceased people, and tried to prevent prostitution. Al-Jabartī also mentioned the French ventilation of homes, especially during epidemics. He then provided an explanation for the logic behind this precaution based on miasma etiology (miasma theory based the origin of disease in pollution emanating from rotten matter found in graveyards, swamps, and sewage).[4]

Al-Jabartī's first treatise discusses the French in an impressed and positive tone, referring to their various instruments and engineering developments.[5] In the second and third chronicle, he included criticism. The change in tone is easily apparent in al-Jabartī's depiction of French rule as being corrupt.[6] Such criticism did not replace appreciative description, but was added to it. In an oft-cited passage, Al-Jabartī described a "miraculous" gristmill, powered by the wind. He was also impressed by the great speed with which the French paved roads and maintained them by paying bonuses to workers using cheap but efficient tools. For example, they exchanged the buckets used by the Egyptian laborers for small barrows with a larger capacity. Having iterated all that, al-Jabartī repeatedly reminds readers that the French destroyed existing structures, including mosques, to make way for new buildings and roads and to create the open spaces they favored in the city.[7]

Al-Jabartī, on his part, did not avoid forming relationships with French scientists even if he did not completely understand some of the things he saw. He described the libraries and laboratories that the French erected in the homes of Egyptian dignitaries left empty when they fled Cairo. He visited French institutions several times, and extensively accounted for the various treatises he studied, the pictures he viewed, and the observation and measuring instruments displayed for him. He described the astronomical instruments he saw as strange, and as "achieving results which minds like ours cannot comprehend."[8]

Al-Jabartī also documented his experience of the "Republic of Letters." The French experts in Cairo happily accepted local guests who wished to visit their libraries and laboratories. They received the visitors with a smile, says al-Jabartī, and cheerfully engaged in discussion and shared their texts and devices if they sensed a fellow scholar.[9] Al-Jabartī built on his own experience in visiting the French scientific institutions, but his description is collaborated by French narratives to reveal that al-Jabartī was far from being alone in such visits.[10]

The social and intellectual spaces—which crossed the borders of politics, religion, and language and merged Europe with the Middle East—continued to expand throughout the early modern period and into the beginning of the modern period. This description may sound too ideal, and we should not gloss over real and meaningful rifts and gaps in understanding between the participants in such encounters. There were barriers of language and worldviews, and encounters were not devoid of political meaning as well, on both parts. All these factors defined the meetings, but even if they charged them with much more than intellectual meaning, they did take place.

OTTOMAN PATTERNS OF SCIENTIFIC ACTIVITY

In many ways, al-Zabīdī and al-Jabartī were atypical of their time. Their breadth of knowledge and the ease with which they passed between types and sources of knowledge and tried to merge them were unusual. Their careers were also unique: how many educated Ottomans devoted their entire lives to studying? This was not just a matter of financial capabilities but also a cultural norm. Numerous examples offered in this book depict the normative practice of combining intellectual activity with a day job to support oneself (including cases in which such a job was not an economic necessity). Moreover, many Ottomans earned a living from work that was not necessarily in their fields of interest. They were compelled to postpone and minimize the time for study to their leisure time. Some utilized the twists and turns their careers took, including assignments to missions throughout the empire, to further their studies with new teachers. However, the volume and scope of their interests matched the style of the era; their careers were not just possible but even worthy of note and praise.

In that case, what do the careers of the teacher and student noted here teach us about the modi operandi of Ottoman science? The following four points serve as a summary of the issues addressed in the book.

Ottoman scientific activity occurred in a multilayered, eclectic, and practical manner. While this description may be broadly applied to other premodern scientific systems as well, the Ottoman case was an extreme example of mixture. Ottoman culture based itself on a rich past and an even richer present. For six hundred years, Ottomans were closely connected to numerous and varied cultures. The social organization in the framework of the household and the process of instilling scientific activity and technology in the administration of the state paint a businesslike and practical approach to science and technology. Pragmatism was not devoid of symbolism of patronage of science and the arts, whether through individual or state patronage. These patterns appeared in all domains of state, societal, and cultural operation—from education, law, and finance to the military—and now we see them also in science. Interests interlaced: those of the center and the periphery, of patrons and scholars, and functional use alongside symbolism of power, status, and identity. All these social components and cultural meanings wove the fabric that was science and technology in the Ottoman Empire.

The Ottoman Turkish language contributed a tool for scientific use by the Ottoman elite. Ottoman was the language in which cultural activities on an imperial level were conducted. Al-Zabīdī, from India, produced magnum opus in Arabic but made use of Ottoman Turkish sources; al-Jabartī wrote the history of Egypt in Arabic and was not disconnected from the rich Ottoman Turkish historiographic traditions of the imperial center (even if he was in no hurry to acknowledge his debt to generations of earlier historians).[11] Ottoman Turkish was the cultural language of the elite (the everyday language was Anatolian Turkish); whoever wanted to attain the recognition and patronage of the authorities had to present work in their language.

This is not to say that the use of local languages for learned writing became redundant. Those who did not seek imperial patronage, were not well versed in Ottoman Turkish, or purposely wanted to address their own community (in addition to or instead of writing in other instances to the imperial center) continued to use local languages. Literary and scientific writing not only continued to exist but even flourished in the various Balkan languages, Arabic, Hebrew, and so forth. In the case of Arabic, it was much more than a local language, as it also retained its position as a link to a wider Islamic audience outside Ottoman domains. Translation, alongside the writing of original works directly in Turkish for the first time, created an important body of knowledge in Ottoman Turkish.

Networks and patronage formed an important organizational factor in scientific activity. Households served as the social organizational unit and, in some cases, also supplied the physical location in which scientific activity took place. Sometimes, official patronage metamorphosed into an endowed institution. In this case, the scholar benefited from the *waqf/vakıf*. He received a salary and had the privilege of eating in the institution's *imaret*, as well as other benefits. But even in the absence of a legal framework, the relationship between members of a social network—especially in the context of a patron (a member of the elite) and a protégé-scholar—was equally binding on both sides. The social interaction influenced scientific activity. Financial backing made it possible for people to devote time to science; the exact choice of a topic or an objective was compatible or in agreement with the patrons' fields of interest (real or imagined).

The Ottoman state had brought a measure of bureaucratization to scientific activity since the early modern period. Elite patronage of science and art was a Middle Eastern Muslim tradition, but the process of methodical organization and hierarchy in scientific activity is traced to the Ottoman state of the early modern era. The relationship between patron and protégé was personal and intimate, but during the Ottoman period it became institutionalized under the wing of the state. Scholars became holders of official posts at the court and in the bureaucracy. Some of these positions had no direct connection to their scientific interests (like Katip Çelebi's post as an army clerk). In other cases, the connection was most evident (like Takiyüddîn's dual hats as imperial astronomer-astrologer at court and at the Istanbul observatory). The process was slow as well as partial. Al-Zabīdī and al-Jabartī, for instance, did not have bureaucratic positions within the Ottoman Empire. Nonetheless, it was important for them to cultivate connections with others who were part of the official system and cooperated with the state; they became part of an unofficial state outreach into the non-state segment of society. Scholars attained pivotal status in the lap of the state. Institutionalization, however, did not make the personal relationship redundant but, rather, added a context to scientific activity.

OTTOMAN INNOVATION

This book reconstructs Ottoman conceptualization of "novelty" and its relevance to science and technology. Innovations migrated back and forth across Eurasia, between the Ottoman Empire, Europe, and Asia alongside (almost) constant conflict. Co-optation of knowledge from other cultures occurred occasionally in conjunction with both official and unofficial political, military, and cultural confrontations with the same cultures. In the words of Eric Dursteler, bazaars and battlefields coexisted as different patterns of interaction, side by side.[12] The relative importance of specific channels of knowledge was a matter of change. During the early modern era, the various channels of knowledge—to and from the Ottoman realm—were more or less balanced. No side was clearly favored or more advanced than the other. The protagonists of this book were not necessarily occupied with the questions of "origin" and "novelty" in the first place.

This situation changed, of course, from the eighteenth century onward, as European sources of knowledge became more and more influential. Christian Europe was always an important source of knowledge for the Ottomans. Even when, in the middle of Süleyman I's reign, a trend emerged toward introversion as part of defining the new Ottoman identity, taste, and fashion,[13] the cultural dialogue with Europe continued. Indeed, already in the seventeenth century, Ottomans marked an accelerated interest in new medical knowledge from Europe. Ottoman observers were perfectly aware that specific knowledge they encountered was new and that its source indeed lay in Europe, as when, for example, chemical medicine entered the Ottoman Empire at the end of the seventeenth century. This development led to significant diversion from humoral medicine founded on botany—the accepted tradition in the Ottoman Empire. Accordingly, chemical medicine was named *tibb-i cedid*, or "new medicine." The title of chemical medicine in the Ottoman language shows that Ottoman authors were enthusiastic about it exactly because of its novelty and newness, or at least they presented it that way. However, this new knowledge had very limited impact outside elite scientific culture. Even within the elite, the new medicine was framed and contained by standard medical concepts of the time.[14]

In the eighteenth century, lively discussion emerged among the Ottoman elite surrounding the concepts of innovation and originality. Words such as *beauty*, *innovation*, *invention*, *fresh*, *original*, and *imagination* often appear in contemporaneous poetry and prose. Similarly, new motifs in design and spatial organization were exhibited in the arts and architecture. People of the era accepted these structures as the height of good taste.[15] Interestingly, in Europe, from the end of the eighteenth century, involvement and experiments with new forms and experiences became something of a fetish as well. However, in Europe the concept of modernity gained momentum to become a category of thinking. There evolved self-interpretation of a new historical path; with it came the distinction between periods and complete separation of the new from the old system.[16]

Only in the nineteenth century did Ottoman discourse give rise to new expectations, experiences, and possibilities departing from traditional concepts and points of references. The new concepts and the enormous amount of new knowledge that was assimilated by the Ottomans determined together changes in the Ottoman way of life that had not occurred in the past—certainly not at such an accelerated pace or as powerfully or profoundly as were taking place at the time. Seemingly minor changes—such as adoption of the French metric system for measuring weight and distance, and the introduction of sewing machines in general and those manufactured by Singer in particular—were made possible by self-assurance and recognition of the need for and legitimacy of new experiences; these in turn brought about profound and irreversible social and economic changes in the way people perceived their physical space, work, and production.

The Ottoman Empire officially adopted the metric system of weight and measurement in 1869, but it was already familiar from the 1830s. It had already been applied in certain areas of the empire and in various fields of commerce—the medications market in Istanbul and the tobacco market, for example, which were connected to the international markets. But in the fall of 1869, a five-year process began to turn the metric system into the obligatory system throughout the empire. This put an end to the various traditional weight and measurement methods used throughout the empire, where even identical terms were differently defined. This situation caused difficulty in the transfer of goods and thus challenged commerce within the empire and hampered efficient supervision of trade. The impetus for regulation and unification was in keeping with the goals of the Tanzimat, the organizational reforms of the structure of the state and society that took place in 1839–1876. Moreover, the metric system was intended to reduce the margin of error and the ability to operate illegally or dishonestly. The reality was less optimistic, as with most other reforms. The level of unification that the metric system was assumed to be able to achieve was perhaps unrealistic in the first place. Inspections after implementation of the new method showed that even a decade following their initiation, the implementation was only very partial, even in government ministries.

The two methods—the old and the new—were applied in conjunction by the public and the authorities. Indeed, the government printer published official exchange tables—proof of its coming to terms with the transition. The former system was so familiar that the public had difficulty making a speedy transition to the new method of measurement. The new system was also essentially different from the traditional method and required new terminology. Hence, the Ottomans were required to accustom themselves to a new way of thinking and to express themselves in a new language, a process that cannot be quickly or easily managed. Only in the 1930s did the enforced implementation of the Turkish law of weights and measures complete the transfer in the core areas of the empire (at this stage, already the "former" empire) to the metric system. The transition period took no less than sixty years—not significantly different from the parallel process in France, the birthplace of the metric system, where it took fifty years for society to fully assimilate the method.[17]

The Singer sewing machine was produced by an American company that established itself in Europe as well, and later in the Middle East. The machines first appeared in Beirut in 1860 and toward the end of the nineteenth century became a familiar household appliance throughout the Middle East. The Singer Company knew how to market the machine very well: its agents were spread out all over the Middle East and were able to offer easy payments (Singer was the first to offer monthly credit payments in the Middle East) as well as training, parts, and repairs in the client's home. The novel marketing strategy and pricing, alongside the prestige of the machine as a high-quality, reliable instrument, allowed the company to enter many homes. The machines also enabled the transfer to industrial production and mass-marketing of finished products, including clothes, footwear, and umbrellas. Until then, many families had purchased raw material and sewed these necessities at home. Tailors and shoemakers upgraded their workshops, and women entered the workforce en masse. Thanks to the household sewing machine, women could continue working at home and produce quantities of quality goods that they could sell. They were able to contribute to their family income without having to leave home and be in contact with strangers (employers and clients).[18]

The new metric system and new sewing machine worked differently in late Ottoman society, but both opened fresh financial horizons and generated new social realities. At the same time, they also reaffirmed the traditional order, whether the centralized state or the gendered, hierarchical family and society. The sewing machine belonged to "small" technologies (to follow Uri Kupferschmidt's term) that were operated in a "democratic" way. Devices, objects, and know-how—including typewriters, cameras, pianos, lightbulbs, electric appliances, and cars—were available on the market and not controlled from above. The metric system, however, was implemented from above. Both inventions required familiarization, but then created new personal environments and brought about new social relations and habits; they also drove individuals and groups toward regional and national integration.[19] Ottoman scientific experience was a complicated and evolving mosaic whose many different pieces coexisted in harmony, competitiveness, and tension.

NOTES

INTRODUCTION

1. Karl R. Popper, *Conjectures and Refutations: The Growth of Scientific Knowledge* (London: Routledge and Kegan Paul, 1963), 216.

2. Peter Dear, "What Is the History of Science the History *Of*? Early Modern Roots of the Ideology of Modern Science," *Isis* 96 (2005): 390–406.

3. Ibid.

4. Naomi Oreskes, "Science and Public Policy: What's Proof Got to Do with It?," *Environmental Science and Policy* 7 (2004): 369–383.

5. Thomas S. Kuhn, *The Structure of Scientific Revolutions* (Chicago: University of Chicago Press, 1962).

6. Daniel Nadav, *Medicine and Nazism* (Jerusalem: Hebrew University Magnes Press, 2010).

7. Paul K. Feyerabend, *Against Method: Outline of an Anarchistic Theory of Knowledge* (London: NLB, 1975); Feyerabend, *Science in a Free Society* (London: NLB, 1978).

8. John Pickstone, *Ways of Knowing: A New History of Science, Technology and Medicine* (Chicago: University of Chicago Press, 2001).

9. A sample of Michel Foucault's monographs pertaining to the history of science include: *Madness and Civilization: A History of Insanity in the Age of Reason* (New York: Pantheon Books, 1965); *The Order of Things: An Archeology of the Human Sciences* (London: Tavistock, 1970); *The Archeology of Knowledge and the Discourse of Knowledge* (New York: Pantheon Books, 1972); and *The Birth of the Clinic: The Archeology of Medical Perception* (London: Routledge, 1973).

10. Yehuda Elkana, "Unmasking Uncertainties and Embracing Contradictions: Graduate Education in the Sciences," in *Envisioning the Future of Doctoral Education: Preparing Stewards of the Discipline—Carnegie Essays on the Doctorate*, edited by Chris M. Golde and George E. Walker (San Francisco: Jossey-Bass, 2006), 65–96.

11. Kapil Raj, *Relocating Modern Science: Circulation and the Construction of Knowledge in South Asia and Europe, 1650–1900* (Basingstoke: Palgrave Macmillan, 2007).

12. Dorothy E. Smith, *The Conceptual Practices of Power: A Feminist Sociology of Knowledge* (Boston: Northeastern University Press, 1990).

13. Sandra Harding and Kathryn Norberg, "New Feminist Approaches to Social Science Methodologies: An Introduction," *Signs* 30 (2005): 2009–2015.

14. David Bloor, *Knowledge and Social Imagery* (London: Routledge and Kegan Paul, 1976); Barry Barnes, David Bloor, and John Henry, *Scientific Knowledge: A Sociological Analysis* (London: Athlone, 1996).

15. Harry M. Collins, *Changing Order: Replication and Induction in Scientific Practice* (London: Sage, 1985); Collins, with Trevor Pinch, *The Golem: What You Should Know about Science* (Cambridge: Cambridge University Press, 1993).

16. An example of the arguments between the different schools is the sharply critical article by Bloor on Latour and Latour's reply: David Bloor, "Anti-Latour," *Studies in the History of Philosophy of Science* 30 (1999): 81–112; Bruno Latour, "For David Bloor . . . and Beyond: A Reply to David Bloor's Anti-Latour," *Studies in the History of Philosophy of Science* 30 (1999): 113–129.

17. Bruno Latour, *Reassembling the Social: An Introduction to Actor-Network-Theory* (Oxford and New York: Oxford University Press, 2005).

18. Bruno Latour and Steve Woolgar, *Laboratory Life: The Construction of Scientific Facts* (Los Angeles: Sage, 1979); Bruno Latour, *Science in Action: How to Follow Scientists and Engineers Through Society* (Cambridge, MA: Harvard University Press, 1987); Latour, *We Have Never Been Modern*, translated by Catherine Parker (Cambridge, MA: Harvard University Press, 1993).

19. Bruno Latour, "On the Partial Existence of Existing and Nonexisting Objects," in *Biographies of Scientific Objects*, edited by Lorraine Daston (Chicago: University of Chicago Press, 2000), 247–269.

20. Timothy Mitchell, *Rule of Experts: Egypt, Techno-Politics, Modernity* (Berkeley: University of California Press, 2002), chap. 1, "Can the Mosquito Speak?," 19–53.

21. Khaled Fahmy, "Women, Medicine, and Power in Nineteenth-Century Egypt," in *Remaking Women: Feminism and Modernity in the Middle East*, edited by Lila Abu-Lughod (Princeton, NJ: Princeton University Press, 1998), 35–72; Fahmy, "The Anatomy of Justice: Forensic Medicine and Criminal Law in Nineteenth-Century Egypt," *Islamic Law and Society* 6 (1999): 224–271; Fahmy, "Modernizing Cairo: A Revisionist Narrative," in *Making Cairo Medieval*, edited by Nezar AlSayyad et al. (Lanham, MD: Lexington Books, 2005), 173–199; Fahmy, "The Essence of Alexandria (Part I)," *Manifesta Journal* 14: 64–72; Fahmy, "The Essence of Alexandria (Part II)," *Manifesta Journal* 16: 22–27.

22. On Barak, *On Time: Technology and Temporality in Modern Egypt* (Berkeley: California University Press, 2013).

23. On Barak, "Three Watersheds in the History of Energy," *Comparative Studies of South Asia, Africa and the Middle East* 34 (2014): 440–453.

24. Marshall Sahlins, "'Sentimental Pessimism' and Ethnographic Experience, or, Why Culture Is Not a Disappearing 'Object,'" in *Biographies of Scientific Objects*, edited by Lorraine Daston (Chicago: University of Chicago Press, 2000), 158–202.

25. Following Pamela H. Smith, *The Body of the Artisan: Art and Experience in the Scientific Revolution* (Chicago: University of Chicago Press, 2004).

26. Recently, Justin Stearns summarized nicely the major trends in the history of premodern Islamic science; see his "Writing the History of the Natural Sciences in the Pre-modern Muslim World: Historiography, Religion, and the Importance of the Early Modern Period," *History Compass* 9, no. 12 (2011): 923–951. Here I am concerned with the historiographical concerns that are relevant to the history of Ottoman science as a subfield of the history of Islamic science, and the next section focusing on the Ottoman period evolves out of this one.

27. Joseph Needham et al., *Science and Civilisation in China*, 7 vols. (Cambridge: Cambridge University Press, 1957–2004). The series continues to be published after Needham's death under the auspices of the Needham Research Institute, commemorating his name by devoting research to science, technology, and medicine in eastern Asia.

28. Nathan Sivin, "Why the Scientific Revolution Did Not Take Place in China—Or Didn't It?," *Chinese Science* 5 (1982): 45–66. This is a much-cited article that appears regularly in anthologies. I relied on the revised version dated August 24, 2005, that includes his current thoughts on this question, which he revisits regularly. The updated version is archived on his private site at University of Pennsylvania: http://ccat.sas.upenn.edu/~nsivin/scirev.pdf.

29. Benjamin A. Elman, *On Their Own Terms: Science in China, 1550–1900* (Cambridge, MA: Harvard University Press, 2005).

30. George Saliba, *Islamic Science and the Making of the European Renaissance* (Cambridge, MA: MIT Press, 2007).

31. The exhibition website is http://www.1001inventions.com. The exhibition and its catalogue have ignited a heated debate on *islamsci* (the listserv of the Commission on History of Science and Technology in Islamic Societies) regarding their academic credibility. From May 2012 until October 2012 and again in October 2014, the listserv was busy with messages, alternatively debating and defending the academic virtues of the exhibition, and this historiographical trend in general. For a review of the exhibition catalogue, see Sonja Brentjes, "1001 Inventions: The Enduring Legacy of Muslim Civilization; edited by Salim T. S. al-Hassani; Washington, D.C.: National Geographic Society, 2012; 3rd ed.," *Aestimatio* 10 (2013): 119–153.

32. Sonja Brentjes raises this claim in her review of Ahmad al-Hassan's book on medieval chemistry and alchemy: "Ahmad Y. al-Hassan, *Studies in al-Kimya': Critical Issues in Latin and Arabic Alchemy and Chemistry*, Texte and Studien zur Wissenschaftsgeschichte, Band 4 (Hildeshein, Zürich, New York: Georg Olms Verlag, 2009), ix, 320pp.," *Centaurus* 53 (2011): 67.

33. Roshdi Rashed, ed., *Encyclopedia of the History of Arabic Science*, 3 vols. (London and New York: Routledge, 1996). See also Sonja Brentjes's book review in *Technology and Culture* 40 (1999): 399–401.

34. Ahmad Dallal, *Islam, Science, and the Challenge of History* (New Haven: Yale University Press, 2010).

35. I wrote on the historiography of Ottoman medicine in Shefer-Mossensohn, "A Tale of Two Discourses: The Historiography of Ottoman-Muslim Medicine," *Social History of Medicine* 21 (2008): 1–12.

36. Adnan Abdülhāk Adıvar, *Osmanlı Türklerinde İlim*, 5th ed. (Istanbul: Remzi Kitabevi, 1991).

37. Marwa Elshakry, "When Science Became Western: Historiographical Reflections," *ISIS* 101 (2010): 98–109.

38. Gönül Cantay, *Anadolu Selçuklu ve Osmanlı Darüşşifaları* (Ankara: Atatürk Kültür, Dil ve Tarih Yüksek Kurumu, 1992).

39. Şerefeddin Sabuncuoğlu, *Cerrahiyyetü'l-Ḥāniyye*, 2 vols., translated and edited by İlter Uzel (Ankara: Atatürk Kültür, Dil ve Tarih Yüksek Kurumu, 1992).

40. Aydın Sayılı, *The Observatory in Islam* (Ankara: Türk Tarihi Kurumu Basımevi, 1988).

41. A collection of his articles was published in Ekmeleddin İhsanoğlu, *Science, Technology and Learning in the Ottoman Empire* (Aldershot, UK: Ashgate, Variorum, 2004).

42. Kemal Çiçek, editor-in-chief, *The Great Ottoman-Turkish Civilisation* (Ankara: Yeni Türkiye, 2000), vols. 3 and 4: *The Ottomans*.

43. Robert Dankoff, *An Ottoman Mentality: The World of Evliya Çelebi* (Leiden: Brill, 2004).

44. Patrick H. Hutton, "The History of Mentalities: The New Map of Cultural History," *History and Theory* 20 (1981): 237–259; Fedwa Malti-Douglas, "*Mentalités* and Marginality: Blindness and Mamlûk Civilization," in *The Islamic World from Classical to Modern Times: Essays in Honor of Bernard Lewis* (Princeton, NJ: Darwin Press, 1989), edited by C. E. Bosworth et al., 211–237.

45. Scott L. Montgomery, *Science in Translation: Movements of Knowledge Through Cultures and Time* (Chicago: Chicago University Press, 2000), 2–3.

46. Following Ronit Ricci, *Islam Translated: Literature, Conversion, and the Arabic Cosmopolis of South and Southeast Asia* (Chicago: University of Chicago Press, 2011); Ricci, "Citing as a Site: Translation and Circulation in Muslim South and Southeast Asia," *Modern Asian Studies* 46, no. 2 (March 2012): 331–353; Ricci and Jan van der Putten, eds., *Translation in Asia: Theories: Practices, Histories* (Manchester: St. Jerome Publishing, 2011).

47. Steven A. Epstein, *Purity Lost: Transgressing Boundaries in the Eastern Mediterranean, 1000–1400* (Baltimore, MD: Johns Hopkins University Press, 2006).

48. The historiographical drive to understand the relationship between Christian and Muslim societies runs throughout Brentjes's studies. For a general and methodological overview, see Brentjes, "Crossing Boundaries: New Approaches to the History of 'Pre-Modern' Science and Technology," *Science in Context* 12, no. 3 (1999): 381–384.

49. Eric R. Dursteler, "On Bazaars and Battlefields: Recent Scholarship on Mediterranean Cultural Contacts," *Journal of Early Modern History* 15 (2011): 413–434.

50. Anna Contadini and Claire Norton, eds., *The Renaissance and the Ottoman World* (Farnham, Surrey, UK, and Burlington, VT: Ashgate, 2013).

51. For example, Gábor Ágoston, "Ottoman Artillery and European Military Tech-

nology in the Fifteenth and Seventeenth Centuries," *Acta Orientalia Academiae Scientiarum Hungaricae* 47, nos. 1–2 (1994): 17–18.

52. Bernard Lewis, "Ottoman Observers of Ottoman Decline," *Islamic Studies* 1 (1962): 71–87.

53. J. Robson, "Bidʿa," *Encyclopaedia of Islam*, 2nd ed. (Brill Online, 2012); Bernard Lewis, "Some Observations on the Significance of Heresy in the History of Islam," *Studia Islamica* 1 (1953): 52–53.

54. Vardit Rispler, "Toward a New Understanding of the Term *bid'a*," *Der Islam* 68 (1991): 320–328.

55. *The Turkish Letters of Ogier Ghiselin de Busbecq*, translated from the Latin of the Elzevir edition of 1633 by Edward Seymour Forester (Oxford: Clarendon Press, 1968), 28, 135–136.

56. Following Keith Krause, *Arms and the State: Patterns of Military Production and Trade* (Cambridge: Cambridge University Press, 1992), 30–31.

57. Virginia H. Aksan, "Enlightening the Ottomans: Tott and Mustafa III," *International Congress on Learning and Education in the Ottoman World, Istanbul, 12–15 April 1999*, edited by Ali Çaksu (Istanbul: IRCICA, 2001), 173.

58. Jonathan Grant, "The Sword of the Sultan: Ottoman Arms Imports, 1854–1914," *Journal of Military History* 66 (2002): 9–36.

CHAPTER 1: FRAMING "KNOWLEDGE" IN THE OTTOMAN EMPIRE

1. See, for instance, the criticism in Kate Fleet, "The Missing Part of the Mediterranean History in the Late Medieval and Early Modern Period," in *The Turks*, vol. 3: *The Ottomans*, edited by Hasan Celâl Güzel et al. (Ankara: Yeni Türkiye, 2000), 40–45.

2. Ernst Diez, "The Zodiac Reliefs at the Portal of the Gök Medreses in Siwas," *Artibus Asiae* 12 (1949): 99–104; Jean-Paul Roux, "Le décor animé du caravansérail de Karatay en Anatolie," *Syria* 49 (1972): 371–397; Katharina Otto-Dorn, "Figural Stone Reliefs on Seljuk Sacred Architecture in Anatolia," *Kunst des Orients* 12, no. 1 (1978–1979): 103–149.

3. See, for example, a question posed to the Saudi scholar Muḥammad Ṣāliḥ al-Munājid (b. 1960): a young Muslim seeks approval of her choice of an academic institution using this hadith. The preacher answers that the hadith is fabricated: http://islamqa.info/en/ref/13637 (accessed June 14, 2013).

4. An example is a fatwa, legal reasoning, of the late Saudi mufti ʿAbd al-ʿAzīz Ibn Bāz (d. 1999), *Majmūʿ Fatāwā* (19th ed.) 30 vols. (Riyadh: Dār al-Qāsim, n.d.), 26:240–242.

5. These two points concern also modern critics of the hadith. Ibn Bāz (above) raises similar claims regarding the distance of China from the Arab world. In a YouTube clip, a Muslim preacher explains that the first part of the hadith—seek knowl-

edge—is indeed correct; the second part, even in China, should be regarded as an addition or explanation of the transmitter, not as an inherent part of the text of the hadith: http://www.youtube.com/watch?v=48_hvPk5Mos (accessed June 14, 2013).

6. Jonathan Brown, *The Canonization of al-Bukhārī and Muslim: The Formation and Function of the Sunnī Ḥadīth Canon* (Leiden: Brill, 2007).

7. Abū al-Faḍl Muḥmmad bin Ṭāhir Ibn al-Qaysarānī, *Maʿrifat al-Tadhkira fi al-Aḥādīth al-Mawḍuʿa* (Beirut: Mu'assasat al-Kutub al-Thaqāfiyya, AH 1406/1985), 101, hadith no. 118.

8. Abū al-Faraj Ibn Jawzī, *Kitāb al-Mawḍuʿāt* (Madina: al-Maktaba al-Salafiyya, 1966–1968), 1:215–216.

9. Taqī al-Dīn Ibn Taymiyya, *Majmūʿ al-Fatāwā* (ʿAbd al-Raḥman bin Muḥammad bin Qāsim; Madina: Majmaʿ al-Malik Fahd: AH 1398), 18:382.

10. One can sense al-Ṣuyūṭī's popularity in the Turkish-speaking regions of the Ottoman Empire from the number of extant manuscripts in what are now Turkish libraries and museums: see the "Collected Catalogue of Manuscripts of Turkey Database" of the Turkish Ministry of Culture and Tourism at http://www.yazmalar.gov.tr/ (accessed June, 22, 2013).

11. E. Geoffroy, "al-Suyūṭī, Abu al-Faḍl ʿAbd al-Raḥmān b. Abī Bakr b. Muḥammad D̲j̲alāl al-Dīn al-K̲h̲uḍayrī," *Encyclopaedia of Islam*, 2nd ed. (Brill Online, 2012); Marlis J. Saleh, "Al-Suyūṭī and His Works: Their Place in Islamic Scholarship from Mamluk Times to the Present," *Mamluk Studies Review* 5 (2001): 73–89.

12. Jalāl al-Dīn al-Ṣuyūṭī, *Al-La'ālī' al-Maṣnūʿa fi al-Aḥādīth al-Mawḍūʿa* ([Cairo]: al-Maktaba al-Ḥusayniyya, [1933/AH 1352]), 1:193.

13. Brinkley Messick, *The Calligraphic State: Textual Domination and History in a Muslim Society* (Berkeley: University of California Press, 1993), 213.

14. Persis Berlekamp, *Wonder, Image, and Cosmos in Medieval Islam* (New Haven, CT: Yale University Press, 2011).

15. Thomas S. Goodrich, *The Ottoman Turks and the New World: A Study of Tarih-i Hind-i Garbi and Sixteenth-Century Ottoman Americana* (Wiesbaden: Otto Harrassowitz, 1990), 15.

16. M. Pinar Emiralioğlu, *Geographical Knowledge and Imperial Culture in the Early Modern Ottoman Empire* (Farnham, UK: Ashgate, 2014); Emiralioğlu, "Relocating the Center of the Universe: China and the Ottoman Imperial Project in the Sixteenth Century," *Osmanlı Araştırmaları/Journal of Ottoman Studies* 39 (2012): 161–187; Kaveh Louis Hemmat, "Children of Cain in the Land of Error: A Central Asian Merchant's Treatise on Government and Society in Ming China," *Comparative Studies of South Asia, Africa and the Middle East* 30 (2010): 434–448.

17. Persis Berlekamp, "The Limits of Artistic Change in Fourteenth-Century Tabriz: The Paradox of Rashid al-Din's Book on Chinese Medicine, part I," *Muqarnas* 27 (2011): 209–250.

18. Gustave E. von Grunebaum, "The Response to Nature in Arabic Poetry," *Journal of Near Eastern Studies* 4 (1945): 137–151.

19. For example, Shah-Khan, "The Song of Creation: Sufi Themes on Nature,"

Sufi (London) 18 (Summer 1993): 27–30; Mine F. Thompson, "Turkey," in *Encyclopedia of Gardens: History and Design*, edited by Candice A. Shoemaker (Chicago: Fitzroy Dearborn, 2001), 3: 1333.

20. Andrew M. Watson, *Agricultural Innovation in the Early Islamic World: The Diffusion of Crops and Farming Techniques, 700–1100* (Cambridge: Cambridge University Press, 1983).

21. Harold J. Cook, *Matters of Exchange: Commerce, Medicine, and Science in the Dutch Golden Age* (New Haven, CT: Yale University Press, 2007), 1.

22. Eleazar Birnbaum, "The Questing Mind: Kātib Chelebi, 1609–1657," in *Corolla Torontonesis: Studies in Honour of Ronald Morton Smith*, edited by Emmet Robbins and Stella Sandahl (Toronto: TSAR, 1994), 145–155; J. D. Pearson, "Bibliography," *Encyclopaedia of Islam*, 2nd ed. (Brill Online, 2012).

23. Ḥājī Khalīfa [Katip Çelebi], *Kashf al-Ẓunūn ʿan Asāmī al-Kutūb wal-Funūn* (Istanbul: Matabaat-i al-Alim, AH 1310 [1891–1892]), 2:203. Alexandor Šopov of Harvard University wrote his doctoral dissertation on early modern Ottoman translations of Arabic agricultural treatises as part of the intersection of environment, food production, science, and literature.

24. Mehmet Öz, "Agriculture in the Ottoman Classical Period," in *The Great Ottoman-Turkish Civilization*, vol. 2: *Economy and Society*, edited by Kemal Çiçek (Ankara: Yeni Türkiye, 2000), 32–40; Alan Mikhail, *Nature and Empire in Ottoman Egypt: An Environmental History* (Cambridge: Cambridge University Press, 2011); Mikhail, "An Irrigated Empire: The View from Ottoman Fayyum," *International Journal of Middle East Studies* 42 (2010): 569–590.

25. See, for example, *Yazma Eserlerden Tıbbi Bitki Hayvan ve Madenler Sergisi/Materia Medica Miniature Pictures Exhibition* (Istanbul: Nobel Tıp Kitabevleri, 2002).

26. Ayşegül Demirhan, *Mısır Çarşısı Drogları* (Istanbul: Sermet Matbaası, 1975); Demirhan, "The Place and the Importance of Mısır Çarşısı (Spice Bazaar) in Ottoman-Turkish Medicine," in *The Great Ottoman-Turkish Civilization*, vol. 3: *Philosophy, Science and Institutions*, edited by Kemal Çiçek (Ankara: Yeni Türkiye, 2000), 447–454.

27. J. Michael Rogers, "The Palace, Potions and the Public: Some Lists of Drugs in Mid-16th Century Ottoman Turkey," in *Studies in Ottoman History in Honour of Professor V. L. Mènage*, edited by Colin Heywood and Colin Imber (Istanbul: Isis, 1994), 273–295; Suraiya Faroqhi and Christoph K. Neumann, eds., *The Illuminated Table, the Prosperous House: Food and Shelter in Ottoman Material Culture* (Würzburg: Ergon, 2003).

28. On hospital gardens, see Miri Shefer-Mossensohn, *Ottoman Medicine: Healing and Medical Institutions, 1500–1700* (Albany, NY: SUNY Press, 2009), 154–166.

29. Evliya Çelebi, *Seyahatname* (Istanbul: İqdam Matbaası, AH 1314 [1894]), 1:391–487; Evliya Çelebi, *The Seyahatname of Evliya Çelebi: Facsimile of Topkapı Sarayı Bağdat 304* (Cambridge, MA: Harvard University, 1993), 1b:237–309; Evliya Efendi, *Narrative of Travels in Europe, Asia, and Africa in the Seventeenth Century*, translated by Ritter Joseph von Hammer (London: Oriental Translation Fund, 1834), 1b:33–34, 40–42, 46, 59–60, 62–63, 64, 82, 84–86.

30. Başbakanlık Osmanlı Arşivi (BOA), Ali Emiri tasnifi, I. Ahmed/851.

31. Shirine Hamadeh, "Public Spaces and the Garden Culture of Istanbul in the Eighteenth Century," in *The Early Modern Ottomans: Remapping the Empire*, edited by Virginia H. Aksan and Daniel Goffman (Cambridge: Cambridge University Press, 2007), 277–312.

32. Otaviano Bon, *The Sultan's Seraglio: An Intimate Portrait of Life at the Ottoman Court* (London: Saqi Books, 1996), 25–26; Douglas Scott Brookes, "*Table of Delicacies Concerning the Rules of Social Gatherings*: An Annotated Translation of Gelibolulu Mustafa Âli's Mevâ'idü'n-Nefâ'is fi Kavâ'idi'l-Mecâlis" (PhD diss., University of California, Berkeley, 1998); Gülru Necipoğlu, *Architecture, Ceremonial, and Power: The Topkapı Palace in the Fifteenth and Sixteenth Centuries* (Cambridge, MA: MIT Press, 1991), chaps. 9 ("The Hanging Garden of the 3rd Court, Its Pavilions, and the Outer Garden") and 10 ("The Pavilions of the Outer Garden"), 184–241.

33. Gülru Necipoğlu, "From International Timurid to Ottoman: A Change of Taste in Sixteenth-Century Ceramic Tiles," *Muqarnas* 7 (1990): 136–170.

34. Shirine Hamadeh, "Ottoman Expressions of Early Modernity and the 'Inevitable' Question of Westernization," *Journal of the Society of Architectural Historians* 63 (2004): 32–51.

35. Gülru Necipoğlu, "The Suburban Landscape of Sixteenth-Century Istanbul as a Mirror of Classical Ottoman Garden Culture," in *Gardens in the Time of the Great Muslim Empires*, edited by Attilio Petruccioli (Leiden: Brill, 1997), 44–45; Doris Behrens-Abouseif, "Gardens in Islamic Egypt," *Der Islam* 69 (1992): 302–312.

36. Cornell Fleischer, *Bureaucrat and Intellectual in the Ottoman Empire: The Historian Mustafa ʿÂlî (1541–1600)* (Princeton, NJ: Princeton University Press, 1986).

37. Gábor Ágoston, "Information, Ideology, and Limits of Imperial Policy: Ottoman Grand Strategy in the Context of Ottoman-Habsburg Rivalry," in *The Early Modern Ottomans: Remapping the Empire*, edited by Virginia H. Aksan and Daniel Goffman (Cambridge: Cambridge University Press, 2007), 75–103. See also the following sample of more recent attempts that met with criticism: Giancarlo Casale, *The Ottoman Age of Exploration* (New York: Oxford University Press, 2010); Pinar Emiralioğlu, *Geographical Knowledge and Imperial Culture*.

38. Franz Rosenthal, *Knowledge Triumphant: The Concept of Knowledge in Medieval Islam*, 2nd ed., with an introduction by Dimitri Gutas (Leiden: Brill, 2007; original 1970).

39. See, for example, Dimitri Gutas, "Classical Arabic Wisdom Literature: Nature and Scope," *Journal of the American Oriental Society* 101 (1981): 49–86.

40. Willi Gorzny, "Meninski, Franz," in *Deutscher Biographischer Index*, edited by Hans-Albrecht Koch et al. (Munich: K. G. Saur, 1986), 1335; Gert A. Zischka, *Allgemeines Gelherten-Lexikon* (Stuttgart: Alfred Kröner, 1961), 421.

41. We have today a reprint of his works in six volumes: Fransicus à Mesgnien Meninski, *Thesaurus linguarum orientalium* (Istanbul: Simurg, 2000).

42. Ron Barkai, "Theoretical and Practical Aspects of Jewish Astrology in the

Middle Ages," in Barkai, *Science, Magic and Mythology in the Middle Ages* (in Hebrew), (Jerusalem: Van Leer Institute, 5747/1987).

43. Foucault, *The Order of Things*; Martin Heidegger, *The Question Concerning Technology, and Other Essays* (New York: Harper and Row, 1977).

44. Meninski, Thesaurus, 2:3316–3318 (ʿilm). See also the article for *hikmet* in 1:1792–1793.

45. On the Ashʿariyya school, see W. Montgomery Watt, "Ashʿariyya," *Encyclopaedia of Islam*, 2nd ed. (Brill Online, 2012).

46. Gerhard Böwering, "God and His Attributes," *Encyclopaedia of the Qurʾān* (Brill Online, 2012).

47. D. Gimaret, "Muʿtazila," *Encyclopaedia of Islam*, 2nd ed. (Brill Online, 2012).

48. For folktales and their justification among Ottoman Jews, see Yaron Ben-Naeh, "Tried and Tested Spells: Magic Beliefs and Acts Among Ottoman Jews" (in Hebrew), *Paʿamim* 85 (2000): 89–111.

49. Following Brinkley Messick, *The Calligraphic State: Textual Domination and History in a Muslim Society* (Berkeley: University of California, 1993).

50. Şerefeddin Sabuncuoğlu, *Mücerreb-nāme*, edited by İlter Uzel and Kenan Süveren (Ankara: Atatürk Kültür Merkezi Yaınları, 1999).

51. Mehmet Gürlek, "Anadolu'da Yazılımış İlk Türkçe Cerrahî Yazmalara Bir Örnek: Alâ'im-i Cerrâhin," *Turkish Studies: International Periodical for the Languages, Literature and History of Turkish or Turkic* 6 (2011): 1423–1434.

52. Evliya Çelebi, *Seyahatname*, edited by Robert Dankoff et al. (Istanbul: Yapı Kredi Yayınları, 2011), 1:261; *The Seyahatname of Evliya Çelebi: Facsimile of Topkapı Sarayı Bağdat 304*, 1b:158v; Evliya Efendi, *Narrative of Travels*, 2:116–117.

53. A. H. M. Zahniser, "Luqmān," *Encyclopaedia of the Qurʾān* (Brill Online, 2012). B. Heller [N. A. Stillman], "Luḳmān," *Encyclopaedia of Islam*, 2nd ed. (Brill Online, 2012).

54. Warren S. Walker and Ahmet E. Uysal, *Tales Alive in Turkey* (Lubbock: Texas Tech University Press, 1990), 24–34 (esp. p. 33).

55. Walker and Uysal, *More Tales Alive in Turkey* (Lubbock: Texas Tech University Press, 1992), 5–70 (esp. p. 60).

56. Kāmil Kāmil al-Bakrī wa-ʿAbd al-Wahāb al-Nūr, "Muqaddimat al-Taḥqīq"; Ahmed bin Mustafa Taşköprüzade, *Miftāḥ al-Saʿāda wa-Miṣbāḥ al-Siyāda fī Mawḍūʿāt al-ʿUlūm* (Cairo: Dār al-Kutub al-Ḥadītha, 1968), 1–25; Pearson, "Bibliography."

57. Magyar Tudományos Akadémia, Könyvtár, manuscript Török F59. I thank my colleague Dr. Guy Burak of New York University for sharing his copy with me. This text is at the center of a collaborative group project directed by Gülru Necipoğlu, Cemal Kafadar, and Cornell Fleischer.

58. I am indebted to Dr. Guy Burak of New York University, who generously shared with me insights from an ongoing project.

59. About the Taşköprüzade family, see Barbara Flemming, F. Babinger [Christine Woodhead], "Tashköprüzāde," *Encyclopaedia of Islam*, 2nd ed. (Brill Online, 2012).

60. Ahmed bin Mustafa Taşköprüzade, *Miftāḥ al-Saʿāda wa-Miṣbāḥ al-Siyāda fī Mawḍūʿāt al-ʿUlūm* (Kāmil Kāmil al-Bakrī wa-ʿAbd al-Wahāb al-Nūr, taḥqīq) (Cairo: Dār al-Kutub al-Ḥadītha, 1968).

61. Katip Çelebi, *Jāmiʿ al-mutūn min jull al-funūn* (manuscript held at the Atıf Efendi Yazma Eser Kütüphanesi, Istanbul, 2012). I thank Dr. Guy Burak for sharing his copy of the manuscript.

62. Paul J. Heck, *The Construction of Knowledge in Islamic Civilization* (Leiden: Brill, 2002); Heck, "The Hierarchy of Knowledge in Islamic Civilization," *Arabica* 49 (2002): 27–54.

63. See, for example, Karen Bauer, "'I Have Seen the People's Antipathy to This Knowledge': The Muslim Exegete and His Audience, 5th/11th-7th/13th Centuries," in *The Islamic Scholarly Tradition: Studies in History, Law and Thought in Honor of Professor Michael Allan Cook*, edited by Asad Q. Ahmed et al. (Leiden: Brill, 2011), 293–314.

64. George Makdisi, *The Rise of Colleges* (Edinburgh: Edinburgh University Press, 1981).

65. See the collection of articles by A. I. Sabra, *Optics, Astronomy, and Logic: Studies in Arabic Science and Philosophy* (Aldershot: Variorum, 1994).

66. For example, *Taʾrīkh ibn Khaldūn*, 1:376–377, 404; *The Muqaddimah*, 346–347, 377–378.

67. See, for instance, Robert Morrison, *Islam and Science: Niẓām al-Dīn al-Nīsābūrī* (London: Routledge, 2007); Nahyan Fancy, *Science and Religion in Mamluk Egypt: Ibn al-Nafīs, Pulmonary Transit and Bodily Resurrection* (London: Routledge, 2013); Justin Stearns, "'All Beneficial Knowledge Is Revealed': The Rational Sciences in the Maghrib in the Age of al-Yūsī (d. 1102/1691)," *Islamic Law and Society* 21 (2014): 49–80.

68. Marijana Kavčić, "Arabic Manuscripts of the National and University Library 'St. Kliment Ohridiski,' Skopje, Republic of Macedonia," in *From Codicology to Technology: Islamic Manuscripts and Their Place in Scholarship*, edited by Stefanie Brinkmann and Beate Wiesmüller (Berlin: Frank and Timme, 2009), 175–193.

69. Aḥmad ibn ʿAbd al-Munʿim Damanhūrī, *Shaykh Damanhūrī on the Churches of Cairo (1739)*, edited and translated by Moshe Perlmann (Berkeley: University of California Press, 1975), 2.

70. ʿAbd al-Raḥmān al-Jabartī, *ʿAjāʾib al-Āthār fī al-Tarājim wa-al-Akhbār* (Cairo: n.p., AH 1236 [1820]), 2:25.

71. Muḥammad Khalīl Abū al-Faḍl al-Murādī, *Silk al-Durar fī Aʿyān al-Qarn al-Thānī ʿAshr* (Baghdad: Maktabat al-Mathnā, 196–), 1:116; H. A. R. Gibb, "Al-Murādī, 5.," *Encyclopaedia of Islam*, 2nd ed. (Brill Online, 2012).

72. Jane H. Murphy, "Aḥmad al-Damanhūrī (1689–1778) and the Utility of Expertise in Early Modern Ottoman Egypt," *Osiris* 25 (2010): 85–103.

73. Lawrence I. Conrad, "Scholarship and Social Context in the Near East," in *Knowledge and the Scholarly Medical Traditions*, edited by Don Bates (Cambridge: Cambridge University Press, 1995), 81–101; Peter E. Pormann, "The Physician and the Other: Images of the Charlatan in Medieval Islam," *Bulletin of the History of Medicine* 79 (2005): 189–207.

74. See Doris Behrens-Abouseif, "The Image of the Physician in Arab Biographies of the Post-Classical Age," *Der Islam* 66 (1989): 331–343, which is based on the biographical lexicons in Arabic from the Levant written in the Mamluk and Ottoman period. To this pool of evidence I add my own acquaintance with the Ottoman lexicons focusing on Anatolia—for example, Ahmed bin Mustafa Taşköprüzade, *Al-shaqā'iq al-nuʿmānīyya fī ʿulamā' al-dawla al-ʿuthmāniyya* (manuscript in the Süleymaniye Library, East Efendi 2308); and 'Alī bin Bālī bin Muḥammad Bey Manq, *al-ʿIqd al-Manẓūm fī Dhikr Afāḍil al-Rūm; Dhayl al-Shaqā'iq* (manuscript in the Süleymaniye Library, Bağadatlı vehbi Efendi 1065).

75. W. Ende, "Mudjāwir, f. mudjāwira," *Encyclopaedia of Islam*, 2nd ed. (Brill Online, 2012).

76. Najm al-Dīn Abū al-Makārim Muḥammad b. Muḥammad al-Amīrī al-Ghazzī, *Lutf al-Samr wa-Qatf al-Thamr min Tarājim Aʿyān al-Ṭabaqa al-Ūlā min al-Qarn al-Ḥādī 'Ashr* (Damascus: Wizārat al-Thaqāfa wal-Irshād al-Qawmī, 1981), 1:30–41.

77. Muḥammad Amīn b. Faḍlallah al-Muḥibbī, *Ta'rīkh Khulaṣat al-Athr fī Aʿyān al-Qarn al-Ḥādī 'Ashr* (Beirut: Maktabat Khayyāṭ, 1966), 4:299–300.

78. Al-Murādī, *Silk al-Durar*, 4:264–265.

79. Alongside the Ḥanafī judge who represented the Ottoman imperial law and was sent accordingly from the imperial center to serve in the urban centers throughout the empire, a local judge also served, representing the local common school, which in al-Shām was Shāfiʿī.

80. Al-Muḥibbī, *Ta'rīkh Khulaṣat al-Athr*, 1:406–408.

81. For further details, see Shefer-Mossensohn, *Ottoman Medicine*, 21–29.

82. Jalāl al-Dīn al-Suyūṭī, *Al-Manhaj al-sawī wal-manhal al-rawī fī al-tib al-nabawī* (manuscript held at the Wellcome Institute for the History of Medicine Library, Wms. Or.90); Fehmi Edhem Karatay, *Topkapı Sarayı Müzesi Kütüphanesi Arapça Kataloğu* (Istanbul: Topkapi Sarayı Müzesi, 1966), 3:859–860.

83. Abdurrahman Atçıl, "Greco-Islamic Philosophy and Islamic Jurisprudence in the Ottoman Empire (1300–1600): Aristotle's Theory of Sciences in Works on *Uṣūl al-Fiqh*," *Osmanlı Araştımaları/Journal of Ottoman Studies* 41 (2013): 33–54.

84. Abū Ḥāmid Al-Ghazzālī, *The Faith and Practice of al-Ghazali*, translated by W. M. Watt (London: G. Allen and Unwin, 1953), 11.

85. Al-Ghazzālī, *Al-Munqidh min al-Ḍalāl wal-Mawṣil ilā dhī al-ʿIzza wal-Jalāl* (Beirut: Al-Lajna al-Lubnāniyya li-Tarjamat al-Rawā'iʿ, 1969), 18–27; R. J. McCarthy, trans., with David Burrell and William Graham, *Al-Ghazali's Path to Sufism; His Deliverance from Error—al-Munqidh min al-Dalal* (Louisville, KY: Fons Vitae, 2000), 27–42.

86. Al-Ghazzālī, *The Incoherence of the Philosophers: A Parallel English-Arabic Text*, translated, introduced, and annotated by Michael E. Marmura (Provo, Utah: Brigham Young University Press, 2000), xv–xvi.

87. See, for example, Majid Fakhry, *A History of Islamic Philosophy*, 2nd ed. (New York: Columbia University Press, 1983); Fakhry, *A Short Introduction to Islamic Philosophy, Theology and Mysticism* (Oxford: Oneworld, 1997); Oliver Leaman, *Islamic Philoso-*

phy, 2nd ed. (Cambridge, UK: Polity, 2009); R. Arnaldez, "Falsafa," *Encyclopaedia of Islam*, 2nd ed. (Brill Online, 2012).

88. Ahmed bin Mustafa Taşköprüzade, *al-shaqā'iq al-nuʿmānīyya*, fols. 208r–209r; ʿAbd al-Ḥayy bin ʿImād, *Shadharāt al-Dhahab fī Akhbār man Dhahab* (Beirut: Maktab al-Tijārī lil-Ṭibāʿa wal-Nashr wal-Tawzīʿ, [1966]), 8:281.

89. Ḥājī Khalīfa, *Kashf al-Ẓunūn*, 2:203–205.

90. Khaled El-Rouayheb, "Sunni Muslim Scholars on the Status of Logic, 1500–1800," *Islamic Law and Society* 11 (2004): 213–232; El-Rouayheb, "Was There a Revival of Logical Studies in Eighteenth-Century Egypt," *Die Welt des Islams* 45 (2005): 1–19; El-Rouayheb, *Relational Syllogisms and the History of Arabic Logic, 900–1900* (Leiden: Brill, 2010).

91. Following Ronit Ricci, *Islam Translated: Literature, Conversion, and the Arabic Cosmopolis of South and Southeast Asia* (Chicago: University of Chicago Press, 2011); Ricci, "Citing as a Site: Translation and Circulation in Muslim South and Southeast Asia," *Modern Asian Studies* 46, no. 2 (March 2012): 331–353; Ricci and Jan van der Putten, eds., *Translation in Asia: Theories, Practices, Histories* (Manchester: St. Jerome, 2011).

92. Ḥājī Khalīfa, *Kashf al-Ẓunūn*, 2:586–589.

93. F. Jamil Ragep, "Astronomy," *Encyclopaedia of Islam*, 2nd ed. (Brill Online, 2012); David A. King, "Mamluk Astronomy and the Institution of *Muwaqqit*," in *The Mamluks in Egyptian Politics and Society*, edited by Thomas Philipp and Ulrich Haarman (Cambridge: Cambridge University Press, 1998), 153–162.

94. David A. King, "The Astronomy of the Mamluks," *Isis* 74 (1983): 531–555; King, "The Astronomy of the Mamluk: A Brief Overview," *Muqarnas* 2 (1984): 73–84; King, "Mamluk Astronomy and the Institution of *Muwaqqit*," 153–162.

95. Ḥājī Khalīfa, *Kashf al-Ẓunūn*, 1:65–66, 96–97, 110–113, 493, 572–576.

96. Daniel A. Stolz, "The Lighthouse and the Observatory: Islam, Authority, and Cultures of Astronomy in Late Ottoman Egypt" (PhD diss., Princeton University, 2013).

97. Ḥājī Khalīfa, *Kashf al-Ẓunūn*, 2:586–589.

98. Ibid., 2:657.

99. Ibid., 2:101.

100. The literature on Takîyüddîn and the observatory in Istanbul is quite considerable. A few typical examples are: A. Süheyl Ünver, *İstanbul Rasathanesi* (Ankara: Türk Tarih Kurumu Basımevi, 1985); Adıvar, *Osmanlı Türklerinde İlim*, 99–109; Sayılı, *The Observatory in Islam*, 289–305; Yavuz Unat, "Takîyüddîn and the Istanbul Observatory," in *The Turks*, vol. 3: *The Ottomans*, edited by Hasan Celâl Güzel et al. (Ankara: Yeni Türkiye, 2000), 819–830; D. A. King, "Taḳī al-Dīn," *Encyclopaedia of Islam*, 2nd ed. (Brill Online, 2012).

101. A copy of the manuscript is archived in the Istanbul University Library. H. Sohrweide, "Luḳmān b.Sayyid Ḥusayn," *Encyclopaedia of Islam*, 2nd ed. (Brill Online, 2012).

102. F. Jamil Ragep, "Astronomy in the Fanārī-Circle: The Critical Background of Qādīzāde al-Rūmī and the Samarqand School," in *Uluslararası Molla Fenârî Sempozyumu (2009 Bursa)—bildiriler; International Symposium on Molla Fanārī (2009 Bursa)—proceedings*, edited by Tevfik Yücedoğru et al. (Bursa: Bursa Yüyükşehir Belediyesi Yayınları, 2010), 165–176; Ragep, "Ḳāḍī-zāde Rūmī," *Encyclopaedia of Islam*, 2nd ed. (Brill Online, 2012).

103. Pinelopi Stathi, "The Seismologia and Their Diffusion During the Ottoman Period," in *Natural Disasters in the Ottoman Empire*, edited by Elizabth Zachariadou (Rethymnon: Crete University Press, 1999), 241–247.

104. Sayılı, *The Observatory in Islam*, 292; Unat, "Takîyüddîn and the Istanbul Observatory," 820–821.

105. This impression may be obtained from Ekmeleddin İhsanoğlu et al., *Osmanlı Astronomi Literaturu Tarihi*, 2 vols. (Istanbul: İslam Tarih, Sanat ve Kultur Arastirma Merkezi, 1997).

106. Gülçin Tunalı Koç, "Osmanlı Siyaset Kültürünü Anlamada Kaynak Olarak—İlm-i Nücûm: Sadullah al-Ankaravî," *Türkiye Araştırmaları Literatür Dergisi* 3 (2004): 183–195; Tunalı Koç, "'Sözüm bu iki gözüm ve vefâ': Müneccim Sadullah el-Ankaravî'nin Kaleminden 19.yy Akarası'ndaki Hizmetkârlar," *Tarih ve Toplum Yeni Yaklaşımalar* 5 (Spring 2007): 41–66; Tunalı Koç, "Sadullah Efendi'nin İlm-i Nücûm Kaynaklarından Tanzimat Ankarasına Bir Katkı," *Türkiyat Araştırmaları Dergisi* 24 (Fall 2008): 369–392.

107. Al-Muḥibbī, *Ta'rīkh Khulaṣat al-Athr*, 4:301; İhsanoğlu, *Osmanlı Astronomi Literaturu Tarihi*, 1:275–276; Boris A. Rosenfeld and Ekmeleddin İhsanoğlu, *Mathematicians, Astronomers, and Other Scholars of Islamic Civilization and Their Works (7th–19th c.)* (Istanbul: Islam Tarih, Sanat ve Kultur Araştırma Merkezi, 2003), 359–360.

108. On the resilience of traditional concepts regarding time and the mechanisms of fixing it, alongside other mechanisms for time fixing in the later Ottoman period, see Avner Wishnitzer, "'Our Time': On the Durability of the Alaturka Hour System in the Late Ottoman Empire," *International Journal of Turkish Studies* 16, nos. 1–2 (2010): 47–69.

109. Rhonda Martens, *Kepler's Philosophy and the New Astronomy* (Princeton, NJ: Princeton University Press, 2000); Elizabeth Spiller, *Science, Reading, and Renaissance Literature: The Art of Making Knowledge, 1580–1670* (Cambridge: Cambridge University Press, 2004).

110. Salim Aydüz, "Osmanlı Devleti'nde Müneccimbaşılık," in *Osmanlı Bilimi Araştırmaları*, edited by Feza Günergün (Istanbul: İstanbul Üniversitesi Edebiyat Fakültesi, 1995), 159–207; Avner Wishnitzer, *Reading Clocks Alla Turca: Time and Society in the Late Ottoman Empire* (Chicago: University of Chicago Press, forthcoming).

111. Fatma Müge Göçek, *East Encounters West: France and the Ottoman Empire in the Eighteenth Century* (New York: Oxford University Press, 1987), 103–115.

112. Wishnitzer, *Reading Clocks Alla Turca*.

113. Maurice Cerasi, "The Urban Perspective of Ottoman Monuments from Sinan

to Mehmet Tahir—Change and Continuity," in *Aptullah Kuran için Yazıları Essays in Honour of Aptullah Kuran*, edited by Çiğdem Kafesçioğlu and Lucienne Thys-Senocak (Istanbul: Yapı Kredi Yayınları, 1999), 180–181.

114. Evliya Çelebi, *Seyahatname*, vol. 7, bk. 2:107–110.

115. Abū al-Qāsim Khalaf ibn ʿAbbās al-Zahrāwī, *Albucasis on Surgery and Instruments*, translated and edited by M. S. Spink and G. L. Lewis (London: Wellcome Institute of the History of Medicine, 1973); Sami Khalaf Hamarneh, *Drawings and Pharmacy in al-Zahrawi's 10th century Surgical Treatise* (Washington, D.C.: Smithsonian Institution, 1961); Emilie Savage-Smith, "Al-Zahrāwī," *Encyclopaedia of Islam*, 2nd ed. (Brill Online, 2012).

116. Şerefeddin Sabuncuoğlu, *Cerrahiyyetü'l-Ḥāniyyet*, edited by İlter Uzel, 2 vols. (Ankara: Atatürk Kültür, Dil ve Tarih Yüksek Kurumu, 1992); Ahmet Süheyl Ünver, "XVinci Asırda Türkiyede Tecrubi Tababete ait İki Misal," *İstanbul Üniversitesi Tıp Fakültesi Mecmuası* 3 (1949): 1–4; Gönül Güreşsever, "Kitab al-Cerrahiyet al-Hāniye (Istanbul Tıp Tarihi Enstitüsü Nüshası) Minyatürler," *I. Milletarası Türkoloji Kongresi. Tebliğler* (Istanbul: İstanbul Üniversitesi, 1979), 3:771–785.

117. Nuran Yıldırım, "XV. Yüzyıla ait Anonim Bir Cerrahnâme Cerrahi Yöntemlerin Kullanıldığı Fasıllar Tıbbı Terminoloji ile Bitki, Drog ve Madde Isimleri," *Yeni Tıp Tarihi Araştırmaları/The New History of Medicine Studies* 10–11 (2004–2005): 325–433.

118. Evliya Çelebi, *Seyahatname*, 7:107–110; Miri Shefer-Mossensohn, "An Ottoman Observer of Central European Surgery in Middle of the Seventeenth Century," *Vesalius* 14, no. 1 (2008): 4–7; J. W. Livingston, "Evliya Çelebi on Surgical Operation in Vienna," *Al-Abhath* 23 (1970): 223–245; Arslan Terzioğlu, "Evliya Çelebi's Beschreibung der Südosteuropäischen Hospitäler und Heilbäder des 17. Jahrhunderts und ihre Kulturgeschichtliche Bedeutung," *Revue des Études Sud-Est Européennes* 13 (1975): 429–442.

119. Jonathan Grant, "Crossing the Eastern Divide: Western Civilization and Islam in the Views of Chaadaev and Gokalp," *History Compass* 3 (2005): 1–7; M. Sait Özervali, "Transferring Traditional Islamic Disciplines into Modern Social Sciences in Late Ottoman Thought: The Attempts of Ziya Gokalp and Mehmed Serefeddin," *Muslim World* 97 (2007): 317–330.

120. Avi Rubin, "East and West: Bahjat and Tamimi in Wilayat Beirut" (in Hebrew), *Jamāʿa* 7 (2001): 54–81.

121. Palmira Brummet, "The Yeni and the Eski Cultural Change and Envisioning the 'Modern' in Late Ottoman Cartoons," in *The Great Ottoman-Turkish Civilization*, vol. 3: *Philosophy, Science and Institutions*, edited by Kemal Çiçek (Ankara: Yeni Türkiye, 2000), 134–140; Nora Şeni, "Fashion and Women's Clothing in the Satirical Press of Istanbul at the End of the 19th Century," in *Women in Modern Turkish Society*, edited by Sirin Tekeli (London: Zed Books, 1995), 25–45.

122. Robert Morrison, "The Reception of Early-Modern European Astronomy by Ottoman Religious Scholars," *Archivum Ottomanicum* 21 (2003): 187–195. Avner Ben-Zaken also discussed Copernican cosmology and advanced technological equipment

in the early modern Ottoman Empire: Avner Ben-Zaken, *Cross-Cultural Scientific Exchanges in the Eastern Mediterranean, 1560–1660* (Baltimore, MD: Johns Hopkins University Press, 2010); Ben-Zaken, "The Heavens of the Sky and the Heavens of the Heart: The Ottoman Cultural Context for the Introduction of Post-Copernican Astronomy," *British Journal for the History of Science* 37 (2004): 1–28; Ben-Zaken, "The Revolving Planets and the Revolving Clocks: Circulating Mechanical Objects in the Mediterranean," *History of Science* 49 (2011): 125–148. Several critics reject his claims, as in the following book review: Sonja Brentjes, "Cross-Cultural Exchange in the Mediterranean," *Journal for the History of Astronomy* 42 (2011): 411–415.

123. Dror Ze'evi, *Producing Desire: Changing Sexual Discourse in the Ottoman Middle East, 1500–1900* (Berkeley: University of California Press, 2006), "Conclusion: Modernity and Sexual Discourse," 167–171.

CHAPTER 2: WHERE AND HOW DOES LEARNING TAKE PLACE?

1. Selçuk Akşın Somel, *The Modernization of Public Education in the Ottoman Empire, 1839–1908* (Leiden: Brill, 2001), 19.

2. Nelly Hanna, *In Praise of Books: A Cultural History of Cairo's Middle Class, Sixteenth to the Eighteenth Century* (Syracuse, NY: Syracuse University Press, 2003).

3. Avner Giladi's work is of central importance in this field. His works in English include "Concepts of Childhood and Attitudes towards Children in Medieval Islam: A Preliminary Study with Special Reference to Infant and Child Mortality," *JESHO* 32 (1989): 121–152; "Infants, Children, and Death in Medieval Muslim Society: Some Preliminary Observations," *Social History of Islam* 3 (1990): 345–368; *Children of Islam: Concepts of Childhood in Medieval Islam Society* (Houndmills, Basingstoke, UK: Macmillan in association with St. Antony's College, Oxford, 1992); "The Child Was Small . . . Not So the Grief for Him: Sources, Structure and Content of al-Sakhāwī's Consolation Treatise for Bereaved Parents," *Poetics Today* 14 (1993): 367–386; "Islamic Consolation Treatises for Bereaved Parents: Some Bibliographical Notes," *Studia Islamica* 81 (1995): 197–202; "Gender Difference in Child Rearing and Education: Some Preliminary Observations with Reference to Medieval Muslim Thought," *Al-Qantara* 16 (1995): 291–308; "Individualism and Conformity in Medieval Islamic Educational Thought: Some Notes with Special Reference to Elementary Education," *Al-Qantara* 26 (2005): 99–121; "The Child in Islam," in *Children and Childhood in World Religions: Primary Sources and Texts*, edited by Don S. Browning and Marcia J. Bunge (New Brunswick, NJ: Rutgers University Press, 2009), 151–216.

4. Gottfried Hagen, "'He Never Took the Path of Pastime and Play': Ideas of Childhood in Ottoman Hagiography," in *Scripta Ottomanica et Res Aitaicae: Festschrift für Barbara Kellner-Heinkele zu ihrem 60. Geburstag*, edited by Ingeborg Hauenschild et al. (Wiesbaden: Harrasowitz Verlag, 2002), 95–118.

5. Miri Shefer, "Medical and Professional Ethics in Sixteenth-Century Istanbul:

Towards an Understanding of the Relationships between the Ottoman State and the Medical Guilds," *Medicine and Law* 21 (2002): 307–319.

6. See, for example, Leslie Peirce, "Haciye Sabah's Story: A Teacher on Trial," in *Morality Tales: Law and Gender in the Ottoman Court of Aintab* (Berkeley: University of California Press, 2003), 251–275.

7. Hagen, "'He Never Took the Path of Pastime and Play,'" 107.

8. Giambattista Toderini, *Letteratura Turchesca* (Venice: Presso G. Storti, 1787), 2:1–28.

9. Cevat İzgi, *Osmanlı Medreselerinde İlim*, 2 vols. (Istanbul: İz Yayıncılık, 1997); İzgi, "Osmanlı Medreselerinde Aritmetik ve Cebir Eğitimi ve Okutulan Kitaplar," in *Osmanlı Bilimi Araştırmaları*, edited by Feza Günergün (Istanbul: İstanbul Üniversitesi Edebiyat Fakültesi, 1995), 129–158.

10. İhsan Fazlıoğlu, "The Samarqand Mathematical-Astronomical School: A Basis for Ottoman Philosophy and Science," *Journal for the History of Arabic Science* 14 (2008): 22–23.

11. Şükran Fazlıoğlu, "*Manzûme fî Tertîb el-Kutûb fî el-Ulûm* ve Osmanlı Medreselerindeki Ders Kitapları," *Değerler Eğitimi Dergisi* 1 (2003): 97–110; Fazlıoğlu, "Nebī Efendi-zāde'nin 'ḳaṣīde fī el-kutub el-meşhūre fī el-ʿulūm' una Göre Bir Medrese Talebesinin Ders ve Kitab Haritası," *Kutadgubilig Felsefe-Bilim Araştırmaları Dergisi* 3 (2003): 191–221.

12. See, for example, İzgi, *Osmanlı Medreselerinde İlim*.

13. Michael Chamberlain, *Knowledge and Social Practice in Medieval Damascus, 1190–1350* (Cambridge: Cambridge University Press, 1994); Jonathan P. Berkey, *The Transmission of Knowledge in Medieval Cairo: A Social History of Islamic Education* (Princeton, NJ: Princeton University Press, 1992).

14. Richard C. Repp, *The Müfti of Istanbul: A Study in the Development of the Ottoman Learned Hierarchy* (London: Ithaca Press, 1986).

15. İ. H. Uzunçarşılı, *Osmanlı Devletinin İlmiye Teşkilatı*, 3rd ed. (Ankara: Türk Tarihi Kurumu Basımevi, 1988), 15–16, 243–246; Colin Imber, *The Ottoman Empire, 1300–1650: The Structure of Power* (Basingstoke, Hampshire: Palgrave, 2002), 228–229; Yasemin Beyazit, "Efforts to Reform Entry into the Ottoman İlmiyye Career towards the End of the 16th Century: The 1598 Ottoman İlmiyye Kanunnamesi," *Turcica* 44 (2012–2013): 201–218.

16. Fazlıoğlu, "*Manzûme fî Tertîb el-Kutûb fî el-Ulûm* ve Osmanlı Medreselerindeki Ders Kitapları," 97–110; Fazlıoğlu, "Nebī Efendi-zāde'nin 'ḳaṣīde fī el-kutub el-meşhūre fī el-ʿulūm,'" 191–221.

17. Şükran Fazlıoğlu, "Ta'lîm ile İrşâd arasında: Erzorumlu İbrahim Hakkı'nın Medrese Ders Müfredatı," *Dîvân İlmi Araştırmalar* 18 (2005): 115–173.

18. See the studies by Berkey and Chamberlain (cited in note 13 above). Berkey and Chamberlain changed the picture that arose from George Makdisi's research (*The Rise of the Colleges*) regarding the centrality of the *medrese*, perhaps even its exclusivity, in the Muslim educational system.

19. Birnbaum, "The Questing Mind: Kātib Chelebi," 133–158; Orhan Şaik Gökyay, "Kātib Čelebi," *Encyclopaedia of Islam*, 2nd ed. (Brill Online).

20. A third work, *Kashf al-Ẓunūn ʿan Asāmī al-Kutūb wal-Funūn* (The revelation of thoughts: Names of the books and the sciences), was discussed in the previous chapter.

21. Katib Çelebi, *Tuhfet ül-Kibar fi Esfār el-Bihar* (Istanbul: Matbaa-yı Bahriye, AH 1329 [1913]).

22. Katip Çelebi, *Mizan al-haqq fi ikhtiyar al-ahaqq* (manuscript in the Cambridge Library, Add. 442). The treatise was translated into English: Katip Çelebi [Haji Khalifa], *The Balance of Truth*, translated by G. L. Lewis (London: G. Allen and Unwin, 1957).

23. Uzunçarşılı, *Osmanlı Devletinin İlmiye Teşkilatı*, 9–10, 242–244; C. E. Bosworth, "Ṣofta," *Encyclopaedia of Islam*, 2nd ed. (Brill Online, 2012).

24. İsmail E. Erünsal, *Ottoman Libraries: A Survey of the History, Development and Organization of Ottoman Foundation Libraries* (Cambridge, MA: Department of Near Eastern Languages and Literatures, Harvard University, 2008).

25. Evliya Çelebi, *Seyahatname*, 1:3, 263.

26. Godfrey Goodwin, *A History of Ottoman Architecture* (London: Thames and Hudson, 1971), 205–206.

27. Hagen, "'He Never Took the Path of Pastime and Play,'" 107.

28. Of course, Gabriel Baer conducted the original research into the Ottoman guilds. In recent years, research has diversified and deepened, and deals with the guilds as economic, social, and religious organizations. Representative samples of such contemporary research, which also addresses vocational training in the framework of the organization, include the following: Amnon Cohen, *The Guilds of Ottoman Jerusalem* (Leiden: Brill, 2001); Eunjeong Li, *Guild Dynamics in Seventeenth-century Istanbul: Fluidity and Leverage* (Leiden: Brill, 2004); Suraiya Faroqhi and Randi Deguilhem, eds., *Crafts and Craftsmen of the Middle East* (London: I. B. Tauris, 2005).

29. İ. H. Uzunçarşılı, *Osmanlı Devletinin Saray Teşkilatı*, 3rd ed. (Ankara: Türk Tarihi Kurumu Basımevi, 1988), 300–357.

30. Goodwin, *A History of Ottoman Architecture*, 197–201; B. O'Kane, "Sinān," *Encyclopaedia of Islam*, 2nd ed. (Brill Online, 2012).

31. Leslie P. Peirce, *The Imperial Harem: Women and Sovereignty in the Ottoman Empire* (New York: Oxford University Press, 1993), 139–143.

32. Al-Khaṭīb al-Baghdādī, *Al-Riḥla fī Ṭalab al-Ḥadīth* ([Beirut:] Dār al-Kutub al-ʿIlmiyya [1985/AH 1395]).

33. Monique Bernards, "*Ṭalab al-ʿIlm* amongst the Linguists of Arabic During the ʿAbbasid Period," in *ʿAbbasid Studies: Occasional Papers of the School of ʿAbbasid Studies, Cambridge, 6–10 July 2002*, edited by James E. Montgomery (Louvain: Peeters, 2004), 33–46.

34. Ignaz Goldziher, *Muslim Studies*, edited by S. M. Stern, translated by C. R. Barber and S. M. Stern, vol. 2 (Chicago: Aldine, 1967), chap. 6, "Ṭalab al-Ḥadīth," 164–180.

35. Suraiya Faroqhi, *Travel and Artisans in the Ottoman Empire: Employment and Mobility in the Early Modern Era* (London: I. B. Tauris, 2014).

36. Paul E. Walker, "Knowledge and Learning," *Encyclopaedia of the Qur'ān* (Brill Online, 2012); Sam I. Gellens, "The Search for Knowledge in Medieval Muslim Societies: A Comparative Approach," in *Muslim Travellers: Pilgrimage, Migration, and the Religious Imagination*, edited by Dale Eickelman and James Piscatori (Berkeley: University of California Press, 1990), 50–65; Abderrahmane El Moudden, "The Ambivalence of *Rihla*: Community Integration and Self-Definition in Moroccan Travel Accounts, 1300–1800," in Eickelman and Piscatori, *Muslim Travellers*, 69–84.

37. Ahmed bin Mustafa Taşköprüzade, *al-Shaqā'iq al-Nuʿmānīyya fi 'Ulamā' al-Dawla al-'Uthmāniyya* (Egypt: Būlāq, AH 1299), 1:84–92 (printed on the margins of Aḥmad bin Muḥammad ibn Khalikān, *Wafayāt al-Aʿyān wa-Anbā' Abnā' al-Zamān* [Egypt: Būlāq, AH 1299]). An English translation for this specific entry is to be found in Ibn Tashköprüzade, "The Biography of an Ottoman Jurist (1350–1431), from *Al-Shaqa'iq al-Nu'maniyya*," in *Islam*, translated and edited by Bernard Lewis (New York: Harper and Row, 1974), 2:45–49.

38. See, for example, the discussion on the possibilities of travel to and from Damascus in the eighteenth century in James Grehan, *Consumer Culture in 18th-century Damascus and Everyday Life* (Seattle: University of Washington Press, 2007), chap. 1, "City and Environment," 21–55.

39. Michael Winter, "Cultural Ties between Istanbul and Ottoman Egypt," in *Turkey: The Ottoman Past and the Republican Present* (in Hebrew), edited by Michael Winter and Miri Shefer (Tel Aviv: University of Tel Aviv, Moshe Dayan Center for Middle Eastern and African Studies, 2007), 27–43.

40. Muḥammad bin Aḥmad bin Iyās, *Badā'iʿ al-Zuhūr Fī Waqā'iʿ al-Duhūr*, taḥrīr Muḥammad Muṣṭafā (Cairo: Dār Iḥyā' al-Kutub al-'Arabiyya, AH 1369/1960), 5:467 and in many other places.

41. Gellens, "The Search for Knowledge in Medieval Muslim Societies," 58–59.

42. Kazuaki Sawai, "Japon Teknolojisi'ne karşı: XVI. Yüzyılda Doğu Asya'da Osmanlı Tüfeğinin Yeri," in *Eskiçağ'dan Modern Çağ'a Ordular: Oluşum, Teşkilat ve İşlev*, edited by Feridun M. Emecen (Istanbul: Kitabevi, 2008), 341–354.

43. Dina Le Gall, *A Culture of Sufism: Naqshbandīs in the Ottoman World, 1450–1700* (Albany: State University of New York Press, 2009).

44. Lâle Can, "Connecting People: A Central Asian Sufi Network in Turn-of-the-Century Istanbul," *Modern Asian Studies* 46, no. 2 (March 2012): 373–401.

45. Bernard Lewis, *From Babel to Dragomans: Interpreting the Middle East* (Oxford: Oxford University Press, 2004), 114.

46. Al-Muḥibbī, *Ta'rīkh Khulaṣat al-Athr*, 2:232.

47. For the large convoy leaving with Selim when he left Cairo, including leading physicians, see Shefer-Mossensohn, *Ottoman Medicine*, 187.

48. Tofiqh Heiderzadeh, "İran Alimlerinin Osmanlı Devletine Gelişi ve Osmanlı Bilimine Katkıları (Timur Döneminin Başından Safevi Döneminin Sonuna Kadar)," *Osmanlı Bilimi Araştırmaları/Studies in Ottoman Science* 2 (1998): 211–242; Nomi Heger,

"The Status and the Image of the Persianate Artist" (PhD diss., Princeton University, 1997).

49. Beatrice F. Manz, "Ulu<u>gh</u> Beg," *Encyclopaedia of Islam*, 2nd ed. (Brill Online, 2012); Manz, "Ulugh Begh, Transoxania and Turco-Mongolian Traditions," in *Iran and Iranisch Geprägte Kulturen: Studien zum 65. Geburstag von Bert G. Fragner*, edited by Markus Ritter et al. (Wiesbaden: Dr. Ludwig Reichert Verlag, 2008), 20–27; George Saliba, "Reform of Ptolemaic Astronomy at the Court of Uḷugh Beg," in *Studies in the History of the Exact Sciences in Honour of David Pingree*, edited by Charles Burnett et al. (Leiden: Brill, 2004), 810–824.

50. Robert Hannah, "The *Meridiana* of Ulugh Beg in Hagia Sophia, Constantinople," *Nuncius: Journal of the History of Science* 22 (2007): 7–14.

51. Adıvar, *Osmanlı Türklerinde İlim*, 20, 47–49, 62–63, 88, 99, 112.

52. Casale, *The Ottoman Age of Exploration*.

53. Lewis, *From Babel to Dragomans*, 108–114. For the Ottoman-Mughal relations in the context of the hajj, see Suraiya Faroqhi, *Pilgrims and Sultans: The Hajj under the Ottomans, 1517–1683* (London: I. B. Tauris, 1994), chap. 6, "The Pilgrimage as a Matter of Foreign Policy," 127–145.

54. Regarding the threat, see Fleischer, *Bureaucrat and Intellectual in the Ottoman Empire*, 134–135; Heger, "The Status and the Image of the Persianate Artist," 87. For Ali's strong Ottoman identity, see Brookes, *Table of Delicacies Concerning the Rules of Social Gatherings*.

55. Christine Woodhead, "Naʿīmā," *Encyclopaedia of Islam*, 2nd ed. (Brill Online, 2012).

56. Mustafa Naima, *Tarih-i Naima: Rawdat al-Husayn fi Khulasat Akhbar al-Khafiqin* (Istanbul: Matbaa-ı Amire, AH 1281), 2:413 (for AH 1036/1626–1627), 3:362 (for 1048/1638), 5:336–37 (for AH 1062/1653), 6:170 (for AH 1066/1656).

57. Wishnitzer, "Teaching Time: Schools, Schedules, and the Ottoman Pursuit of Progress," *New Perspective on Turkey* (2010), 8.

58. Rhoads Murphey, "The Ottoman Attitude towards the Adoption of Western Technology: The Role of the Efrenci Technicians in Civil and Military Applications," in *Contributions à l'histoire économique et sociale de l'Empire Ottoman*, edited by Jean-Louis Bacqué-Grammont and Paul Dumont (Louvain: Peeters, 1983), 287–298.

59. Tuncay Zorlu, *Innovation and Empire in Turkey: Sultan Selim III and the Modernisation of the Ottoman Navy* (London: I. B. Tauris, 2008), chap. 3, "The Role of Foreign Missions in the Ottoman Naval Transformation," 77–109.

60. Bernard Lewis, *The Emergence of Modern Turkey*, 2nd ed. (London: Oxford University Press, 1968), 82.

61. Mehmed Süreyya, *Sicill-i Osmani* (Istanbul: Darülmaarif, AH 1311 [1893–1894]), 1:246, 2:441; Hans Georg Majer, "Aḥmed Pasha, Bonneval," *Encyclopaedia of Islam*, 3rd ed. (Brill Online, 2015); H. Bowen, "Aḥmad Pa<u>sh</u>a Bonneval," *Encyclopaedia of Islam*, 2nd ed. (Brill Online, 2012); Lewis, *The Emergence of Modern Turkey*, 47–48.

62. Miri Shefer, "Ṭibbiyye-i ʿAdliyye-i <u>Sh</u>āhāne," *Encyclopaedia of Islam*, 2nd ed. (Brill Online, 2012).

63. Avner Wishnitzer, "Teaching Time: Schools, Schedules, and the Ottoman Pursuit of Progress," *New Perspectives on Turkey* 43 (2010): 5–32.

64. Eugene L. Rogan, "Aşiret Mektebi: Abdülhamid II's School for Tribes (1892–1907)," *IJMES* 28 (1996): 83–107.

65. Emine Önhan Evered, "An Educational Prescription for the Sultan: Hüseyin Hilmi Paşa's Advice for the Maladies of Empire," *Middle Eastern Studies* 43 (2007): 439–459.

66. K. E. Fleming, "Women as Preservers of the Past: Ziya Gökalp and Women's Reform," in *Deconstructing Images of "The Turkish Woman,"* edited by Zehra F. Arat (New York: Palgrave, 2000), 127–138.

67. Benjamin C. Fortna, *Imperial Classroom* (Oxford: Oxford University Press, 2002); Somel, *The Modernization of Public Education in the Ottoman Empire, 1839–1908*; Wishnitzer, "Teaching Time."

68. Douglas Scott Brookes, trans. and ed., *The Concubine, the Princess, and the Teacher: Voices from the Ottoman Harem* (Austin: University of Texas Press, 2008), 194–272.

69. Aron Rodrigue, *French Jews, Turkish Jews: The Alliance Israelite Universelle and the Politics of Jewish Schooling in Turkey, 1860–1925* (Bloomington: Indiana University Press, 1990).

70. Feyyat Gökçe and Nilüfer Oğuz, "Minority and Foreign Schools on [*sic*] the Ottoman Education System," *E-International Journal of Educational Research* 1, no. 1 (2010): 42–57.

71. Barbara Reeves-Ellington, "A Vision of Mount Holyoke in the Ottoman Balkans: American Cultural Transfer, Bulgarian Nation-Building and Women's Educational Reform, 1858–1870," *Gender and History* 16 (2004): 146–171; Reeves-Ellington, "Education: Missionary—The Ottoman Empire, Nineteenth Century," *Encyclopedia of Women and Islamic Cultures* (Brill Online, 2012).

72. A. H. Shissler, "A Student Abroad in Late Ottoman Times: Ahmet Ağaoğlu and French Paradigms in Turkish Thought," in *Iran and Beyond: Essays in Middle Eastern History in Honor of Nikki R. Keddie*, edited by Rudi Matthee and Beth Baron (Costa Mesa, CA: Mazda, 2000), 35–55.

73. Fortna, *Imperial Classroom.*

74. Vamik D. Volkan and Norman Itzkowitz, *The Immortal Atatürk: A Psychobiography* (Chicago: University of Chicago Press, 1984), 12–37.

CHAPTER 3: THE TRANSFER OF KNOWLEDGE TO, FROM, AND WITHIN THE OTTOMAN EMPIRE

1. Y. Tzvi Langermann, "No Reagent, No Reaction: The Barren Transmission of Avicennan Dynamics to Ḥasdai Crexas," *Aleph* 12, no. 1 (2012): 161–188.

2. Sonja Brentjes, "Medieval Portolan Charts as Documents of Shared Cultural Spaces," in *Acteurs des transferts culturels en Méditerranée médiévale*, edited by R. Abdellatif et al. (Munich: Oldenbourg Velag, 2012), 135; John-Paul A. Ghobrial, *The*

Whispers of Cities: Information Flows in Istanbul, London, and Paris in the Age of William Trumbull (Oxford: Oxford University Press, 2013).

3. Following Kostas Gavroglu, Manolis Patiniotis, Faidra Papanelopoulou et al., "Science and Technology in the European Periphery: Some Historiographical Reflections," *History of Science* 46 (2008): 153–175; Manolis Patiniotis, "Eclecticism and Appropriation of the New Scientific Methods by the Greek-Speaking Scholars in the Ottoman Empire," in *Science between Europe and Asia: Historical Studies on the Transmission, Adoption, and Adaptation of Knowledge*, edited by Feza Günergun and Dhruv Raina (New York: Springer, 2011), 193–206.

4. Sebastian Günther, "Literacy," in *Encyclopaedia of the Qur'ān* (Brill Online, 2012).

5. David Sheffler, "Late Medieval Education: Continuity and Change," *History Compass* 8, no. 9 (2010): 1067–1082; Maristella Botticini and Zvi Eckstein, *The Chosen Few: How Education Shaped Jewish History, 70–1492* (Princeton, NJ: Princeton University Press, 2012).

6. Jack Goody, *The Logic of Writing and the Organization of Society* (Cambridge: Cambridge University Press, 1986); Goody, *The Interface between the Written and the Oral* (Cambridge: Cambridge University Press, 1987); Goody, *The Power of the Written Tradition* (Washington, D.C.: Smithsonian Institution Press, 2000).

7. Emine Fetvacı, *Picturing History at the Ottoman Court* (Bloomington: Indiana University Press, 2013), esp. chap. 1, "Circulation, Audience, and the Creation of a Shared Court Culture," 25–58.

8. Maurits H. van den Boogert, "Patrick Russell and the Republic of Letters in Aleppo," in *The Republic of Letters and the Levant*, edited by Alastair Hamilton et al. (Leiden: Brill, 2005), 244.

9. M. Çağatay Uluçay, *Osmanlı Sulranlarına Aşk Mektupları* (Istanbul: Ufuk Kitapları, 2001 [Vakıt Matbaası, 1950]); Çağatay Uluçay, *Harem II* (Ankara: Türk Tarih Kurumu Basımevi, 1992), 86–87.

10. Leslie Peirce, "Polyglottism in the Ottoman Empire: A Reconsideration," in *Braudel Revisted: The Mediterranean World, 1600–1800*, edited by Gabriel Piterberg, Teofilo F. Ruiz, and Geoffrey Symcox (Toronto: University of Toronto Press, 2010), 76–98.

11. M. Şükrü Hanioğlu, *A Brief History of the Late Ottoman Empire* (Princeton, NJ: Princeton University Press, 2008), 33.

12. Hanioğlu, *A Brief History of the Late Ottoman Empire*, 34–37.

13. Musa Duman, "Turkish Language During the Reform Period," in *The Turks*, edited by Hasan Celâl Güzel et al. (Ankara: Yeni Türkiye, 2002), vol. 4: *The Ottomans*, 723–724; Geoffrey L. Lewis, *The Turkish Language Reform: A Catastrophic Success* (Oxford: Oxford University Press, 1999), chap. 2, "Ottoman Turkish," 7–12; Uriel Heyd, *Language Reform in Modern Turkey* (Jerusalem: Israel Oriental Society, 1954), "Introduction: An Outline of Early Turkish Language Reform," 9–10.

14. Duman, "Turkish Language," 724–725; Lewis, *Turkish Language Reform*, 12.

15. Duman, "Turkish Language," 725–730; Lewis, *Turkish Language Reform*, 12–13; Heyd, *Language Reform in Modern Turkey*, 10–12.

16. Duman, "Turkish Language," 730–733; Lewis, *Turkish Language Reform*, 14–26; Heyd, *Language Reform in Modern Turkey*, 12–12.

17. Benjamin C. Fortna, *Learning to Read in the Late Ottoman Empire and the Early Turkish Republic* (Basingstoke: Palgrave Macmillan, 2011), 2–7. For the transition to the early republic period see also Yılmaz Çolak, "Language Policy and Official Ideology in Early Republican Turkey," *Middle Eastern Studies* 40, no. 6 (November 2004): 69–70.

18. Ibid.

19. J. Sourdel-Thomine, "K͟haṭṭ; i. In the Arab World," *Encyclopaedia of Islam* , 2nd ed. (Brill Online, 2012).

20. Süreyya, *Sicill-i Osmanı*, 2:243–244.

21. On the relationship between the state and calligraphy in the late Ottoman period, see Zoe Griffith, "Calligraphy and the Art of Statecraft in the Late Ottoman Empire and Modern Turkish Republic," *Comparative Studies of South Asia, Africa and the Middle East* 31 (2011): 601–614.

22. Emine Fetvacı, "Enriched Narratives and Empowered Images in Seventeenth-Century Ottoman Manuscripts," *Ars Orientalis* 40 (2011): 243–266.

23. M. Uğur Derman, *Letters in Gold: Ottoman Calligraphy from the Sakıp Sabancı Collection, Istanbul* (New York: Metropolitan Museum of Art, 1998), 21.

24. Sheila S. Blair, *Islamic Calligraphy* (Edinburgh: Edinburgh University Press, 2006), chap. 11, "The Ottomans in Anatolia, the Balkans, and the Eastern Mediterranean," 476–533; Ali̇ Alparslan, "K͟haṭṭ; iii. In Turkey," *Encyclopaedia of Islam*, 2nd ed. (Brill Online, 2012).

25. Amy Singer, "The Mülknāmes of Hürrem Sultan's Waqf in Jerusalem," *Muqarnas* 14 (1997): 96–102; Blair, *Islamic Calligraphy*, 509–513; Carol G. Fisher, "Naḳḳās͟h-K͟hāna," *Encyclopaedia of Islam*, 2nd ed. (Brill Online, 2012).

26. Singer, "The Mülknāmes," Jerusalem," 99.

27. Elizabeth L. Eisenstein, *The Printing Revolution in Early Modern Europe*, 2nd ed. (Cambridge: Cambridge University Press, 2005).

28. Jonathan M. Bloom, *Paper before Print: The History of and Impact of Paper in the Islamic World* (New Haven, CT: Yale University Press, 2001), 221. On the history of printing in the Muslim world in general, see G. Oman et al., "Maṭbaʿa," *Encyclopaedia of Islam*, 2nd ed. (Brill Online, 2012).

29. Orlin Sabev, *İbrahim Müteferrika ya da İlk Osmanlı Matbaa Serüveni (1726–1746): Yeniden Değerlendirme* (Istanbul: Yeditepe Yayınevi, 2006); Sabev, "The First Ottoman-Turkish Printing Enterprise: Success or Failure?," in *Ottoman Tulips, Ottoman Coffee: Leisure and Lifestyle in the Eighteenth Century*, edited by Dana Sajdi (London: I. B. Tauris, 2007), 63–89 (188–194, notes); Sabev, "Formation of Ottoman Print Culture (1726–1746): Some General Remarks," *New Europe College Yearbook: Regional Program 2003–2004, 2004–2005* (Bucharest: New Europe College, 2007), 293–333; Yasemin Gencer, "İbrahim Mütefrrika and the Age of Printed Manuscript," in *The Islamic Manuscript Tradition*, edited by Christiane Gruber (Bloomington: Indiana University Press, 2010), 155–193; Maurits H. van den Boogert, "The Sultan's Answer

to the Medici Press? Ibrahim Müteferrika's Printing House in Istanbul," in *The Republic of Letters and the Levant*, edited by Alastair Hamilton et al. (Leiden: Brill, 2005), 265–291.

30. İbrahim Peçevi, *Tarih-i Peçevi* (Istanbul: Matbaa-ı Amire, AH 1283 [1867], 1:107; Fr. Babinger and Christine Woodhead, "Pečewī," *Encyclopaedia of Islam*, 2nd ed. (Brill Online, 2012).

31. Bekir Harun Küçük, "Early Enlightenment in Istanbul" (PhD diss., University of California, San Diego, 2013).

32. Bloom, *Paper before Print*, 220.

33. Orlin Sabev, "Rich Men, Poor Men: Ottoman Printers and Booksellers Making Fortune or Seeking Survival (Eighteenth-Nineteenth Centuries)," *Oriens* 37 (2009): 178.

34. Van den Boogert, "The Sultan's Answer to the Medici Press?," 277.

35. Hanna, *In Praise of Books*, 83–84, 89–90.

36. Messick, *The Calligraphic State*, chap. 12 "Spiral Texts," 231–250.

37. Francis Robinson, "Technology and Religious Change: Islam and the Impact of Print," *Modern Asian Studies* 27 (1993): 229–251; Bloom, *Paper before Print*, 10, 220.

38. Bloom, *Paper before Print*, 222.

39. Evliya Çelebi, *Seyahatname*, 1:525, 609. The information is not consistent and includes various contradictions in quoting numbers and in identifying patrons or the founding fathers of the various guilds.

40. Sabev, "Rich Men, Poor Men," 180.

41. Fortna, *Learning to Read in the Late Ottoman Empire and the Early Turkish Republic*, 141, 143–148. For a scholarly interdisciplinary discussion of "Visual Literacy," see "What Is Visual Literacy?" on the International Visual Literacy Association [IVLA] website (Aug. 2, 2012), http://www.ivla.org/org_what_vis_lit.htm.

42. Fetvacı, "Enriched Narratives and Empowered Images in Seventeenth-Century Ottoman Manuscripts."

43. *Yazma Eserlerden Tıbbi Bitki Hayvan ve Madenler Sergisi/Materia Medica Miniature Pictures Exhibition*, viii, x, xii–xvi; Jean A. Givens et al., eds., *Visualising Medieval Medicine and Natural History, 1200–1550* (Aldershot: Ashgate, 2006); Jaclynne J. Kerner, "Art in the Name of Science: The Kitāb al-Diryāq in Text and Image," in *Arab Painting: Text and Image in Illustrated Arabic Manuscripts*, edited by Anna Contadini (Leiden: Brill, 2007), 25–39; George Saliba and Linda Komoroff, "Illustrated Books May Be Hazardous to Your Health: A New Reading of the Arabic Perception and Rendition of the Materia Medica of Dioscorides," *Ars Orientalis* 35 (2008): 6–65; Sarıcıoğlu, "Ottoman Cartography," 836.

44. Karen Pinto, "Searchin' his eyes, lookin' for traces: Piri Reis' World Map of 1513 and Its Islamic Iconographic Connections (A Reading through Bağdat 334 and Proust)," *Osmanlı Araştırmaları/Journal of Ottoman Studies* 39 (2012): 64.

45. A good introduction to Ottoman cartography is Svat Soucek, "Ottoman Cartography," in Soucek, *Studies in Ottoman Naval History and Maritime Geography* (Istanbul: Isis, 2009), 225–238; Fikret Sarıcaoğlu, "Ottoman Cartography," in *The Turks*,

vol. 3: *The Ottomans*, edited by Hasan Celâl Güzel et al. (Ankara: Yeni Türkiye, 2000), 831–840.

46. Ahmet T. Karamustafa, "Military, Administrative, and Scholarly Maps and Plans," in *The History of Cartography*, vol. 2, book 1: *Cartography in the Traditional Islamic and South Asian Societies*, edited by J. B. Harley and David Woodward (Chicago: Chicago University Press, 1987), 221–222; Sonja Brentjes, "On Two Manuscripts by Abū Bakr b. Bahrām al-Dimashqī (d. 1102/1691) to W. and J. Blaeu's *Atlas Minor*," *Osmanlı Araştırmaları/Journal of Ottoman Studies* 40 (2012): 171–192.

47. Evliya Çelebi, *Seyahatname*, 1:548; *The Seyahatname of Evliya Çelebi: Facsimile of Topkapı Sarayı Bağdat 304*, 1b:329.

48. Pinto, "Piri Reis' World Map of 1513 and Its Islamic Iconographic Connections," 63–94; Muharrem Cerabregu, "Scientific Benefits from Piri Reis's Kitab-i Bahriye and Its Position in the History of Cartography," *XI. Türk Tarih Kongresi, Ankara . . . 1990: Kongreye sunulan bildiriler* (Ankara: Türk Tarih Kurumu Basımevi, 1994), 3:1105–1125; Emily Zoss, "An Ottoman View of the World: The Kitab Cihanüma and Its Cartographic Contexts," in *The Islamic Manuscript Tradition*, edited by Christiane Gruber (Bloomington: Indiana University Press, 2010), 194–219; S. Soucek, "Pīrī Reʾīs," *Encyclopaedia of Islam*, 2nd ed. (Brill Online, 2012).

49. Norman J. Johnson, "The Urban World of the Matraki Manuscript," Journal of Near Eastern Studies 30 (1971): 159–176; Hüseyin G. Yurdaydin, "Maṭrāḳčī," *Encyclopaedia of Islam*, 2nd ed. (Brill Online, 2012).

50. Elizabeth B. Frierson, "Cheap and Easy: The Creation of Consumer Culture in Late Ottoman Society," in *Consumption Studies and the History of the Ottoman Empire, 1559–1922: An Introduction*, edited by Donald Quataert (Albany: State University of New York Press, 2000), 243–260; Şeni, "Fashion and Women's Clothing in the Satirical Press of Istanbul at the End of the 19th Century."

51. Ramazan Şeşen, "Onbeşinci Yüzyılda Türkçeye Tercumeler," *XI. Türk Tarih Kongresi, Ankara . . . 1990: Kongreye sunulan bildiriler* (Ankara: Türk Tarih Kurumu Basımevi, 1994), 3:899–919.

52. Ünver, "XVinci Asırda Türkiyede Tecrubi Tababete ait İki Misal"; Yıldırım, "XV. Yüzyıla ait Anonim Bir Cerrahnâme Cerrahi Yöntemlerin Kullanıldığı Fasıllar Tıbbı Terminoloji ile Bitki, Drog ve Madde Isimleri."

53. Gottfried Hagen, "Translations and Translators in a Multilingual Society: A Case Study of Persian-Ottoman Translations, Late Fifteenth to Early Sixteenth Century," *Eurasian Studies* 2 (1) (2003): 95–134; Tijana Krstic, "Of Translation and Empire: Sixteenth-Century Ottoman Imperial Interpreters as Renaissance Go-Betweens," in *The Ottoman World*, edited by Christine Woodhead (London and New York: Routledge, 2012), 130–142.

54. Following Karen L. Fresco and Charles D. Wright, eds., *Translating the Middle Ages* (Farnham, Surrey: Ashgate, 2012).

55. Şemsüddin İtaki, *Teşrih-ī Ebdan* (Islamabad: al Majlis al-Watanī, lilhijra, AH 1410 [1990]), 244–249; Şemsüddin İtaki, *Şemseddîn-i İtâkî'nin Resimli Anatomi Kitabı*, edited by Esin Kâhya (Ankara: Atatürk Kültür Merkezi Yayını, 1996), 1–2, 231–232

(transliteration to modern Turkish); 236–238 (in the appendix, a transcription of the Ottoman text). The English translation is found in Şemsüddin İtaki, *The Treatise on Anatomy of the Human Body and Interpretation of Philosophers* (Islamabad: National Hijra Council, AH 1410/AD 1990), 122–124.

56. Esin Kâhya, "One of the Samples of the Influences of Avicenna on the Ottoman Medicine, Shams al-Din Itaqi," *Belleten* 64, no. 4 (2000): 63–68.

57. Şemsüddin İtaki, *Teşrih-ī Ebdan*, 60–62, 64, 77, 82–83, 85–87, 89–95, 97, 99, 112, 137–138, 157, 178, 203, 223, 232–235, 239–240; Gül Russell, "'The Owl and the Pussycat': The Process of Cultural Transmission in Anatomical Illustration," in *Transfer of Modern Science and Technology to the Muslim World*, edited by Ekmeleddin İhsanoğlu (Istanbul: Research Centre for Islamic History, Art and Culture, 1992), 191–195; Adıvar, *Osmanlı Türklerinde İlim*, 129–130; Esin Kâhya and Aysegül D. Erdemir, *Işığında Osmanlıdan Cumhuriyete Tıp ve Sağlık Kurumları* (Ankara: Türkiye Diyanet Vakfı Yayınları, 2000), 188–179.

58. Ṣāliḥ bin Naṣrallāh Ibn Sallūm, *Ghāyat al-itqān fi tadbīr badan al-insān* (manuscript held Cambridge University Library, Add. 3532).

59. Some examples are *Ghayat al-bayan fi tadbir badan al-insan* (manuscript held at the Cambridge University Library, Cambridge, P.27 Brown); *Ghayat al-bayan fi tadbir badan al-insan* (manuscript held at the Princeton University Library, Princeton, NJ, Garret 1181H); *Ghayat al-bayan fi tadbir badan al-insan* (manuscript held at the Princeton University Library, Princeton NJ, New Series 998).

60. See, for example, two manuscripts in the Cambridge University Library from the first half of the nineteenth century: Edward G. Browne, *A Supplementary Hand-List of the Muhammadan Manuscripts including all those Written in the Arabic Character, Preserved in the Libraries of the University and Colleges of Cambridge* (Cambridge: Cambridge University Press, 1922), 169.

61. Emilie Savage-Smith, "Drug Therapy of Eye Disease in Seventeenth-Century Islamic Medicine: The Influence of the 'New Chemistry' of the Paracelsians," *Pharmacy in History* 29 (1987): 3–28; Savage-Smith, "The Influence of 'New Chemistry' of the Paracelsians upon Seventeenth-Century Arabic Medicine and Its Application to the Treatment of Eye Disease." I thank Professor Savage-Smith for making her unpublished article available.

62. Natalia Bachour, *Oswaldus Crollius und Daniel Sennert in frühneuzeitlichen Istanbul: Studien zur Rezeption des Paracelsismus im Werk des osmanischen Arztes Ṣāliḥ b. Naṣrallāh Ibn Sallūm al-Ḥalabī* (Freiburg: Centaurus, 2012).

63. Küçük, "Early Enlightenment in Istanbul," 115.

64. Nil Sarı, "18. ve 19. Asırda Kimyager Hekimlerin Kullandıkları Âletler," *Tıp Tarihi Araştırmaları* 1 (1986): 51–78.

65. Küçük, "Early Enlightenment in Istanbul," 104–126.

66. Eric R. Dursteler, "Speaking in Tongues: Language and Communication in the Early Modern Mediterranean," *Past and Present* 217 (2012): 47.

67. Ibid., 52–53.

68. Semavi Eyice, "Dr. Karl Ambros Bernard (Charles Ambroise Bernard) ve

Mekteb-i Tibbiye-i Şahane'ye Dair Bir Kaç Not," in *Türk Tıbbının Batılılaşması*, edited by Arslan Terzioğlu and Erwin Lucius (Istanbul: Arkeoloji ve Sanat Yayınları, 1993), 97–98; Shefer, "Ṭibbiyye-i ʿAdliyye-i Shāhāne."

69. R. H. Davison, "Shānī-zāde Meḥmed ʿAṭāʾ Allāh Efendi," *Encyclopaedia of Islam*, 2nd ed. (Brill Online, 2012).

70. Carter V. Findley, *Bureaucratic Reform in the Ottoman Empire: The Sublime Porte, 1789–1922* (Princeton, NJ: Princeton University Press, 1980), 186; Findley, *Ottoman Civil Officialdom* (Princeton, NJ: Princeton University Press, 1989), 133–134, 153, 258, 260, 262–264, 280; Lewis, *Emergence of Modern Turkey*, 86–87.

71. An international conference in February-March 2013 at the Center for Middle East Studies at the University of Chicago was dedicated to translation and transmission of knowledge in the Ottoman Empire during the long seventeenth century, seeking to highlight the people involved in this process (http://cmes.uchicago.edu/page/translations-translators-and-converts-transmission-knowledge-seventeenth-century-ottoman-land).

72. Göçek, *East Encounters West*, 116–135.

73. For the Venetian-Latin example, see E. Natalie Rothman, "Interpreting Dragomans: Boundaries and Crossings in the Early Modern Mediterranean," Comparative Studies in Society and History 51 (2009): 771–800. For an example of dragomans' accumulation of property, see Colin Heywood, "A Buyuruldu of AH 1100/A.D. 1689 for the Dragomans of the English Embassy of Istanbul," in *The Balance of Truth: Essays in Honour of Professor Geoffrey Lewis*, edited by Çiğdem Balım-Harding and Colin Imber (Istanbul: Isis Press, 2000), 125–144.

74. V. Miović Perić, "Dragomans of the Dubrovnik Republic: Their Training and Career," *Dubrovnik Annals* 5 (2001): 85–87.

75. Alexander H. de Groot, "The Changing National Character of the Dragoman (1756–1863)," in *Fremde Erfahrungen: Asiaten und Afrikaner in Deutschland, Österreich und in der Schweiz bis 1945*, edited by Gerhard Höpp (Berlin: Das Arabische Buch, 1996), 297–317; de Groot, "Protection And Nationality: The Decline of The Dragomans," in *Istanbul et les langues orientales. Actes du colloque . . . Istanbul . . . 1995*, edited by Frédéric Hitzel (Paris: L'Harmattan, 1997), 235–255.

76. Christiane Phillio, "Mischief in the Old Regime: Provincial Dragomans and Social Change at the Turn of the Nineteenth Century," *New Perspectives on Turkey* 25 (2001): 103–121.

77. Frank Castiglione, "'Levantine' Dragomans in Nineteenth Century Istanbul: The Pisans, the British, and Issues of Subjecthood," *Osmanlı Araştırmaları/Journal of Ottoman Studies* 44 (2014): 169–195.

78. Kemal Çiçek, "Interpreters of the Court in the Ottoman Empire as Seen from the Sharia Court Records of Cyprus," *Islamic Law and Society* 9 (2002): 1–15.

79. Suraiya Faroqhi, "Selānīk," *Encyclopaedia of Islam*, 2nd ed. (Brill Online, 2012).

80. Speros Vryonis Jr., "Religious Changes and Patterns in the Balkans, 14th–16th Centuries," in *Aspects of the Balkans: Continuity and Change*, edited by Henrik Birnbaum and Speros Vryonis Jr. (The Hague: Mouton, 1972), 163.

81. Eyal Ginio, "Marginals in an Ottoman Town: The Case of Eighteenth Century Salonika" (PhD diss., Hebrew University of Jerusalem, 1998).

82. Mark Mazower, *Salonica, City of Ghosts: Christians, Muslims and Jews, 1430–1950* (New York: Knopf, 2004).

83. Victoria Hislop, *The Thread* (London: Headline Review, 2011).

84. Annelies Kuyt, "With One Foot in the Renaissance: Shlomo Almoli and His Dream Interpretation," *Jewish Studies Quarterly* 6 (1999): 205–217; "Almoli (Almuli), Solomon ben Jacob," *Encyclopaedia Judaica*, edited by Michael Berenbaum and Fred Skolnik, 2nd ed. (Detroit: Macmillan Reference USA, 2007), 1:682, Gale Virtual Reference Library (web) (accessed Aug. 4, 2011).

85. Ron Barkai, "Between East and West: A Jewish Doctor from Spain," *Mediterranean Historical Review* 10 (1995): 49–63; Manfred Ullman, *Die Medizin im Islam* (Leiden: Brill, 1970), 249, 348–349.

86. Avner Ben-Zaken, "Bridging Networks of Trust: Practicing Astronomy in Late Sixteenth-Century Salonika," *Jewish History* 23 (2009): 343–361.

87. Y. Tzvi Langermann, "Medicine, Mechanics and Magic from Moses ben Judah Galeano's *Ta'alumot Ḥokmah*," *Aleph* 9 (2009): 353–377; Robert Morrison, "A Scholarly Intermediary between the Ottoman Empire and Renaissance Europe," *Isis* 105 (2014): 32–57.

88. Marc David Baer, *The Dönme: Jewish Converts, Muslim Revolutionaries, and Secular Turks* (Stanford, CA: Stanford University Press, 2010), esp. the second chapter, "Religious and Mortal Education, Schools and Their Effects," 44–64.

89. For example, Sonja Brentjes, "On the Relation between the Ottoman Empire and the West European Republic of Letters (17th–18th Centuries)," in *Proceedings of the International Congress of Learning and Education in the Ottoman World, Istanbul, 12–15 April 1999*, edited by A. Çaksu (Istanbul: Research Centre for Islamic History, Art and Culture, 2001), 121–148.

90. Sonja Brentjes, "The Interests of the Republic of Letters in the Middle East, 1550–1700," *Science in Context* 12 (1999): 465.

91. Van den Boogert, "Patrick Russell and the Republic of Letters in Aleppo," 223–264.

92. In recent years, much has been written about intercultural contact in the Mediterranean and the Ottoman Empire. Noted here are only a few of the most prominent researchers and their works: Gerald MacLean, *The Rise of Oriental Travel: English Visitors to the Ottoman Empire, 1580–1720* (New York: Palgrave Macmillan, 2004); Eric Dursteler, *Venetians in Constantinople: Nation, Identity, and Coexistence in the Early Modern Mediterranean* (Baltimore, MD: Johns Hopkins University Press, 2006); Nabil Matar, *Turks, Moors and Englishmen in the Age of Discovery* (New York: Columbia University Press, 1999).

93. Billie Melman, *Women's Orient: English Women and the Middle East, 1718–1918: Sexuality, Religion, and Work* (Houndmills, Basingstoke, UK: Macmillan, 1992).

94. *The Complete Letters of Lady Mary Wortley Montagu*, edited by R. Halsbad, 3 vols. (Oxford: Clarendon Press, 1965–1967), 1:337–340.

95. Nadav Davidovitch and Zalman Greenberg, "Public Health, Culture, and Colonial Medicine: Smallpox and Variolation in Palestine during the British Mandate," *Public Health Chronicles* 122 (May–June 2007): 398–406.

96. On the transfer of scientific knowledge from the "high" to the "low" levels and vice versa, to the extent that its origin is completely forgotten, see Ghada Karmi, "The Colonisation of Traditional Arabic Medicine," in *Patients and Practitioners: Lay Perceptions of Medicine in Pre-Industrial Society*, edited by Roy Porter (Cambridge: Cambridge University Press, 1985), 315–339.

97. Studies that focus on North Africa and less on the Levant include Nabil Matar, ed. and trans., *In the Lands of the Christians: Arabic Travel Writing in the 17th Century* (New York: Routledge, 2003); and Matar, *Europe through Arab Eyes, 1578–1727* (New York: Columbia University Press, 2009).

98. Dankoff, *An Ottoman Mentality: The World of Evliya Çelebi.*

99. Neşe Erim, "Trade, Traders and the State in Eighteenth-Century Erzurum," *New Perspectives on Turkey* 5–6 (1991): 123–141.

100. Marc Baer, "Globalization, Cosmopolitanism, and the Dönme in Ottoman Salonica and Turkish Istanbul," *Journal of World History* 18 (2007): 141–170.

101. On this point I benefited from my PhD student Ms. Irena Fliter, who is working on her doctoral project titled "Ottoman Diplomats and the Culture of Diplomacy: Ambassadors, Chargés d'Affairs and Dragomans between the Ottoman Empire and Prussia (1761–1821)."

CHAPTER 4: STATE IN SCIENCE

1. Graham Burchell et al., eds., *The Foucault Effect: Studies in Governmentality* (Chicago: University of Chicago Press, 1991).

2. Sonja Brentjes, "Courtly Patronage of the Ancient Sciences in Post-Classical Islamic Societies," *Al-Qanṭara* 29 (2008): 403–436.

3. Sonja Brentjes, "The Language of 'Patronage' in Islamic Societies before 1700," *Cuadernos del Cemyr* 20 (2012): 11–22.

4. Ehud R. Toledano, "The Emergence of Ottoman-Local Elites (1700–1800): A Framework for Research," in *Middle Eastern Politics and Ideas: A History from Within*, edited by I. Pappé and M. Maʿoz (London: Tauris Academic Studies, 1997), 145–162.

5. Dror Ze'evi, "A Chaotic Empire: The Ottoman Household as a Dynamic Vector," in *Turkey: The Ottoman Past and the Republican Presence* (in Hebrew), edited by Michael Winter and Miri Shefer (Tel Aviv: Tel Aviv University, the Moshe Dayan Center for Middle Eastern and African Studies, 2007), 15–26; Claudia Derichs and Diane E. King, "Patronage and Clientage," *Encyclopedia of Women and Islamic Cultures* (Brill Online, 2012).

6. Brentjes, "The Language of 'Patronage'" in Islamic Societies before 1700."

7. Ibid.

8. Orhan Pamuk, *Benim Adım Kırımızı* (Istanbul: İletişim, 1998).

9. Esin Atil, ed., *Islamic Art and Patronage* (New York: Rizzoli, 1990).

10. Gülru Necipoğlu, "A Kānūn for the State, a Canon for the Arts: Conceptualizing the Classical Synthesis of Ottoman Arts and Architecture," in *Soliman le Magnifique et son temps*, edited by Gilles Veinstein (Paris: Rencontres de l'Ecole du Louvre, 1992), 195–216.

11. Fetvacı, *Picturing History at the Ottoman Court*, esp. chap. 2, "Making Books at the Ottoman Court," 59–98.

12. Marshall G. S. Hodgson, *The Venture of Islam: Conscience and History in a World Civilization* (Chicago: University of Chicago Press, 1974), vol. 3: *The Gunpowder Empires and Modern Times*, 14–15.

13. Terence Kealey, *The Economic Laws of Scientific Research* (Basingstoke, UK: Macmillan, 1996).

14. Terence Kealey, *Sex, Science and Profits* (London: William Heinemann, 2008).

15. Kealey may be right that governmental "neglect" in fact leads to better science, but does that mean that this science is necessarily better for us? Kealey would like the system to evolve on its own, but exogenous moral and cultural considerations should affect the scientific system as well.

16. Hodgson, *The Venture of Islam*, 15.

17. Amy Singer, *Constructing Ottoman Beneficence: An Imperial Soup Kitchen in Jerusalem* (Albany: State University of New York Press, 2002); Singer, *Charity in Islamic Societies* (Cambridge: Cambridge University Press, 2008).

18. Avner Ben-Zaken, "Political Economy and Scientific Activity in the Ottoman Empire," in *The Turks*, edited by Hasan Celal Güzel et al., vol. 3: *The Ottomans* (Ankara: Yeni Türkiye Publications, 2002), 776–794.

19. Al-Muḥibbī, *Ta'rīkh Khulaṣat al-Athr*, 2:240–242; Mehmed bin Mustafa Raşed Efendi, *Tarih-i Raşed* (Istanbul: Matbaa-i Amire, 1282AH [1865]), 1:96, 164.

20. N. A. Stillmann, "Khilʿa," *Encyclopaedia of Islam*, 2nd ed. (Brill Online, 2012); Stewart Gordon, ed., *Robes and Honor: The Medieval World of Investiture* (New York: Palgrave, 2001).

21. Miri Shefer, "Old Patterns, New Meaning: The 1845 Hospital of Bezm-i ʿAlem in Istanbul," *Dynamis: Acta hispanica ad medicinae scientiarumque historiam illustrandam* 25 (2005): 329–350.

22. Feza Günergün and Şeref Etker, "Waqf Endowments and the Emergence of Modern Charitable Hospitals in the Ottoman Empire: The Case of Zeynep-Kamil Hospital in Istanbul," in *The Development of Modern Medicine in Non-Western Countries*, edited by Hormoz Ebrahimnejad (London: Routledge, 2009), 82–107.

23. Franz Babinger, *Mehmed the Conqueror and His Time* (Princeton, NJ: Princeton University Press, 1978), 462, 473, 485.

24. Gabor Ágoston, *Guns for the Sultan: Military Power and the Weapons Industry in the Ottoman Empire* (Cambridge: Cambridge University Press, 2005), 43.

25. Karen Pinto, "The Maps Are the Message: Mehmet II's Patronage of an 'Ottoman Cluster,'" *Imago Mundi* 63, no. 2 (2011): 155–179.

26. Maria Mavroudi, "Translators from Greek into Arabic at the Court of Mehmet

the Conqueror," in *The Byzantine Court: Source of Power and Culture*, edited by A. Ödekan et al. (Istanbul: Koç University Press, 2013), 202.

27. Karamustafa, "Military, Administrative, and Scholarly Maps and Plans," 210–215.

28. Gábor Ágoston, "Where Environmental and Frontier Studies Meet: Rivers, Forests, Marshes and Forts along the Ottoman-Hapsburg Frontier in Hungary," in *The Frontiers of the Ottoman World*, edited by A. C. S. Peacock (Oxford: The British Academy, by Oxford University Press, 2009), 66.

29. Mavroudi, "Translators from Greek into Arabic at the Court of Mehmed the Conqueror," 195–207.

30. Pinto, "The Maps Are the Message."

31. Ágoston, "Ottoman Artillery and European Military Technology," 21, 23–24; Ágoston, *Guns for the Sultan*, 17.

32. Ágoston, *Guns for the Sultan*, 21.

33. Halil İnalcık, "Military and Fiscal Transformation in the Ottoman Empire, 1600–1700," *Archivum Ottomanicum* 6 (1980): 293–294.

34. Ágoston, "Ottoman Artillery and European Military Technology in the Fifteenth and Seventeenth Centuries," 25–26.

35. Babinger, *Mehmed the Conqueror*, 78, 80–81, 82; Ágoston, "Ottoman Artillery and European Military Technology in the Fifteenth and Seventeenth Centuries," 27–28.

36. Babinger, *Mehmed the Conqueror*, 138, 231, 335, 396–397; Ágoston, "Ottoman Artillery and European Military Technology in the Fifteenth and Seventeenth Centuries," 28–29; Ágoston, *Guns for the Sultan*, 44.

37. Ágoston, "Ottoman Artillery and European Military Technology in the Fifteenth and Seventeenth Centuries," 30.

38. Maria Pia Pedari, "Ottoman Ships and Venetian Craftsmen in the Sixteenth Century," in *Seapower, Technology, and Trade: Studies in Turkish Maritime History*, edited by Dejanirah Conto et al. (Istanbul: Denizler Kitabevi, 2014), 460–464.

39. Jonathan Grant, "Rethinking the Ottoman 'Decline'": Military Technology Diffusion in the Ottoman Empire, Fifteenth to Eighteenth Centuries," *Journal of World History* 10 (1999): 200.

40. Thus, for example, the naval reforms of Selim III: Zorlu, *Innovation and Empire in Turkey*, chap. 3, "The Role of Foreign Mission in the Ottoman Naval Transformation," 77–109, 191–200.

41. Virginia Aksan, "Breaking the Spell of the Baron de Tott: Reframing the Question of Military Reform in the Ottoman Empire, 1760–1830," *The International History Review* 24 (2002): 253–277. On other Frenchmen like de Tott, see Mustafa Kaçar, "Osmanlı İmaparatorluğu'nda Askerî Teknik Eğitimde Modernleşme Çalışmaları ve Mühendishanelerin Kuruluşu (1880'e kadar)," *Osmanlı Bilimil Araştırmaları* 2 (1998): 69–137; Kaçar, "Osmanlı Ordusunda Görevli Fransız Subayı Saint-Rémy'nin İsyanbul'daki Top Döküm Çalışmaları (1785–87)," *Osmanlı Bilimil Araştırmaları* 5 (2003): 33–50.

42. Gábor Ágoston, "Empires and Warfare in East-Central Europe, 1550–1750: The Ottoman-Habsburg Rivalry and Military Transformation," in *European Warfare, 1350–1750*, edited by D. Trim and F. Tallett (Cambridge: Cambridge University Press, 2010), 110–134.

43. Helmuth von Moltke, *Under dem Halbmond: Erlebnisse in der alten Türkei 1835–1839*, edited and annotated by Ernst Bartsc (Stuttgart: Erdmann, 1997); Murat Gül and Richard Lamb, "Mapping, Secularizing and Modernizing Ottoman Istanbul: Aspects of Genesis of the 1839 Development Policy," *Urban History* 31 (2004): 421–436.

44. Glen W. Swanson, "War, Technology, and Society in the Ottoman Empire from the Reign of Abdülhamid II to 1913: Mahmud Şevket and the German Military Mission," in *War, Technology and Society in the Middle East*, edited by V. J. Parry and M. E. Yapp (London: Oxford University Press, 1975), 367–385.

45. Friedrich Frieherr Kress von Kressenstein, *Mit den Turken zum Suezkanal* (Berlin: O. Schlegel, 1938).

46. Ulrich Trumpener, "Liman von Sanders and the German-Ottoman Alliance," *Journal of Contemporary History* 1 (1966): 179–192.

47. Hodgson, *The Venture of Islam*, vol. 3: *The Gunpowder Empires and Modern Times*.

48. Ágoston, *Guns for the Sultan*, "Introduction: Firearms and Armaments Industries," 1–14.

49. J. M. Rogers, *Sinan*, Makers of Islamic Civilization, (London: Oxford Centre for Islamic Studies; New York: I. B. Tauris, 2006); Doğan Kuban, "Sinan," in *The Great Ottoman-Turkish Civilization*, vol. 4: *Culture and Arts*, edited by Kemal Çiçek (Ankara: Yeni Türkiye, 2000), 450–463; İsmail Yakıt, "The Modular System in Mimar Sinan's Works of Arts and Ebced Accounting," in *The Great Ottoman-Turkish Civilization*, vol. 4: *Culture and Arts*, 480–485; B. O'Kane, "Sinān," *Encyclopaedia of Islam*.

50. Zeynep Çelik, *Empire, Architecture, and the City: French-Ottoman Encounters, 1830–1914* (Seattle: University of Washington Press, 2008).

51. Zeynep Çelik, *The Remaking of Istanbul: Portrait of an Ottoman City in the Nineteenth Century* (Berkeley: University of California Press, 1993), chap. 6, "Architectural Pluralism and the Search of a Style," 126–154; Filiz Yenişehirlioğlu, "Continuity and Change in Nineteenth-Century Istanbul: Sultan Abdülaziz and the Beylerbeyi Palace," in *Islamic Art in the 19th Century: Tradition, Innovation, and Eclecticism*, edited by Doris Behrens-Abouseif and Stephen Vernoit (Leiden and Boston: Brill, 2006), 63–66.

52. On the Balyans, see Daphna Sharef-Davidovich, "The Imperial Palaces in Istanbul, 1856–1909" (in Hebrew), PhD diss., Ben-Gurion University of the Negev, 2010, 43–49.

53. S. Yerasimos, "Istanbul—VIII. Monuments," *Encyclopaedia of Islam*, 2nd ed. (Brill Online, 2012).

54. Yenişehirlioğlu, "Continuity and Change in Nineteenth-Century Istanbul," 76–77.

55. Shirine Hamadeh, "Public Spaces and the Garden Culture of Istanbul in the Eighteenth Century," in *The Early Modern Ottomans: Remapping the Empire*, edited by

Virginia H. Aksan and Daniel Goffman (Cambridge: Cambridge University Press, 2007), 277–312.

56. Soraya Faroqhi, "Camels, Wagons, and the Ottoman State in the Sixteenth and Seventeenth Centuries," *International Journal of Middle East Studies* 14 (1982): 523–539; Fatih Müderrisoğlu, "Menzil Roads and Menzil Complexes in the Ottoman Empire," in *The Great Ottoman-Turkish Civilization*, vol. 4: *Culture and Arts*, edited by Kemal Çiçek (Ankara: Yeni Türkiye, 2000), 380–388.

57. Grehan, *Everyday Life and Consumer Culture in 18th-Century Damascus*, 35–55.

58. Yakup Bektas, "The Sultan's Messenger: Cultural Constructions of Ottoman Telegraphy," *Technology and Culture* 41 (2000): 671.

59. Soli Shahvar, "Concession Hunting in the Age of Reform: British Companies and the Search for Government Guarantees; Telegraph Concessions in Ottoman Territories, 1855–58," *Middle Eastern Studies* 38, no. 4 (2002): 169–193; Shahvar, "Technology, Diplomacy and European Financial Entrepreneurship in the Ottoman Middle East During the Second Half of the Nineteenth Century: The Indo-European Telegraph Line and the Anglo-Ottoman Conflict of Interests," in *Turkey: The Ottoman Past and the Republican Present* (in Hebrew), edited by Michael Winter and Miri Shefer (Tel Aviv: Dayan Center for Middle Eastern and African Studies, 2007), 211–237.

60. Bektas, "The Sultan's Messenger," 671–672.

61. Ibid., 672–676; Shahvar, "Concession Hunting in the Age of Reform," 169–170; Shahvar, "Technology, Diplomacy and European Financial Entrepreneurship in the Ottoman Middle East," 215–216.

62. Soli Shahvar, "Tribes and Telegraph in Lower Iraq: The Muntafiq and the Baghdad-Basrah Telegraph Line of 1863–65," *Middle Eastern Studies* 39 (2003): 89–116; Shahvar, "Iron Poles, Wooden Poles: The Electric Telegraph and the Ottoman-Iranian Boundary Conflict, 1863–1865," *British Journal of Middle Eastern Studies* 34 (2007): 23–42.

63. Mustafa Kaçar, "Osmanlı Telegraf İşlemetmesi," in *Çağını Yakalayan Osmanlı!*, edited by Ekmeleddin İhsanoğlu (Istanbul: İslam Tarih, Sanat ve Kültür Araştırma Merkezi, 1995), 45–120; Eugene Rogan, "Instant Communication: The Impact of the Telegraph in Ottoman Syria," in *The Syrian Land: Processes of Integration and Fragmentation Bilad al-Sham from the 18th to the 20th Century*, edited by Thomas Philipp and Birgit Schaebler (Stuttgart: Steiner, 1998), 113–128; R. H. Davison, "Effect of the Electric Telegraph on the Conduct of Ottoman Foreign Relations," in *Decision Making and Change in the Ottoman Empire*, edited by Caesar E. Farah (Kirksville: Thomas Jefferson University Press, 1993), 53–66.

64. Yuval Ben-Bassat, *Petitioning the Sultan: Protests and Justice in Late Ottoman Palestine* (London: I. B. Tauris, 2013).

65. On some of the train projects in Anatolia and the Levant, see Michael E. Bonine, "The Introduction of Railroads in the Eastern Mediterranean: Economic and Social Aspects," in *The Syrian Land: Processes of Integration and Fragmentation, Bilad al-Sham from the 18th to the 20th Century*, edited by Thomas Philipp and Birgit Schaebler (Stuttgart: Steiner, 1998), 53–78; Ruth Kark, "Transportation in Nineteenth-Century

Palestine: Reintroduction of the Wheel," *The Land that Became Israel*, edited by Ruth Kark (Jerusalem: Magnes Press, 1989), 57–76.

66. Selim Deringil, "Legitimacy Structures in the Ottoman State: The Reign of Abdulhamid II (1876–1909)," *International Journal of Middle East Studies* 23 (1991): 345–359; Deringil, *The Well-Protected Domains: Ideology and Legitimation of Power in the Ottoman Empire, 1876–1909* (London: I. B. Tauris, 1998).

67. Hakkı Acun, "Anatolia Clock Towers," in *The Great Ottoman-Turkish Civilization*, 4:374–379.

68. Wishnitzer, *Reading Clocks Alla Turca*; Mehmet B. Uluengin, "Secularizing Anatolia Tick by Tick: Clock Towers in the Ottoman Empire and in the Turkish Republic," *International Journal of Middle East Studies* 42 (2010): 17–36; Avner Wishnitzer, "A Comment on Mehmet Bengü Uluengin, 'Secularizing Anatolia Tick by Tick: Clock Towers in the Ottoman Empire and the Turkish Republic,'" *International Journal of Middle East Studies* 42 (2010): 537–540; Wishnitzer, "Our Time," 47–69; Wishnitzer, "On Schedules, Clock Towers, and Urban Rhythms in the Ottoman Empire" (in Hebrew), *Zmanim* 119 (Summer 2012): 18–31.

69. Amy Singer, "The Persistence of Philanthropy," *Comparative Studies of South Asia, Africa and the Middle East* 31 (2011): 557–568.

70. Jacob M. Landau, *The Hejaz Railway and the Muslim Pilgrimage: A Case of Ottoman Political Propaganda* (Detroit: Wayne State University Press, 1971), 16.

71. Roy S. Fischel and Ruth Kark, "Sultan Abdülhamid II and Palestine: Private Lands and Imperial Policy," *New Perspectives on Turkey* 29 (2008): 142.

72. Ibid., 144–156.

73. Murat Özyüksel, "Hicaz Demiryolu'nun Finanmanı," in *Hicaz Demiryolu* (Istanbul: Tarih Vakfı Yurt Yayınları, 2000), 99–114.

74. For a discussion of the treatise, the Arabic text, and an English translation, see Landau, *The Hejaz Railway and the Muslim Pilgrimage*.

75. William L. Ochsenwald, "The Financing of the Hijaz Railroad," *Die Welt des Islams*, n.s., 14 (1973): 129–149; Ochsenwald, "A Modern Waqf: The Hijaz Railway, 1900–48," *Arabian Studies* 3 (1976): 1–12; Özyüksel, *Hicaz Demiryolu*, 85–98.

76. Özyüksel, *Hicaz Demiryolu*, 124–127, 127–135, 135–140; James Nicholson, *The Hejaz Railway* (London: Stacey International, 2005), 18–22.

77. Walter Pinchas Pick, "Meissner Pasha and the Construction of Railways in Palestine and Neighboring Countries," in *Ottoman Palestine, 1800–1914: Studies in Economic and Social History*, edited by Gad G. Gilbar (Leiden: Brill, 1990), 179–218; Nicholson, *The Hejaz Railway*, 20–24.

78. Daniel R. Headrick, *The Tools of an Empire: Technology and European Imperialism in the Nineteenth Century* (Oxford: Oxford University Press, 1981).

79. Martha Hanson, "Visualizing the Geography of Disease in China, 1870s–1920s," a paper presented at the conference "From Qing to China: Rethinking the Interplay of Tradition and Modernity, 1860–1949," held at Tel Aviv University, May 2012.

80. On Barak, "Scraping the Surface: The Techno-Politics of Modern Streets in Turn-of-Twentieth-Century Alexandria," *Mediterranean Historical Review* 24 (2009):

187–205. See also his forthcoming book *On Time: Technology and Temporality in Modern Egypt* (California University Press).

81. Çelik, *The Remaking of Istanbul.*

82. Nancy Elizabeth Gallagher, *Medicine and Power in Tunisia, 1780–1900* (Cambridge: Cambridge University Press, 1983), 5–6.

83. An international conference convened in January 2012 at the Institute for Advanced Studies at the Hebrew University of Jerusalem was dedicated to this transformation in the Middle East. http://www.as.huji.ac.il/isf/on_the_move (accessed Oct. 27, 2012).

84. Mark Harrison, *Disease and the Modern World, 1500 to the Present Day* (Cambridge, UK: Polity, 2004), 103, 128; Harrison, *Contagion: How Commerce Has Spread Disease* (New Haven, CT: Yale University Press, 2012), 140–141, 147.

85. Patrick Zylberman, "Civilizing the State: Borders, Weak States and International Health in Modern Europe," in *Medicine at the Border: Disease, Globalization and Security, 1850 to the Present*, edited by Alison Bashford (New York: Palgrave Macmillan, 2006), 21–40.

86. Harrison, *Disease and the Modern World*, 131–132.

87. Michael Christopher Low, "Empire and the Hajj: Pilgrims, Plagues, and Pan-Islam under British Surveillence, 1865–1908," *International Journal of Middle East Studies* (2008): 269–290.

88. Valeska Huber, "The Unification of the Globe by Disease? The International Sanitary Conferences on Cholera, 1851–1894," *Historical Journal* 49 (2006): 453–476.

89. Mahmoud Yazbak, *Haifa in the Late Ottoman Period, 1864–1914: A Muslim Town in Transition* (Leiden: Brill, 1998), 35, 38–39, 77, 79–81, 110; Michelle U. Campos, *Ottoman Brothers: Muslims, Christians, and Jews in Early Twentieth-Century Palestine* (Stanford, CA: Stanford University Press, 2011), 169–170. For a detailed discussion of transmissible disease in Ottoman Palestine, see Miri Shefer-Mossensohn, "Communicable Disease in Ottoman Palestine: Local Thoughts and Actions," *Korot* 21 (2011–2012): 19–49.

90. See, for example, BOA, A.MKT.MHM, 309/19, 341/19, DH. MKT, 1581/37, 2246/45, 2331/84, 2459/119, 2657/98, ŞD 2281/7, ŞD.ML, 2271/58; published in *Osmanlı Belgelerinde Filistin* (Istanbul: T. C. Republic of Turkey, General Directorate of State Archives, 2009), documents 10–18, pp. 87–117.

91. Jens Hanssen, *Fin de Siècle Beirut: The Making of an Ottoman Provincial Capital* (Oxford: Clarendon Press, 2005), chap. 4, "War, Health, and the Making of Municipal Beirut," 115–137; Leila Fawaz, "Foreign Presence and Perception of Ottoman Rules in Beirut," in *The Empire in the City: Arab Provincial Capitals in the Late Ottoman Empire*, edited by Jens Hanssen et al. (Würzberg: Ergon, 2002), 93–104.

CONCLUSION

1. Al-Jabartī, *ʿAjāʾib al-Āthār* 2:196–210; Stefan Reichmuth, *The World of Murtada al-Zabidi (1732–91): Life, Networks and Writings* (Cambridge: Gibb Memorial Trust, 2009); Reichmuth, "Murtada al-Zabidi (d. 1791) in Biographical and Autobiographical Accounts: Glimpses of Islamic Scholarship in the 18th Century," *Die Welt des Islams* 39 (1999): 64–102; Reichmuth, "The Interplay of Local Developments and Transnational Relations in the Islamic World: Perception and Perspectives," in *Muslim Culture in Russia and Central Asia from the 18th to the Early 20th Century*, vol. 2: *Inter-Regional and Inter-Ethnic Relations*, edited by A. von Kögelgen et al. (Berlin: K. Schwarz, 1998), 32–37; C. Brockelmann, "Muḥammad Murtaḍa," *Encyclopaedia of Islam*, 2nd ed. (Brill Online, 2012).

2. Jane Hathaway, ed., *Al-Jabartī's History of Egypt* (Princeton, NJ: Markus Wiener, 2009), "Introduction," xi–xxxiv.

3. Jane H. Murphy, "Locating the Sciences in Eighteenth-Century Egypt," *British Journal for the History of Science* 43 (2010): 557–571.

4. Al-Jabartī, *ʿAjāʾib al-Āthār*, 3:21, 52, 57, 86, 149–150, 156. For the English translation, see Thomas Philipp and Moshe Perlmann, eds., *ʿAbd al-Rahman al-Jabartī's History of Egypt: ʿAjāʾib al-Āthār fi'l-Tarājim wa'l-Akhbār* (Stuttgart: Franz Steiner Verlag, 1994), 3:33, 81–82, 90, 135, 235–236, 244.

5. *Al-Jabartī's Chronicle of the First Seven Months of the French Occupation: Muḥarram–Rajab 1213 = 15 June–December 1798*, edited and translated by Shmuel Moreh (Leiden: Brill, 1975), 89–93; for the English translation, see 115–117.

6. See, for example, al-Jabartī, *ʿAjāʾib al-Āthār*, 3:113. For the English translation, see Philipp and Perlmann, 3:176.

7. Al-Jabartī, *ʿAjāʾib al-Āthār*, 3:33–35, 54–55, 160; Philipp and Perlmann, 3:52–55, 85–86, 250–251. Part of the translation was included in Hathaway, *Al-Jabartī's History of Egypt*, 191–193.

8. Al-Jabartī, *ʿAjāʾib al-Āthār*, 33–35; Philipp and Perlmann, 3:52–55. Part of the translation was included in Hathaway, *Al-Jabartī's History of Egypt*, 191–193.

9. Al-Jabartī, *ʿAjāʾib al-Āthār*, 34; Philipp and Perlmann, 3:54.

10. Murphy, "Locating the Sciences in Eighteenth-century Egypt."

11. Hathaway, *Al-Jabartī's History of Egypt*, xxv–xxx.

12. Dursteler, "On Bazaars and Battlefields."

13. Necipoğlu, "A Kānūn for the State, a Canon for the Arts."

14. Miri Shefer, "An Ottoman Physician and His Social and Intellectual Milieu: The Case of Salih bin Nasrallah Ibn Sallum," *Studia Islamica*, n.s., 1 (2011): 133–158.

15. Hamadeh, "Ottoman Expressions of Early Modernity."

16. See, for example, Reinhart Koselleck, *Futures Past: On the Semantics of Historical Time* (New York: Columbia University Press, 2004).

17. Feza Günergün, "The Metric System in Turkey," in *The Great Ottoman-Turkish Civilization*, vol. 3: *Philosophy, Science and Institutions*, edited by Kemal Çiçek (Ankara: Yeni Türkiye, 2000), 487–491; Günergün, "Introduction of the Metric System

to the Ottoman State," in *Transfer of Modern Science and Technology to the Muslim World*, edited by Ekmeleddin İhsanoğlu (Istanbul: Islam Tarih, Sanat ve Kultur Arastirma Merkezi, 1992), 297–316.

18. Uri M. Kupferschmidt, "The Social History of the Sewing Machine in the Middle East," *Die Welt des Islams* 44 (2004): 195–213.

19. Uri M. Kupferschmidt, "On the Diffusion of 'Small' Western Technologies and Consumer Goods in the Middle East During the Era of the First Modern Globalization," in *A Global Middle East: Mobility, Materiality and Culture in the Modern Age, 1880–1940*, edited by Liat Kozma, Cyrus Schayegh, and Avner Wishnitzer (London and New York: I. B. Tauris, 2015), 229–260.

BIBLIOGRAPHY

PRIMARY SOURCES

Başbakanlık Osmanlı Arşivi (BOA)

Ali Emiri, I. Ahmed (AE.SAMD.I) 851
Dahiliye Nezâreti, Mektubî Kalemi (DH.MKT), 1581/37, 2246/45, 2331/84, 2459/119, 2657/98
Sedâret Mektubî Kalemi, Mühimme Odası (A.MKT.MHM), 309/19, 341/19
Şûrâ-yı Devlet (ŞD), 2281/7
Şûrâ-yı Devlet Maliye (ŞD.ML), 2271/58

Manuscripts

Ibn Sallūm, Ṣāliḥ bin Naṣrallāh. *Ghayat al-bayan fi tadbir badan al-insan.* Manuscript held at the Cambridge University Library, Cambridge, P.27 Brown.

———. *Ghayat al-bayan fi tadbir badan al-insan.* Manuscript held at the Princeton University Library, Princeton, NJ, Garret 1181H.

———. *Ghayat al-bayan fi tadbir badan al-insan.* Manuscript held at the Princeton University Library, Princeton, NJ, n.s. 998.

———. *Ghāyat al-itqān fi tadbīr badan al-insān.* Manuscript held at Cambridge University Library, Cambridge, Add. 3532.

Katip Çelebi. *Jāmiʿ al-mutūn min jall al-funūn.* Manuscript held at the Atıf Efendi Yazma Eser Kütüphanesi, Istanbul, 2812.

———. *Mizan al-haqq fi ikhtiyar al-ahaqq.* Manuscript held at the Cambridge University Library, Add. 442.

Manq, ʿAlī bin Bālī bin Muḥammad Bey. *Al-ʿiqd al-manẓūm fi dhikr afāḍil al-rūm; dhayl al-shaqāʾiq.* Manuscript held at the Süleymaniye Library, Istanbul, Bağadatlı vehbi Efendi 1065.

Al-Suyūṭī, Jalāl al-Dīn. *Al-Manhaj al-sawī wal-manhal al-rawī fi al-tib al-nabawī.* Manuscript held at the Wellcome Institute for the History of Medicine Library, London, Wms.Or.90.

Taşköprüzade, Ahmed bin Mustafa. *Al-Shaqā'iq al-nu'māniyya fi 'ulamā al-dawla al-'uthmāniyya*. Manuscript held at the Süleymaniye Library, Istanbul, East Efendi 2308.

Published Primary Sources

Bon, Otaviano. *The Sultan's Seraglio: An Intimate Portrait of Life at the Ottoman Court*. London: Saqi Books, 1996.

Brookes, Douglas Scott, trans. and ed. *The Concubine, the Princess, and the Teacher: Voices from the Ottoman Harem*. Austin: University of Texas Press, 2008.

———. "*Table of Delicacies concerning the Rules of Social Gatherings*: An Annotated Translation of Gelibolulu Mustafa Âli's *Mevâ'idü'n-Nefâ'is fi Kavâ'idi'l-Mecâlis*." PhD diss., University of California, Berkeley, 1998.

Damanhūrī, Aḥmad ibn 'Abd al-Mun'im. *Shaykh Damanhūrī on the Churches of Cairo (1739)*. Edited and translated by Moshe Perlmann. Berkeley: University of California Press, 1975.

Evliya Çelebi. *Narrative of Travels in Europe, Asia, and Africa in the Seventeenth Century*. Translated by Ritter Joseph von Hammer. London: Oriental Translation Fund, 1834.

———. *Seyahatname*. 10 vols. in 2. Istanbul: Yapı Kredi Yayıları, 2011.

———. *The Seyahatname of Evliya Çelebi: Facsimile of Topkapı Sarayı Bağdat 304*. 3 vols. Cambridge, MA: Harvard University Press, 1993.

Ghazzālī, Abū Ḥāmid al-. *Al-Ghazali's Path to Sufism; His Deliverance from Error—al-Munqidh min al-Dalal*. Translated by R. J. McCarthy, with David Burrell and William Graham. Louisville, KY: Fons Vitae, 2000.

———. *Al-Munqidh min al-Ḍalāl wal-Mawṣil ilā dhī al-'Izza wal-Jalāl*. Beirut: Al-Lajna al-Lubnāniyya li-Tarjamat al-Rawā'i', 1969.

———. *The Faith and Practice of al-Ghazali*. Translated by W. M. Watt. London: G. Allen and Unwin, 1953.

———. *The Incoherence of the Philosophers: A Parallel English-Arabic Text*. Translated, introduced, and annotated by Michael E. Marmura. Provo, UT: Brigham Young University Press, 2000.

Ghazzī, Najm al-Dīn Abū al-Makārim Muḥammad b. Muḥammad al-Amīrī al-. *Lutf al-Samr wa-Qatf al-Thamr min Tarājim A'yān al-Ṭabaqa al-Ūlā min al-Qarn al-Ḥādī 'Ashr*. 2 vols. Damascus: Wizārat al-Thaqāfa wal-Irshād al-Qawmī, 1981.

Ḥājī Khalīfa [Katip Çelebi]. *The Balance of Truth*. Translated by G. L. Lewis. London: G. Allen and Unwin, 1957.

———. *Kashf al-Ẓunūn 'an Asāmī al-Kutūb wal-Funūn*. Istanbul: Matabaat-i al-Alim, AH 1310 [1891–1892].

———. *Tuhfet ül-Kibar fi Esfar el-Bihar*. Istanbul: Matbaa-i Bahriye, AH 1329 [1913].

Ibn Bāz, 'Abd al-'Azīz. *Majmū' Fatāwā*. 10th ed. 30 vols. Riyadh: Dār al-Qāsim, n.d.

Ibn 'Imād, 'Abd al-Ḥayy. *Shadharāt al-Dhahab fī Akhbār man Dhahab*. 8 vols. Beirut: Maktab al-Tijārī lil-Ṭibā'a wal-Nashr wal-Tawzī' [1966].

Ibn Iyās, Muḥammad bin Aḥmad. *Badāʾiʿ al-Zuhūr fī Waqāʾiʿ al-Duhūr*. Taḥrīr Muḥammad Muṣṭafā. 5 vols. Cairo: Dār Iḥyāʾ al-Kutub al-ʿArabiyya, AH 1369/1960.

Ibn Jawzī, Abū al-Faraj. *Kitāb al-Mawḍuʿāt*. 3 vols. Madina: al-Maktaba al-Salafiyya, 1966–1968.

Ibn Khaldūn, ʿAbd al-Raḥmān ibn Muḥammad. *The Muqaddimah*. Translated by Franz Rosenthal; abridged by N. J. Dawood. London: Routledge and Kegan Paul, 1967.

———. *Taʾrīkh ibn Khaldūn al-Musammī bi-Kitāb al-ʿIbar*. Beirut: Manshūrāt Muʾassassat al-Aʿlamī, lil-Maṭbūʿāt, AH 1391/1961.

Ibn al-Qaysarānī, Abū al-Faḍl Muḥmmad bin Ṭāhir. *Maʿrifat al-Tadhkira fī al-Aḥādīth al-Mawḍuʿa*. Beirut: Muʾassasat al-Kutub al-Thaqāfiyya, AH 1406/1985.

Ibn Taymiyya, Taqī al-Dīn. *Majmūʿ al-Fatāwā*. ʿAbd al-Raḥman bin Muḥammad bin Qāsim. Al-Madīa al-Nabawiyya: Majmaʿ al-Malik Fahd: 1398h.

İtâkî, Şemsüddîn. *Şemseddîn-i İtâkî'nin Resimli Anatomi Kitabı*. Edited by Esin Kâhya. Ankara: Atatürk Kültür Merkezi Yayını, 1996.

———. *Teşrih-i Ebdan*. Islamabad: al-Majlis al-Watanī, lilhijra AH 1410/AD 1990.

———. *The Treatise on Anatomy of the Human Body and Interpretation of Philosophers*. Translated by Esin Kahya. Islamabad: National Hijra Council, AH 1410/1990.

Jabartī, ʿAbd al-Raḥmān, al-. *ʿAbd al-Rahman al-Jabartī's History of Egypt: ʿAjāʾib al-Āthār fīʾl-Tarājim waʾl-Akhbār*. Translated and edited by Thomas Philipp and Moshe Perlmann. 4 vols. Stuttgart: Franz Steiner Verlag, 1994.

———. *ʿAjāʾib al-Āthār fī al-Taraājim wa-al-Akhbār*. 4 vols. Cairo: n.p., AH 1236 [1820].

———. *Al-Jabartī's Chronicle of the First Seven Months of the French Occupation: Muḥarram–Rajab 1213 = 15 June–December 1798*. Edited and translated by Shmuel Moreh. Leiden: Brill, 1975.

———. *Al-Jabartīs History of Egypt*. Edited by Jane Hathaway. Princeton, NJ: Markus Wiener, 2009.

Al-Khaṭīb al-Baghdādī. *Al-Riḥla fī Ṭalab al-Ḥadīth*. [Beirut]: Dār al-Kutub al-ʿIlmiyya, [AH 1395/1985].

Kress von Kressenstein, Friedrich Frieherr. *Mit den Turken zum Suezkanal*. Berlin: O. Schlegel, 1938.

Matar, Nabil, ed. and trans. *Europe through Arab Eyes, 1578–1727*. New York: Columbia University Press, 2009.

———. *In the Lands of the Christians: Arabic Travel Writing in the 17th Century*. New York: Routledge, 2003.

Meninski, Franciscus à Mesgnien. *Thesaurus linguarum orientalium*. 6 vols. Istanbul: Simurg, 2000.

Moltke, Helmuth von. *Under dem Halbmond: Erlebnisse in der alten Türkei 1835–1839*. Edited and annotated by Ernst Bartsc. Stuttgart: Erdmann, 1997.

Muḥibbī, Muḥammad Amīn b. Faḍlallah, al-. *Taʾrīkh Khulaṣat al-Athr fī Aʿyān al-Qarn al-Ḥādī ʿAshr*. 4 vols. Beirut: Maktabat Khayyāṭ, 1966.

Murādī, Muḥammad Khalīl Abū al-Faḍl al-. *Silk al-Durar fī Aʿyān al-Qarn al-Thānī ʿAshr*. 4 vols. in 2. Baghdad: Maktabat al-Mathnā, 196–.

Naima, Mustafa. *Tarih-i Naima: Rawdat al-Husayn fi Khulasat Akhbar al-Khafiqin.* 6 vols. Istanbul: Matbaa-i Amire, AH 1281.

Osmanlı Belgelerinde Filistin. Istanbul: T. C. Republic of Turkey, General Directorate of State Archives, 2009.

Peçevi, İbrahim. *Tarih-i Peçevi.* Istanbul: Matbaa-i Amire, AH 1283 [1867].

Raşed Efendi, Mehmed bin Mustafa. *Tarih-i Raşed.* Istanbul: Matbaa-i Amire, AH 1282 [1865].

Sabuncuoğlu, Şerefeddin. *Cerrahiyyetü'l-Ḥāniyye.* Edited by İlter Uzel. 2 vols. Ankara: Atatürk Kültür, Dil ve Tarih Yüksek Kurumu, 1992.

———. *Mücerrebname.* Edited by İlter Uzel and Kenan Süveren. Ankara: Atatürk Kültür Merkezi Yaınları, 1999.

Süreyya, Mehmed. *Sicill-i Osmani.* 4 vols. Istanbul: Darülmaarif, AH 1311 [1893–1894].

Taşköprüzade, Ahmed bin Mustafa. *Al-Shaqā'iq al-Nuʿmānīyya fi ʿUlamā al-Dawla al-ʿUthmāniyya.* Egypt: Būlāq, AH 1299. Printed on the margins of Aḥmad bin Muḥammad ibn Khalikān, *Wafayāt al-Aʿyān wa-Anbā' Abnā' al-Zamān* (Egypt: Būlāq, AH 1299).

———. *Miftāḥ al-Saʿāda wa-Miṣbāḥ al-Siyāda fi Mawḍūʿāt al-ʿUlūm.* Kāmil Kāmil al-Bakrī wa-ʿAbd al-Wahāb al-Nūr: Taḥqīq. Cairo: Dār al-Kutub al-Ḥadītha, 1968.

Toderini, Giambattista. *Letteratura Turchesca.* 3 vols. Venice: G. Storti, 1787.

The Turkish Letters of Ogier Ghiselin de Busbecq, The. Translated from the Latin of the Elzevir edition (1633) by Edward Seymour Forester. Oxford: Clarendon, 1968.

Wortley Montagu, Mary. *The Complete Letters of Lady Mary Wortley Montagu.* Edited by R. Halsbad. 3 vols. Oxford: Clarendon, 1965–1967.

Yazma Eserlerden Tıbbi Bitki Hayvan ve Madenler Sergisi/Materia Medica Miniature Pictures Exhibition. Istanbul: Nobel Tıp Kitabevleri, 2002.

Zahrāwī, Abū al-Qāsim Khalaf ibn ʿAbbās al-. *Albucasis on Surgery and Instruments.* Translated and edited by M. S. Spink and G. L. Lewis. London: Wellcome Institute of the History of Medicine, 1973.

SECONDARY LITERATURE

"Almoli (Almuli), Solomon ben Jacob." *Encyclopaedia Judaica.* 2nd ed. Vol. 1. Edited by Michael Berenbaum and Fred Skolnik, 682. Detroit: Macmillan Reference USA, 2007; Gale Virtual Reference Library (web) (accessed Aug. 4, 2011).

Abdülhāk Adıvar, Adnan. *Osmanlı Türklerinde İlim.* 5th ed. Istanbul: Remzi Kitabevi, 1991.

Acun, Hakkı. "Anatolia Clock Towers." In *The Great Ottoman-Turkish Civilization,* edited by Kemal Çiçek, vol. 4: *Culture and Arts,* 374–379. Ankara: Yeni Türkiye, 2000.

Ágoston, Gábor. "Empires and Warfare in East-Central Europe, 1550–1750: The Ottoman-Habsburg Rivalry and Military Transformation." In *European Warfare,*

1350–1750, edited by D. Trim and F. Tallet, 110–134. Cambridge: Cambridge University Press, 2010.

———. *Guns for the Sultan: Military Power and the Weapons Industry in the Ottoman Empire*. Cambridge: Cambridge University Press, 2005.

———. "Information, Ideology, and Limits of Imperial Policy: Ottoman Grand Strategy in the Context of Ottoman-Habsburg Rivalry." In *The Early Modern Ottomans: Remapping the Empire*, edited by Virginia H. Aksan and Daniel Goffman, 75–103. Cambridge: Cambridge University Press, 2007.

———. "Ottoman Artillery and European Military Technology in the Fifteenth and Seventeenth Centuries." *Acta Orientalia Academiae Scientiarum Hungaricae* 47, nos. 1–2 (1994): 15–48.

———. "Where Environmental and Frontier Studies Meet: Rivers, Forests, Marshes and Forts along the Ottoman-Hapsburg Frontier in Hungary." In *The Frontiers of the Ottoman World*, edited by A. C. S. Peacock, 57–79. Oxford: Oxford University Press, for the British Academy, 2009.

Aksan, Virginia. "Breaking the Spell of the Baron de Tott: Reframing the Question of Military Reform in the Ottoman Empire, 1760–1830." *International History Review* 24 (2002): 253–277.

———. "Enlightening the Ottomans: Tott and Mustafa III." *International Congress on Learning and Education in the Ottoman World, Istanbul, 12–15 April 1999*, edited by Ali Çalesu, 163–174. Istanbul: IRCICA, 2001.

Alparslan, Ali. "K͟haṭṭ; iii. In Turkey." *Encyclopaedia of Islam*. 2nd ed. Brill Online, 2012.

Arnaldez, R. "Falsafa." *Encyclopaedia of Islam*. 2nd ed. Brill Online, 2012.

Atgil, Abdurrahman. "Greco-Islamic Philosophy and Islamic Jurisprudence in the Ottoman Empire (1300–1600): Aristotle's Theory of Sciences the Works of Usūl I. Figh," *Osmanlı Araştırmaları/Journal of Ottoman Studies* 41 (2013): 33–54.

Atil, Esin, ed. *Islamic Art and Patronage*. New York: Rizzoli, 1990.

Aydüz, Salim. "Osmanlı Devleti'nde Müneccimbaşılık." In *Osmanlı Bilimi Araştırmaları*, edited by Feza Günergün, 159–207. Istanbul: İstanbul Üniversitesi Edebiyat Fakültesi, 1995.

Babinger, Franz. *Mehmed the Conqueror and His Time*. Princeton, NJ: Princeton University Press, 1978.

Babinger, Franz, and Christine Woodhead. "Pečewī." *Encyclopaedia of Islam*. 2nd ed. Brill Online, 2012.

Bachour, Natalia. *Oswaldus Crollius und Daniel Sennert in frühneuzeitlichen Istanbul: Studien zur Rezeption des Paracelsismus im Werk des osmanischen Arztes Ṣāliḥ b. Naṣrallāh Ibn Sallūm al-Ḥalabī*. Freiburg: Centaurus, 2012.

Baer, Marc David. *The Dönme: Jewish Converts, Muslim Revolutionaries, and Secular Turks*. Stanford, CA: Stanford University Press, 2010.

———. "Globalization, Cosmopolitanism, and the Dönme in Ottoman Salonica and Turkish Istanbul." *Journal of World History* 18 (2007): 141–170.

Barak, On. *On Time: Technology and Temporality in Modern Egypt*. Berkeley: California University Press, 2013.

———. "Scraping the Surface: The Techno-Politics of Modern Streets in Turn-of-Twentieth-Century Alexandria." *Mediterranean Historical Review* 24 (2009): 187–205.

———. "Three Watersheds in the History of Energy." In *Comparative Studies of South Asia, Africa and the Middle East* 34 (2014): 440–453.

Barkai, Ron. "Between East and West: A Jewish Doctor from Spain." *Mediterranean Historical Review* 10 (1995): 49–63.

———. *Science, Magic and Mythology in the Middle Ages*. [In Hebrew.] Jerusalem: Van Leer Institute, 5747/1987.

Barnes, Barry, David Bloor, and John Henry. *Scientific Knowledge: A Sociological Analysis*. London: Athlone, 1996.

Bauer, Karen. "'I Have Seen the People's Antipathy to This Knowledge': The Muslim Exegete and His Audience, 5th/11th–7th/13th Centuries." In *The Islamic Scholarly Tradition: Studies in History, Law and Thought in Honor of Professor Michael Allan Cook*, edited by Asad Q. Ahmed, Behnam Sadeghi, and Michel Bonner, 293–314. Leiden: Brill, 2011.

Behrens-Abouseif, Doris. "Gardens in Islamic Egypt." *Der Islam* 69 (1992): 302–312.

———. "The Image of the Physician in Arab Biographies of the Post-Classical Age." *Der Islam* 66 (1989): 331–343.

Bektas, Yakup. "The Sultan's Messenger: Cultural Constructions of Ottoman Telegraphy." *Technology and Culture* 41 (2000): 669–696.

Ben-Bassat, Yuval. *Petitioning the Sultan: Protests and Justice in Late Ottoman Palestine*. London: I. B. Tauris, 2013.

Ben-Naeh, Yaron. "Tried and Tested Spells: Magic Beliefs and Acts among Ottoman Jews." [In Hebrew.] *Pa'amim* 85 (2000): 89–111.

Ben-Zaken, Avner. "Bridging Networks of Trust: Practicing Astronomy in Late Sixteenth-Century Salonika." *Jewish History* 23 (2009): 343–361.

———. *Cross-Cultural Scientific Exchanges in the Eastern Mediterranean, 1560–1660*. Baltimore, MD: Johns Hopkins University Press, 2010.

———. "The Heavens of the Sky and the Heavens of the Heart: The Ottoman Cultural Context for the Introduction of Post-Copernican Astronomy." *British Journal for the History of Science* 37 (2004): 1–28.

———. "Political Economy and Scientific Activity in the Ottoman Empire." In *The Turks*, edited by Hasan Celal Güzel et al., vol. 3: *The Ottomans*, 776–794. Ankara: Yeni Türkiye Publications, 2002.

———. "The Revolving Planets and the Revolving Clocks: Circulating Mechanical Objects in the Mediterranean." *History of Science* 49 (2011): 125–148.

Berkey, Jonathan P. *The Transmission of Knowledge in Medieval Cairo: A Social History of Islamic Education*. Princeton, NJ: Princeton University Press, 1992.

Berlekamp, Persis. "The Limits of Artistic Change in Fourteenth-Century Tabriz:

The Paradox of Rashid al-Din's Book on Chinese Medicine, part I." *Muqarnas* 27 (2011): 209–250.

———. *Wonder, Image, and Cosmos in Medieval Islam*. New Haven, CT: Yale University Press, 2011.

Bernards, Monique. "*Ṭalab al-ʿIlm* amongst the Linguists of Arabic during the ʿAbbasid Period." In *ʿAbbasid Studies: Occasional Papers of the School of ʿAbbasid Studies, Cambridge, 6–10 July 2002*, edited by James E. Montgomery, 33–46. Louvain: Peeters, 2004.

Beyazit, Yasemin. "Efforts to Reform Entry into the Ottoman İlmiyye Career towards the End of the 16th Century: The 1598 Ottoman İlmiyye Kanunnamesi." *Turcica* 44 (2012–2013): 201–218.

Birnbaum, Eleazar. "The Questing Mind: Kātib Chelebi, 1609–1657." In *Corolla Torontonesis: Studies in Honour of Ronald Morton Smith*, edited by Emmet Robins and Stella Sandahl, 133–158. Toronto, Ont.: TSAR, 1994.

Blair, Sheila S. *Islamic Calligraphy*. Edinburgh: Edinburgh University Press, 2006.

Bloom, Jonathan M. *Paper before Print: The History of and Impact of Paper in the Islamic World*. New Haven, CT: Yale University Press, 2001.

Bloor, David. "Anti-Latour." *Studies in the History of Philosophy of Science* 30 (1999): 81–112.

———. *Knowledge and Social Imagery*. London: Routledge and Kegan Paul, 1976.

Bonine, Michael E. "The Introduction of Railroads in the Eastern Mediterranean: Economic and Social Aspects." In *The Syrian Land: Processes of Integration and Fragmentation, Bilad al-Sham from the 18th to the 20th Century*, edited by Thomas Philipp and Birgit Schaebler, 53–78. Stuttgart: Steiner, 1998.

Boogert, Maurits H. van den. "Patrick Russell and the Republic of Letters in Aleppo." In *The Republic of Letters and the Levant*, edited by Alastair Hamilton, Maurits H. van den Boogert, and Bart Westerweel, 223–264. Leiden: Brill, 2005.

———. "The Sultan's Answer to the Medici Press? Ibrahim Müteferrika's Printing House in Istanbul." In *The Republic of Letters and the Levant*, edited by Alastair Hamilton, Maurits H. van den Boogert, and Bart Westerweel, 265–291. Leiden: Brill, 2005.

Bosworth, C. E. "Ṣofta." *Encyclopaedia of Islam*. 2nd ed. Brill Online, 2012.

Botticini, Maristella, and Zvi Eckstein. *The Chosen Few: How Education Shaped Jewish History, 70–1492*. Princeton, NJ: Princeton University Press, 2012.

Bowen, H. "Aḥmad Pas͟ha Bonneval." *Encyclopaedia of Islam*. 2nd ed. Brill Online, 2012.

Böwering, Gerhard. "God and His Attributes." *Encyclopaedia of the Qurʾān*. Brill Online, 2012.

Brentjes, Sonja. "Cross-Cultural Exchange in the Mediterranean." *Journal for the History of Astronomy* 42 (2011): 411–415.

———. "Crossing Boundaries: New Approaches to the History of 'Pre-Modern' Science and Technology." *Science in Context* 12, no. 3 (1999): 381–384.

———. "The Interests of the Republic of Letters in the Middle East, 1550–1700." *Science in Context* 12 (1999): 435–468.

———. "The Language of 'Patronage' in Islamic Societies before 1700." *Cuadernos del Cemyr* 20 (2012): 11–22.

———. "Medieval Portolan Charts as Documents of Shared Cultural Spaces." In *Acteurs des transferts culturels en Méditerranée médiévale*, edited by R. Abdellatif, Yassir Benhima, Daniel König, and Elisabeth Ruchaud, 135–146. Munich: Oldenbourg Velag, 2012.

———. "On the Location of the Ancient or 'Rational' Sciences in Muslim Educational Landscapes (AH 500–1100)." *Bulletin of the Royal Institute for Inter-Faith Studies* 4, no. 1 (2002): 47–71.

———. "On the Relation between the Ottoman Empire and the West European Republic of Letters (17th–18th Centuries)." In *Proceedings of the International Congress of Learning and Education in the Ottoman World, Istanbul, 12–15 April 1999, edited by* A. Çaksu, 121–148. Istanbul: Research Centre for Islamic History, Art and Culture, 2001.

———. "On Two Manuscripts by Abū Bakr b. Bahrām al-Dimashqī (d. 1102/1691) to W. and J. Blaeu's *Atlas Minor*." *Osmanlı Araştırmaları/Journal of Ottoman Studies* 40 (2012): 171–192.

———. Review of "1001 Inventions: The Enduring Legacy of Muslim Civilization," edited by Salim T. S. al-Hassani. *Aestimatio* 10 (2013): 119–153.

———. Review of *Studies in al-Kimya': Critical Issues in Latin and Arabic Alchemy and Chemistry*, by Ahmad Y. al-Hassan. *Centaurus* 53 (2011): 67.

Brockelmann, C. "Muḥammad Murtaḍa." *Encyclopaedia of Islam*. 2nd ed. Brill Online, 2012.

Brown, Jonathan. *The Canonization of al-Bukhārī and Muslim: The Formation and Function of the Sunnī Ḥadīth Canon*. Leiden: Brill, 2007.

Browne, Edward G. *A Supplementary Hand-List of the Muhammadan Manuscripts including all those Written in the Arabic Character, Preserved in the Libraries of the University and Colleges of Cambridge*. Cambridge: Cambridge University Press, 1922.

Brummet, Palmira. "The Yeni and the Eski Cultural Change and Envisioning the 'Modern' in Late Ottoman Cartoons." In *The Great Ottoman-Turkish Civilization*, edited by Kemal Çiçek, vol. 3: *Philosophy, Science and Institutions*, 134–140. Ankara: Yeni Türkiye, 2000.

Burchell, Graham, Colin Gordon, and Peter Miller, eds. *The Foucault Effect: Studies in Governmentality*. Chicago: University of Chicago Press, 1991.

Campos, Michelle U. *Ottoman Brothers: Muslims, Christians, and Jews in Early Twentieth-Century Palestine*. Stanford, CA: Stanford University Press, 2011.

Can, Lâle. "Connecting People: A Central Asian Sufi Network in Turn-of-the-Century Istanbul." *Modern Asian Studies* 46, no. 2 (March 2012): 373–401.

Cantay, Gönül. *Anadolu Selçuklu ve Osmanlı Darüşşifaları*. Ankara: Atatürk Kültür, Dil ve Tarih Yüksek Kurumu, 1992.

———. [Güreşsever.] "Kitab al-Cerrahiyet al-Hāniye (İstanbul Tıp Tarihi Enstitüsü

Nüshası) Minyatürler." *I. Milletarası Türkoloji Kongresi. Tebliğler*, 3:771–785. Istanbul: İstanbul Üniversitesi, 1979.

Casale, Giancarlo. *The Ottoman Age of Exploration*. New York: Oxford University Press, 2010.

Castiglione, Frank. "'Levantine' Dragomans in Nineteenth-Century Istanbul: The Pisanis, the British, and Issues of Subjecthood," *Osmanlı Araştırmaları/Journal of Ottoman Studies* 44 (2014): 169–195.

Çelik, Zeynep. *Empire, Architecture, and the City: French-Ottoman Encounters, 1830–1914*. Seattle: University of Washington Press, 2008.

———. *The Remaking of Istanbul: Portrait of an Ottoman City in the Nineteenth Century*. Berkeley: University of California Press, 1993.

Cerabregu, Muharrem. "Scientific Benefits from Piri Reis's *Kitab-ı Bahriye* and Its Position in the History of Cartography." In *XI. Türk Tarih Kongresi, Ankara . . . 1990: Kongreye sunulan bildiriler*, 3:1105–1125. Ankara: Türk Tarih Kurumu Basımevi, 1994.

Cerasi, Maurice. "The Urban Perspective of Ottoman Monuments from Sinan to Mehmet Tahir: Change and Continuity." In *Aptullah Kuran için Yazıları: Essays in Honour of Aptullah Kuran*, edited by Çiğdem Kafesçioğlu and Lucienne Thys-Senocak, 171–190. Istanbul: Yapı Kredi Yayınları, 1999.

Chamberlain, Michael. *Knowledge and Social Practice in Medieval Damascus, 1190–1350*. Cambridge: Cambridge University Press, 1994.

Çiçek, Kemal. "Interpreters of the Court in the Ottoman Empire as Seen from the Sharia Court Records Of Cyprus." *Islamic Law and Society* 9 (2002): 1–15.

Cohen, Amnon. *The Guilds of Ottoman Jerusalem*. Leiden: Brill, 2001.

Çolak, Yılmaz. "Language Policy and Official Ideology in Early Republican Turkey." *Middle Eastern Studies* 40, no. 6 (November 2004): 67–91.

Collins, Harry M. *Changing Order: Replication and Induction in Scientific Practice*. London: Sage, 1985.

Collins, Harry M., with Trevor Pinch. *The Golem: What You Should Know about Science*. Cambridge: Cambridge University Press, 1993.

Conrad, Lawrence I. "Scholarship and Social Context in the Near East." In *Knowledge and the Scholarly Medical Traditions*, 81–101. Cambridge: Cambridge University Press, 1995.

Contadini, Anna, and Claire Norton, eds. *The Renaissance and the Ottoman World*. Farnham, UK: Ashgate, 2013.

Cook, Harold J. *Matters of Exchange: Commerce, Medicine, and Science in the Dutch Golden Age*. New Haven, CT: Yale University Press, 2007.

Dankoff, Robert. *An Ottoman Mentality: The World of Evliya Çelebi*. Leiden: Brill, 2004.

Davidovitch, Nadav, and Zalman Greenberg. "Public Health, Culture, and Colonial Medicine: Smallpox and Variolation in Palestine during the British Mandate." *Public Health Chronicles* 122 (May–June 2007): 398–406.

Davison, R. H. "Effect of the Electric Telegraph on the Conduct of Ottoman Foreign Relations." In *Decision Making and Change in the Ottoman Empire*, edited by Caesar E. Farah, 53–66. Kirksville, MO: Thomas Jefferson University Press, 1993.

———. "S͟hānī-zāde Meḥmed 'Aṭā' Allāh Efendi." *Encyclopaedia of Islam*. 2nd ed. Brill Online, 2012.

Dear, Peter. "What Is the History of Science the History *Of*? Early Modern Roots of the Ideology of Modern Science." *Isis* 96 (2005): 390–406.

de Groot, Alexander H. "The Changing National Character of the Dragoman (1756–1863)." In *Fremde Erfahrungen: Asiaten und Afrikaner in Deutschland, Österreich und in der Schweiz bis 1945*, edited by Gerhard Höpp, 297–317. Berlin: Das Arabische Buch, 1996.

———. "Protection and Nationality: The Decline of the Dragomans." In *Istanbul et les langues orientales: Actes du colloque . . . Istanbul . . . 1995*, edited by Frédéric Hitzel, 235–255. Paris: L'Harmattan, 1997.

Demirhan, Ayşegül. *Mısır Çarşısı Drogları*. Istanbul: Sermet Matbaası, 1975.

———. "The Place and the Importance of Mısır Çarşısı (Spice Bazaar) in Ottoman-Turkish Medicine." In *The Great Ottoman-Turkish Civilization*, edited by Kemal Çiçek, vol. 3: *Philosophy, Science and Institutions*, 447–454. Ankara: Yeni Türkiye, 2000.

Derichs, Claudia, and Diane E. King. "Patronage and Clientage." In *Encyclopedia of Women and Islamic Cultures*. Brill Online, 2012.

Deringil, Selim. "Legitimacy Structures in the Ottoman State: The Reign of Abdulhamid II (1876–1909)." *International Journal of Middle East Studies* 23 (1991): 345–359.

———. *The Well-Protected Domains: Ideology and Legitimation of Power in the Ottoman Empire, 1876–1909*. London: I. B. Tauris, 1998.

Derman, M. Uğur. *Letters in Gold: Ottoman Calligraphy from the Sakıp Sabancı Collection, Istanbul*. New York: Metropolitan Museum of Art, 1998.

Diez, Ernst. "The Zodiac Reliefs at the Portal of the Gök Medreses in Siwas." *Artibus Asiae* 12 (1949): 99–104.

Duman, Musa. "Turkish Language during the Reform Period." In *The Turks*, edited by Hasan Celâl Güzel, C. Cem Oğuz, and Osman Karatay, vol. 4: *The Ottomans*, 723–724. Ankara: Yeni Türkiye, 2002.

Dursteler, Eric R. "On Bazaars and Battlefields: Recent Scholarship on Mediterranean Cultural Contacts." *Journal of Early Modern History* 15 (2011): 413–434.

———. "Speaking in Tongues: Language and Communication in the Early Modern Mediterranean." *Past and Present* 217 (2012): 47–77.

———. *Venetians in Constantinople: Nation, Identity, and Coexistence in the Early Modern Mediterranean*. Baltimore, MD: Johns Hopkins University Press, 2006.

Eisenstein, Elizabeth L. *The Printing Revolution in Early Modern Europe*. 2nd ed. Cambridge: Cambridge University Press, 2005.

Elkana, Yehuda. "Unmasking Uncertainties and Embracing Contradictions: Graduate Education in the Sciences." In *Envisioning the Future of Doctoral Education: Pre-*

paring Stewards of the Discipline, edited by Chris M. Golde and George E. Walker, 65–69. Carnegie Essays on the Doctorate. San Francisco: Jossey-Bass, 2006.

El-Moudden, Abderrahmane. "The Ambivalence of *Rihla*: Community Integration and Self-Definition in Moroccan Travel Accounts, 1300–1800." In *Muslim Travellers: Pilgrimage, Migration, and the Religious Imagination*, edited by Dale F. Eickelman and James Piscatori, 69–84. London: Routledge, 1990.

Elshakry, Marwa. "When Science Became Western: Historiographical Reflections." *ISIS* 101 (2010): 98–109.

Emiralioğlu, M. Pinar. *Geographical Knowledge and Imperial Culture in the Early Modern Ottoman Empire*. Farnham, UK: Ashgate, 2014.

———. "Relocating the Center of the Universe: China and the Ottoman Imperial Project in the Sixteenth Century." *Osmanlı Araştırmaları/Journal of Ottoman Studies* 39 (2012): 161–187.

Ende, W. "Mudjāwir, f. mudjāwira." *Encyclopaedia of Islam*. 2nd ed. Brill Online, 2012.

Epstein, Steven A. *Purity Lost: Transgressing Boundaries in the Eastern Mediterranean, 1000–1400*. Baltimore, MD: Johns Hopkins University Press, 2006.

Erim, Neşe. "Trade, Traders and the State in Eighteenth-Century Erzurum." *New Perspectives on Turkey* 5–6 (1991): 123–141.

Ерünsal, İsmail E. *Ottoman Libraries: A Survey of the History, Development, and Organization of Ottoman Foundation Libraries*. Cambridge, MA: Department of Near Eastern Languages and Literatures, Harvard University, 2008.

Evered, Emine Önhan. "An Educational Prescription for the Sultan: Hüseyin Hilmi Paşa's Advice for the Maladies of Empire." *Middle Eastern Studies* 43 (2007): 439–459.

Eyice, Semavi. "Dr. Karl Ambros Bernard (Charles Ambroise Bernard) ve Mekteb-i Tibbiye-i Şahane'ye Dair Bir Kaç Not." In *Türk Tıbbının Batılılaşması*, edited by Arslan Terzioğlu and Erwin Lucius, 97–124. Istanbul: Arkeoloji ve Sanat Yayınları, 1993.

Fahmy, Khaled. "The Anatomy of Justice: Forensic Medicine and Criminal Law in Nineteenth-Century Egypt." *Islamic Law and Society* 6 (1999): 224–271.

———. "The Essence of Alexandria (Part I)." *Manifesta Journal* 14: 64–72.

———. "The Essence of Alexandria (Part II)." *Manifesta Journal* 16: 22–27.

———. "Modernizing Cairo: A Revisionist Narrative." In *Making Cairo Medieval*, edited by Nezar AlSayyad, Irene A. Bierman, and Nasser Rabbat, 173–199. Lanham, MD: Lexington Books, 2005.

———. "Women, Medicine, and Power in Nineteenth-Century Egypt." In *Remaking Women: Feminism and Modernity in the Middle East*, edited by Lila Abu-Lughod, 35–72. Princeton, NJ: Princeton University Press, 1998.

Fakhry, Majid. *A History of Islamic Philosophy*. 2nd ed. New York: Columbia University Press, 1983.

———. *A Short Introduction to Islamic Philosophy, Theology and Mysticism*. Oxford: Oneworld, 1997.

Fancy, Nahyan. *Science and Religion in Mamluk Egypt: Ibn al-Nafis, Pulmonary Transit and Bodily Resurrection*. London: Routledge, 2013.

Faroqhi, Suraiya. "Camels, Wagons, and the Ottoman State in the Sixteenth and Seventeenth Centuries." *International Journal of Middle East Studies* 14 (1982): 523–539.

———. *Pilgrims and Sultans: The Hajj under the Ottomans, 1517–1683*. London: I. B. Tauris, 1994.

———. "Selānīk." *Encyclopaedia of Islam*. 2nd ed. Brill Online, 2012.

———. *Travel and Artisans in the Ottoman Empire: Employment and Mobility in the Early Modern Era*. London: I. B. Tauris, 2014.

Faroqhi, Suraiya, and Randi Deguilhem, eds. *Crafts and Craftsmen of the Middle East*. London: I. B. Tauris, 2005.

Faroqhi, Suraiya, and Christoph K. Neumann, eds. *The Illuminated Table, the Prosperous House: Food and Shelter in Ottoman Material Culture*. Würzburg: Ergon, 2003.

Fawaz, Leila. "Foreign Presence and Perception of Ottoman Rules in Beirut." In *The Empire in the City: Arab Provincial Capitals in the Late Ottoman Empire*, edited by Jens Hanssen, Thomas Philipp, and Stefan Weber, 93–104. Würzberg: Ergon, 2002.

Fazlıoğlu, İhsan. "The Samarqand Mathematical-Astronomical School: A Basis for Ottoman Philosophy and Science." *Journal for the History of Arabic Science* 14 (2008): 3–68.

Fazlıoğlu, Şükran. "*Manzûme fî Tertîb el-Kutûb fî el-Ulûm* ve Osmanlı Medreselerindeki Ders Kitapları." *Değerler Eğitimi Dergisi* 1 (2003): 97–110.

———. "'Nebī Efendi-zāde'nin "ḳaṣīde fī el-kutub el-meşhūre fī el-'ulūm' una Göre Bir Medrese Talebesinin Ders ve Kitab Haritası." *Kutadgubilig Felsefe-Bilim Araştırmaları Dergisi* 3 (2003): 191–221.

———. "Ta'lîm ile İrşâd arasında: Erzorumlu İbrahim Hakkı'nın Medrese Ders Müfredatı." *Dîvân İlmi Araştırmalar* 18, no. 1 (2005): 115–173.

Fetvacı, Emine. "Enriched Narratives and Empowered Images in Seventeenth-Century Ottoman Manuscripts." *Ars Orientalis* 40 (2011): 243–266.

———. *Picturing History at the Ottoman Court*. Bloomington: Indiana University Press, 2013.

Feyerabend, Paul K. *Against Method: Outline of an Anarchistic Theory of Knowledge*. London: NLB, 1975.

———. *Science in a Free Society*. London: NLB, 1978.

Findley, Carter V. *Bureaucratic Reform in the Ottoman Empire: The Sublime Porte, 1789–1922*. Princeton, NJ: Princeton University Press, 1980.

———. *Ottoman Civil Officialdom*. Princeton, NJ: Princeton University Press, 1989.

Fischel, Roy S., and Ruth Kark. "Sultan Abdülhamid II and Palestine: Private Lands and Imperial Policy." *New Perspectives on Turkey* 29 (2008): 129–166.

Fisher, Carol G. "Naḳḳā<u>sh</u>-<u>Kh</u>āna." *Encyclopaedia of Islam*. 2nd ed. Brill Online, 2012.

Fleet, Kate. "The Missing Part of the Mediterranean History in the Late Medieval and Early Modern Period." In *The Turks*, edited by Hasan Celâl Güzel, C. Cem

Oğuz, and Osman Karatay, vol. 3: *The Ottomans*, 40–45. Ankara: Yeni Türkiye, 2000.

Fleischer, Cornell. *Bureaucrat and Intellectual in the Ottoman Empire: The Historian Mustafa ʿÂlî*. Princeton, NJ: Princeton University Press, 1986.

Fleming, K. E. "Women as Preservers of the Past: Ziya Gökalp and Women's Reform." In *Deconstructing Images of "The Turkish Woman,"* edited by Zehra F. Arat, 127–138. New York: Palgrave, 2000.

Flemming, Barbara, and F. Babinger [Christine Woodhead]. "Ṭas̲h̲köprüzāde." *Encyclopaedia of Islam*. 2nd ed. Brill Online, 2012.

Fortna, Benjamin C. *Imperial Classroom*. Oxford: Oxford University Press, 2002.

———. *Learning to Read in the Late Ottoman Empire and the Early Turkish Republic*. Basingstoke, UK: Palgrave Macmillan, 2011.

Foucault, Michel. *The Archeology of Knowledge and the Discourse of Knowledge*. New York: Pantheon Books, 1972.

———. *The Birth of the Clinic: The Archeology of Medical Perception*. London: Routledge, 1973.

———. *Madness and Civilization: A History of Insanity in the Age of Reason*. New York: Pantheon Books, 1965.

———. *The Order of Things: An Archeology of the Human Sciences*. London: Tavistock, 1970.

Fresco, Karen L., and Charles D. Wright, eds. Translating the Middle Ages. Farnham, Surrey: Ashgate, 2012.

Frierson, Elizabeth B. "Cheap and Easy: The Creation of Consumer Culture in Late Ottoman Society." In *Consumption Studies and the History of the Ottoman Empire, 1559–1922: An Introduction*, edited by Donald Quataert, 243–260. Albany: SUNY Press, 2000.

Gallagher, Nancy Elizabeth. *Medicine and Power in Tunisia, 1780–1900*. Cambridge: Cambridge University Press, 1983.

Gavroglu, Kostas, Manolis Patiniotis, Faidra Papanelopoulou et al. "Science and Technology in the European Periphery: Some Historiographical Reflections." *History of Science* 46 (2008): 53–75.

Gellens, Sam I. "The Search for Knowledge in Medieval Muslim Societies: A Comparative Approach." In *Muslim Travellers: Pilgrimage, Migration, and the Religious Imagination*, edited by Dale Eickelman and James Piscatori, 50–65. Berkeley: University of California Press, 1990.

Gencer, Yasemin. "İbrahim Mütefrrika and the Age of Printed Manuscript." In *The Islamic Manuscript Tradition*, edited by Christiane Gruber, 155–193. Bloomington: Indiana University Press, 2010.

Geoffroy, E. "al-Suyūṭī, Abu ʾl-Faḍl ʿAbd al-Raḥmān b. Abī Bakr b. Muḥammad D̲j̲alāl al-Dīn al-K̲h̲uḍayrī." *Encyclopaedia of Islam*. 2nd ed. Brill Online, 2012.

Ghobrial, John-Paul. *The Whispers of Cities: Information Flows in Istanbul, London, and Paris in the Age of William Trumbull*. Oxford: Oxford University Press, 2013.

Gibb, H. A. R. "Al-Murādī, 5." *Encyclopaedia of Islam*. 2nd ed. Brill Online, 2012.

Giladi, Avner. "The Child in Islam." In *Children and Childhood in World Religions: Primary Sources and Texts*, Don S. Browning and Marcia J. Bunge, 151–216. New Brunswick, NJ: Rutgers University Press, 2009.

———. *Children of Islam: Concepts of Childhood in Medieval Islam Society*. Houndmills, Basingstoke, UK: Macmillan, in association with St. Antony's College, Oxford, 1992.

———. "The Child was Small . . . Not so the Grief for Him: Sources, Structure and Content of al-Sakhāwī's Consolation Treatise for Bereaved Parents." *Poetics Today* 14 (1993): 367–386.

———. "Concepts of Childhood and Attitudes towards Children in Medieval Islam: A Preliminary Study with Special Reference to Infant and Child Mortality." *Journal of the Economic and Social History of the Orient* 32 (1989): 121–152.

———. "Gender Difference in Child Rearing and Education: Some Preliminary Observations with Reference to Medieval Muslim Thought." *Al-Qantara* 16 (1995): 291–308.

———. "Individualism and Conformity in Medieval Islamic Educational Thought: Some Notes with Special Reference to Elementary Education." *Al-Qantara* 26 (2005): 99–121.

———. "Infants, Children, and Death in Medieval Muslim Society: Some Preliminary Observations." *Social History of Islam* 3 (1990): 345–368.

———. "Islamic Consolation Treatises for Bereaved Parents: Some Bibliographical Notes." *Studia Islamica* 81 (1995): 197–202.

Gimaret, D. "Muʿtazila." *Encyclopaedia of Islam*. 2nd ed. Brill Online, 2012.

Ginio, Eyal. "Marginals in an Ottoman Town: The Case of Eighteenth Century Salonika." PhD diss., Hebrew University of Jerusalem, 1998.

Givens, Jean A., Karen M. Reeds, and Allain Touwaide, eds. *Visualising Medieval Medicine and Natural History, 1200–1550*. Aldershot, UK: Ashgate, 2006.

Göçek, Fatma Müge. *East Encounters West: France and the Ottoman Empire in the Eighteenth Century*. New York: Oxford University Press, 1987.

Gökçe, Feyyat, and Nilüfer Oğuz. "Minority and Foreign Schools on [*sic*] the Ottoman Education System." *E-International Journal of Educational Research* 1, no. 1 (2010): 42–57.

Gökyay, Orhan Şaik. "Kātib Čelebi." *Encyclopaedia of Islam*. 2nd ed. Brill Online, 2012.

Goldziher, Ignaz. *Muslim Studies*. Edited by S. M. Stern; translated by C. R. Barber and S. M. Stern. Chicago: Aldine, 1967.

Goodrich, Thomas S. *The Ottoman Turks and the New World: A Study of Tarih-i Hind-i Garbi and Sixteenth-Century Ottoman Americana*. Wiesbaden: Otto Harrassowitz, 1990.

Goodwin, Godfrey. *A History of Ottoman Architecture*. London: Thames and Hudson, 1971.

Goody, Jack. *The Interface between the Written and the Oral*. Cambridge: Cambridge University Press, 1987.

———. *The Logic of Writing and the Organization of Society*. Cambridge: Cambridge University Press, 1986.

———. *The Power of the Written Tradition*. Washington, DC: Smithsonian Institution Press, 2000.

Gordon, Stewart, ed. *Robes and Honor: The Medieval World of Investiture*. New York: Palgrave, 2001.

Grant, Jonathan. "Crossing the Eastern Divide: Western Civilization and Islam in the Views of Chaadaev and Gokalp." *History Compass* 3 (2005): 1–7.

———. "Rethinking the Ottoman 'Decline': Military Technology Diffusion in the Ottoman Empire, Fifteenth to Eighteenth Centuries." *Journal of World History* 10 (1999): 179–201.

———. "The Sword of the Sultan: Ottoman Arms Imports, 1854–1914." *Journal of Military History* 66 (2002): 9–36.

Grehan, James. *Consumer Culture in 18th-Century Damascus and Everyday Life*. Seattle: University of Washington Press, 2007.

Griffith, Zoe. "Calligraphy and the Art of Statecraft in the Late Ottoman Empire and Modern Turkish Republic." *Comparative Studies of South Asia, Africa and the Middle East* 31 (2011): 601–614.

Grunebaum, Gustave E. von. "The Response to Nature in Arabic Poetry." *Journal of Near Eastern Studies* 4 (1945): 137–151.

Gül, Murat, and Richard Lamb, "Mapping, Secularizing and Modernizing Ottoman Istanbul: Aspects of Genesis of the 1839 Development Policy." *Urban History* 31 (2004): 421–436.

Günergün, Feza. "Introduction of the Metric System to the Ottoman State." In *Transfer of Modern Science and Technology to the Muslim World*, edited by Ekmeleddin İhsanoğlu, 297–316. Istanbul: Islam Tarih, Sanat ve Kultur Arastirma Merkezi, 1992.

———. "The Metric System in Turkey." In *The Great Ottoman-Turkish Civilization*, edited by Kemal Çiçek, vol. 3: *Philosophy, Science and Institutions*, 487–491. Ankara: Yeni Türkiye, 2000.

Günergün, Feza, and Şeref Etker. "Waqf Endowments and the Emergence of Modern Charitable Hospitals in the Ottoman Empire: The Case of Zeynep-Kamil Hospital in Istanbul." In *The Development of Modern Medicine in Non-Western Countries*, edited by Hormoz Ebrahimnejad, 82–107. London: Routledge, 2009.

Günther, Sebastian. "Literacy." In *Encyclopaedia of the Qur'ān*. Brill Online, 2012.

Gürlek, Mehmet. "Anadolu'da Yazılımış İlk Türkçe Cerrahî Yazmalara Bir Örnek: Alâ'im-i Cerrâhin." *Turkish Studies: International Periodical for the Languages, Literature and History of Turkish or Turkic* 6 (2011): 1423–1434.

Gutas, Dimitri. "Classical Arabic Wisdom Literature: Nature and Scope." *Journal of the American Oriental Society* 101 (1981): 49–86.

Hagen, Gottfried. "'He Never Took the Path of Pastime and Play': Ideas of Childhood in Ottoman Hagiography." In *Scripta Ottomanica et Res Aitaicae: Festschrift für*

Barbara Kellner-Heinkele zu ihrem 60. Geburstag, edited by Ingeborg Hauenschild et al., 95–118. Wiesbaden: Harrasowitz Verlag, 2002.

———. "Translations and Translators in a Multilingual Society: A Case Study of Persian-Ottoman Translations, Late Fifteenth to Early Seventeenth Century." *Eurasian Studies* 2, no. 1 (2003): 95–134.

Hamadeh, Shirine. "Ottoman Expressions of Early Modernity and the 'Inevitable' Question of Westernization." *Journal of the Society of Architectural Historians* 63 (2004): 32–51.

———. "Public Spaces and the Garden Culture of Istanbul in the Eighteenth Century." In *The Early Modern Ottomans: Remapping the Empire*, edited by Virginia H. Aksan and Daniel Goffman, 277–312. Cambridge: Cambridge University Press, 2007.

Hamarneh, Sami Khalaf. *Drawings and Pharmacy in al-Zahrawi's 10th-Century Surgical Treatise*. Washington, DC: Smithsonian Institution, 1961.

Hanioğlu, M. Şükrü. *A Brief History of the Late Ottoman Empire*. Princeton, NJ: Princeton University Press, 2008.

Hanna, Nelly. *In Praise of Books: A Cultural History of Cairo's Middle Class, Sixteenth to the Eighteenth Century*. Syracuse, NY: Syracuse University Press, 2003.

Hannah, Robert. "The *Meridiana* of Ulugh Beg in Hagia Sophia, Constantinople." *Nuncius: Journal of the History of Science* 22 (2007): 7–14.

Hanson, Martha. "Visualizing the Geography of Disease in China, 1870s–1920s." Paper presented at the conference "From Qing to China: Rethinking the Interplay of Tradition and Modernity, 1860–1949," Tel Aviv University, May 2012.

Hanssen, Jens. *Fin de Siècle Beirut: The Making of an Ottoman Provincial Capital*. Oxford: Clarendon Press, 2005.

Harding, Sandra, and Kathryn Norberg. "New Feminist Approaches to Social Science Methodologies: An Introduction." *Signs* 30 (2005): 2009–2015.

Harrison, Mark. *Contagion: How Commerce Has Spread Disease*. New Haven, CT: Yale University Press, 2012.

———. *Disease and the Modern World, 1500 to the Present Day*. Cambridge: Polity, 2004.

Headrick, Daniel R. *The Tools of an Empire: Technology and European Imperialism in the Nineteenth Century*. Oxford: Oxford University Press, 1981.

Heck, Paul J. *The Construction of Knowledge in Islamic Civilization*. Leiden: Brill, 2002.

———. "The Hierarchy of Knowledge in Islamic Civilization." *Arabica* 49 (2002): 27–54.

Heger, Nomi. "The Status and the Image of the Persianate Artist." PhD diss., Princeton University, 1997.

Heidegger, Martin. *The Question Concerning Technology, and Other Essays*. New York: Harper and Row, 1977.

Heiderzadeh, Tofiqh. "İran Alimlerinin Osmanlı Devletine Gelişi ve Osmanlı Bilimine Katkıları (Timur Döneminin Başından Safevi Döneminin Sonuna Kadar)." *Osmanlı Bilimi Araştırmaları/Studies in Ottoman Science* 2 (1998): 211–242.

Heller, B. [N. A. Stillman]. "Luḳmān." *Encyclopaedia of Islam*. 2nd ed. Brill Online, 2012.

Hemmat, Kaveh Louis. "Children of Cain in the Land of Error: A Central Asian Merchant's Treatise on Government and Society in Ming China." *Comparative Studies of South Asia, Africa and the Middle East* 30 (2010): 434–448.

Heyd, Uriel. *Language Reform in Modern Turkey*. Jerusalem: Israel Oriental Society, 1954.

Heywood, Colin. "A Buyuruldu of A.H. 1100/A.D. 1689 for the Dragomans of the English Embassy of Istanbul." In *The Balance of Truth: Essays in Honour of Professor Geoffrey Lewis*, edited by Çiğdem Balım-Harding and Colin Imber, 125–144. Istanbul: Isis, 2000.

Hislop, Victoria. *The Thread*. London: Headline Review, 2011.

Hodgson, Marshall G. S. *The Venture of Islam: Conscience and History in a World Civilization*, vol. 3: *The Gunpowder Empires and Modern Times*. Chicago: University of Chicago Press, 1974.

Huber, Valeska. "The Unification of the Globe by Disease? The International Sanitary Conferences on Cholera, 1851–1894." *Historical Journal* 49 (2006): 453–476.

Hutton, Patrick H. "The History of Mentalities: The New Map of Cultural History." *History and Theory* 20 (1981): 237–259.

İhsanoğlu, Ekmeleddin. *Osmanlı Astronomi Literaturu Tarihi*. 2 vols. Istanbul: İslam Tarih, Sanat ve Kultur Arastirma Merkezi, 1997.

———. *Science, Technology, and Learning in the Ottoman Empire*. Aldershot, UK: Ashgate, Variorum, 2004.

Imber, Colin. *The Ottoman Empire, 1300–1650: The Structure of Power*. Basingstoke, Hampshire, UK: Palgrave, 2002.

İnalcik, Halil. "Military and Fiscal Transformation in the Ottoman Empire, 1600–1700." *Archivum Ottomanicum* 6 (1980): 283–337.

International Visual Literacy Association [IVLA]. "What Is 'Visual Literacy'?" http://www.ivla.org/drupal2/content/what-visual-literacy.

İzgi, Cevat. "Osmanlı Medreselerinde Aritmetik ve Cebir Eğitimi ve Okutulan Kitaplar." In *Osmanlı Bilimi Araştırmaları*, edited by Feza Günergün, 129–158. Istanbul: İstanbul Üniversitesi Edebiyat Fakültesi, 1995.

———. *Osmanlı Medreselerinde İlim*. 2 vols. Istanbul: İz Yayıncılık, 1997.

Johnson, Norman J. "The Urban World of the Matraki Manuscript." *Journal of Near Eastern Studies* 30 (1971): 159–176.

Kaçar, Mustafa. "Osmanlı İmaparatorluğu'nda Askerî Teknik Eğitimde Modernleşme Çalışmaları ve Mühendishanelerin Kuruluşu (1880'e kadar)." *Osmanlı Bilimil Araştırmaları* 2 (1998): 69–137.

———. "Osmanlı Ordusunda Görevli Fransız Subayı Saint-Rémy'nin İsyanbul'daki Top Döküm Çalışmaları (1785–87)." *Osmanlı Bilimil Araştırmaları* 5 (2003): 33–50.

———. "Osmanlı Telegraf İşlemetmesi." In *Çağını Yakalayan Osmanlı!*, edited by Ekmeleddin İhsanoğlu, 45–120. Istanbul: İslam Tarih, Sanat ve Kültür Araştırma Merkezi, 1995.

Kâhya, Esin. "One of the Samples of the Influences of Avicenna on the Ottoman Medicine, Shams al-Din Itaqi." *Belleten* 64, no. 4 (2000): 63–68.

Kâhya, Esin, and Aysegül D. Erdemir. *Işığında Osmanlıdan Cumhuriyete Tıp ve Sağlık Kurumları*. Ankara: Türkiye Diyanet Vakfı Yayınları, 2000.

Karamustafa, Ahmet T. "Military, Administrative, and Scholarly Maps and Plans." In *The History of Cartography*, edited by J. B. Harley and David Woodward, vol. 2, book 1: *Cartography in the Traditional Islamic and South Asian Societies*, 209–227. Chicago: University of Chicago Press, 1987.

Karatay, Fehmi Edhem. *Topkapı Sarayı Müzesi Kütüphanesi Arapça Kataloğu*. 4 vols. Istanbul: Topkapi Sarayı Mūzesi, 1962–1969.

Kark, Ruth. "Transportation in Nineteenth-Century Palestine: Reintroduction of the Wheel." In *The Land That Became Israel*, edited by Ruth Kark, 57–76. Jerusalem: Magnes Press, 1989.

Karmi, Ghada. "The Colonisation of Traditional Arabic Medicine." In *Patients and Practitioners: Lay Perceptions of Medicine in Pre-Industrial Society*, edited by Roy Porter, 315–339. Cambridge: Cambridge University Press, 1985.

Kavčić, Marijana. "Arabic Manuscripts of the National and University Library 'St. Kliment Ohridiski,' Skopje, Republic of Macedonia." In *From Codicology to Technology: Islamic Manuscripts and Their Place in Scholarship*, edited by Stefanie Brinkmann and Beate Wiesmüller, 175–193 Berlin: Frank and Timme, 2009.

Kealey, Terence. *The Economic Laws of Scientific Research*. Basingstoke, UK: Macmillan, 1996.

———. *Sex, Science and Profits*. London: William Heinemann, 2008.

Kerner, Jaclynne J. "Art in the Name of Science: The Kitāb al-Diryāq in Text and Image." In *Arab Painting: Text and Image in Illustrated Arabic Manuscripts*, edited by Anna Contadini, 25–39. Brill: Leiden, 2007.

King, David A. "The Astronomy of the Mamluk: A Brief Overview." *Muqarnas* 2 (1984): 73–84.

———. "The Astronomy of the Mamluks." *Isis* 74 (1983): 531–555.

———. "Mamluk Astronomy and the Institution of *Muwaqqit*." In *The Mamluks in Egyptian Politics and Society*, edited by Thomas Philipp and Ulrich Haarman, 153–162. Cambridge: Cambridge University Press, 1998.

———. "Taḳī al-Dīn." *Encyclopaedia of Islam*. 2nd ed. Brill Online, 2012.

Koch, Hans-Albrecht, Uta Koch, Angelika Koller, eds. *Deutscher Biographischer Index*. Munich: K. G. Saur, 1986.

Koselleck, Reinhart. *Futures Past: On the Semantics of Historical Time*. New York: Columbia University Press, 2004.

Krause, Keith. *Arms and the State: Patterns of Military Production and Trade*. Cambridge: Cambridge University Press, 1992.

Krstic, Tijana. "Of Translation and Empire: Sixteenth-Century Ottoman Imperial Interpreters as Renaissance Go-Betweens." In *The Ottoman World*, edited by Christine Woodhead, 130–142. London and New York: Routledge, 2012.

Kuban, Doğan. "Sinan." In *The Great Ottoman-Turkish Civilization*, edited by Kemal Çiçek, vol. 4: *Culture and Arts*, 450–463. Ankara: Yeni Türkiye, 2000.

Küçük, Bekir Harun. "Early Enlightenment in Istanbul." PhD diss., University of California, San Diego, 2012.

Kuhn, Thomas S. *The Structure of Scientific Revolutions.* Chicago: University of Chicago Press, 1962.

Kupferschmidt, Uri M. "On the Diffusion of 'Small' Western Technologies and Consumer Goods in the Middle East During the Era of the First Modern Globalization." In *A Global Middle East: Mobility, Materiality and Culture in the Modern Age, 1880–1940*, edited by Liat Kozma, Cyrus Schayegh, and Avner Wishnitzer, 229–260. London and New York: I.B. Tauris, 2015.

———. "The Social History of the Sewing Machine in the Middle East." *Die Welt des Islams* 44 (2004): 195–213.

Kuyt, Annelies. "With One Foot in the Renaissance: Shlomo Almoli and His Dream Interpretation." *Jewish Studies Quarterly* 6 (1999): 205–217.

Landau, Jacob M. *The Hejaz Railway and the Muslim Pilgrimage: A Case of Ottoman Political Propaganda.* Detroit, MI: Wayne State University Press, 1971.

Langermann, Y. Tzvi. "No Reagent, No Reaction: The Barren Transmission of Avicennan Dynamics to Ḥasdai Crexas." *Aleph* 12, no. 1 (2012): 161–188.

Latour, Bruno. "For David Bloor . . . and Beyond: A Reply to David Bloor's Anti-Latour." *Studies in the History of Philosophy of Science* 30 (1999): 113–129.

———. "On the Partial Existence of Existing and Nonexisting Objects." In *Biographies of Scientific Objects*, edited by Lorraine Daston, 247–269. Chicago: University of Chicago Press, 2000.

———. *Reassembling the Social: An Introduction to Actor-Network-Theory.* Oxford: Oxford University Press, 2005.

———. *Science in Action: How to Follow Scientists and Engineers through Society.* Cambridge, MA: Harvard University Press, 1987.

———. *We Have Never Been Modern.* Translated by Catherine Parker. Cambridge, MA: Harvard University Press, 1993.

Latour, Bruno, and Steve Woolgar. *Laboratory Life: The Construction of Scientific Facts.* Los Angeles: Sage, 1979.

Leaman, Oliver. *Islamic Philosophy.* 2nd ed. Cambridge: Polity, 2009.

Le Gall, Dina. *A Culture of Sufism: Naqshbandīs in the Ottoman World, 1450–1700.* Albany: SUNY Press, 2009.

Lewis, Bernard. *The Emergence of Modern Turkey.* 2nd ed. London: Oxford University Press, 1968.

———. *From Babel to Dragomans: Interpreting the Middle East.* Oxford: Oxford University Press, 2004.

———. "Ottoman Observers of Ottoman Decline." *Islamic Studies* 1 (1962): 71–87.

———. "Some Observations on the Significance of Heresy in the History of Islam." *Studia Islamica* 1 (1953): 43–63.

———, trans. and ed. *Islam*. New York: Harper and Row, 1974.

Lewis, Geoffrey L. *The Turkish Language Reform: A Catastrophic Success*. Oxford: Oxford University Press, 1999.

Li, Eunjeong. *Guild Dynamics in Seventeenth-Century Istanbul: Fluidity and Leverage*. Leiden: Brill, 2004.

Livingston, J. W. "Evliya Çelebi on Surgical Operation in Vienna." *Al-Abhath* 23 (1970): 223–245.

Low, Michael Christopher. "Empire and the Hajj: Pilgrims, Plagues, and Pan-Islam under British Surveillance, 1865–1908." *International Journal of Middle East Studies* (2008): 269–290.

MacLean, Gerald. *The Rise of Oriental Travel: English Visitors to the Ottoman Empire, 1580–1720*. New York: Palgrave Macmillan, 2004.

Majer, Hans Georg. "Aḥmed Pasha, Bonneval." *Encyclopaedia of Islam*. 3rd ed. Brill Online, 2015.

Makdisi, George. *The Rise of Colleges*. Edinburgh: Edinburgh University Press, 1981.

Malti-Douglas, Fedwa. "*Mentalités* and Marginality: Blindness and Mamlûk Civilization." In *The Islamic World from Classical to Modern Times: Essays in Honor of Bernard Lewis*, edited by C. E. Bosworth, Charles Issawi, Roger Savory, and A. L. Udovitch, 211–237. Princeton, NJ: Darwin, 1989.

Manz, Beatrice F. "Ulu<u>gh</u> Beg." *Encyclopaedia of Islam*. 2nd ed. Brill Online, 2012.

———. "Ulugh Begh, Transoxania and Turco-Mongolian Traditions." In *Iran and Iranisch Geprägte Kulturen: Studien zum 65: Geburstag von Bert G. Fragner*, edited by Markus Ritter, Ralph Kauz, and Birgitt Hoffmann, 20–27. Wiesbaden: Dr. Ludwig Reichert Verlag, 2008.

Martens, Rhonda. *Kepler's Philosophy and the New Astronomy*. Princeton, NJ: Princeton University Press, 2000.

Matar, Nabil. *Turks, Moors and Englishmen in the Age of Discovery*. New York: Columbia University Press, 1999.

Mavroudi, Maria. "Translators from Greek into Arabic at the Court of Mehmet the Conqueror." In *The Byzantine Court: Source of Power and Culture*, edited by A. Ödekan et al., 202. Istanbul: Koç University Press, 2013.

Mazower, Mark. *Salonica, City of Ghosts: Christians, Muslims and Jews, 1430–1950*. New York: Knopf, 2004.

Melman, Billie. *Women's Orient: English Women and the Middle East, 1718–1918: Sexuality, Religion, and Work*. Houndmills, Basingstoke, UK: Macmillan, 1992.

Messick, Brinkley. *The Calligraphic State: Textual Domination and History in a Muslim Society*. Berkeley: University of California Press, 1993.

Michot, Yahya J. "Ibn Taymiyya on Astrology: Annotated Translation of Three Fatwas." *Journal of Islamic Studies* 11 (2000): 147–208.

Mikhail, Alan. "An Irrigated Empire: The View from Ottoman Fayyum." *International Journal of Middle East Studies* 42 (2010): 569–590.

———. *Nature and Empire in Ottoman Egypt: An Environmental History*. Cambridge: Cambridge University Press, 2011.

Miović-Perić, Vesna. "Dragomans of the Dubrovnik Republic: Their Training and Career." *Dubrovnik Annals* 5 (2001): 81–94.

Mitchell, Timothy. *Rule of Experts: Egypt, Techno-Politics, Modernity*. Berkeley: University of California Press, 2002.

Montgomery, Scott L. *Science in Translation: Movements of Knowledge through Cultures and Time*. Chicago: University of Chicago Press, 2000.

Morrison, Robert. *Islam and Science: The Intellectual Career of Nī*. London: Routledge, 2007.

———. "The Reception of Early-Modern European Astronomy by Ottoman Religious Scholars." *Archivum Ottomanicum* 21 (2003): 187–195.

———. "A Scholarly Intermediary between the Ottoman Empire and Renaissance Europe." *Isis* 105 (2014): 32–57.

Murphey, Rhoads. "The Ottoman Attitude towards the Adoption of Western Technology: The Role of the Efrenci Technicians in Civil and Military Applications." In *Contributions à l'histoire économique et sociale de l'Empire Ottoman*, edited by Jean-Louis Bacqué-Grammont and Paul Dumont, 287–298. Louvain: Peeters, 1983.

Murphy, Jane H. "Aḥmad al-Damanhūrī (1689–1778) and the Utility of Expertise in Early Modern Ottoman Egypt." *Osiris* 25 (2010): 85–103.

———. "Locating the Sciences in Eighteenth-Century Egypt." *British Journal for the History of Science* 43 (2010): 557–571.

Müderrisoğlu, Fatih. "Menzil Roads and Menzil Complexes in the Ottoman Empire." In *The Great Ottoman-Turkish Civilization*, edited by Kemal Çiçek, vol. 4: *Culture and Arts*, 380–388. Ankara: Yeni Türkiye, 2000.

Nadav, Daniel. *Medicine and Nazism*. Jerusalem: Hebrew University/Magnes Press, 2010.

Necipoğlu, Gülru. *Architecture, Ceremonial, and Power: The Topkapı Palace in the Fifteenth and Sixteenth Centuries*. Cambridge, MA: MIT Press, 1991.

———. "From International Timurid to Ottoman: A Change of Taste in Sixteenth-Century Ceramic Tiles." *Muqarnas* 7 (1990): 136–170.

———. "A *Kānūn* for the State, a Canon for the Arts: Conceptualizing the Classical Synthesis of Ottoman Arts and Architecture." In *Soliman le Magnifique et son temps*, Gilles Veinstein, 195–216. Paris: Rencontres de l'Ecole du Louvre, 1992.

———. "The Suburban Landscape of Sixteenth-Century Istanbul as a Mirror of Classical Ottoman Garden Culture." In *Gardens in the Time of the Great Muslim Empires*, edited by Attilio Petruccioli, 32–71. Leiden: Brill, 1997.

Needham, Joseph, et al. *Science and Civilisation in China*. 7 vols. Cambridge: Cambridge University Press, 1957–2004.

Nicholson, James. *The Hejaz Railway*. London: Stacey International, 2005.

Ochsenwald, William L. "The Financing of the Hijaz Railroad." *Die Welt des Islams*, n.s., 14 (1973): 129–149.

———. "A Modern Waqf: The Hijaz Railway, 1900–48." *Arabian Studies* 3 (1976): 1–12.

O'Kane, B. "Sinān." *Encyclopaedia of Islam*. 2nd ed. Brill Online, 2012.

Oman, G., Günay Alpay Kut, W. Floor, and G. W. Shaw. "Maṭbaʿa." *Encyclopaedia of Islam*. 2nd ed. Brill Online, 2012.

Oreskes, Naomi. "Science and Public Policy: What's Proof Got to Do with It?" *Environmental Science and Policy* 7 (2004): 369–383.

Otto-Dorn, Katharina. "Figural Stone Reliefs on Seljuk Sacred Architecture in Anatolia." *Kunst des Orients* 12, no. 1 (1978–79): 103–149.

Öz, Mehmet. "Agriculture in the Ottoman Classical Period." In *The Great Ottoman-Turkish Civilization*, edited by Kemal Çiçek, vol. 2: *Economy and Society*, 32–40. Ankara: Yeni Türkiye, 2000.

Özervali, M. Sait. "Transferring Traditional Islamic Disciplines into Modern Social Sciences in Late Ottoman Thought: The Attempts of Ziya Gokalp and Mehmed Serefeddin." *Muslim World* 97 (2007): 317–330.

Özyüksel, Murat. *Hicaz Demiryolu*. Istanbul: Tarih Vakfı Yurt Yayınları, 2000.

Pamuk, Orhan. *Benim Adım Kırmızı*. Istanbul: İletişim, 1998.

Patiniotis, Manolis. "Eclecticism and Appropriation of the New Scientific Methods by the Greek-Speaking Scholars in the Ottoman Empire." In *Science between Europe and Asia: Historical Studies on the Transmission, Adoption, and Adaptation of Knowledge*, edited by Feza Günergun and Dhruv Raina, 193–206. New York: Springer, 2011.

Pearson, J. D. "Bibliography." *Encyclopaedia of Islam*. 2nd ed. Brill Online, 2012.

Pedari, Maria Pia. "Ottoman Ships and Venetian Craftsmen in the Sixteenth Century." In *Seapower, Technology, and Trade: Studies in Turkish Maritime History*, edited by Dejanirah Conto et al., 460–464. Istanbul: Denizler Kitabevi, 2014.

Peirce, Leslie P. *The Imperial Harem: Women and Sovereignty in the Ottoman Empire*. New York: Oxford University Press, 1993.

———. *Morality Tales: Law and Gender in the Ottoman Court of Aintab*. Berkeley: University of California Press, 2003.

———. "Polyglottism in the Ottoman Empire: A Reconsideration." In *Braudel Revisted: The Mediterranean World, 1600–1800*, edited by Gabriel Piterberg, Teofilo F. Ruiz, and Geoffrey Symcox, 76–98. Toronto: University of Toronto Press, 2010.

Pellat, Ch. "Fahrasa." *Encyclopaedia of Islam*. 2nd ed. Brill Online, 2012.

Phillio, Christiane. "Mischief in the Old Regime: Provincial Dragomans and Social Change at the Turn of the Nineteenth Century." *New Perspectives on Turkey* 25 (2001): 103–121.

Pick, Walter Pinchas. "Meissner Pasha and the Construction of Railways in Palestine and Neighboring Countries." In *Ottoman Palestine, 1800–1914: Studies in Economic and Social History*, edited by Gad G. Gilbar, 179–218. Leiden: Brill, 1990.

Pickstone, John. *Ways of Knowing: A New History of Science, Technology, and Medicine*. Chicago: University of Chicago Press, 2001.

Pinto, Karen. "The Maps Are the Message: Mehmet II's Patronage of an 'Ottoman Cluster.'" *Imago Mundi* 63, no. 2 (2011): 155–179.

———. "Searchin' his eyes, lookin' for traces: Piri Reis' World Map of 1513 and Its

Islamic Iconographic Connections (A Reading through Bağdat 334 and Proust)." *Osmanlı Araştırmaları/Journal of Ottoman Studies*, 39 (2012): 63–94.

Popper, Karl R. *Conjectures and Refutations: The Growth of Scientific Knowledge*. London: Routledge and Kegan Paul, 1963.

Pormann, Peter E. "The Physician and the Other: Images of the Charlatan in Medieval Islam." *Bulletin of the History of Medicine* 79 (2005): 189–207.

Ragep, F. Jamil. "Astronomy." *Encyclopaedia of Islam*. 3rd ed. Brill Online, 2015.

———. "Astronomy in the Fanārī-Circle: The Critical Background of Qāḍīzāde al-Rūmī and the Samarqand School." In *Uluslararası Molla Fenârî Sempozyumu (2009 Bursa)—bildiriler/International Symposium on Molla Fanārī (2009 Bursa)—Proceedings*, edited by Tevfik Yücedoğru, Orhan Ş. Koloğlu, U. Murat Kılavuz, and Kadir Gömbeyaz, 165–176. Bursa: Bursa Yüyükşehir Belediyesi Yayınları, 2010.

———. "Ḳāḍī-zāde Rūmī." *Encyclopaedia of Islam*. 2nd ed. Brill Online, 2012.

Raj, Kapil. *Relocating Modern Science: Circulation and the Construction of Knowledge in South Asia and Europe, 1650–1900*. Basingstoke, UK: Palgrave Macmillan, 2007.

Rashed, Roshdi, ed. *Encyclopedia of the History of Arabic Science*. 3 vols. London: Routledge, 1996.

Reeves-Ellington, Barbara. "Education: Missionary—The Ottoman Empire, Nineteenth Century." In *Encyclopedia of Women and Islamic Cultures*. Brill Online, 2012.

———. "A Vision of Mount Holyoke in the Ottoman Balkans: American Cultural Transfer, Bulgarian Nation-Building and Women's Educational Reform, 1858–1870." *Gender and History* 16 (2004): 146–171.

Reichmuth, Stefan. "The Interplay of Local Developments and Transnational Relations in the Islamic World: Perception and Perspectives." In *Muslim Culture in Russia and Central Asia from the 18th to the Early 20th Century*, edited by A. von Kögelgen, M. Kemper, and A. J. Frank, vol. 2: *Inter-Regional and Inter-Ethnic Relations*, 32–37. Berlin: K. Schwarz, 1998.

———. "Murtada al-Zabidi (d. 1791) in Biographical and Autobiographical Accounts: Glimpses of Islamic Scholarship in the 18th Century." *Die Welt des Islams* 39 (1999): 64–102.

———. *The World of Murtada al-Zabidi (1732–91): Life, Networks and Writings*. Cambridge: Gibb Memorial Trust, 2009.

Repp, Richard C. *The Müfti of Istanbul: A Study in the Development of the Ottoman Learned Hierarchy*. London: Ithaca Press, for the Board of the Faculty of Oriental Studies, Oxford University, 1986.

Ricci, Ronit. "Citing as a Site: Translation and Circulation in Muslim South and Southeast Asia." *Modern Asian Studies* 46, no. 2 (March 2012): 331–353.

———. *Islam Translated: Literature, Conversion, and the Arabic Cosmopolis of South and Southeast Asia*. Chicago: University of Chicago Press, 2011.

Ricci, Ronit, and Jan van der Putten, eds. *Translation in Asia: Theories, Practices, Histories*. Manchester: St. Jerome, 2011.

Rispler, Vardit. "Toward a New Understanding of the Term *bid'a*." *Der Islam* 68 (1991): 320–328.

Robinson, Francis. "Technology and Religious Change: Islam and the Impact of Print." *Modern Asian Studies* 27 (1993): 229–251.

Robson, J. "Bidʿa." *Encyclopaedia of Islam.* 2nd ed. Brill Online, 2012.

Rodrigue, Aron. *French Jews, Turkish Jews: The Alliance Israélite Universelle and the Politics of Jewish Schooling in Turkey, 1860–1925.* Bloomington: Indiana University Press, 1990.

Rogan, Eugene L. "Aşiret Mektebi: Abdülhamid II's School for Tribes (1892–1907)." *International Journal of Middle East Studies* 28 (1996): 83–107.

———. "Instant Communication: The Impact of the Telegraph in Ottoman Syria." In *The Syrian Land: Processes of Integration and Fragmentation, Bilad al-Sham from the 18th to the 20th Century*, edited by Thomas Philipp and Birgit Schaebler, 113–128. Stuttgart: Steiner, 1998.

Rogers, J. Michael. "The Palace, Potions and the Public: Some Lists of Drugs in Mid-16th Century Ottoman Turkey." In *Studies in Ottoman History in Honour of Professor V. L. Mènage*, edited by Colin Heywood and Colin Imber, 273–295. Istanbul: Isis, 1994.

———. *Sinan.* Makers of Islamic Civilization. London: I. B. Tauris in association with Oxford Centre for Islamic Studies, 2006.

Rosenfeld, Boris A., and Ekmeleddin İhsanoğlu. *Mathematicians, Astronomers, and Other Scholars of Islamic Civilization and Their Works (7th–19th c.).* Istanbul: Islam Tarih, Sanat ve Kultur Araştırma Merkezi, 2003.

Rosenthal, Franz. *Knowledge Triumphant: The Concept of Knowledge in Medieval Islam.* 2nd ed. Introduction by Dimitri Gutas. 1970. Reprint, Leiden: Brill, 2007.

Rothman, E. Natalie. "Interpreting Dragomans: Boundaries and Crossings in the Early Modern Mediterranean." Comparative Studies in Society and History 51, no. 4 (2009): 771–800.

Rouayheb, Khaled El-. *Relational Syllogisms and the History of Arabic Logic, 900–1900.* Leiden: Brill, 2010.

———. "Sunni Muslim Scholars on the Status of Logic, 1500–1800." *Islamic Law and Society* 11 (2004): 213–232.

———. "Was There a Revival of Logical Studies in Eighteenth-Century Egypt?" *Die Welt des Islams*, n.s., 45, no. 1 (2005): 1–19.

Roux, Jean-Paul. "Le décor animé du caravansérail de Karatay en Anatolie." *Syria* 49 (1972): 371–397.

Rubin, Avi. "East and West: Bahjat and Tamimi in Wilayat Beirut" (in Hebrew). *Jamaʿa* 7 (2001): 54–81.

Russell, Gül. "'The Owl and the Pussycat': The Process of Cultural Transmission in Anatomical Illustration." In *Transfer of Modern Science and Technology to the Muslim World*, edited by Ekmeleddin Ihsanoğlu, 191–195. Istanbul: Research Centre for Islamic History, Art and Culture, 1992.

Sabev, Orlin. "The First Ottoman-Turkish Printing Enterprise: Success or Failure?" In *Ottoman Tulips, Ottoman Coffee: Leisure and Lifestyle in the Eighteenth Century*, edited by Dana Sajdi, 63–89. London: I. B. Tauris, 2007.

———. "Formation of Ottoman Print Culture (1726–1746): Some General Remarks." In *New Europe College Yearbook: Regional Program 2003–2004 and 2004–2005*, 293–333. Bucharest: New Europe College, 2007.

———. *İbrahim Müteferrika ya da İlk Osmanlı Matbaa Serüveni (1726–1746). Yeniden Değerlendirme*. Istanbul: Yeditepe Yayınevi, 2006.

———. "Rich Men, Poor Men: Ottoman Printers and Booksellers Making Fortune or Seeking Survival (Eighteenth–Nineteenth Centuries)." *Oriens* 37 (2009): 177–90.

Sabra, A. I. *Optics, Astronomy, and Logic: Studies in Arabic Science and Philosophy*. Aldershot, UK: Variorum, 1994.

Sahlins, Marshall. "'Sentimental Pessimism' and Ethnographic Experience, or, Why Culture Is Not a Disappearing 'Object.'" In *Biographies of Scientific Objects*, edited by Lorraine Daston, 158–202. Chicago: University of Chicago Press, 2000.

Saleh, Marlis J. "Al-Suyūṭī and His Works: Their Place in Islamic Scholarship from Mamluk Times to the Present." *Mamluk Studies Review* 5 (2001): 73–89.

Saliba, George. *Islamic Science and the Making of the European Renaissance*. Cambridge, MA: MIT Press, 2007.

———. "Reform of Ptolemaic Astronomy at the Court of Ulugh Beg." In *Studies in the History of the Exact Sciences in Honour of David Pingree*, edited by Charles Burnett, Jan P. Hogendijk, Kim Plofker, and Michio Yano, 810–824. Leiden: Brill, 2004.

———. "The Role of the Astrologer in Medieval Islamic Society." *Bulletin d'Études Orientales* 44 (1992): 45–67.

Saliba, George, and Linda Komoroff. "Illustrated Books May Be Hazardous to Your Health: A New Reading of the Arabic Perception and Rendition of the Materia Medica of Dioscorides." *Ars Orientalis* 35 (2008): 6–65.

Sarı, Nil. "18. ve 19. Asırda Kimyager Hekimlerin Kullandıkları Âletler." *Tıp Tarihi Araştırmaları* 1 (1986): 51–78.

Sarıcaoğlu, Fikret. "Ottoman Cartography." In *The Turks*, edited by Hasan Celâl Güzel, C. Cem Oğuz, and Osman Karatay, vol. 3: *The Ottomans*, 831–840. Ankara: Yeni Türkiye, 2000.

Savage-Smith, Emilie. "Al-Zahrāwī." *Encyclopaedia of Islam*. 2nd ed. Brill Online, 2012.

———. "Drug Therapy of Eye Disease in Seventeenth-Century Islamic Medicine: The Influence of the 'New Chemistry' of the Paracelsians." *Pharmacy in History* 29 (1987): 3–28.

———. "The Influence of 'New Chemistry' of the Paracelsians upon Seventeenth-Century Arabic Medicine and Its Application to the Treatment of Eye Disease." Unpublished manuscript.

Sawai, Kazuaki. "Japon Teknolojisi'ne karşı: XVI. Yüzyılda Doğu Asya'da Osmanlı Tüfeğinin Yeri." In *Eskiçağ'dan Modern Çağ'a Ordular: Oluşum, Teşkilat ve İşlev*, edited by Feridun M. Emecen, 341–354. Istanbul: Kitabevi, 2008.

Sayılı, Aydın. *The Observatory in Islam*. Ankara: Türk Tarihi Kurumu Basımevi, 1988.

Şeni, Nora. "Fashion and Women's Clothing in the Satirical Press of Istanbul at the

End of the 19th Century." In *Women in Modern Turkish Society*, edited by Sirin Tekeli, 25–45. London: Zed Books, 1995.

Şeşen, Ramazan. "Onbeşinci Yüzyılda Türkçeye Tercumeler." In *XI. Türk Tarih Kongresi, Ankara . . . 1990: Kongreye sunulan bildiriler*, 3:899–919. Ankara: Türk Tarih Kurumu Basımevi, 1994.

Shah-Khan. "The Song of Creation: Sufi Themes on Nature." *Sufi* (London) 18 (Summer 1993): 27–30.

Shahvar, Soli. "Concession Hunting in the Age of Reform: British Companies and the Search for Government Guarantees; Telegraph Concessions in Ottoman Territories, 1855–58." *Middle Eastern Studies* 38, no. 4 (2002): 169–193.

———. "Iron Poles, Wooden Poles: The Electric Telegraph and the Ottoman-Iranian Boundary Conflict, 1863–1865." *British Journal of Middle Eastern Studies* 34 (2007): 23–42.

———. "Technology, Diplomacy and European Financial Entrepreneurship in the Ottoman Middle East during the Second Half of the Nineteenth Century: The Indo-European Telegraph Line and the Anglo-Ottoman Conflict of Interests" (in Hebrew). In *Turkey: The Ottoman Past and the Republican Present*, edited by Michael Winter and Miri Shefer, 211–237. Tel Aviv: Dayan Center for Middle Eastern and African Studies, 2007.

———. "Tribes and Telegraph in Lower Iraq: The Muntafiq and the Baghdad-Basrah Telegraph Line of 1863–65." *Middle Eastern Studies* 39 (2003): 89–116.

Sharef-Davidovich, Daphna. "The Imperial Palaces in Istanbul, 1856–1909" (in Hebrew). PhD diss., Ben-Gurion University of the Negev, Be'er Sheva, 2010.

Shefer-Mossensohn, Miri. "Communicable Disease in Ottoman Palestine: Local Thoughts and Actions." *Korot* 21 (2011–2012): 19–49.

———. "Medical and Professional Ethics in Sixteenth-Century Istanbul: Towards an Understanding of the Relationships between the Ottoman State and the Medical Guilds." *Medicine and Law* 21 (2002): 307–319.

———. "Old Patterns, New Meaning: The 1845 Hospital of Bezm-i ʿAlem in Istanbul." *Dynamis: Acta Hispanica ad Medicinae Scientiarumque Historiam Illustrandam* 25 (2005): 329–350.

———. *Ottoman Medicine: Healing and Medical Institutions 1500–1700*. Albany: SUNY Press, 2009.

———. "An Ottoman Observer of Central European Surgery in Middle of the Seventeenth Century." *Vesalius* 14, no. 1 (2008): 4–7.

———. "An Ottoman Physician and His Social and Intellectual Milieu: The Case of Salih bin Nasrallah Ibn Sallum." *Studia Islamica*, n.s., 1 (2011): 133–158.

———. "A Tale of Two Discourses: The Historiography of Ottoman-Muslim Medicine." *Social History of Medicine* 21 (2008): 1–12.

———. "Ṭibbiyye-i ʿAdliyye-i S͟hāhāne." *Encyclopaedia of Islam*. 2nd ed. Brill Online, 2012.

Sheffler, David. "Late Medieval Education: Continuity and Change." *History Compass* 8, no. 9 (2010): 1067–1082.

Shissler, A. H. "A Student Abroad in Late Ottoman Times: Ahmet Ağaoğlu and French Paradigms in Turkish Thought." In *Iran and Beyond: Essays in Middle Eastern History in Honor of Nikki R. Keddie*, edited by Rudi Matthee and Beth Baron, 35–55. Costa Mesa, CA: Mazda, 2000.

Singer, Amy. *Charity in Islamic Societies*. Cambridge: Cambridge University Press, 2008.

———. *Constructing Ottoman Beneficence: An Imperial Soup Kitchen in Jerusalem*. Albany: SUNY Press, 2002.

———. "The Mülknāmes of Hürrem Sultan's Waqf in Jerusalem." *Muqarnas* 14 (1997): 96–102.

———. "The Persistence of Philanthropy." *Comparative Studies of South Asia, Africa and the Middle East* 31 (2011): 557–568.

Sivin, Nathan. "Taoism and Science." In *Medicine, Philosophy and Religion in Ancient China: Researches and Reflections*, chap. 7, 1–72. Aldershot, UK: Variorum, 1995.

———. "Why the Scientific Revolution Did Not Take Place in China—Or Didn't It?" *Chinese Science* 5 (1982): 45–66. Revised version, August 24, 2005, http://ccat.sas.upenn.edu/~nsivin/scirev.pdf.

Smith, Pamela H. *The Body of the Artisan: Art and Experience in the Scientific Revolution*. Chicago: University of Chicago Press, 2004.

Sohrweide, H. "Luḳmān b. Sayyid Ḥusayn." *Encyclopaedia of Islam*. 2nd ed. Brill Online, 2012.

Somel, Selçuk Akşın. *The Modernization of Public Education in the Ottoman Empire, 1839–1908*. Leiden: Brill, 2001.

Soucek, Svat. "Ottoman Cartography." In *Studies in Ottoman Naval History and Maritime Geography*, 225–238. Istanbul: Isis, 2009.

———. "Pīrī Reʾīs." *Encyclopaedia of Islam*. 2nd ed. Brill Online, 2012.

Sourdel-Thomine, J. "Khaṭṭ; i. In The Arab World." *Encyclopaedia of Islam*. 2nd ed. Brill Online, 2012.

Spiller, Elizabeth. *Science, Reading, and Renaissance Literature: The Art of Making Knowledge, 1580–1670*. Cambridge: Cambridge University Press, 2004.

Stathi, Pinelopi. "The Seismologia and Their Diffusion During the Ottoman Period." In *Natural Disasters in the Ottoman Empire*, edited by Elizabeth Zachariadou, 241–247. Rethymnon: Crete University Press, 1999.

Stearns, Justin. "'All Beneficial Knowledge Is Revealed': The Rational Sciences in the Maghrib in the Age of al-Yūsī (d. 1102/1691)." *Islamic Law and Society* 21 (2014): 49–80.

———. "The Legal Status of Science in the Muslim World in the Early Modern Period: An Initial Consideration of *Fatwās* from Three Maghribī Sources." In *The Islamic Scholarly Tradition: Studies in History, Law and Thought in Honor of Professor Michael Allan Cook*, edited by Asad Q. Ahmed, Behnam Sadeghi, and Michael Bonner, 265–290. Leiden: Brill, 2011.

———. "Writing the History of the Natural Sciences in the Pre-modern Muslim World: Historiography, Religion, and the Importance of the Early Modern Period." *History Compass* 9, no. 12 (2011): 923–951.

Stillmann, N. A. "Khil'a." *Encyclopaedia of Islam*. 2nd ed. Brill Online, 2012.

Stolz, Daniel A. "The Lighthouse and the Observatory: Islam, Authority, and Cultures of Astronomy in Late Ottoman Egypt." PhD diss., Princeton University, 2013.

Swanson, Glen W. "War, Technology, and Society in the Ottoman Empire from the Reign of Abdülhamid II to 1913: Mahmud Şevket and the German Military Mission." In *War, Technology and Society in the Middle East*, edited by V. J. Parry and M. E. Yapp, 367–385. London: Oxford University Press, 1975.

Terzioğlu, Arslan. "Evliya Çelebi's Beschreibung der südosteuropäischen Hospitäler und Heilbäder des 17. Jahrhunderts und ihre kulturgeschichtliche Bedeutung." *Revue des Études Sud-Est Européennes* 13 (1975): 429–442.

Thompson, Mine F. "Turkey." In *Encyclopedia of Gardens: History and Design*, edited by Candice A. Shoemaker, 3:1333. Chicago: Fitzroy Dearborn, 2001.

Toledano, Ehud R. "The Emergence of Ottoman-Local Elites (1700–1800): A Framework for Research." In *Middle Eastern Politics and Ideas: A History from Within*, edited by I. Pappé and M. Ma'oz, 145–162. London: Tauris Academic Studies, 1997.

Trumpener, Ulrich. "Liman von Sanders and the German-Ottoman Alliance." *Journal of Contemporary History* 1 (1966): 179–192.

Tunalı Koç, Gülçin. "Osmanlı Siyaset Kültürünü Anlamada Kaynak Olarak—İlm-i Nücûm: Sadullah al-Ankaravî." *Türkiye Araştırmaları Literatür Dergisi* 2 (2004): 183–195.

———. "Sadullah Efendi'nin İlm-i Nücûm Kaynaklarından Tanzimat Ankarasına Bir Katkı." *Türkiyat Araştırmaları Dergisi* 24 (Autumn 2008): 369–392.

———. "'Sözüm bu iki gözüm ve vefâ': Müneccim Sadullah el-Ankaravî'nin Kaleminden 19.yy Akarası'ndaki Hizmetkârlar." *Tarih ve Toplum Yeni Yaklaşımalar* 5 (Spring 2007): 41–66.

Ullman, Manfred. *Die Medizin im Islam*. Leiden: Brill, 1970.

Uluçay, Çağatay M. *Harem II*. Ankara: Türk Tarih Kurumu Basımevi, 1992.

———. *Osmanlı Sulranlarına Aşk Mektupları*. 1950. Reprint, Istanbul: Ufuk Kitapları, 2001.

Uluengin, Mehmet B. "Secularizing Anatolia Tick by Tick: Clock Towers in the Ottoman Empire and in the Turkish Republic." *International Journal of Middle East Studies* 42 (2010): 17–36.

Unat, Yavuz. "Takîyüddîn and the Istanbul Observatory." In *The Turks*, edited by Hasan Celâl Güzel, C. Cem Oğuz, and Osman Karatay, vol. 3: *The Ottomans*, 819–830. Ankara: Yeni Türkiye, 2000.

Ünver, Ahmet Süheyl. *İstanbul Rasathanesi*. Ankara: Türk Tarih Kurumu Basımevi, 1985.

———. "Xvinci Asırda Türkiyede Tecrubi Tababete ait İki Misal." *İstanbul Üniversitesi Tıp Fakültesi Mecmuası* 3 (1949): 1–4.

Uzunçarşılı, İ. H. *Osmanlı Devletinin İlmiye Teşkilatı*. 3rd ed. Ankara: Türk Tarihi Kurumu Basımevi, 1988.

———. *Osmanlı Devletinin Saray Teşkilatı*. 3rd ed. Ankara: Türk Tarihi Kurumu Basımevi, 1988.

Volkan, Vamik D., and Norman Itzkowitz. *The Immortal Atatürk: A Psychobiography*. Chicago: University of Chicago Press, 1984.

Vryonis, Speros, Jr. "Religious Changes and Patterns in the Balkans, 14th–16th Centuries." In *Aspects of the Balkans: Continuity and Change*, edited by Henrik Birnbaum and Speros Vryonis Jr., 151–176. The Hague: Mouton, 1972.

Walker, Paul E. "Knowledge and Learning." *Encyclopaedia of the Qur'ān*. Brill Online, 2012.

Walker, Warren S., and Ahmet E. Uysal. *More Tales Alive in Turkey*. Lubbock: Texas Tech University Press, 1992.

———. *Tales Alive in Turkey*. Lubbock: Texas Tech University Press, 1990.

Watson, Andrew M. *Agricultural Innovation in the Early Islamic World: The Diffusion of Crops and Farming Techniques, 700–1100*. Cambridge: Cambridge University Press, 1983.

Watt, W. Montgomery. "Ash'ariyya." *Encyclopaedia of Islam*. 2nd ed. Brill Online, 2012.

"What Is Visual Literacy?" International Visual Literacy Association [IVLA]. http://www.ivla.org/drupal2/content/what-visual-literacy.

Winter, Michael. "Cultural Ties between Istanbul and Ottoman Egypt." In *Turkey: The Ottoman Past and the Republican Present*, edited by Michael Winter and Miri Shefer, 27–43. [In Hebrew.] Tel Aviv: University of Tel Aviv, Moshe Dayan Center for Middle Eastern and African Studies, 2007.

Wishnitzer, Avner. "A Comment on Mehmet Bengü Uluengin, 'Secularizing Anatolia Tick by Tick: Clock Towers in the Ottoman Empire and the Turkish Republic.'" *International Journal of Middle East Studies* 42 (2010): 537–540.

———. "On Schedules, Clock Towers, and Urban Rhythms in the Ottoman Empire" (in Hebrew). *Zmanim* 119 (Summer 2012): 18–31.

———. "'Our Time': On the Durability of the Alaturka Hour System in the Late Ottoman Empire." *International Journal of Turkish Studies* 16, nos. 1–2 (2010): 47–69.

———. *Reading Clocks Alla Turca: Time and Society in the Late Ottoman Empire*. University of Chicago Press, forthcoming.

———. "Teaching Time: Schools, Schedules, and the Ottoman Pursuit of Progress." *New Perspectives on Turkey* 43 (2010): 5–32.

———. "The Transformation of Ottoman Temporal Culture during the Long Nineteenth Century." PhD diss., Tel Aviv University, 2009.

Woodhead, Christine. "Na'īmā." *Encyclopaedia of Islam*. 2nd ed. Brill Online, 2012.

Yakıt, İsmail. "The Modular System in Mimar Sinan's Works of Arts and Ebced Accounting." In *The Great Ottoman-Turkish Civilization*, edited by Kemal Çiçek, vol. 4: *Culture and Arts*, 480–485. Ankara: Yeni Türkiye, 2000.

Yazbak, Mahmoud. *Haifa in the Late Ottoman Period, 1864–1914: A Muslim Town in Transition*. Leiden: Brill, 1998.

Yenişehirlioğlu, Filiz. "Continuity and Change in Nineteenth-Century Istanbul: Sultan Abdülaziz and the Beylerbeyi Palace." In *Islamic Art in the 19th Century: Tradition, Innovation, and Eclecticism*, edited by Doris Behrens-Abouseif and Stephen Vernoit, 57–87. Leiden: Brill, 2006.

Yerasimos, S. "Istanbul—VIII. Monuments." *Encyclopaedia of Islam*. 2nd ed. Brill Online, 2012.

Yıldırım, Nuran. "XV. Yüzyıla ait Anonim Bir Cerrahnâme Cerrahi Yöntemlerin Kullanıldığı Fasıllar Tıbbı Terminoloji ile Bitki, Drog ve Madde Isimleri." *Yeni Tıp Tarihi Araştırmaları/New History of Medicine Studies* 10–11 (2004–2005): 325–433.

Yurdaydin, Hüseyin G. "Maṭrāḳčī." *Encyclopaedia of Islam*. 2nd ed. Brill Online, 2012.

Zahniser, A. H. M. "Luqmānm." In *Encyclopaedia of the Qur'ān*. Brill Online, 2012.

Ze'evi, Dror. "A Chaotic Empire: The Ottoman Household as a Dynamic Vector." In *Turkey: The Ottoman Past and the Republican Presence*, edited by Michael Winter and Miri Shefer, 15–26. [In Hebrew.] Tel Aviv: Tel Aviv University, Moshe Dayan Center for Middle Eastern and African Studies, 2007.

———. *Producing Desire: Changing Sexual Discourse in the Ottoman Middle East, 1500–1900*. Berkeley: University of California Press, 2006.

Zischka, Gert A. *Allgemeines Gelehrten-Lexikon*. Stuttgart: Alfred Kröner, 1961.

Zorlu, Tuncay. *Innovation and Empire in Turkey: Sultan Selim III and the Modernisation of the Ottoman Navy*. London: I. B. Tauris, 2008.

Zoss, Emily. "An Ottoman View of the World: The Kitab Cihanüma and Its Cartographic Contexts." In *The Islamic Manuscript Tradition*, edited by Christiane Gruber, 194–219. Bloomington: Indiana University Press, 2010.

Zylberman, Patrick. "Civilizing the State: Borders, Weak States and International Health in Modern Europe." In *Medicine at the Border: Disease, Globalization and Security, 1850 to the Present*, edited by Alison Bashford, 21–40. New York: Palgrave Macmillan, 2006.

INDEX

Lightning Source UK Ltd.
Milton Keynes UK
UKHW010615070922
408458UK00001B/16

9 781477 312216